SANGHARAKSHITA

THROUGH BUDDHIST EYES

TRAVEL LETTERS

WINDHORSE PUBLICATIONS

Published by Windhorse Publications
11 Park Road
Birmingham
B 13 8AB

Printed by Interprint Ltd, Marsa, Malta

British Library Cataloguing in Publication Data
A catalogue record for this book is available from the British Library

ISBN 1 899579 23 0

Contents

The publishers acknowledge with gratitude permission to quote extracts from the following:

pp.303–6 reproduced by permission of Oxford University Press Australia and New Zealand and Mrs J. Baxter from *Collected Poems James K. Baxter*, Oxford University Press 1980 © The Estate of James K. Baxter,

pp.320–1 reproduced by permission of the Artful Publishing Co, Onehunga, Auckland. *The Epistles of the Sincere Brethren* translated by Eric van Reijn, Auckland 1988.

Every effort has been made to trace copyright in the following, but if any omission has been made please let us know in order that this may be acknowledged in the next edition.

pp.292–4 William Langland, *The Vision of Piers Plowman*, trans. Henry W. Wells.

pp. 295–8 Herb Goldberg, *The Hazards of Being Male*.

About the Author

Sangharakshita was born Dennis Lingwood in South London, 1925. Largely self-educated, he developed an interest in the cultures and philosophies of the East early on, and realized that he was a Buddhist at the age of sixteen.

The Second World War took him, as a conscript, to India, where he stayed on to become the Buddhist monk Sangharakshita ('protected by the spiritual community'). After studying for some years under leading teachers from the major Buddhist traditions, he went on to teach and write extensively. He also played a key part in the revival of Buddhism in India, particularly through his work among the most socially deprived people in India, often treated as untouchables.

After twenty years in India, he returned to England to establish the Friends of the Western Buddhist Order (FWBO) in 1967, and the Western Buddhist Order (called Trailokya Bauddha Mahasangha in India) in 1968. A translator between East and West, between the traditional world and the modern, between principles and practices, Sangharakshita's depth of experience and clear thinking have been appreciated throughout the world. He has always particularly emphasized the decisive significance of commitment in the spiritual life, the paramount value of spiritual friendship and community, the link between religion and art, and the need for a 'new society' supportive of spiritual aspirations and ideals.

The FWBO is now an international Buddhist movement with centres in sixteen countries world-wide. In recent years Sangharakshita has been handing on most of his responsibilities to his senior disciples in the Order. From his base in Birmingham, he is now focusing on personal contact with people, and on his writing.

Foreword

I have known Sangharakshita for thirty years. I have attended his lectures, retreats, and Dharma classes, participated in some of his seminars on Buddhist texts, accompanied him on an extensive lecture tour of Central India, read, edited, and published his books, and lived with him in two residential communities. I think I can say I have got to know him pretty well. Indeed he has become a friend.

In saying this I recognize my luck. Already, an increasingly small proportion of his followers have even met Sangharakshita, let alone got to know him. He is founder and head of the Western Buddhist Order and of the Friends of the Western Buddhist Order, a movement that is growing all the time. When I first came along in 1970 Sangharakshita met up with about forty of us once a week in a hired room; now we are a worldwide community of Dharma practitioners, interrelated via a network of public centres, residential communities, 'Right Livelihood' businesses, artistic ventures, and social welfare projects. Meanwhile, age has naturally curtailed Sangharakshita's freedom to get about. Although he still takes himself out on the road occasionally, he spends most of his time in his study keeping up with correspondence, composing brief papers, and producing rather less brief volumes of memoirs.

For many people, even in the UK, who regard him as their teacher and whose lives he has touched, he has become something of a distant figure, glimpsed from time to time at festive gatherings or during a brief visit to a residential community or public centre. On such occasions, as when delivering a lecture, he speaks and deports himself with a kind of classical formality. When manifesting publicly in less ceremonious mode he transmits himself via a rather self-conscious carrier wave of avuncular charm. He still grants private interviews. But how many people, I wonder, tangled up as they are in their own questions and a perhaps daunting sense of occasion, gain more than a superficial impression of the rather urbane gentleman who receives them with warm attention and unnerving self-possession? There are of course the books. But most of these reveal – behind the treasure-trove of knowledge and insight – a mind that places lucidity of expression above – well, certainly above popularity of style, and which eschews self-reference or illustrative personal anecdote.

So who is Sangharakshita, the man? What is he really like? How is one to get to know him, to feel some kind of meaningful human connection with him? And how is one to make – more to the point perhaps – a meaningful assessment of the character of a man to whose advice one might be entrusting one's life? Because one cannot help sensing that there must be more to him than so often meets the eye. This is the man, after all, who wandered barefoot across fifties India in search of spiritual teachings, who beheld visions in caves and befriended hermits and lamas, who lived through all the extraordinary events of an early life so vividly, yet gracefully, described in those memoirs. Here is the author of poems such as 'The Mask', 'New', and 'The Veil of Stars'. Just a few conversations with him inspired B.R. Ambedkar to ask this unknown young Westerner to conduct the first ceremony of 'mass-conversion' (of so-called 'untouchable' Hindus to Buddhism), while certain aspects of his teaching approach and perceived behaviour induced some members of Britain's Buddhist establishment of the 1960s to ask him to stay out of England, even, so rumour had it, to threaten his life.

Once, when asked what he thought might have happened to him had he not discovered Buddhism, he replied that he would probably have gone mad. 'It was as if the forces of my nature were so powerful and in some ways so contradictory that, had I not discovered an integrating ideal as powerful and as worthy as the Three Jewels, then they would most probably have ripped me apart.' Surely, some must think, if one could only get close enough to him to see these powerful and contradictory forces at play, one might see a rather different man to the one who embodies such conscious gentility so much of the time.

When preparing for the trip to India in 1981 I packed my cameras with anticipation. I had heard Sangharakshita talk so much about India. It was clear that he loved the place and perhaps felt more at home there than he did in England. Maybe I would see – and record

THROUGH BUDDHIST EYES

– a different Sangharakshita there, some feral Sangharakshita, Sangharakshita with his hair down? So when I saw him descending from the 'Deccan Queen' at Poona Station into a surging mass of cheering, chanting, garland-bearing well-wishers I was rather surprised, and I confess a little disappointed, to make out exactly the same friendly but controlled expression and the almost ponderous mindfulness of movement with which I was so familiar from the grey streets of London or the wind-chilled expanses of Norfolk. As the weeks went by, and as Sangharakshita maintained his poise and mindfulness throughout a roller-coaster adventure that kept me in a perpetual state of emotional and sensory overdrive, I came to see that he was indeed very happy to be in India, he did register the sights and sounds, was totally committed to meeting as many people as possible and making the maximum possible impact on their difficult lives, and he was occasionally frustrated by sickness or the (almost predictable) collapse of logistical arrangements. He was absolutely present and alive to things, all of the time. It was just that he never demonstrated this by losing himself, losing his self-possession, and so dribbling away his energy, in the mood, magic, or catastrophe of the moment, in the way that so many of us do so much of the time. And even if there was something crude and undisciplined in me that never quite felt comfortable with what I now saw as a defining characteristic of the man, I came more and more to appreciate and respect it.

With this volume of Letters in your hands you too have a kind of double opportunity to see what Sangharakshita is really like. For here you are being invited not only to travel with him, but also to sit with him as he tries to record as accurately as he can the most recent sights, thoughts, and impressions of his life and travels.

The words reproduced here were composed as letters to *Shabda*, the monthly journal that circulates among members of the Western Buddhist Order (Dharmacharis and Dharmacharinis). They were written while actually on the move, or in fairly immediate retrospect. This, however, does not mean that there is anything accidental about them. They were not dashed off in a hurry, or thrown together without thought. They were written with exactly the same five-hundred-words-a-day discipline that Sangharakshita brings to all his literary work. Sangharakshita's purpose in writing them, however, was not to produce another volume of memoirs, in which experience is selected, highlighted, and virtually recreated so as to form an artistic whole. Rather it was to communicate as completely as he could the outstanding moments and aspects of his immediate experience to a number of his close friends around the world.

As such they reveal what is uppermost in his mind, almost from moment to moment, as he goes about his life in London, Italy, New Zealand, Wales, the USA, Spain.... Sometimes he is 'on duty', attending a conference, visiting an FWBO centre, conducting ordinations, sometimes he is 'at play', sightseeing in a Renaissance capital or travelling through a series of beautiful landscapes, and sometimes he is at rest, wrapped in a newly-discovered poet, philosopher, or novelist. Sometimes the sweep is broad, general, and sublime; sometimes it is very specific to the situation in which he finds himself, while at others it is so incidental as to seem unconnected. Sometimes the sweep can seem minute and prosaic, almost to the point of superfluity.

Among his original readers there were some I know who found this extraordinary mixture baffling, even irritating. How could a man write so movingly about an aspect of Buddhist philosophy, a beautiful painting, or the prospect of his own approaching old age and death, and then devote so much space to an account of his search for a decent hotel or a vegetarian pizza? Where was the discipline? Where was the discrimination? I think they missed the point. In these letters Sangharakshita sets out to share, more intimately than perhaps such readers appreciated, exactly what it is like to be Sangharakshita. And while Sangharakshita does enjoy, even adore, high art, and loves to dwell in the realms of philosophy and metaphysics, he also has to feed himself and find a bed for the night. Don't we all? Well, er, no, actually. We're probably rather less concerned with art, philosophy, and metaphysics than is Sangharakshita.

In writing this way, I believe Sangharakshita reveals above all two of his strongest characteristics, which happen also to be his greatest pleasures. He is a man who loves to ruminate on his experience. He does not simply slide from moment to moment, encounter to encounter, allowing each new impression to override the last. He likes to dwell, reflect, make connections, savour all the tastes and after-tastes. And he is a man who really wants to share himself with others. Whatever physical, psychological, or spiritual distances separate us from him should not lure us into the mistaken idea that he inhabits an ivory tower of proud self-sufficiency. As so many passages in these letters demonstrate, Sangharakshita places an exceptionally high value on friendship, even companionship, not merely as an ideal, as some necessary dimension of one's refuge in the Sangha Jewel, but as a lived, day-to-day reality. In offering these letters to us he is offering us the chance to partake of his friendship, to become if only in imagination the companions not only of his travels, but of his heart and mind.

The essential quality of the human state is our capacity to be aware that we are aware. The challenge and the opportunity presented by Buddhism is to develop, maximize, and refine that capacity for 'reflexive self-awareness' to the uttermost. So far as I know I have not yet met a Buddha. I have, however, known and observed for thirty years a man who embodies that capacity to a degree greater than that I have encountered anywhere else during my life. I have had the good fortune to spend a great deal of time in his company and to observe him at close quarters. Having been so close to him, and having observed him, then I can only say that these Travel Letters are as comprehensive and detailed a substitute for that 'close observation' as it is possible to find. In these letters you can find out for yourself what Sangharakshita is really like.

Nagabodhi
Stroud
December 1999

To
Prasannasiddhi and Paramartha
and all my other travelling companions
both literal and metaphorical

Sangharakshita at Il Convento

LETTER FROM ITALY

Pisa – Santa Maria della Spina – Il Convento – Frari, Venice – messages from Yama: old age, disease, and death – Maha Dhammavira – The Caves of Bhaja – Blickling Hall – 'Buddhism, Art and Faith' exhibition at the British Museum – Lord Tonypandy and the Night Thoughts programme – dinner at Khadiravani community – The Glory of the Literary World – visit to Uncle Dick at Cheriton House – Naples – Naples Archaeological Museum – San Paolo Maggiore – San Lorenzo Maggiore – Capodimonte Museum – Italian Renaissance art – Pope Paul III – St Jerome – Basilica of Santa Chiara – Jesù Nuovo – San Domenico Maggiore – Pompeii – counter-drawings – the House of the Vettii – the Street of the Tombs – the Villa of Cicero – the Large Theatre – Vesuvian mineral specimens – Villa La Floridiana – Certosa di San Martino

Dear Dharmacharis and Dharmacharinis,

There was no moon when I reached Il Convento, and on getting out of the car I stumbled through the darkness in the direction of the lofty, faintly illuminated blind arch at the far end of the roofless nave. Half an hour earlier Prasannasiddhi and I had been met at Grosseto station by Suvajra and Buddhapalita, after an uneventful two-hour journey from Pisa in the course of which there was little that was worthy of remark other than the redness of the sun as it sank behind the blue waters of the Tyrrhenian Sea (or was it still the Gulf of Genoa?) and the politeness with which our Italian fellow-passengers bade us 'Buona sera!' as they left the compartment on reaching one of the tiny, oleander-surrounded stations at which the train was constantly stopping. Driving through the deserted streets of Grosseto, and along the broad tree-lined avenues that led to the hills, none of us had much to say, but once the lights of Batignano were seen twinkling in the distance tongues were loosened and Prasannasiddhi started questioning Suvajra and Buddhapalita about the retreat. By the time we pulled up outside Il Convento contact had been re-established and my young companion and I began to feel that we really were in Italy, really were in Tuscany, and that we really had, at last, come to the end of our journey. It was my fifth visit to Il Convento. I had already spent a year of my life, altogether, within its walls, and now I was about to spend another three months there. As I made my way up the two flights of worn stone steps, and along the bare, barrel-vaulted corridor that led to my room, I asked myself what my predominant impression was on finding myself back in those now familiar surroundings. The answer came as soon as I asked the question. My predominant impression was one of silence, emptiness, and simplicity.

Prasannasiddhi and I had arrived in Italy eight hours earlier. On our emergence from the plane the first thing of which we became conscious was the heat. London had been hot when we left but Italy – or at least Pisa – was even hotter. According to an announcement made shortly before we landed the ground temperature at Pisa was 80° Fahrenheit. We could well believe it. Waiting in the queue that was slowly edging its way across the tarmac in the direction of Immigration and Customs we could feel the hot, beneficent sun beating down on our backs and penetrating our bodies in a way that it seemed we had not felt for years. For once I was content to stand there without wishing that the queue would move faster. It was enough simply to see the intense blue of the sky overhead and feel the heat not just on one's skin but soaking into one's flesh, one's bones, one's sinews, and drying up all the cold unwholesome humours that one had brought with one from the damp regions of the North. It was enough to know that we were in Italy and on our way to Il Convento. Not that the journey from England had been an unpleasant one. That was far from being the case. Though our flight from Heathrow was delayed by more than an hour (there had been a power failure in Milan, and the plane could not take off until radio contact had been restored), the two hours that we spent in the air were quite enjoyable. Sunshine streamed in at the cabin windows, and looking out we could see first the smooth grey waters of the English Channel, then the green and brown patchwork of fields (Paris, we were informed, was on our left), and finally the huge masses of the French and Italian Alps, where snow-filled valleys alternated with jagged black crags and where, every now and then, appeared the intense turquoise of the little mountain lakes. When we had crossed the Gulf of Genoa the plane banked steeply and flew slowly up a narrow gorge in (I supposed) the Apennines, its wings almost touching the tree-lined cliffs on either side. Peering over Prasannasiddhi's shoulder I could see huts perched on seemingly inaccessible ridges and slopes criss-crossed with a multitude of tiny paths. Ten minutes later the plane landed at Pisa airport and we emerged into the hot Italian sun.

The fact that the flight had been delayed and we had arrived late meant that we might not be able to do as much sightseeing as we had hoped. There was no time to be lost. As soon as we had collected our luggage we caught a taxi to Pisa Central station, deposited our luggage, bought our tickets (that is Prasannasiddhi bought them, his Italian being better than mine), tried to telephone Il Convento (there was no reply), had a snack at the station cafeteria, caught another taxi, and within little more than half an hour of our arrival in Italy we were standing within the Quadrangle and gazing across the greensward up at the gleaming white Romanesque beauty of the Leaning Tower, the Cathedral, and the Baptistery, all of which we had seen a number of times before. On its southern side the Quadrangle is lined with souvenir stalls, of which there must be upwards of a hundred. Most of these contain nothing but junk, but on our way to last year's Tuscany retreat Prasannasiddhi and I had found one stall that was selling pottery of a rather unusual colour, peacock blue streaked with green, and decided to buy a pair of flower vases for Padmaloka. Not wanting the trouble of carrying the vases with us to Il Convento, we decided to make our purchases on our way back to England after the retreat, when we would in any case be passing through Pisa again. The result might have been foreseen. Returning three months later we found the stall closed. Our disappointment was not very great. We knew that we would most likely be passing that way again the following year and would probably be able to buy the vases then, even if this did mean that we would, after all, have to carry them with us to Il Convento. Having gazed our fill at the white marble shapes opposite, therefore, we turned left and, slipping into the stream of bronzed and scantily clad holidaymakers, went in search of our pottery stall.

It did not take us long to find it. In fact we found two other stalls that were selling pottery of the same peacock blue streaked with green which was, I suspected, a speciality of the district. But though it did not take us long to find the stall we found it filled with so many vases, of so many shapes and sizes, as well as with pots, bowls, and dishes, all of the same peacock blue streaked with green, that it took us a long time to make up our minds what to buy. So much so, indeed, that we found it necessary to repair to a restaurant just outside the city wall and discuss the matter over a cup of tea and a bun. By the time we had made up our minds, returned to the stall, bought the vases (plus a pot and another, smaller vase), and had each item separately wrapped, the afternoon was more than half over and we had not yet done any real sightseeing. We therefore went and sat in the Cathedral and for a few minutes gazed up at the mosaic of the great bearded Christ in the apse and at the small stained-glass window, with its brilliant reds and blues, immediately above. I then noticed hanging against a pillar to the right a large painting of St Jerome, the red of his cardinal's robes scarcely visible through the gloom. On walking over to it I saw squeezed into the bottom left-hand corner the figure of the faithful lion, no bigger than a small dog, and called Prasannasiddhi over to take a look. After we had chuckled over the lion, we strolled round the transepts, pausing to take a particularly close look at the famous pulpit on the way, and so passed down the nave and from pillared gloom out through the west door into a world of blue sky, green grass, and brilliant sunshine reflected from dazzlingly white marble.

Our original intention had been to visit not only the Cathedral but the Baptistery and the Campo Santo, where I particularly wanted to have another look at *The Triumph of Death* and the other fourteenth-century frescoes we had seen the previous year. In the end, however, we decided that rather than seeing the frescoes and having to hurry back to the station we would see them on our return journey and walk back to the station in a leisurely manner. After Prasannasiddhi had bought a reproduction of Holiday's *Dante and Beatrice* at a bookshop, we accordingly plunged into a quiet street that ran parallel to the main thoroughfare and eventually emerged on the bank of the River Arno. We had just crossed over the main bridge when Prasannasiddhi's sharp eyes noticed that the door of the Santa Maria della Spina, which stood a short distance down a street to the left, immediately adjoining the river, was actually open. On all our previous visits to Pisa it had been firmly closed, and we had had to content ourselves with admiring the delicately carved statues, arches, canopies, crockets, and water-spouts with which the exterior of the tiny Gothic building – no bigger than an ordinary house – was richly embellished, and with peering through a missing pane in the mullioned windows. Thinking the opportunity too good to be missed, we followed the two elderly Americans who had just turned up into the building. The interior was bare and rather barnlike, though of pleasing proportions, and the light that filtered through the alabaster panes of the windows overlooking the river filled it with a soft amber glow. At the far end stood two rather fine statues of saints (Peter and Paul, I think), similar in style to those decorating the outside of the building, and the inevitable Madonna and Child. In the wall to the left of the altar was a niche that had once contained the spina or sacred thorn (i.e. the thorn from Christ's crown of thorns) to which the place had been dedicated and from which it derived its name.

After lingering inside the Spina – as it was generally called – for a few minutes, and taking another look at the magnificently decorated exterior of the building, we resumed walking and in little more than twenty minutes were back at the station. After Prasannasiddhi had telephoned Il Convento, and left a message for Suvajra and Buddhapalita informing them of the time of our arrival in Grosseto, all that we had to do was have supper, collect our luggage, and catch the 6.30 train. Easier said than done! The station restaurant did not open until 7 o'clock, so that we had to make do with a pizza at the bar of the cafeteria, and the train was more than half an hour late. Not that any of this really mattered. We were in Italy, we were on our way to Il Convento, and I for one was quite content to pass the time observing the Italians in the cafeteria and on the platform. Eventually the train came along. Though it was quite full – Pisa was, after all, on the main line between Genoa and Rome – we managed to squeeze into a compartment occupied by an elderly married couple who dozed most of the way, a rather restless young man, and a girl student who flirted violently with two boy students standing in the corridor and eventually succeeded in luring one of them into the compartment. Two hours later we arrived in Grosseto and were warmly welcomed by Suvajra and Buddhapalita.

Partly because I was so familiar with the place, partly because this year there were no days of strenuous sightseeing to recover from, it did not take me long to settle in at Il Convento and get back to my normal daily routine. It took me, in fact, less than forty-eight hours. On the second morning after our arrival I started editing the transcript of my lecture on 'The Path of Regular Steps and the Path of Irregular Steps', which Windhorse Publications hopes to bring out in book form next year together with three or four other lectures given at about the same time; the same afternoon I started tackling arrears of correspondence, while three days later I took the first of the evening question-and-answer sessions on Gampopa's *Jewel Ornament of Liberation*, which would continue – with intermissions – for about a month. The first part of the daily routine to be established, however, was my afternoon constitutional, which I generally take with Prasannasiddhi immediately after lunch. Only three days earlier this had meant a walk along a quiet Norfolk road between lush green hedgerows thickly interwoven with late summer and early autumn flowers. Now, on the day after our arrival, as on many subsequent days, it meant a walk along an even quieter Tuscany hillside track between dry bushes so thickly covered in white dust as to resemble the 'frosted' leaves that one sees in shops at Christmas time. In England the summer had been so wet that there had hardly been a summer at all. In Italy summer had begun early and in Tuscany, at least, not a drop of rain had fallen for many months, so that even the evergreens that covered the surrounding hills were tinged, here and there, with yellow. The long, hot summer had been preceded by an exceptionally cold winter, in the course of which two thirds of the country's olive trees had died. Il Convento had had two feet of snow, and now more than a dozen of the olive trees nearest the front of the building were gaunt grey skeletons with hardly a leaf between them. There were other skeletons further down the hillside, as well as in the various olive groves that we passed in the course of our walk. We noticed other changes. There seemed to be fewer lizards about than in previous years, and we saw only one bright green iguana. There also seemed to be fewer butterflies, or at least fewer species, though we saw an unusually large number both of swallowtails and of small blues. As for the birds, apart from the pigeons nesting in the crevices of Il Convento, whose numbers had apparently doubled, and whose loud coo-coos resounded throughout the day, there were as few of them as ever. In Tuscany, as elsewhere in Italy, the guns and dogs of the weekend sportsman have prevented them from multiplying, so that one hardly ever sees more than a few sparrows or a solitary magpie. Once again I wondered how it was that St Francis of Assisi, who preached to the birds and called them his little sisters, had come to be declared – along with St Catherine of Siena – one of the two patron saints of modern Italy.

What with editing in the morning and clearing up arrears of correspondence in the afternoon, the greater part of my time was necessarily spent in my room, a noble apartment more than twenty feet square, the rafters of which were supported on two enormous beams that ran right across it. Indeed, the greater part of my time was spent not just in my room but at my desk which on account of the unevenness of the tiled floor had been placed two feet away from the tall double case-ment window that extended practically to the ceiling. From this win-dow I had an even finer view than from the window of my study at Padmaloka. From the window of my study at Padmaloka I could see an expanse of vivid green lawn backed by trees which, at the time of my departure, were still in the full glory of their summer foliage. From the window of my room at Il Convento I could see a stretch of brown hillside that, bare save for two or three small Mediterranean oaks, descended in terraces to meet the olive trees and evergreens that came surging up from below. Away to the left, clustered around a low hill on the other side of the valley, were the red roofs and dirty white walls of the hundred or so houses and one church that make up the village of Batignano. Farther away to the right, covering the lower portion of another hill, were two or three olive groves, their grey trunks and silver-green foliage making a pleasing contrast with the pinkish-brown of the earth. Between the two hills was a broad gap, to the left of which, below the road that skirted Batignano, extended a line of some fifteen or twenty dark green cypresses. From the window of my room they looked like toy trees, but having stood beneath them a number of times I knew that they were of enormous height and that they formed an avenue leading to a kind of cemetery. This cemetery comprised not only a graveyard but an open-fronted structure, about as high as a two-storeyed house and twice as wide, divided into a number of square pigeonholes into which, it seemed, the coffins were inserted lengthwise and the opening sealed up with a tablet inscribed with the name and other particulars of the deceased. From the window of my room this curious structure was clearly visible, and at night I would sometimes see row upon row of tiny lamps twinkling in the midst of the surrounding blackness and, with their collective golden radiance, illuminating the entire front of the structure and, though more faintly, the last two or three cypresses.

Behind the cemetery the gap between the two hills widened out into a broad valley that was, in fact, an extension of the coastal plain. The floor of the valley was entirely covered with olive groves, which indeed had begun to encroach on the lower slopes of the foothills that, rising some three or four miles away, stretched from one end of the horizon to the other. Behind the foothills rose more foothills, their long flowing lines growing fainter and fainter with the distance. In the more outlying foothills to the extreme right there was a gap, and through this gap I was sometimes able to see the roofs and spires of Grosseto, half a dozen miles away, glittering through the haze. Indeed, if I walked to the window I was sometimes able to see, half a dozen miles beyond Grosseto itself, the narrow ribbon of burnished silver that was the sea. On exceptionally clear days I could even make out, half hidden by a distant headland, the dim blue shape of the island of Elba. When not actually writing, I sometimes just sat at my desk and, looking out of the window, allowed my eyes to rest on the red roofs, on the olive groves, on the line of dark green cypresses, on the foothills. In the course of the last four years they had all become very familiar to me. Tuscany had become very familiar to me. Italy had become very familiar to me. Indeed, one of the more unforeseen consequences of the three-month men's ordination retreats that, since 1981, we have been holding at Il Convento, has been that I have had the opportunity of seeing more of Italy than I had ever expected to see. This was not to say that I had seen much of modern Italy – no more, in fact, than had been necessary. The Italy which had become so familiar to me, and of which I had tried to see a little more each year, either on the way to Il Convento or on the way back to England, or both, had been the Italy of Classical, Medieval, and Renaissance civilization and culture. It was of this Italy that I sometimes allowed myself to dream as I looked out of the window. I thought of the great centres of culture I had visited, and of the great works of art I had seen. I thought of the glories of Pisa, Florence, Siena, Venice, Ravenna, and Rome, most of which I had visited several times. I reflected, moreover, on the kind of effect a particular mosaic, or painting, or sculpture, or building had had on me. I also recollected some of my more striking experiences. One of these had taken place in the Frari in Venice, which Prasannasiddhi and I visited in 1983. While we were walking around I became aware that about two hundred years ago there had been held, in the right-hand transept, a meeting of considerable spiritual importance to humanity. By whom the meeting had been held, and for precisely what purpose, I could not tell. Perhaps it had been held by the Franciscans (to whom the place belonged), or, as seemed more likely, by the Rosicrucians or the Illuminati or one of the other occult fraternities of the time. Whatever the truth might be, the meeting had been of sufficient importance to leave on the atmosphere of the place an impression that was still strong enough to be perceived.

Besides thinking of Italy, after settling in at Il Convento and getting back to my normal daily routine I also thought of England. That is to say, I thought not of strikes, unemployment figures, and by-election results, but rather of all the things that had happened in my own life – and in the larger life of the Movement – during the nine months that had elapsed since my return to England after the last Tuscany retreat. Quite a lot of things had happened. There had been trips to Norwich, London (Bethnal Green and Croydon), Rayleigh, Rottingdean, Manchester, Corwen, and Leeds. There had been meetings and consultations of various kinds. There had been Men's Events, pujas, and name-giving ceremonies. There had been question-and-answer sessions. There had been literary work, including correspondence. There had been visitors. Above all, perhaps, there had been the Order Convention, or rather, there had been the three Order Conventions (the Women's, the Combined, and the Men's), all of which I had attended. As I thought of all the things that had happened since the last Tuscany retreat I realized that to give even a brief account of them would require a longer 'Letter from Italy' than I have time to write and than many of you, probably, have time to read. But fortunately I do not have to produce a Letter of such mammoth proportions. For the last year there has appeared in the *FWBO Newsletter*, in addition to the usual thematic articles and round-up of centre news, an item entitled 'Order Office'. Under this prosaic, not to say unimaginative, heading Subhuti (I think it usually is) gives a report on the work of the Order Office team, and a résumé of Bhante's activities, for the previous quarter. These résumés, informative though they are, for obvious reasons do not have much to say about matters of a more personal nature. It was of matters of a more personal nature too that I thought, however, when I thought of all the things that had happened since my return to England nine months ago; and since the majority of you will have no other means of knowing about them – or at least, no other means of knowing about my personal feelings with regard to them – it is about three such matters that I want to write. These were concerned, respectively, with old age, with disease, and with death, though not quite in that order. Old age, disease, and death are, of course, the three messengers that Yama, the king and judge of the dead, sends to each one of us from time to time in order to remind us of the contingent and evanescent character of human existence, and in the course of the previous nine months I had seen all three of them at rather close quarters, either in my own person or in the person of someone near and dear to me.

The first messenger to come was disease, and he came in the form of the serious illness that, at the beginning of the year, confined my mother to bed for six weeks and left her considerably weakened afterwards. Since she is in her late eighties the illness, which was brought on by over-exertion (she is of a very active nature, and cannot bear to sit still for long), could easily have proved fatal. Indeed, for a time it seemed that she might not have more than a few months to live. Further over-exertion was in any case absolutely out of the question and to be avoided at all costs. If she over-exerted herself in that sort of way again, she was warned (and for a long time even the slightest exertion exhausted her), she would certainly not survive the after-effects for more than a few hours. Though I was naturally concerned for my mother (as were the rest of the family), the only practical difference her illness made to me was that my trips to Rayleigh became more frequent than usual. Instead of going every three or four months I now went every three or four weeks. Since I was extremely busy, and did not really like to disrupt my routine, this was not always easy; but nonetheless I was glad to go since I knew that my mother greatly looked forward to my visits (to see me, she said, was what she wanted more than anything else) and that they had a positive effect on her and hastened her (partial) recovery. In between visits I sent her letters and cards and, during the worst of her illness, telephoned every few days to Tynia, the cheerful and sensible wife of my elder nephew John, for the latest news of her condition. Slowly she recovered, and when I made my last trip to Rayleigh prior to my departure for Italy I had the satisfaction of seeing that she was able to walk from the sitting room to the kitchen and back without becoming too exhausted in the process. She did not, it seemed, mind my going to Italy, from which I could in any case return within a few hours if necessary, but when in the course of a previous visit I had mentioned that I would be going to India in December she had become so agitated that, after thinking the matter over, I promised her that I would postpone my visit until the following year. Since by December at least a dozen Indian Mitras* would, I knew, be ready for ordination, this meant that either the ordinations would have to be postponed for a year or more or – as I had been thinking of doing for some time – I would have to start

---

* Mitra: Sanskrit for 'friend'. Someone in the process of deepening their spiritual commitment through active involvement in the FWBO.

handing over the responsibility for conferring ordinations to some of the more senior and spiritually experienced members of the Order.

Thinking about the first of the three messengers that Yama had sent to me that year, I realized that my personal feelings with regard to my mother's illness were quite clear and straightforward. I was undoubtedly very fond of her, and would be sorry to 'lose' her, but she had already reached an advanced age, and I had long accepted the prospect of her death with the same equanimity as I accepted the prospect of my own. Whether it came soon or late, therefore, her death would certainly not be a shock to me, and I doubted if I would feel any real grief. The same could not, of course, be said of the rest of the family. My sister, I knew, would probably accept my mother's death with her customary phlegm, but my nephew John, my sister's son, whom my mother had brought up and who was deeply attached to her, would no doubt feel it very keenly indeed. On one of my more recent visits to Rayleigh I had noticed that his eyes never left her and that he followed every movement that she made with an anxiety that was truly pitiable. My mother was not unaware of this, and whenever she made one of her little journeys to the kitchen gave him a smile that said, quite clearly, that while she fully appreciated his concern she had no intention of spending the rest of her life sitting idly in a chair, whatever the consequences might be. Idleness and inactivity were, in fact, more difficult for her to bear than anything else. In the course of an earlier visit, when she was still confined to bed, she had complained bitterly about her situation, exclaiming, 'for me, lying here like this is *murder!*' Naturally I had consoled her as best I could, and counselled patience, but I knew quite well that, in the same way that some people would rather be dead than Red, my mother would rather be dead than inactive, and in my heart of hearts I could not blame her for feeling as she did.

During even the worst of her illness, however, when from her ashen looks it seemed she did not have much longer to live, my mother was mentally as bright and alert as ever, and it did not take much effort on my part to cheer her up and even make her laugh. As I sat on the edge of her bed, with the afternoon sun falling on the counterpane, and lighting up her withered cheeks and sparse grey curls, we in fact had some quite worthwhile conversations. (As I had known for a long time, it was always possible to have a worthwhile conversation with my mother, provided I could get her on her own, away from the other female members of the family.) As we generally did when we were

alone together, we talked about her early life, about the work of the
FWBO in India (as usual, there was money to be taken out of the drawer
and sent to Padmasuri 'for the children'), and about my own life and
work at Padmaloka. She also took the opportunity of telling me about
her worries, which as usual related mainly to members of the family
and distant friends. During the period of her illness she was particularly worried about her youngest (and only surviving) brother Dick,
who at the age of eighty-four had taken to wandering the streets at
night in his pyjamas and visiting wine bars. My mother was insistent
that he should be admitted to an old people's home, where he would
be properly looked after (he lived alone in a big house in Norbury, and
never bothered to cook), and wanted me to telephone his ex-wife
Audrey, who still kept in touch with him, and his daughter Gillian, and
make sure that this was done as soon as possible. Since I knew that my
mother was extremely fond of her scapegrace brother, who until quite
recently had visited her regularly every two or three weeks, I naturally
assured her that I would do as she wished. It was, however, quite a
while before arrangements could be made for Uncle Dick to be admitted to a suitable home and in the meantime my mother worried about
him to such an extent that she was in danger of making herself more
ill than she was already. 'If I wasn't lying in bed like this,' she declared
on one of my visits, 'I'd have the poor chap here and look after him
myself.' From the energy with which she said this I knew that these
were no empty words and that there was, in fact, very little that she
was not prepared to do for the members of her immediate family or
for her friends.

But once she had told me about her worries, which she always did
quite unreservedly, my mother was able to put them aside and turn to
other things. (She worried about her brother most, she said, when she
was on her own and had nothing to occupy her mind.) By far the
greater part of the time I spent with her, therefore, was devoted not to
her worries but to talking about more positive things. As we talked,
touching now on Buddhism and the FWBO and now on more mundane
topics, it not infrequently happened that we reached a deeper level of
communication and were able to share our more intimate thoughts
and feelings to a degree that circumstances did not usually permit. At
such times I felt a profound satisfaction that, despite the vast differ-
ences that there were between us in so many ways, I had in the course
of the last ten or twelve years – but particularly since her visit to the
London Buddhist Centre in 1979 – succeeded in establishing between

my mother and myself an understanding which, though it had its limits, was deep and genuine.

The second messenger to come was death, and he came – as he so often does come – in a particularly unexpected and dramatic form. I was in my study at Padmaloka, working on my memoirs, when there came an unexpected knock on the door and Subhuti entered to inform me that Lokamitra had just telephoned from Poona with the news that Maha Dhammavira had committed suicide by setting fire to himself while on the Order retreat at Bhaja. Lokamitra wanted to know whether or not they should return to Bhaja and finish the retreat after performing his obsequies. The news was so sudden and so unexpected that it was at first difficult to grasp. I had seen Maha Dhammavira less than a year and a half ago. Despite his age (he was only ten or twelve years younger than my mother) he had been so full of life and vigour. He had been so emotionally positive, so radiant with happiness and good will. It seemed impossible to think of him as dead. Gradually, however, the news sank in, and I realized that the Order had lost one of its brightest ornaments. I was not surprised that he should have taken his own life, and taken it in such a way. But I was surprised that he should have taken it so soon, even though I knew that he had been seriously ill the previous winter and that he had no wish to be a burden either to his children and grandchildren or to his fellow Order members. Clearly he had been much more seriously ill than anyone had suspected and, knowing that if he fell ill again he would probably be unable to look after himself, had made arrangements to leave the world in the best possible place, under the best possible conditions, and at the best possible time, i.e. at Bhaja, during the annual Order retreat, and on the night of the full moon. With an indescribably poignant feeling of sadness that was, at the same time, not gloomy but touched with exhilaration at the thought of the heroic nature of his death, I realized that I would never again see Maha Dhammavira's virtually toothless mouth break into a beaming smile on seeing me, never again experience the warmth of his affection for me and for the rest of the Order.

A few nights later I woke up in the early hours of the morning, unable to sleep. The thought of Maha Dhammavira, and of the way in which he had died, was still very much with me. As I lay there in the darkness, there came flooding into my consciousness memories of my last visit to India, memories of Bhaja, memories of meetings with Maha Dhammavira and of conversations we had had. Eventually, these memories started crystallizing and, as they crystallized, there came to me the udāna-like lines:

> *Often, now, I find myself*
> *Thinking of the Caves of Bhaja,*
> *Thinking of the silent valley*
> *Where they look down on the rice-fields.*

As I heard these lines (or as I composed them – it was difficult to say which was the case) I realized that this might well be the beginning of a poem, though I did not immediately think of it as a poem about Maha Dhammavira. Four lines having 'come', and my more consciously creative energies being now engaged, I therefore set myself to continue the poem, if poem it was to be. By the time dawn came I had composed between thirty and forty more lines and hastened to get up and write them down before I forgot them. Already I had realized that the poem was in the metre of Longfellow's *Hiawatha*, which he had derived from the Finnish *Kalevala*, that it would consist of paragraphs of unequal length and not of four-line stanzas as I had at first thought, and that it would be a poem on the death of Maha Dhammavira. Having had my usual early breakfast (a meal which I always take on my own, and before anyone else in the community) I therefore decided that instead of working on my memoirs I would spend the rest of the day trying to complete the poem that had so unexpectedly arisen from the depths of my unconscious mind. It would be a kind of tribute to Maha Dhammavira. By 10 o'clock that night I had written altogether 100 lines but the poem was still not finished. The next day I wrote another 100 lines, and the next day another. It was only towards the end of the third day that I was able to write out the virtual repetition of the first four lines with which the poem concludes. During these three days I remained completely immersed in my thoughts and feelings about Maha Dhammavira. I did not even take part in the *puṇyānumodanā* ceremonies which, on the second (I think it was) of these three days, were held at Padmaloka and elsewhere throughout the Movement on his behalf. In carrying on with the writing of the poem I was, I felt, performing the best *puṇyānumodanā* ceremony for my old friend and disciple that I possibly could.

But although I wrote approximately 100 lines on each of the three days that I devoted to the writing of the poem, which on completion I decided to call 'The Caves of Bhaja', I did not write each century of lines with the same ease. The second century was much more difficult to write than the first, and the third so difficult that at times I felt that I might not be able to finish the poem. This was not due to any drying up of the sources of inspiration, so much as to the fact that the longer the poem became the more careful I had to be in drawing together all the different threads of which it was composed. There was also the fact that I knew very little about the actual circumstances of Maha Dhammavira's death, and had to keep the concluding paragraphs of the poem sufficiently general to cover a number of possible contingencies. (As it happened, I was not completely successful in this.) I could, of course, have postponed the writing of the poem until I had received a full account of Maha Dhammavira's death from Lokamitra. But if I did this there was the danger that the sources of inspiration would dry up, in the sense that the feelings that had been aroused by the sudden shock of Maha Dhammavira's death would inevitably subside after a while and by the time Lokamitra's letter arrived might not be sufficiently strong to sustain me throughout the composition of a long poem. Besides, from a purely poetic point of view it might even be an advantage not to know very much about the circumstances of Maha Dhammavira's death. There was, after all, such a thing as poetic tact or poetic discretion. By its very nature a death such as Maha Dhammavira's made detailed description impossible. Concentration on the minutiae of that death would serve, in fact, only to obscure its sublimity.

From the time that I had realized that 'The Caves of Bhaja' would be a poem about Maha Dhammavira, and that it would be a kind of tribute to him, I had known that this tribute would be a public one. In other words, I knew that I did not want simply to give expression to my thoughts and feelings about Maha Dhammavira; I also wanted to communicate them to other people. In particular, I wanted to communicate them to Order members, Mitras, and Friends. After all, as a member of the Western Buddhist Order, or Trailokya Bauddha Mahasangha, Maha Dhammavira was part of the Movement, and inasmuch as he was part of the Movement he belonged to us all, so that his death concerned us all, and affected us all. Moreover, inasmuch as I was myself part of the Movement, in the sense that my life was intimately connected with the life of every one of its members, and theirs with mine, my thoughts and feelings about Maha Dhammavira's death were of concern to all, and affected all. They were, so speak, public property. Indeed, I felt that until I had communicated my thoughts and feelings about Maha Dhammavira's death to at least some Order members, Mitras, and Friends I would not have given full expression to those thoughts and feelings. 'The Caves of Bhaja' was essentially a public poem. It existed not in the written or printed words on the page but in those words as spoken to a live audience, and until I had spoken them in this way 'The Caves of Bhaja' would not really be finished.

As soon as I had typed out what I had written, I therefore asked Subhuti to telephone Kulamitra and (if possible) make arrangements for me to read the poem at the London Buddhist Centre on the coming full moon day, when they would be celebrating Dharma Day. This was quickly done and, exactly one lunar month after Maha Dhammavira's death, I had the opportunity of reading 'The Caves of Bhaja' in the main shrine-room of the Centre immediately before the evening puja, which I had undertaken to lead. To my right, seated on his throne of English oak, rose the majestic golden figure of the Buddha, flanked by vases of crimson flowers and with the various offerings that had been made in the course of the day piled up before him. To my left, and in front of me, were packed the 150 or more Order members, Mitras, and Friends who had gathered for the occasion – a few of whom had not only been to India but had actually met Maha Dhammavira. After speaking a few words about Maha Dhammavira, and eulogizing his many positive qualities, especially his intense appreciation of the Movement, I took up the typescript of my poem (it had already been printed in booklet form) and amidst pin-drop silence read it to one of the most receptive audiences that it has ever been my good fortune to encounter. I had paid my tribute to Maha Dhammavira! I had given full expression to my thoughts and feelings about him! 'The Caves of Bhaja' was now really finished! It was therefore with quiet satisfaction that, having led the puja, I sat in the reception room afterwards, returning people's greetings and watching them buy copies of the booklet of the poem, proceeds from the sale of which were to be devoted to a suitable memorial for Maha Dhammavira.

Though the second of the three messengers that Yama had sent to me that year had come in a particularly unexpected and dramatic form, this was not the only form in which he had come. In the course of the previous nine months he had come in several other forms. Besides the death of Maha Dhammavira there had been the deaths of Lama Govinda, of the Venerable M. Sangharatana, formerly one of the Joint Secretaries of the Maha Bodhi Society of India, and of the Venerable U. Dhammaratana, who had succeeded me in the virtual editorship of the *Maha Bodhi Journal*, all three of whom were old friends of mine, as well as the death of my old friend and disciple Sherab Nangwa

(Prajnaloka), about which I had heard (from his daughter) six months after it had taken place. Like Maha Dhammavira's, each one of these deaths was a reminder that I too would have to die – though in justice to myself I must add that it was a long time since I had really needed any such reminders. But truly sorry though I was to 'lose' all these old friends, the fact was that they belonged to my past life (that is, my pre-FWBO Indian life) rather than to my present life, and their deaths did not affect me nearly so deeply as the death of Maha Dhammavira. Partly for this reason, therefore, and partly on account of its particularly unexpected and dramatic nature, it was in the shape of Maha Dhammavira's death that, for me, the second of Yama's messengers had really come that year.

The third and last messenger to come was old age, and unlike the two previous messengers he came (perhaps rather deceptively) in a joyful and even celebratory form. On Monday 26 August I reached the age of sixty! Though at sixty I felt no different from what I had felt at fifty-nine (just as at fifty-nine I had felt no different from what I had felt at fifty-eight), it seemed that inasmuch as the completion of one's sixth decade of life somehow marked a turning point the occasion had to be signalized in some way. Birthday cards, presents, and letters of felicitation had, in fact, been arriving at Padmaloka all the week, and the morning's mail brought a particularly large batch of them. Left to my own devices, I would probably have spent the day working as usual, but from the atmosphere that prevailed in the Order Office community I gathered not only that the day was to be celebrated but that I was expected to join in the celebrations. Prasannasiddhi went so far as to insist that on one day of the year, at least, I ought to take a holiday and not do any work. Though I did not quite see the logic of this, I acquiesced, and spent the greater part of the time between breakfast and lunch arranging my cards, reading the letters that had come that morning (usually, I do not read the day's mail until the afternoon, mornings being devoted to literary work), and perusing the magnificently illustrated history of London that I had found lying on the armchair when I entered my study: a birthday gift from Prasanna-siddhi. After all, it was in a remote and undistinguished corner of London that I had been born all those years ago, and it seemed not inappropriate that, on the morning of my sixtieth birthday, I should be perusing a history of my natal city. From time to time I raised my eyes from the book and listened, as it were, for whatever the messenger who had come to me in that joyful and celebratory form – the messenger of old age – might have to say.

In the afternoon, the sky being only slightly overcast, Prasannasiddhi and I decided to have a little outing. Accompanied by Subhuti and Sona, and closely followed by Ratnaprabha and Dhirananda, we accordingly drove to Blickling Hall, a famous stately home situated some twenty miles north of Norwich. Though it was so near to Padmaloka, and though I had heard so much about it, I had not been there before, and it was with a thrill of delight that, as the car turned a bend, I saw against the sky the harmonious south or entrance front of the old Jacobean house, with its mullioned windows, its corner turrets, its heavily decorated porch, its dominating central clock tower, and its clusters of tall, ornamental chimney stacks. The interior was no less delightful than the exterior. Many stately homes, though interesting and impressive, having been built and rebuilt, decorated and redecorated, furnished and refurnished over the centuries, tend to be a jumble of different periods and styles. At Blickling Hall this was by no means the case. There the predominant styles were those of the early seventeenth and late eighteenth centuries, and as we mounted the monumental staircase in the Great Hall and, reaching the first floor, walked through the magnificent staterooms, I could not but agree with the author of *The Great Houses of Britain* (which Prasannasiddhi and I had discovered in the Il Convento library the previous year) that the marriage that had been arranged at Blickling between these two quite distinctive styles was a very happy one. After we had spent an hour or more walking round, and I had particularly admired the subtle harmony that characterized the colour scheme of each room, we made our way to the cafeteria and treated ourselves to tea and cakes. After all, we were supposed to be celebrating my sixtieth birthday! Next door to the cafeteria was a gift shop, and there I bought a book of colour photographs of the English countryside for Lokamitra. The photographs must have been taken by an exceptionally fine photographer, for they were undoubtedly the most beautiful of their kind that I had seen. They were so beautiful that the thought crossed my mind that Lokamitra *might* think that I had sent him the book in order to make him homesick and entice him back to England. This was certainly not the case. I knew very well that, for Lokamitra, 'home' now meant India, and I had bought the book because someone had told me that he wanted some 'English views' – presumably to help keep alive his feeling for the old country and to show his friends what England was like.

Prasannasiddhi

Before leaving Blickling Hall we walked through the formal garden on the eastern side of the house, with its clipped yews and classical urns, and thence up the formal avenue that stretched beyond. On either hand towered rows of magnificent old beeches and oaks, under which grew azaleas, rhododendrons, and magnolias. By the time we reached the white pavilion that stood at the far end of the avenue the sky, which had been becoming more and more overcast for some time, suddenly grew quite dark, and drops of rain started to fall. We therefore hurriedly retraced our steps and, regaining the car, were soon on our way back to Padmaloka and dinner, having thoroughly enjoyed our afternoon's outing.

As the car drew up outside the front door, I saw the figure of Kovida emerging from a car parked further down the drive. With him were two other figures, both unidentifiable, whom he proceeded to hurry past the shrubbery and, apparently, into the house by the further of the two side entrances. At the time I attached no significance to the incident. Shortly afterwards I was informed that dinner would be an hour late, that it would be served in the small barn (which ever since the Convention had been functioning as a retreat dining room), and that I was on no account to enter the barn before 7 o'clock. The plot was beginning to thicken. A few minutes later, on happening to look out of my study window, I saw a car draw up in front of the portico.

Out of it stepped Nagabodhi, whom I was not expecting to see, and Ashvajit, to whom I had said goodbye only a few days earlier when he left Padmaloka for (eventually) India. Something suspicious was indeed going on. As though in confirmation of this impression, there came from somewhere downstairs the sound of a familiar laugh. It was the laugh of Kulananda who (I afterwards learned) had driven Nagabodhi and Ashvajit up from London but whom I had not seen when I looked out of the window as he was still inside the car. Since we had not met for some time, and since dinner would not be ready for nearly an hour, I asked Prasannasiddhi to call him up to my study for a chat. Thus the time passed very pleasantly, until, at exactly 7 o'clock, I made my way down the back stairs and across the gravelled courtyard to the small barn. There a big surprise awaited me. On opening the door I found the place brilliantly illuminated, while from two loudspeakers came the well-known strains of Handel's *Water Music*, one of my favourite items from the baroque repertoire. Beneath rows of Chinese lanterns tables covered in red and white cloths had been arranged round three out of the four sides of a long rectangle, the open end of which was towards me. On the tables stood tall red candles. As I took my seat at the head of the table, so to speak, with Subhuti on my right and Prasannasiddhi on my left, I saw on the wall opposite a colourful landscape across which was written, in huge letters, 'HAPPY 60TH BIRTHDAY, BHANTE', while to one side a putto (no doubt one of the 'Yashos' in disguise) blew on a horn. Prasannasiddhi also drew my attention to the fact that in the corner of some of the white Chinese lanterns, which had been decorated with colourful paper cutouts, could be seen the diminutive but distinctly recognizable figure of St Jerome. Someone must have taken a lot of trouble with the decoration of the barn.

Indeed, someone must have taken a lot of trouble with the organization of the whole function, of the nature of which I had no inkling until almost the last minute. Though I had taken it for granted that there would be the usual special birthday meal in the Order Office community kitchen-cum-dining room, I had had no idea that anything so elaborate was being planned or that so many people would be coming. To Subhuti's right and Prasannasiddhi's left, and all the way down the longer sides of the rectangle, shone the beaming faces of as many of those who (among the men in the Movement) had had a particularly long and close contact with me as it had been possible to muster at short notice. With one exception all were Order members (the exception was Kevin Brooks, with whom, towards the end of 1970, Siddhiratna and I had started what was in effect the first FWBO men's community), and with one exception all wore suits and even ties. While I was still looking round, seeing who was there, and admiring the decorations, there arrived from the Retreat Community kitchen the first course of a very well-cooked meal which was served with the greatest care and devotion by Satyaloka, Dhirananda, and Chris Morris. At the end of the meal a flat, square birthday cake was carried in, and after I had blown out the six candles, and cut the cake into pieces with a big knife (being careful to keep one piece for my mother, whom I would be seeing the following day), Subhuti rose to his feet and, calling everybody to order, announced that there would now be speeches. These were by no means of the usual after-dinner type. Besides being carefully prepared and well delivered, they were all remarkable for the strength of feeling with which Abhaya, Ashvajit, Nagabodhi, Devaraja, Padmavajra, Kulananda, and Prasannasiddhi in turn, as well as Subhuti himself as chairman, delivered the verbal equivalent of a series of truly magnificent 'floral tributes', as our Indian friends would say. Indeed, it might be said that if in the TBMSG they 'say it with flowers' in the FWBO they 'say it with speeches'. And, just as in India I am sometimes overwhelmed by all the sweet-smelling garlands and bouquets that I am offered, so, on the present occasion, I was overwhelmed by all the words of appreciation that were addressed to me for what I had done in the course of my sixty years – especially since the founding of the FWBO and the WBO. Had anyone from outside the Movement been listening they might have thought that the speakers were indulging in exaggeration and hyperbole; but I knew that this was not the case, and that every one of the speakers was speaking directly from the heart and saying exactly what he really thought and felt.

As if an excellent meal and seven superlative speeches were not more than enough, Subhuti next announced that Sthirananda would entertain us by singing musical settings of poems by William Blake to his own guitar accompaniment. I was already familiar with one of these settings and, since I always enjoyed hearing Sthirananda sing, so far as I was concerned there could hardly have been a better way of concluding the evening. Sthirananda was in very good voice, and to great applause sang four or five songs with his usual combination of musicality and expressiveness. So well did he sing, in fact, that in the course of a little impromptu speech that I made immediately afterwards, thanking everybody for giving me 'the best birthday I had ever had', I was moved to remark that Sthirananda's performance illustrated how well the 'folk' type of music was adapted to celebrations of this sort and that we ought, perhaps, to think in terms of developing the musical side of the Movement from comparatively humble beginnings of this kind rather than going in for something more ambitiously 'classical'. I also admitted that, listening to Sthirananda, I could not help wondering if it would be possible for him to set some of my own poems to music. Perhaps 'St Francis and the Birds' would lend itself to this kind of treatment.

The next day Kulananda drove Prasannasiddhi, Chintamani, and me down to London. On the way we called in at Rayleigh, and while the others spent the afternoon on the beach at Southend I talked with my mother. Though still very easily exhausted, she looked considerably better than she had done at the time of my previous visit. She was, however, still very worried about her brother. Uncle Dick (or Kets, as everybody called him) had at last been admitted to an old people's home in Thornton Heath, but since she had had no news of him except from Audrey, whose letters she found rather vague, she was anxious to know whether he was being properly looked after and what sort of mental state he was in. I therefore promised that, if I possibly could, I would go and see him before my departure for Italy and send her a full report of his condition. By the time the others came to collect me she had brightened up considerably and insisted on their coming in and having a cup of tea and a biscuit before we left for London and Sukhavati. At Sukhavati further celebrations awaited me, in the form of the birthday cake that was brought in at the end of the meal which, as usual, I had with the community. Once again I had to blow out the candles and cut the cake into pieces.

In the morning Prasannasiddhi and I went to see the 'Buddhism, Art and Faith' exhibition at the British Museum. The exhibition was quite a comprehensive one, and included some very interesting material; but I was forced to admit that very few of the images and paintings on display could be considered really first-class from a purely artistic point of view. Had Buddhism not succeeded in inspiring great and supreme art in the way that Christianity had done? (If not, why not?) Or were the masterpieces of Buddhist art hidden away in the monasteries and temples (and museums) of the East? Or was I, perhaps, judging Buddhist art in accordance with criteria that were really foreign to its genius? One of the most interesting items in the

exhibition was an early nineteenth-century Thai drawing of the traditional Buddhist model of the universe, in which the different god
realms were depicted one on top of the other like the storeys of an
immensely tall and slender pagoda, with a god sitting at the window
of each storey. The drawing gave one a better idea of the amount of
'space' occupied by the god realms relative to that occupied by the four
(or five) other realms of sentient existence than does the Tibetan Wheel
of Life, where they are all squeezed into a single segment (or half-
segment) of the third circle of the Wheel. Unfortunately, the exhibition
catalogue reproduces only the upper portion of the drawing (p.179,
fig.258). Having seen the exhibition, and bought a few postcards, we
had lunch at an Indian (Gujarati) restaurant in Great Russell Street
and, after doing a little shopping, made our way back to Bethnal
Green, where I had a short rest before taking a taxi to the Thames
Television studios in Euston Road.

Earlier in the year I had been invited to give a series of seven short
talks in the *Night Thoughts* programme on some aspect of Buddhism
and, after thinking the matter over, had decided to accept the invita-
tion. Besides giving me an opportunity of bringing the Dharma to the
attention of a larger audience than usual, the extreme shortness of the
talks (three of them 280 words long and four of them 200) would be an
interesting test of my ability to condense rather than (as usual) to
expand what I had to say. The researcher of the programme had
originally suggested to Subhuti that I might talk about a particular
Buddhist festival, but I decided that pilgrimage would be a better
subject and, this having proved acceptable, set to work on the scripts
about half-way through the Women's Order Convention. After a number of false starts I eventually got on to the right wavelength, so to
speak, and produced my tiny scripts with increasing facility. Indeed,
when I came to write a talk of 280 words after writing two or three of
only 200 words I felt as though I had ample room in which to express
myself. Unfortunately, after the scripts had been submitted to the
producer of the programme, and pronounced excellent, I was asked to
reduce the longer talks by ten words each and the shorter ones by
twenty! This was because a sign language translator was being used
and it had been discovered that fewer words could be fitted into the
allotted time than had originally been supposed. Since I had already
eliminated every inessential word it was impossible for me to make the
talks shorter without some sacrifice of meaning, and I therefore com-
plied with the producer's request with the greatest reluctance and

only after making a vigorous protest. Eventually the necessary adjustments were made and thus it was that, a little after 2.30 on the afternoon of 28 August, I found myself in the Thames Television studios.

The producer, the director, and the researcher of the *Night Thoughts* programme, as well as the director's secretary, were all women. The studio technicians, of whom there seemed to be seven or eight, were all men. After I had met the producer and director I was shown the recording studio and introduced to Viscount Tonypandy (the former George Thomas, the Speaker of the House of Commons), who had just finished recording his own contribution to the *Night Thoughts* series. Presumably because the producer had introduced me as the *Venerable* Sangharakshita, Lord Tonypandy (who is, I believe, of the Welsh Methodist persuasion) raised his eyebrows in mock surprise and ejaculated, 'Church of England?' to which I retorted, 'No. Buddhist.' This seemed to stagger him and for a few moments he was at a loss what to say. However, he soon recovered himself, and by the time we joined the producer and the other women for a cup of tea he had resumed what was apparently his customary flow of conversation. He was, of course, far too sophisticated a person to show any open curiosity about me, but he managed to elicit the main facts of my curriculum vitae and it transpired that we had several friends in common, among them the late Dr G.P. Malalasekera, the former Sri Lankan High Commissioner in London, whom I had known since the early fifties and whom I had once defended in a famous controversy. Malalasekera was the only Buddhist Lord Tonypandy had known (they had met, I gathered, in the thirties, at a gathering of the World Congress of Faiths), and he commended him warmly for his tolerance, his kindliness, and other peaceable qualities. There proved to be a sting in the tail of the commendation, however, for after observing that Buddhism was in fact a very peaceable religion the ex-Speaker suddenly remarked, 'But the Buddhists of Sri Lanka aren't behaving very peaceably nowadays, are they?' This was in allusion, of course, to the increasingly bloody conflict between the Sinhalese and the Tamil inhabitants of that unhappy island. There was little I could say in reply. Indeed, Lord Tonypandy obviously did not expect a reply. Throughout our conversation he had carried on a violent flirtation with all the women present, especially with the young and pretty secretary, and seemed to be far more interested in that than in Buddhism, or Malalasekera, or the peaceableness or otherwise of the Buddhists of Sri Lanka. The flirtation was conducted mainly in terms of mildly suggestive remarks, and having frequently heard his voice on the radio calling 'Ord—*er*, ord—*er!*' during parliamentary debates I found it strange to hear him talking in this kind of way and I wondered why a man of his age should have so little respect for his own grey hairs as to behave in such a way with women who were young enough to be his granddaughters. Was he of a genuinely lecherous temperament (like Lloyd George, another Welsh-man), or did he feel that he was obliged to behave as he did simply in order to show everybody that there was still some life left in the old man? The women, including the youthful secretary, responded to his clumsy advances with polite indifference, and seemingly were no more bothered by them than they would have been by the creaking of a door or the dripping of a tap. Nonetheless, I could not help wonder-ing what they really thought of Lord Tonypandy's behaviour – if, indeed, they thought about it at all, which they gave no sign of doing.

Lord Tonypandy having taken his departure, boisterously assuring the director that if her secretary, who had undertaken to show him where the toilets were located, was not back within half an hour she would have to send someone to see what the two of them were up to, I was ushered back into the recording studio. Here I found the sign language translator, a rather ordinary middle-aged woman in a black dress whose duty it was to 'translate' my talks for the benefit of deaf-and-dumb viewers. After we had gone over the two or three specifically Buddhist terms I would be using, and she had consulted her sign language dictionary (the first time I knew that such a thing existed), the recording session started. The technicians, I thought, looked rather jaded, probably because they were recording 365 talks, by 51 different speakers (Lord Tonypandy had a double innings), within the space of 21 days, which was probably rather too much of a good thing. One of the speakers (the producer told me), an Anglican bishop, had tried to give his talks impromptu, but the results had been far from satisfactory, and he had been sent away to write out his scripts in the usual manner. In my case there was of course no such difficulty, and in a few minutes the script of my first talk started to appear on the autocue and at a signal from the studio manager (as I think he is called) I started to read. Including rehearsals and retakes (the sign language translator had difficulty with several passages) the sessions lasted altogether two hours. Though the producer and the director were satisfied with the results I was not, mainly because in order to fit the talks into the allotted time I had to speak faster than was natural to me and faster than, in my opinion, the nature of the talks required. However, the producer and the director both assured me that, by television standards, I was not speaking fast at all, and both seemed slightly amused that I should be so concerned about the matter. Before leaving the studio I asked the sign language translator whether she had found my talks easier to translate than those of my predecessors in the series or more difficult. Rather to my surprise, she replied that she had found them much easier. My language was very concrete, whereas the language used by some of the other speakers had been very abstract, and it was extremely difficult to translate abstract language into sign language.

Back in the reception room I had a cup of tea with the producer and the other women working on the *Night Thoughts* programme and, a more relaxed atmosphere prevailing now that the day's work was over, we chatted for a few minutes before parting. The conversation having naturally turned to Buddhism, the producer confessed that she and her colleagues had looked forward to meeting me with a certain amount of apprehension. The reason for this was that one of them (I think it was the researcher) had been told by a friend who knew a little about Buddhism that she should on no account offer to shake hands with me; if she did, I would be deeply offended, since Buddhist monks were not allowed to touch women. They had therefore been pleasantly surprised when I *had* shaken hands with them as this made them feel more at ease with me. On my enquiring whether they knew anything about Buddhism other than that Buddhist monks were not allowed to touch women they admitted that they did not. To me it was strange that four intelligent women (or five, including the sign language translator, who had also joined us) should know no more about Buddhism than that Buddhist monks were 'not allowed' to come into physical contact with members of the opposite sex. It was strange, and it was unfortunate, and in the few minutes at my disposal it was obviously difficult for me to give them a more balanced picture of Buddhism (though they had, of course, heard my seven talks). I therefore contented myself with remarking that while in the Buddhist countries of Asia it was certainly the custom for monks to avoid physical contact with women (and nuns with men), many English Buddhists did not think it necessary to adhere to those aspects of Asian Buddhist praxis that were liable to give rise to misunderstanding in the West. At the same time, I pointed out that in countries like Sri Lanka and Tibet men often became monks at an early age, and since monks were supposed to be celibate it was no more than a common-sense precaution that they should avoid coming into contact with women. It was for much the same reason, I added, that in the FWBO we had single-sex communities for those who took their commitment to the spiritual life more seriously. The women's reaction to these remarks was interesting. While they were quite prepared to accept that in Buddhism it was 'not the done thing' for a monk to shake hands with a woman, they were quite unable to understand why it should be so. When I tried to pursue the matter a little further, explaining that in the case of a young monk, especially, physical contact with a woman might lead to the arising of sexual desire, and that sexual desire was a hindrance to spiritual development, I met with looks of blank incomprehension. Clearly I was speaking a language with which they were not acquainted. Nonetheless, they remained friendly enough, and showed no disposition to argue, and I therefore backtracked a little and told them about the country retreat centre that the women in the FWBO were working to establish. When it was open, I suggested, it would be a good subject for a television programme.

By this time it was nearly 5.30, and the height of the rush hour. The women therefore suggested that it would be quicker to go by tube than to take a taxi and I left the Thames Television studios with the researcher, who was going the same way as I was. Despite the crush, which was the worst I could remember experiencing on the Underground and made me feel slightly giddy, we managed to secure seats and had a lively conversation – mainly about marriage – all the way to Liverpool Street, where I had to change to another line. On my arrival at Sukhavati I found Vanda Chivers waiting to drive me down to the new Khadiravani community in Streatham, where I had a dinner engagement, and as soon as I had had a wash and brush-up we were speeding from Bethnal Green to Whitechapel and from Whitechapel across Tower Bridge through Walworth, Camberwell, and Brixton to Streatham (Vanda seemed to know all the short cuts). As we drove down Streatham High Street we passed the Streatham Public Library, to which I had belonged in my teens, and which I had visited on Saturday afternoons. I could still remember some of the books I had borrowed then. Among them were King's *The Gnostics and Their Remains*, Kant's *Critique of Pure Reason*, and Dean Inge's *The Philosophy of Plotinus*, in two volumes.

Though I have spoken of the 'new' Khadiravani community it was really only the location that was new, Ashokashri and the other members of the community having moved into that particular building from their old premises about a year ago. Since then they had been busy painting and decorating, and though the work was still not *quite* finished they were naturally eager for me to see the results of their labours. A three-storeyed Victorian building, the new Khadiravani was situated in a quiet street round the corner, so to speak, from Streatham High Street, and not far from Tooting Bec Station – another haunt of my boyhood. On my arrival I was welcomed by Ashokashri, and after I had had a cup of tea with her and Ratnasuri in a very pleasant little room overlooking the back garden Ashokashri took me on a guided tour of the premises, which had certainly been decorated to a very high standard indeed. In fact Khadiravani is probably the best-decorated community in the whole Movement (though I have yet to see Aryaloka), besides being the biggest women's community. In one of the study-bedrooms I saw a quite remarkable picture of a female head that had been executed in mosaic by one of the Mitras and which owed, I thought, something to the mosaic of the Empress Theodora and her court at San Vitale in Ravenna. It was so good that I spent several minutes in front of it lost in admiration. In fact I admired it so much that – Ashokashri having no doubt commented on my enthusiasm – it arrived at Padmaloka a few days later with the best wishes of the artist.

On completing my tour of the premises I found that the table had been laid in the dining room, the walls of which were hung with colourful abstract paintings by Vanda, and with the nine or ten members of the community, plus Vanda and Pam Cooper from Brighton, I sat down to an excellent meal. After nourishment for the body came nourishment for the mind. The room having been cleared, Luise Holtbernd and Elizabeth English brought in their violoncellos and for upwards of an hour entertained us with a performance of French, Italian, and German baroque music, the last item on the programme being by Telemann. It was interesting to see how the differing temperaments of the two musicians were reflected in the way in which they played. Luise took the performance very seriously indeed, bending over her instrument with an intensity of concentration that wrinkled her brow into a slight frown. Elizabeth sat upright, bowing away gaily, and smiling at the audience in sheer delight. Despite the striking difference between them the two women played together extremely well. So well did they play, and such an attractive picture did they make, that there flashed across my inward eye an image of the angels I had seen in a Renaissance painting in Venice playing on their viols at the foot of the throne of the Madonna. In between the musical items Pam Cooper read some of her own poems in a measured manner and with considerable feeling. By the end of the performance I was left with the distinct impression that there was a lot of talent at Khadira-vani and a lot of positive emotion.

But the evening was not yet over. Hardly had the applause died away than the lights suddenly went out and, with a golden blaze of candles, there came into the blackness of the room – a birthday cake.

The next day passed more quietly, at least until the evening, when I went along to Friends House in Euston Road and read my paper on 'The Glory of the Literary World' to an audience of more than 450 people. Originally the reading of the paper had been intended to mark the launching of *The Eternal Legacy*, my long-awaited book on Buddh-ist canonical literature, but owing to a series of accidents the date of publication had had to be postponed. Nonetheless, since the paper was ready, and since I would shortly be leaving for Italy, it had been decided to hold the meeting on 29 August as planned. If we were unable actually to launch *The Eternal Legacy* we could at least give it some advance publicity, besides helping to launch Tharpa (the new Buddhist publication house that was bringing out the book) and drawing attention to the appearance of my *Travel Letters*, which had just been issued by Windhorse Publications and which was on sale that evening together with the text of 'The Glory of the Literary World' in booklet form. What with having to introduce a paper that was now being read on its own account, so to speak, to explain the non-appear-ance of the book that we were supposed to be launching, to draw attention to the presence on the bookstall of a publication that we were *not* launching (for this was not, strictly speaking, an FWBO occasion), to help launch a new Buddhist publication house that did not as yet have any publications to its credit, and to bestow congratulations all round, the chairman of the meeting did not have an enviable assign-ment, but since the chairman happened to be Nagabodhi he acquitted himself with ease and confidence. Listening to him, I in fact marvelled at the way in which he trod his particular tightrope without a moment's hesitation and with the greatest aplomb. So far as my own part in the proceedings was concerned, I read my paper reasonably well and was not dissatisfied with the impression it seemed to pro-duce, though subsequently I heard that some members of the audience had complained (if that is the right word) that I had included in the lecture more material than they were able to take in at a single sitting.

Perhaps there is something to be said for my reverting, at least occasionally, to the more popular type of lecture that I used to give in the early days of the Movement. Having read my paper, and listened appreciatively to Nagabodhi's concluding remarks, I retired to a corner of the hall, where I sat and had a cup of tea and exchanged a few words with friends both old and new. Among the old friends was Stephen Hall (Shantideva), who presented me with a beautiful crystal lotus blossom, and among the new friends Estelle Lovett, who is currently helping Devamitra translate *The Essence of Zen* into Italian.

The following morning Subhuti (thanks to whose heroic efforts *Travel Letters* and *The Glory of the Literary World* had been brought out in time for the meeting) drove Prasannasiddhi and me up to Padmaloka for the weekend Men's Event and the study group leaders' retreat that was to follow. On the way we stopped at the Temple tea house, where we sat in the garden in the warm sunshine and had our morning coffee. The study group leaders' retreat represented my last major engagement before I left for Italy and the Men's Ordination Course. In the evenings and afternoons I attended to my usual work, and in the evenings I joined the retreatants and for two hours or more dealt with questions arising out of my lectures on the Buddha's Noble Eightfold Path, which they had studied during the earlier part of the day. On the last day of the retreat, however, I dealt with the questions not in the evening but in the afternoon, so that Prasannasiddhi and I could leave Padmaloka immediately afterwards and thus have one whole day in London before flying to Pisa on the morning of 11 September. The reason for this was that, mindful of my promise to my mother, I wanted to go and see my uncle in the old people's home at Thornton Heath. Kulamitra (who on my arrival at Sukhavati had presented me with a copy of the magnificent facsimile edition of Johnson's *Dictionary*) kindly offered to chauffeur us for the day, and we accordingly set out soon after lunch. Our first stop was not Thornton Heath but the South Bank, where the exhibition of the work of Edward Burra was being shown at the Hayward Gallery. Not being very interested in the moderns, I had scarcely heard the name of this twentieth-century British artist before, but a review of the exhibition that I had read having aroused my curiosity I wanted to see what his work was like. Prasannasiddhi was not very enthusiastic (having acquired from me some rather 'pre-Raphaelite' tendencies) but Kulamitra was willing to investigate, and the three of us spent an hour looking round the extensive and quite impressive exhibition. Some of the later paintings depicted hilly landscapes along the winding roads of which were strung out enormous lorries that dominated the entire scene – obviously an 'ecological' warning of some kind. Having seen the exhibition we adjourned to the cafeteria and chatted over a cup of tea before continuing our journey to Thornton Heath – and Croydon, where we were to have dinner at Hockneys and attend Jayamati's talk on 'Towards a Buddhist Theatre'.

Cheriton House, as the old people's home was called, was situated in a quiet side street off the London Road about a mile further on from Khadiravani. It was a featureless brick building, rather like a small block of flats, and with no sign of an entrance. On leaving the car (Kulamitra and Prasannasiddhi were going to wait for me) I saw a stout West Indian woman, evidently a nurse who had just come off duty, emerging from a small gate and asked her where the main entrance was. She directed me down the side of the building, where there was a narrow door. On passing through this door I found myself in a large and very hot kitchen beyond which I could see a dining room where five or six old people were already waiting impatiently for their after-noon tea. Obviously I had not come in at the main entrance, but nobody seemed to mind, and a cheerful young kitchen assistant directed me to the reception area where I found another stout West Indian woman, in nurse's uniform, sitting behind a desk in a tiny office. After I had explained that I was Mr Ketskemety's nephew she asked me to wait as he was shaving. About half an hour having elapsed, I heard my uncle's voice in the distance complaining that he had lost his jacket. Several people appeared to be trying to help him find it. A few more minutes elapsed, and Uncle Dick appeared – without his jacket – in the door of the office. On seeing me his face lit up, but not being quite sure of my identity (we had met only twice in the last twenty years) he asked 'Who is it?' When I had identified myself we shook hands warmly (I noticed that his handshake was quite firm) and he exclaimed, 'Well I'll be blowed, fancy seeing *you* here!' Despite his eighty-four years he held himself erect, and though he was extremely thin he had a good colour and in fact looked quite healthy. He was also quite smartly dressed. Before I could ask him anything about himself, however, a nurse intervened and marched him away to the dining room for his tea. I sat and waited for him out in the garden (as the little patch of lawn was called) and the same nurse – a young English girl – brought me a cup of tea that must have contained at least three teaspoonfuls of sugar. Sitting there I could see the old people passing backwards and forwards through the reception area and walking up and down the stairs. After a few minutes I realized that it was usually the same ten or twelve old people who kept passing backwards and forwards through the reception area and walking up and down the stairs. It was as though they were simply unable to sit still. This was all the more remarkable in that they were for the most part extremely frail and emaciated (some had crutches and walking frames) and besides moving stiffly stared fixedly in front of them without the slightest change of expression. They all looked well cared for, and some of the women were smartly and even stylishly dressed, but with their jerky wooden movements they resembled puppets controlled by invisible wires rather than living human beings.

After fifteen or twenty minutes Uncle Dick returned, no doubt having had his tea, and we moved to the centre of the garden where it was still sunny. Having ascertained that he was being properly looked after and that his mental state was (so far as I could tell) better than my mother's fears had led me to expect, my main concern was to obtain a message from him for her, since she had been greatly perturbed at not receiving any reply to her letters. We had not talked for more than five or ten minutes before I noticed that he kept repeating himself and that he sometimes replied to me at random. From this I concluded that he was probably a little deaf. A few experiments proved that this was, in fact, the case, and that he was deafer in his right ear than in his left. Drawing my chair as close to him as I could, I therefore positioned my lips a few inches from his left ear. Communication between us at once improved, and after making sure that he still remembered my mother (Audrey had written and told her that he had completely lost his memory) I gave him news of her and asked if he would like to send her a message. To my relief he at once said, 'Give her my love and tell her I'll come and see her soon.' He also talked about the dates of their respective birthdays, and told me that my mother was a year younger than she thought she was. By this time we had talked for nearly an hour, and since I had completed my mission and moreover did not want to keep Kulamitra and Prasannasiddhi waiting any longer I therefore brought the meeting to an end. Not wanting my uncle to think that I was in a hurry to get away (he had complained that no one ever came to see him) I did this as tactfully as I could. As it happened, my tactfulness was wasted. Though pleased to see me, Uncle Dick was not sorry to see me go, and on my showing signs of leaving jumped up with shouts of, 'Bring the key! Bring the key!' Our conversation had probably tired him, and I recalled that on my last two or three visits to Christmas Humphreys the latter had not been able to sustain the conversation for more than an hour and a half. As for the key, this was the key to the front door, the door by which I had *not* entered, which apparently was kept locked. Though no doubt it was kept locked in the interest of the old people themselves, some of whom might have wandered out and got lost or knocked down by a passing car, nonetheless it underlined in a slightly sinister manner the fact that old age can bring not only helplessness but loss of freedom.

On our arrival at the Croydon Buddhist Centre I telephoned Tynia and asked her to tell my mother that I had seen Kets and that I would send her a full report of our meeting from Italy. This done, I rejoined Kulamitra and Prasannasiddhi in Hockneys, where Padmaraja and other members of the Aryatara chapter entertained us in their customarily hospitable fashion. After a very pleasant meal I spent some time browsing in the well-stocked and (evidently) well-patronized bookshop and from there made my way to the meeting room in readiness for Jayamati's talk 'Towards a Buddhist Theatre.' The talk proved to be rather shorter than I had expected, but in it Jayamati made a number of important points. One of the most striking of these was to the effect that a Buddhist theatre would not need a permanent company of professional actors. Actors could be recruited on an ad hoc basis from the ranks of Order members, Mitras, and Friends and trained for a particular production. Jayamati seemed to think that emotional positivity and a willingness to communicate – such as one finds in the 'Friends' – were more important than professional expertise.

The morning of the following day, Wednesday 11 September, saw Prasannasiddhi and me on our way to Heathrow, Amoghachitta driving. As we sped westward along the M4 the sky was so ethereally blue, and the sun so bright, it seemed a pity to be leaving England, and we consoled ourselves with the reflection that in Italy the sky would probably be even bluer and the sun even brighter. Not that we could count on this. Last year it had actually been raining when we arrived in Pisa. Since the journey from Bethnal Green did not take much more than an hour we arrived at Heathrow with plenty of time to spare, and after Prasannasiddhi and I had checked in the three of us made our way upstairs to the cafeteria for a farewell coffee. All around us was the mingled excitement and melancholy of departure, the boredom of waiting, the fatigue of the continually revolving crowd, punctuated every few minutes by the muffled roar of an aircraft taking off. Eventually our flight was called and having said goodbye to Amoghachitta and, in his person, to all the friends we were leaving behind us, Prasannasiddhi and I passed through Passport Control and Customs to the departure lounge. Here there was a half-hour wait before we could board the aircraft. In the aircraft itself there was an hour-long wait until radio contact with Milan could be restored. At last, contact having been restored, at about midday the plane took off and after quite an enjoyable flight (as described at the beginning of this Letter) my companion and I found ourselves standing on the tarmac of Pisa airport with the unaccustomed heat of the sun soaking into our bodies.

That was a month ago. Or rather, it would have been a month ago if time had stood still since I started writing this Letter. During that month I continued to follow the daily routine into which I had so quickly settled after my arrival within the familiar walls of Il Convento. In the morning I wrote and edited. In the afternoon, after taking my constitutional with Prasannasiddhi or (occasionally) one of the Mitras, I attended to correspondence, the arrears of which had already been supplemented by the bulky packets of redirected mail that had started arriving from Padmaloka. In the evening (except when it was a Special Day of some kind) I took the question-and-answer sessions on Gampopa's *Jewel Ornament of Liberation*, a text which seemed not to be adapted to the spiritual needs of all the retreatants. Since I started writing this Letter a week ago, however, there have been two important changes as well as one important new development. The question-and-answer sessions on *The Jewel Ornament of Liberation*, eighteen in number, have come to an end, which means that for the time being, at least, I have more time for writing and editing and for correspondence. Since at Il Convento I have no secretarial help of any kind (except that Suvajra and Buddhapalita post my letters) this is very welcome, the more especially since the postponement of my visit to India, and the consequent necessity of handing over the responsibility for conferring ordinations there this year to a team of senior Order members from England, has already involved me in a good deal of extra letter-writing. The other important change is that Gary Pierpont, a Mitra from Manchester, has started making a videotape record of the Course – something that has not been done before and which will, I hope, give the rest of the Movement a better idea of what happens at Il Convento. When the videotaping should start, and how it should be done, has been the subject of much earnest discussion between

Vessantara and the rest of the team on the one hand and Gary on the other, with the result that instead of being an intrusion into the privacy of the Course the making of the videotape is an integral part of it. As to the important new development, this consists in the fact that I have accepted the team's recommendation that all twenty-three of the Mitras participating in this year's Course should be ordained, so that Il Convento is currently pervaded by a sense of joy not unmixed with relief. In a few days' time the private ordinations will begin and, therewith, eight days of virtually uninterrupted silence.

* * *

Three weeks have now passed. The private and public ordinations having taken place in the usual manner, Prasannasiddhi and I felt free to go on a short trip to Naples, from which we returned just over two weeks ago, that is to say, about a week before I was due to start taking the fifteen small 'private' discussion groups which have just concluded. In previous years I have done most of my sightseeing either before the Course began or after it had ended. This year I decided that it would be better to do it a month earlier, immediately after the completion of the ordinations. Not only would the weather be warmer then but, as experience had shown, the four or five days following the ordinations tended to be taken up with the systematic 'briefing' of the new Order members, or else with building work, and my presence was not really needed. Suvajra and Buddhapalita having driven us into Grosseto, and treated us to coffee and pastries at one of their favourite bars, on the morning of Tuesday 29 October Prasannasiddhi and I therefore caught the express train to the South. I had spent a day (I think it was) in Naples in the summer of 1966, on the way back to England from Greece, and my two most vivid memories of the place were of the enormous piles of rotting garbage at the end of the streets and the alabaster and bronze image of the many-breasted Diana of Ephesus in the National Archaeological Museum. Apart from the northerner's natural attraction to the warmth and colour of the South, there were two main reasons for the present expedition. I wanted to see if Campania might not be a more suitable area for a retreat centre than Tuscany, and I wanted to extend my acquaintance with the historically and artistically important cities of Italy, as did Prasannasiddhi.

For the first half of our journey the landscape was not unlike that through which we had passed on our way down from Pisa to Grosseto.

On our right (for part of the distance) was the sea, and on our left, beyond the olive groves, the little white farmhouses, and the patches of cultivation, were ranges of low green hills very similar to those behind Grosseto. We had found seats in a no-smoking compartment with a couple of young Italians who seemed to be friends, or at least acquaintances, and who sat opposite each other in the window seats. A few stations further on the thinner and darker of the two, who I noticed was carrying a copy of an Italian translation of a book by Carlos Castaneda, left us with the usual 'Buongiorno!' The other was a well-built, pleasant-looking young man in his early twenties clad in blue jeans and a brown sweater. Within minutes of his friend's departure the three of us had entered into conversation. At least, what we entered into would have been conversation if he had known any English and if Prasannasiddhi and I had had more than a couple of dozen words of Italian between us. As things were, it was only with the help of a good deal of gesticulation and (on his part at least) some very expressive rollings of the eyes that we were able to make ourselves mutually intelligible. He was in the Parachute Police, he informed us (this was a force that we did not have in England, I somehow managed to explain) and quite enjoyed the experience of jumping from the plane at a height of 2,000 feet and counting six (I think it was) before pulling the safety cord that caused the parachute to open. He had made more than twenty such jumps and had not yet completed his training. No, his friend was not in the Parachute Police. He worked in the port that we had seen from the station where he had got down. He himself lived not far from Rome, and would be changing trains at Rome Central. He was going home on leave. In this way a sort of friendship sprang up between us, a friendship that was consolidated by the sharing of our crispbread sandwiches, with the result that when he got down at Rome Central he shook hands with us with genuine warmth and a cordial 'Arrivederci!' Though he had told us a good deal about himself, we had not been able to tell him very much about ourselves, or about what we were doing in Italy. More important still, we had not been able to tell him anything about Buddhism. As on similar occasions in previous years, I wished that we had had with us a booklet in Italian that we could have given him as a parting gift.

In Rome Central we had more than an hour to wait before the train resumed its journey to the South. During that time the compartment gradually filled up with short, plump Italians, most of them swarthy-complexioned and wearing dark suits. Several pulled out newspapers.

Half-way down the front page I noticed a headline with the words 'Rajneesh' and 'FBI' in close juxtaposition. What was happening? At Il Convento we had had no news of the outside world for nearly two months, and it would seem that in Rajneeshpuram, at least, some dramatic developments had been taking place unbeknown to us. Not being able to read Italian, however, we had to contain our curiosity. In any case, by this time the train had slid out of the station and our attention was claimed by the scenery through which we were now passing. This was of a grander and more rugged character than that between Grosseto and Rome. The hills to the east, bordering the coastal plain, were so big as to be almost mountains and instead of being covered with evergreens they were grey and stony. As for the towns and villages, these were not perched on the hilltops but strung out along the edge of enormous ridges, the dirty grey of the houses making them virtually indistinguishable from the rock on which they were built. At regular intervals a stone quarry made an ugly grey hole in the mountainside. Cacti started appearing, and I noticed that many of the trees growing in the stony orchards, or bordering the roads, were half dead – presumably the result of the exceptionally heavy snowfalls last winter.

Italian engineers have a great fondness for tunnels. During the latter part of our journey we passed through quite a number of them, three of which were of considerable length. From the second of these we emerged on to the very edge of a sparkling blue sea, but this fascinating vision did not last for more than a few minutes. From the third tunnel, which must have been at least four or five miles long, we emerged into a greater width of coastal plain than we had as yet traversed. There were plenty of olive groves, as well as orchards and market gardens of various kinds. Among the few vegetables that I was able to recognize was the artichoke, the grey-green crowns of which poked up out of the reddish-brown soil in neat rows. Despite all the cultivation, the general impression was one of comparative wilderness, probably because the farmhouses were few in number and because the mountains seemed to have grown bigger and to have withdrawn into the distance. At one point I saw a herd of buffalo in a field, so that for a moment I could easily imagine that I was in India. Half an hour later the mountains, which tended to be grey and rather sinister in appearance, started coming closer again, and soon Prasannasiddhi and I were on the lookout for Mount Vesuvius. After several wrong identifications we eventually saw it, though from an angle that was quite unfamiliar to us from the guidebooks we had perused. Moreover, the train having by this time reached the suburbs of Naples we saw its purplish-brown shape through a perfect forest of aluminium factory chimneys.

Ten minutes later we had arrived and were making our way across the enormous width of the very modern, not to say futuristic, Central Station in the direction of the glass-walled bar and cafeteria. Here we found a quiet corner, an attentive waiter, and a pot of tea for two as we pored over our map of Naples. Originally we had intended to stay at a hotel on St Elmo's Hill, which was said to command a fine view of the city and the bay, but when Vessantara had telephoned on our behalf he had been unable to get a reply. Prasannasiddhi had therefore picked out from the Hotel Directory a third-class hotel called the Coral, which was situated quite near the station and was sufficiently central for our purpose. Having located it on the map we left the station and, cutting across a corner of the Piazza Garibaldi (there was a monument to that hero in the centre), made our way through some rather dirty back streets to the Hotel Coral. There were no problems. Within minutes of our arrival we had booked in and were being ushered into a double room on the second floor. On opening the shutters and drawing aside the curtain we saw that our room overlooked an inner courtyard, the most striking feature of which was that it was entirely filled with lines of washing, which were stretched across it at as many different levels as there were storeys in the buildings that made up its four sides. Since there were at least five or six storeys that was quite a lot of washing. In the days that followed we were to see those lines of washing festooning courtyards, and stretched across streets and alleys, all over Naples, and came to think of that colourful city as the City of Washing.

But we had not come simply to stare out of the window, even though the washing hanging outside was indeed a picturesque sight and one that would have made the reputations – and perhaps the fortunes – of a whole school of painters and photographers. After a brief rest, and a wash and brush up, we therefore left the key of our room at the reception desk and set out to explore the neighbourhood. On stepping into the street I noticed that although it was late October the air was mild, even balmy. Our intention was to walk down to the Marina, which according to the map was quite near, on the way keeping a lookout for a restaurant where we could take our evening meal later on. Once we had found the Marina we could have a quiet stroll along the sea front and see, perhaps, something of the famous bay. In my mind's eye I saw Prasannasiddhi and myself proceeding peacefully along what I must have imagined would be a sort of cross between the promenade at Brighton and Marine Drive, Bombay. The reality proved to be far otherwise. Having threaded a maze of narrow streets, all of them lined with tiny shops crammed with goods, we finally emerged into the Via Garibaldi, one of the busiest and noisiest thoroughfares I had seen – or heard – for a long time. The narrow pavements were thronged with rather poorly dressed people, many of them women with shopping bags, while along the roadway thundered and shrieked and roared a densely packed stream of traffic. The traffic consisted mainly of small, shabby motor cars, though there were also quite a number of motor scooters and mustard yellow, single-decker trolley buses, the latter apparently having only recently replaced the trams, the iron rails of which could still be seen embedded in the cobbled surface of the road. Whenever the traffic slowed down, or became so congested as to grind to a temporary halt, there would be a furious blaring of horns from two or three dozen vehicles – a blaring that would not stop until the traffic was moving sufficiently fast again, and sometimes not even then. Moving in what we hoped was the right direction, Prasannasiddhi and I allowed ourselves to be borne along by the flow. On the other side of the road, flanking a comparatively narrow opening in what was originally the city wall, there stood two enormous round Aragonese towers, their calm and immobility contrasting strangely with the frenzied movements of the crowds and the traffic below. When we had progressed a few hundred yards, passing the Vesuviana (the main station on the circular route round mount Vesuvius), and had crossed several busy roads, the crowds (though not the traffic) started to thin out. Perhaps we were approaching the Marina. After negotiating an extremely complicated and dangerous crossroads, where the traffic came hurtling towards us from at least three different directions, we found ourselves in the comparative emptiness and tranquillity not of the Marina but the docks. Naples was a much bigger city than we had realized, and anything of the nature of a sea front was several miles further along the bay. By this time night had fallen. With some difficulty we made our way to the quayside, where we had the satisfaction of peering down into the black water, while above us the bow of a ship towered sharply against the stars. Far away to the north-west we could see rows of coloured lights: probably the Marina.

Having had our fill of the solitude and quietness of the docks we retraced our steps and so gained the Piazza Garibaldi. Since we were now beginning to feel rather tired, as well as a little hungry, we walked round the broad, comparatively unfrequented pavements of the Piazza scrutinizing the menus displayed in the restaurant windows in the hope of finding one that included a few vegetarian dishes. Not meeting with much success, we eventually decided to make do with a pizza (Naples was, after all, supposed to be the original home of that ubiquitous comestible) and, having found a pizzeria, we had our first and last full meal of the day and returned to the hotel. Before we went upstairs I had a coffee in the bar-cum-dining room. What with the upended chairs, the general air of untidiness, and the slovenly – though cheerful – service, it was not a very attractive place, and Prasannasiddhi and I resolved not to have breakfast there in the morning but to go, instead, to a bar somewhere in the neighbourhood.

Before retiring we consulted the guidebook we had brought with us from Il Convento (indeed, from England) and made provisional plans for the following day's sightseeing. (Where we went, and what we did, would depend to some extent on the state of the weather, and our plans covered various possible contingencies.) This done, we got into our respective beds and put out the light. Though it was quite dark within the room I was unable to sleep for what seemed like several hours. This was not because I was not tired, or because I was mentally over-stimulated. The reason was that although light could not penetrate the wooden shutters and the curtains, sound certainly could. As in India, people with record-players, radios, and television sets seemed to think themselves obliged to turn the volume up as much as possible for the benefit of their less fortunate neighbours. Eventually, however, there was only one loudspeaker left, though whether it belonged to a radio or a television set or whether it was amplifying the performance of a live singer it was difficult to tell. Whichever it was, the song that floated in through the window was of an extraordinary sweetness, and was sung over and over again, as if in response to inaudible encores. I could not distinguish the words (they were probably in Italian), but they were sung in a clear but impassioned tenor voice that rose and fell in one of the most beautiful melodies I have ever heard. Perhaps it was a Neapolitan folk song. Or perhaps it came from an Italian opera. It was difficult to tell. At any rate, such was the unearthly sweetness of the song that despite my tiredness I could not help listening to it. Indeed, after a brief struggle between my desire to go to sleep and my desire to enjoy the sweetness of the song I surrendered myself unreservedly to the latter as though to a voice from paradise. Whether the song eventually ceased, or whether I dropped off to sleep in spite of it, I do not know; but sleep I eventually did, and awoke the next morning feeling rested and refreshed.

Our first full day in Naples dawned clear and bright, with very little cloud in the sky. Having walked through the Piazza Garibaldi (where the man with the umbrella stall was already displaying his wares) to Central Station, we took a mustard yellow taxi to the Royal Palace, having decided that we would spend the morning seeing this and the National Archaeological Museum. The journey took fifteen or twenty minutes, much of it taking us through streets and squares more splendid than any we had as yet seen as well as along a section of the Marina. Whenever the traffic slowed down, there was the usual impatient blaring of horns from all sides. Turning off the Marina, we passed a park-like area with smooth green lawns and magnificent date palms. On our left was the fifteenth-century Castel Nuovo or New Castle, with its massive round towers, all crenellated and built of grey stone. The celebrated 'triumphal arch' gateway was obscured by scaffolding, so that we were unable to see the sculptures with which it is decorated. Beyond the Castel Nuovo was the Royal Palace, an even more extensive building, and beyond the Royal Palace the Piazza Plebiscito. Here the taxi-driver deposited us at the edge of an enormous fleet of mustard yellow single-decker buses (the place seemed to be a terminus of some kind), behind which rose a building not unlike the Pantheon in Rome, except that the atrium formed the centrepiece of a semicircular colonnade. Having passed through the enormous gate of the palace, and located the courtyard in which the entrance to the State Apartments was situated, our first concern was to track down the Tourist Information Office, which was supposedly housed somewhere in the vast building. Beside a door in a corridor off another courtyard we found a discoloured marble plaque inscribed with the barely decipherable legend 'Ufficio Informazioni Turistico', or words to that effect. This did not look very promising, especially as through the door there was only a badly lit flight of stone steps. Prasannasiddhi was, however, for some reason or other convinced that we had found the right place and disappeared up the steps while I, more sceptical and wanting to save my breath, waited below. Ten minutes later he returned smiling and triumphant, clutching a fistful of maps and leaflets. At the top of seven or eight flights of steps he had found a corridor, and half-way down the corridor he had found the Tourist Information Office. This was fortunate, since the leaflets he had been given showed the opening and closing times of the various places we wanted to visit, so that we could now plan our sightseeing with greater confidence.

After satisfying ourselves that the National Archaeological Museum opened on Wednesdays, we returned to the courtyard in which the entrance to the State Apartments was situated and, having waited a short while for the ticket office to open, ascended the superb grand staircase. This consisted of three flights of stairs, the first of which was considerably shorter than the two others – or rather, than the four others, since from the first landing there were two successive flights of stairs on either side, the two last flights being situated at right angles to the ones immediately below. The whole staircase, as well as the pilastered walls and the lofty vaulted and coffered ceiling, was magnificently decorated with polychrome marbles, but owing to the sunshine that came streaming in through the spacious entrance and, still more brightly, through the rows of tall windows above it and in the opposing wall, the effect was not oppressive. On the contrary, far from being simply one of richness and grandeur the overall impression was one of space, harmony, and light. This was rather surprising, since the staircase had been constructed in the middle of the seventeenth century, fifty years after the completion of the palace itself. From the staircase we proceeded straight to the Court Theatre, all red plush and gilded scroll-work, and from there to the State Apartments, which after the staircase came as something of an anti-climax. Not that they were not grand. They were very grand indeed. But what with their polychrome marble floors, their painted and gilded ceilings, their heavily carved and elaborately inlaid furniture, their crystal chandeliers, their damask-covered walls, their tapestries, their oil paintings, and their porcelain Chinese vases (each one as large as a man), the twenty enormous rooms through which we passed – including a throne-room and a chapel – were suggestive of opulence and power rather than of sound artistic taste, and it was with something like relief that, on finding a pair of French windows ajar, we peered out over a broad terrace at the famous blue waters of the bay and at the deeper blue of the Tyrrhenian Sea beyond. Some of the decorative work in the State Apartments was, however, of a very high order, and there were a few fine paintings, among them a portrait of Pier Luigi Farnese in gala dress by Titian.

Descending the grand staircase (on the way pausing to examine the ancient bronze doors from the Castel Nuovo that stood on the second landing down) we regained the courtyard and from there walked back through the corridor with the discoloured marble plaque and so out into the gardens that lay partly within the angle formed by the longer and the shorter sides of the approximately L-shaped building. It being our intention to visit the Castel Nuovo, we walked along the side of the palace, past the National Library, which occupied much of the ground floor, and came to a kind of terrace from which there was an excellent view of the castle but, unfortunately, no means of access to it owing to the excavations that were going on. Since it was already 10.30, and since there would be a lot to see at the Archaeological Museum, we decided that for the time being at least we would rest content with seeing the Castel Nuovo from the outside. We therefore walked back through the palace to the Piazza Plebiscito and, after walking from there to the Piazza Trento e Trieste, took another mustard yellow taxi to the Archaeological Museum. Our route lay straight along the Via Roma, a busy cobbled thoroughfare that seemed to become steeper the further up it we went. So dense was the traffic that the driver had to put us down a short distance before the square in which the museum was situated. On the corner there was a bar and restaurant. Here we had a hot drink and a pastry (we had already refreshed ourselves in similar fashion on leaving the hotel) and rested for a few minutes before tackling the Archaeological Museum.

The museum building itself was a two-storeyed pink and white structure between the front of which and the road there stood a row of dusty palm trees. According to the guidebook it had been started in 1585 and finished in 1616 and was originally intended as a cavalry barracks. Subsequently it became part of the University of Naples, among the professors who lectured there being the long-neglected thinker Giambattista Vico. On entering the vestibule we found rather more visitors there than we had encountered in the State Apartments of the Royal Palace, which we had had practically to ourselves. The rooms to the right of the vestibule were, however, comparatively deserted, and we spent the next half hour wandering round the Gallery of the Great Masters (Phidias, Polyclitus, and others, either in the original or in early copies), as well as round the Gallery of the Tyrannicides and the Gallery of the Palestrita, admiring the serene and majestic forms of the gods and heroes of the ancient world. Many of the finest items, I noticed, came from the Farnese Collection, the nucleus of which had been created at the beginning of the sixteenth century by Cardinal Alessandro Farnese, who subsequently became pope and who is better known to history as Paul III. Unfortunately, the remaining galleries on that side of the building were closed for renovations, so that we were unable to see some of the most important works in the museum – including the alabaster and bronze Diana of Ephesus and the group known as the Farnese Bull, both of which also came from the Farnese Collection. This did not mean that there was not much left for us to see. There was the whole of the first floor, or practically the whole of it (a few rooms were closed), the mezzanine floor, and the ground floor rooms on the other side of the building. There were, in short, fifty or more rooms filled with paintings, weapons, ivories, glassware, silverware, gold jewellery, coloured and plain glass, ceramics, marbles, small bronzes, large bronzes, portrait busts, surgical instruments, mosaics, and coins, and through all these rooms Prasannasiddhi and I slowly made our way, pausing in front of whatever had happened to catch our eye or was of special interest or importance. Quite a few of the items, particularly in the case of the wall paintings and the mosaics, were from Pompeii and Herculaneum, at least one of which we were hoping to visit the following day. The majority of the wall paintings depicted episodes from classical mythology, and we had an interesting time identifying the various personages involved and observing the way in which the artist had handled his subject. Few of the paintings were of real artistic merit, though as examples of the level attained even by provincial Roman painting in the first century BCE and the first century CE they showed how great the achievements of the ancient world in this department of the visual arts must have been. From a purely artistic point of view the most impressive items from Pompeii and Herculaneum were, I thought, some of the bronzes, particularly the Hermes at Rest, the Sleeping Satyr, the Dancing Faun, the Ephebus, and the two Wrestler and the two Deer figures, as well as certain portrait busts.

On emerging from the last of the rooms on the mezzanine floor Prasannasiddhi and I realized that we were feeling a little tired. More than two hours had passed since we entered the museum. Descending to the ground floor we found a bench in the garden of one of the courtyards and rested for a while. After seeing so immense an array of man-made treasures it was very pleasant to behold the green grass and the palm trees and to feel the warmth of the sun on our bodies. Behind us, as yet unvisited, was the gallery containing the Egyptian collection, but not wanting to confuse our impressions of Graeco-Roman civilization by mixing them with impressions of the very different civilization of Ancient Egypt we reluctantly decided that that part of the museum should remain unvisited. In any case, as Prasannasiddhi remarked, the British Museum had a very much bigger Egyptian collection which we could go and see whenever we liked. From the courtyard we therefore went straight to the museum shop, pausing only to take a final look at some of the sculptures in the spacious atrium, where I particularly admired a marble sarcophagus on one side of which was depicted the creation of man by Prometheus and the gods – an interesting parallel to the more familiar Medieval and Renaissance representations of the corresponding Judaeo-Christian myth. Unlike God, Prometheus was shown not standing erect but seated on the ground, the head of as yet inanimate man resting on his knees as the latter, instead of having the breath of life breathed into his nostrils by an omnipotent Creator, was showered with gifts by all the gods.

In the museum shop we bought at least three dozen picture postcards, including postcards of some of the sculptures we had not been able to see, and then made our way down through the narrow oblong gardens that were the Piazza Cavour to the metro station at the far end. From this station we took a train to Naples Central, which was only one stop further on. This was our first experience of the local equivalent of the London Underground system, and we found it so quick and so convenient that from that time onwards it became our principal means of transport. Our usual practice was to have recourse to the metro for our outward journey, which would take us to those parts of the city which were situated at a higher altitude, and then to make the return journey on foot, when we would be able to walk down hill all the way. From Naples Central, which was located in – and under – Central Station, we walked back to the hotel, on the way stopping to buy some fruit and bread rolls for our lunch. Already the days were beginning to fall into a particular pattern: museums and art galleries in the morning, a siesta in the middle of the afternoon, churches in the evening. Now it was time for our siesta. Having eaten our fruit and bread rolls we therefore rested on our beds until it was time to go out again.

The Duomo or Cathedral and the churches of San Lorenzo Maggiore and San Paola Maggiore, which according to the guidebook were well worth seeing, were situated within easy walking distance of one another, and all were within walking distance of the Piazza Cavour.

After having our afternoon cup of tea at a bar in the Piazza Garibaldi we therefore took the metro to the Piazza Cavour and, having found our way to the Via Duomo, walked down it in the direction of the Cathedral. By this time the sky had become grey and overcast and there were a few drops of rain in the wind, which blew rather coldly up the long narrow street. On arriving at the Cathedral, a rather small building (rather small for a cathedral, that is) that fronted almost directly on to the road, we found that it was closed. According to the proprietor of a sweet stall opposite it would not be open until five o'clock, which meant that we had more than half an hour to wait. We therefore decided to walk on to the two churches and see what luck we had there. Continuing down the Via Duomo, we passed a number of rather fashionable shops, some of which were already open. Since we wanted to give the churches time to open too, we stopped and looked in the brilliantly lit windows. Quite a high proportion of the shops sold nothing but model human and animal figures of china, glass, crystal, plastic, and every other conceivable material, together with such things as flower vases and fancy boxes. Shops of this kind seemed to be very popular with the Neapolitans, for we saw large numbers of them in every part of the city. A few hundred yards from the Cathedral we turned right into a street so narrow that it was not so much a street as an alley. On either side were houses four or five storeys in height, with lines of washing between. There were a number of shops, mostly bakeries, greengrocers, and general stores, some of which had encroached on to the meagre strip of pavement. Though the street was really too narrow for vehicular traffic (not that the occasional motor car did not squeeze its way through), it was not too narrow for motor bikes and motor scooters. These roared up and down at a tremendous speed all the time, ridden mostly by youths who seemed to be joy-riding rather than bent on serious business and who showed a complete disregard for the convenience and even the safety of pedestrians.

A few hundred yards down this noisy and dismal alley we came upon what was officially a piazza but which in fact was not much more than a sort of crossroads on which abutted several churches. The most prominent of these was San Paolo Maggiore, the rather dingy baroque façade of which could be seen rising behind the bepedestalled figure of a haloed and wildly gesticulating saint. The place was closed. Indeed, there was no sign of life about it at all. Turning left, and passing through a gloomy archway, we tried to find the entrance to San

Lorenzo Maggiore; but here too we encountered only locked doors. Feeling a trifle disappointed, and more than a little weary, we retraced our steps to the Cathedral, which was still not open. Fortunately, we happened to see on the other side of the road the modest façade of a building that, according to a discreet plaque, was the Monastery of the Gerolomini. In the middle of the façade there was a door, and this door was open. Slipping through it, we found ourselves in a beautiful Renaissance cloister the style of which reminded me of Brunelleschi's work in San Lorenzo in Florence, particularly the cloister there. A flight of steps led to a library, but as we started climbing them a custodian suddenly appeared and told us rather curtly that it was closed. Neither our Italian nor his English was sufficient to enable us to find out at what time it would be open. Later on, in a book on Naples, I found a picture of this library, which was housed in a magnificently decorated hall and was evidently well worth seeing.

The clocks in the neighbourhood were now striking five. On issuing from the monastery we saw that the door of the Cathedral stood cautiously open. In order to reach it we had to climb a broad flight of marble steps that extended the whole width of the building. On these steps a boisterous – not to say violent – game of football was in progress, the players being five or six overweight boys who, as we set foot on the steps, glared at us with undisguised hostility – as though the steps were *their* territory and all visitors to the Cathedral were intruders and, therefore, enemies. Inside the Cathedral it was almost completely dark, two or three feeble electric bulbs and the red lamp that indicated the presence of the Blessed Sacrament providing the sole illumination. As soon as our eyes had grown accustomed to the gloom we slowly made our way round the building, peering into the darkness of the side chapels and gazing at the shadowy forms carved on the tombs. Everything we touched seemed to be covered with a layer of dust and the whole place breathed an atmosphere of decay and neglect. This was strange, for besides being the principal church of the diocese the Cathedral possessed the famous liquefying blood of St Januarius, the patron saint of Naples. Together with the saint's cranium, the blood was enshrined in the most prominent of the side chapels, the extravagantly baroque interior of which we could just make out through the elaborate grillework of the fine bronze gates. (Writing more than three weeks after our visit, I *may* have confused these particular bronze gates with those of another chapel into which we looked.) On the whole, our visit to the Cathedral had not proved very rewarding. Nonetheless, we decided to return to San Paolo Maggiore and San Lorenzo Maggiore and see whether they too were now open, since we would in any case have to go down to the Via Duomo as far as the alley on our way back to the hotel and might as well have another look.

Fortunately, San Paolo Maggiore was open. Or rather, it was half open. On climbing the rather operatic staircase that led to the main entrance we had found the door closed, but as we regained ground floor level there emerged from a sort of cubbyhole underneath the staircase the black figure of a friendly priest who, it transpired, spoke a little English, as well as some French. The upper church was closed, he explained, because there was no lighting and one would not be able to see anything anyway. But the lower church was open. If we went through that door (here he indicated a narrow opening a few feet away) we would be able to see everything. Through the door we therefore went and at once found ourselves in a brilliantly illuminated crypt or grotto. So brilliantly was it illuminated in fact, that we paused for a moment, in order that our eyes might grow as accustomed to the brightness of the place as previously to the gloom of the Cathedral. On looking about us, we saw that the ceiling was quite low, and that the greater part of the crypt, which was not very wide, was fitted out with highly polished wooden pews, complete with hassocks. So much space did these occupy that, as we made our way round the place, it was not always easy for us to squeeze past the little shrines and altars lining the walls. Though there was nobody about at the time, it was obvious that the place was not only much used but well cared for. Everything was scrubbed and polished, painted and gilded, to the highest possible degree, as though a small army of painters and decorators had been at work on the place and had only just left. Unfortunately, despite all the care – and expense – that had been lavished on the crypt the result was far from happy. With its abundance of marble (both real and imitation), its heavily carved woodwork, its plaster saints, its simpering Madonnas and arch Bambinos, as well as its artificial flowers, its electric candles, and its religious trinkets of every kind, the place was furnished and decorated in the worst possible taste, and Prasannasiddhi and I were not sorry to escape into the open air and to cross to the other side of the little piazza. San Lorenzo Maggiore itself was not open, but on passing for the second time through the gloomy archway we discovered a little door, and beyond this door an ancient cloister, the middle of which had been excavated to a depth of twelve or fifteen feet. According to the guidebook, the thirteenth-century church (which technically was a basilica) had been built on the site of a much smaller sixth-century structure, and this – according to tradition – had stood on the site of the ancient pagan basilica of Neapolis. With its 2,500 years of history Naples was a many-layered place, and vestiges of most of the layers were to be seen in one or another part of the city. According to the same guidebook, San Paolo Maggiore stood on the site of the ancient temple of the Dioscuri, two columns from which still formed part of the church's baroque façade.

As we left San Lorenzo Maggiore and made our way back to the Via Duomo I recalled that it was in this church that Boccaccio had first seen his Fiammetta. In those days Naples had been a much smaller and a much more beautiful place – how much smaller and how much more beautiful was evident from a fifteenth-century painting that we saw the following day. Within their encircling walls, the white, red-roofed houses and churches crowded to the very edge of the green waters of the bay. On the far left rose the prodigious grey bulk of the Castel Nuovo, while from between the city and the castle there extended into the sea a massive L-shaped pier, on the broad white pavement of which tiny human figures were walking up and down and in front of which the gaily beflagged galleys were riding at anchor. Behind the city rose steep green hills, the lower slopes of which were dotted with little white churches and hermitages. In an eighteenth-century painting of the Departure of King Charles from Naples, which we also saw the following day, the buildings extended further along the bay in both directions, and had begun to creep up the hillside. On an eminence to the far right, a long, low building was faintly seen breaking the skyline, while in the foreground the galleys had grown into galleons with three masts instead of one and a multitude of sails. Today Naples is the third largest city in Italy, and the hills immediately behind it are completely covered with buildings. Much of the old city still remains, and many of the old streets and squares, and it was into the labyrinth formed by some of these that Prasannasiddhi and I plunged after crossing the Via Duomo. On either side of the alleys – as narrow as those of Venice – the four- and five-storeyed houses formed a continuous wall of grimy red stone, relieved only by iron-barred gratings and heavily shuttered windows. At intervals the wall would be pierced by an enormous archway, through which we could see flights of dimly lit steps, desolate courtyards, and, of course, festoons upon festoons of washing. Though it was not yet six o'clock, there were not many people about and when the motor scooters were not roaring up and down at top speed it was strangely quiet. After walking for ten or fifteen minutes we turned into a broader and better lit thoroughfare and from this soon emerged into the wide open spaces of the Piazza Garibaldi.

The problem now was to find a restaurant that made at least rudimentary provision for the needs of the vegetarian, since we did not want to subsist on pizzas indefinitely. Having scrutinized the menus in several windows with no better success than the previous evening, we eventually decided to take a chance with a corner restaurant not far from the hotel where the waiters were not very busy and where the television set was not in operation. As it happened, we were quite fortunate. The elderly waiter who served us knew a little English and we were able to explain our needs. 'No problem!' he exclaimed with a benign smile, and no problem there indeed was, except that the tomato sauce that came with the spaghetti turned out to contain tiny pieces of meat which we carefully pushed to one side. Nevertheless, we were on the whole well satisfied with our meal and ate at the corner restaurant every evening for the remainder of our stay, always taking good care not to order those dishes which despite their innocent appearance on the menu and our waiter's reassuring 'No problem!' we knew from experience would contain a small admixture of meat. On the present occasion, having lingered for a while over our concluding drinks (a white coffee for me and a lemon tea for Prasannasiddhi) we took a stroll down one side of the Piazza Garibaldi and then returned to the Hotel Coral. Though it was not yet eight, we had had a long and tiring day and did not feel inclined to do much more than look at our guidebooks and (in my case) write a few picture postcards before going to bed. Fortunately or unfortunately, the people with the record-players, radios, and television sets did not seem to be in such a generous mood that night as the night before, and I was therefore able to get off to sleep without any trouble.

Our second full day in Naples dawned neither clear nor bright, and there was a good deal of cloud in the sky. In fact it was raining. Pompeii being out of the question, we decided to spend the morning at the Capodimonte Museum and accordingly took the metro to Piazza Cavour and then a taxi to the gates of the park in which the museum was situated. During the last part of the journey the road became very steep, with sharp bends and a lot of heavy traffic; but there were compensations, mainly in the form of a fine view of a very big, very new church built in what could only be described as the neo-baroque style of architecture, and after our mustard yellow taxi had skirted an enormous length of wall we eventually were deposited at the park gates. Owing to the rain, which was now falling steadily, the smooth lawns and clusters of magnificent trees – including palm trees – by which the museum was surrounded showed a particularly vivid green, which contrasted admirably with the pink and white mass of the vast neoclassical building. That the building should be vast was hardly surprising. Erected in the middle of the eighteenth century, it had been built not only as a royal palace but also to contain the Farnese Collection and was, in fact, the long, low building on an eminence to the far right that broke the skyline in the painting of the departure of King Charles from Naples. The sculptures and *objets d'art* belonging to the original nucleus of the collection were, of course, in the Archaeological Museum, while the paintings – after a lengthy sojourn in the Archaeological Museum – were now housed on the second floor of the Capodimonte, and it was these paintings that we had come to see.

After looking at the seven enormous Brussels tapestries, depicting episodes from the Battle of Pavia, that covered the walls of a sort of vestibule, we accordingly made our way through a series of rooms containing works by the masters of the thirteenth to the sixteenth centuries, among them Simone Martini, Masaccio, Botticelli, Raphael, Sebastiano del Piombo, Correggio, Giovanni Bellini, Mantegna, Lorenzo Lotto, Titian, Cranach, Holbein, and Breughel. The collection thus was a very rich one. As in other art galleries where the paintings were arranged in chronological order I was, however, painfully aware of the fact that, despite the unequalled brilliance of its achievements, in certain important respects the art of the (Italian) Renaissance represented a decline. In what that decline consisted it was difficult to say, for the technical competence of the great masters of that period often enabled them not only to express much but, also, to conceal much and compensate for much. But though it was difficult to say in what the decline consisted, as on previous occasions it seemed to me that it had something to do with a certain coarsening of feeling that set in towards the end of the fifteenth century (set in, that is, so far as the visual arts, at least, were concerned). This coarsening was particularly noticeable in the treatment of faces. In the works of the earlier masters, including some who were comparatively unknown and even anonymous, faces – whether those of saints, angels, or ordinary human beings – were generally treated with a sensitiveness and delicacy of feeling, and (dare I say it?) with an *intelligence*, that more often than not were entirely absent from the works of their more distinguished successors. In order to substantiate this thesis it would, of course, be necessary for me to cite specific examples, but since no catalogue of the Capodimonte Museum was available (and no picture postcards, even), and since my recollection of individual paintings is not sufficiently detailed, I am unable to do this. Certain paintings – not necessarily illustrative of my thesis – did, however, leave me with a very strong impression. These were for the most part paintings with which I was already familiar from reproductions. Among them were Simone Martini's great painting of St Louis of Toulouse crowning his brother, Robert of Anjou, King of Naples, Bellini's *Transfiguration*, Titian's portrait of Pope Paul III with his nephews Ottavio and Alessandro Farnese, and Breughel's *Parable of the Blind*. The last of these was in process of being photographed by a three-man team of professional photographers, so that the room was better lighted than those through which we had already passed and we were able to have a particularly good look not only at the Breughel but also at the other paintings in the room, including a fine portrait of Erasmus by (I think) Cranach.

This room happened to be the last on that side of the building. Leaving it, we found ourselves in a lobby and at the foot of a flight of steps that led, as Prasannasiddhi soon discovered, to the flat roof of the museum and to a kind of solarium. From this eyrie, which may have been as much as 2,000 feet above sea level, we could see – through the fine silver veil of the rain – how extensive Naples was, as well as the way in which the greater part of the present city was distributed over the slopes below. When we had gazed our fill, and identified a few landmarks, we returned to the lobby and sought to continue our progress through the remaining twenty rooms of the second-floor gallery and the forty or fifty rooms of the first-floor gallery. These were, however, all closed. Since they contained mainly nineteenth-century Neapolitan paintings we were as much relieved as disappointed and at once retraced our steps through the rooms we had already seen, on the way stopping for a second look at those paintings by which we had been particularly struck. One of these was Titian's portrait of Pope Paul III with his two nephews, which it was interesting to compare with the same artist's portrait of the Pope *solus*, as well as with della Porta's slightly 'idealized' bust. The first portrait, which was of historical no less than of artistic importance – Paul III having been the creator of the original nucleus of the Farnese Collection, which had reached Naples through the descendants of his son Pier Luigi, the first duke of Parma

– has been well described by the historian of the popes, Dr Ludwig Pastor:

> In a chamber of the Vatican hung with red tapestry sits Paul III in an armchair, his small head covered with the red *camauro*; the shrunken figure speaks of old age and the burden of care – the hour-glass on the table gives warning of the flight of time. On the Pope's right hand, behind his chair, stands Cardinal Alessandro Farnese in his robes, wearing on his head the red biretta, while on the left, in the front of the group, the youthful Ottavio Farnese bends before the Pope, whose diminutive stature is accentuated by the lofty presence of the younger man. The latter appears to be presenting some petition or apology, and the Pope to be speaking in a low voice; but the energy with which the Pontiff addresses him, the piercing look with which he regards him, betoken the fiery soul still aglow under the weight of years.*

The character of the Pope, whose long life embraced both Renaissance and Catholic Reaction, was indeed depicted with remarkable psychological penetration. I particularly admired the way in which the great artist had used a realistic rendering of the spotted-fur lining of the Pope's cream-coloured outer garment to impart to the whole aged, shrunken figure a look of almost animal cunning and ferocity.

Another painting by which we had been particularly struck, and at which we now stopped for a second look, was the Neapolitan Colantonio's *St Jerome and the Lion*. I had not heard of Colantonio before (he is not listed in *The Penguin Dictionary of Art and Artists*), though to judge from this painting and a companion piece belonging to the same polyptych, showing St Francis giving the Rule to the Poor Clares, he was an artist of no small merit. St Jerome was shown seated in his study, extracting a thorn from the lion's uplifted paw, the figure of the king of beasts being depicted on the same scale as that of the saint. What was remarkable about the painting, apart from the predominance of brown tints, was its loving attention to detail. This was particularly noticeable in the way in which the artist had depicted the books on the surrounding shelves, as well as the saint's hour-glass and writing instruments and – a delightful touch – a mouse nibbling a piece of bread in the bottom right-hand corner. Altogether it was a serene, harmonious, honest composition which it did one good to look at and

* *The History of the Popes, From the Close of the Middle Ages*, London 1923, vol.XI, p.31.

which I was overjoyed to have 'discovered'. My only regret was that it was not reproduced in our guide to Naples, which contained a section on the museum, and that no picture postcard of it was available either. Order members who want to gain a better idea of Colantonio's *St Jerome and the Lion* will therefore have to make the journey to Naples.

Having taken a second look at some of the paintings we descended to the ground floor and explored the lofty arcades surrounding the inner courtyard, where loose planks, heaps of sand, and various items of machinery suggested that building and decorating work was in progress – though not just then. Since the rain had not quite ceased, and since we were in any case beginning to feel a little tired, we sat and had a hot drink and a pastry at a cafeteria that had been improvised in a corner of the courtyard. We had not sat there for more than fifteen minutes when the sky began to clear and the sun to shine forth from the puddles that had formed on the enormous flagstones. It was time for us to depart. Negotiating the puddles, we crossed to the other side of the courtyard and, having passed through the vestibule of the building, made our way along the winding path that led, between green lawns and even greener trees, back to the park gate. We had not quite finished with the Capodimonte Museum and its paintings, however. In the hope of finding a shop that sold reproductions, or even picture postcards, we walked up the road from the park gates for a short distance and then, turning right down a narrow, cobbled side street, proceeded to look in the windows of all the shops. But these, though they sold practically everything else, did not sell picture postcards. We therefore retraced our steps to the park gates and from there returned to the Piazza Cavour by the same route that we had followed some three or four hours earlier – though this time we made the journey not by taxi but on foot. On our way down Prasannasiddhi dived into a small general shop to buy some bread rolls and a few other things while I waited outside. While waiting I was shocked to see what a high proportion of the passers-by were either maimed, or deformed, or suffering from some kind of mental disturbance. One stout, rather showily dressed woman of about forty with a shopping basket, whom I particularly noticed, staggered past me with painted features horribly distorted and muttering furiously to herself.

By the time we reached the hotel we had again begun to feel a little tired, and were not sorry that it was nearly time for our siesta, which that afternoon we prolonged somewhat beyond its usual limits. We were planning to see three more churches that evening and since, as we now knew, the churches of Naples did not open until five o'clock there was in any case no point in our going out much before half-past four. The three churches in question were the Chiara, the Jesù Nuovo, and the San Domenico Maggiore, all of which were situated in roughly the same quarter of the old city as the Duomo, though at about twice the distance from the Piazza Cavour. We therefore had a fairly long walk from the metro and it was with some relief that, on turning a corner, we saw the severe and lofty form of the Chiara towering above the rooftops. The Basilica of Santa Chiara – to give it its full title – had been built early in the fourteenth century by King Robert of Anjou and his wife Sancha of Majorca and was said to be the church that was dearest to the Neapolitans – a fact which perhaps helped to explain the comparatively neglected state of the Cathedral. During the Second World War the building had suffered severe damage. Indeed, much of it had been totally destroyed. But the disaster had not been without its compensations, for on its being rebuilt the church had been restored to its original Gothic and Provençal form, minus the baroque encrustations of the last few centuries. With its well-lit single nave, its unadorned side chapels, its Gothic windows, and its wooden ceiling, the serene and spacious interior was once again the epitome of Franciscan simplicity. The only fault we had to find with it was that the tall lancet windows of the clerestory had been filled with *modern* stained glass, the crude reds and blues of which contrasted oddly with the soft golden hues of the surrounding stonework. The building was evidently the centre of a certain amount of activity, such as we had not seen in the Cathedral. Besides a few worshippers in the side chapels, and a sprinkling of tourists, there was also a wedding party of some three or four dozen people. We had already encountered half the party at the entrance to the church, standing on the strip of red carpet that ran from the porch to the door of the waiting car. The remaining half including, presumably, the bride and bridegroom, we encountered as we crossed the presbytery – and the other end of the red carpet – to get a better view of the tomb of King Robert of Anjou, an elaborate four-storeyed structure that rose from behind the unpretentious high altar to a height sufficient to obscure the lower part of the four-lighted Gothic window in the centre of the wall. In a niche of the topmost storey the King sat enthroned, wearing his royal regalia, while in the storey below he lay in a sort of sepulchral cave, dressed in the simple Franciscan habit.

On emerging from the church we had to turn right and walk down the side of the massive building in order to reach the celebrated Cloister of the Poor Clares, also known as the Majolica Cloister. It was a very quiet place, and all the quieter for the fact that night had now begun to fall. Round the four sides ran a fourteenth-century colonnade of pointed arches supported on pillars, the central space of the cloister being occupied by an eighteenth-century rustic garden laid out in the form of a Greek cross. On either side of the broad paths were low walls and benches alternating with octagonal pillars, all of them entirely covered with square Majolica tiles in which the predominant colours – apart from white – were golden yellow, green, and turquoise. The backs of the benches were framed in volutes, and contained panels depicting country landscapes and festive scenes of an apparently mythological character. Round the pillars ran spirals of flowers, leaves, and fruit and these pillars supported a horizontal wooden trellis across which had been trained the centuries-old vines. These vines were now almost bare, and the beautifully shaped yellow leaves lay thick on the ground beneath our feet as we wandered down the rapidly darkening paths. Many of the trees in the four principal sections into which the garden was divided had also lost their leaves, though a few orange trees still bore their diminutive golden fruits. Both in form and in colour the works of man and the works of nature had achieved an unusual harmony, albeit a harmony wherein the autumnal nature of the prevailing tints, the fading light, the fallen leaves, and the ever-deepening silence, combined to impart to the garden and to the cloister an atmosphere of not unpleasing melancholy.

There was nothing melancholy about the atmosphere of the Jesù Nuovo, or New Church of the Jesuits, which we visited immediately afterwards. Rather was it one of mystery and grandeur. The mystery and the grandeur were all the more unexpected for being hidden away behind a sober Renaissance façade of lozenge-shaped stone blocks that had been preserved from an earlier structure, the Palazzo Sanseverino. As in the famous Jesù in Rome, which we had seen the previous year, the play of the architectural masses and the dramatic alternations of light and darkness had been combined with the lavish use of striking polychrome marbles, and an abundance of bronze and wooden sculptures, to produce a definite effect, and one had to admit that in the Neapolitan as in the Roman church that effect had been triumphantly achieved. Whether for this reason or because, as the candles flickering in front of the numerous altars seemed to indicate, the place was much used for purposes of devotion, there was an intenser vibration in the Jesù than we had as yet encountered in Naples. On our way round the building we did in fact see a small group of women praying in one of the side chapels. Nearby there was a placard carrying a black and white photograph of a youngish-looking priest who, as it appeared from the accompanying inscription, had recently been beatified and whose body now rested in a sort of cavity beneath the altar of that very chapel. One end of the coffin was visible, the rest of it being hidden by the white frontlet of the altar. Observing the scene, I wondered who the youngish-looking priest in the photograph was, and why he had been beatified. Was he, perhaps, a Jesuit missionary, and had he given his life for the faith somewhere in Darkest Africa? Were the women just ordinary worshippers, or were they related to him in some way? As I wondered, I noticed that one of the group, a quite elderly woman, remained kneeling on the steps of the altar after the others had risen to their feet and started moving towards the door. With the palm of her hand she was stroking the side of the coffin in a slow, strangely insistent manner. Was she begging the dead priest's intercession in some matter close to her heart, or was she his aunt or sister, or even his mother, stroking the side of the coffin as she might have stroked his cheek, unable to accept the fact of his death and vainly seeking to bring him back to life? There was no answer to these questions, and as we left the church I saw that the woman was still on her knees before the altar, still slowly stroking the side of the coffin in that gentle, patient, insistent manner.

On emerging into the Piazza del Jesù Nuovo and turning in the direction of San Domenico we saw glimmering white through the darkness the fantastic shape of an 'ornamental obelisk'. Between forty and fifty feet in height, it resembled nothing so much as a gigantic baroque candlestick, with the statue of the Madonna at the top for a candle. We did not stay to examine it, however, and pressed on through the narrow streets until we came to the Piazza San Domenico Maggiore. This was surrounded by the fronts of what were, or had been, palaces, and by the *back* of the church that gave the square its name. Traversing a tawdry marble vestibule, and climbing several flights of stone steps, we eventually came out beside the high altar of a magnificent church which, despite later additions, was obviously Gothic. We at once admired the smooth, soaring multiple columns and pointed arches, the richness of the furnishings, and the good taste with which the ribs of the arches had been picked out in gold. The place was, in fact, extremely well cared for, and conveyed an overall impression of wealth, dignity, and refinement. Like the Chiara and the Jesù Nuovo the church was evidently the centre of a certain amount of activity, and I wondered what connection this had with the fact that all three of them were, unlike the Cathedral and most of the other churches, associated with a religious order. In the case of San Domenico Maggiore that order was, of course, the Order of Preachers, known also as the Dominicans or Black Friars. The badge of the order, a black and white dog carrying a torch in its mouth (for according to medieval punditry the Dominicans were the Domini Canes or 'Dogs of the Lord')* was repeated in the blue and gold ceiling of the nave and elsewhere in the building. Besides being of architectural importance, the church was rich in historical and religious associations. St Thomas Aquinas had taught theology there, and in one of the side chapels was preserved the thirteenth-century crucifix that – according to tradition – had once spoken to him. This was not a carved but a painted crucifix, and we admired the delicacy and refinement of the work and the purity of its colours. We also admired the fourteenth-century frescoes, particularly a fine *noli me tangere*. There was, indeed, much to admire in the San Domenico Maggiore, and as we left it by the same way that we had entered (the main door being closed), I reflected that artistically speaking the place could be regarded as representing a *via media* between the simplicity of the Chiara and the extravagance of the Jesù. In this respect San Domenico indeed seemed quite 'Anglican', standing in much the same relation to the Chiara and the Jesù as a Church of England cathedral did to a nonconformist chapel on the one hand and a Roman Catholic oratory on the other.

But these reflections were soon dispelled by the sights and sounds by which we were confronted on our way back to the Piazza Garibaldi and our corner restaurant. Our route was roughly parallel to that of the previous evening, and lay through much of the same kind of territory, except that we seemed to have stumbled on that part of the old city in which different streets were still devoted to different trades. Thus we passed through the street of the cabinet-makers, the street of the makers of musical instruments (mainly guitars), and what I mentally christened the street of the Bambinos, though Bambinos were far from being the only figures produced there. Both Prasannasiddhi and I were fascinated by the shops in this street, and not only stopped and

---

* He used them for hunting heretics.

looked in the windows but even ventured inside. Originally the Bambino-makers had concentrated on the production of crib sets, i.e. representations of the manger in which Jesus was laid at birth plus the Virgin Mary, Joseph, the three kings, the shepherds, cows, donkeys, and so on, and in the course of time (apparently since the eighteenth century) these crib sets had not only become extremely elaborate, comprising hundreds of figures, but had also led to the production of a whole range of figures having no direct connection with the biblical episode. Since Christmas was approaching, crib sets occupied every available inch of space in the shop windows and the premises behind. There were sets consisting of no more than a dozen tiny figures and sets consisting of a hundred figures all as big as an ordinary child's doll. There were sets costing a thousand lire and sets costing a million. But whether small and simple or large and elaborate, and whether they were cheap or expensive, all the figures were beautifully made and, in the case of some of the larger ones, beautifully dressed in real clothes. Even on the cows and donkeys, as well as on the horses and camels accompanying the three kings, incredible artistry had been lavished. So numerous in fact were the figures, and so lifelike, that they seemed to constitute a world of their own – a world in which one could very easily lose oneself. Having quite happily lost ourselves in it for half an hour or so, Prasannasiddhi and I resumed our journey and before long had passed through the city gate (the one flanked by the two massive Aragonese towers that we had seen on the evening of our arrival) and were picking our way through the muddy space between the gate and the road that was, it seemed, the preserve of the fishmongers. Eels wriggled in great shallow vats of water, fish gleamed and gasped in enormous wicker baskets, and strange marine creatures lifted claws and trailed whiskers on broad wooden trays. There was a strong fishy smell in the air.

Friday, 1 November, was All Saints' Day, and since this was a public holiday (quite an important one in Italy) we had not been sure if anything would be open. However, on our making enquiries at the small Tourist Information Office that we had discovered in a corner of Central Station we had learned that the Pompeii 'excavations' (as the publicity material invariably called them) would definitely be open that day. We had therefore decided that, weather permitting, Friday, 1 November, would be devoted to seeing Pompeii, since we had only two more full days left in Naples and did not want to risk leaving the excursion to the last day of our visit. I myself had seen Pompeii in the summer of 1966, on the occasion of my visit to Naples, but I had not spent much time there, and my most distinct recollection of the place was of being surprised to find that everything was on a much smaller scale than I had expected. So little did I remember of Pompeii, in fact, that it was almost as though I had not been there before at all, and I looked forward to our excursion with hardly less eagerness than Prasannasiddhi.

Fortunately our third full day in Naples dawned even clearer and brighter than had the first. On opening the shutters and looking up through the lines of washing I saw that the sky was already more blue than grey and completely free from cloud. We lost no time in getting to Central Station and after a brief wait on a downstairs platform caught the local (Salerno) train to Pompeii. As we relaxed in our seats the sun streamed in through the windows of the compartment with a warmth that we had not felt for a couple of weeks. Opposite us sat an old Italian couple, both rather shabbily dressed in dark clothes, the woman wearing a headscarf. The husband (from the way in which he behaved to his companion he could hardly have been anything else) was evidently afflicted with a particularly savage temper. Whenever his wife spoke to him or made as though to speak to us, as well as when she started making ready to get down at their station, he checked her with a sudden forward jerk of the head and a really ferocious snarl, for all the world as though he had been a particularly vicious animal rather than a human being. Every time she was checked in this way the old woman subsided into her seat, but after a few minutes she would return to the attack (if anything so inoffensive could be described as an attack), and say or do something that would provoke another snarl, after which she would again subside, sometimes casting in our direction a smile that was half apologetic, half ingratiating. With her soft brown eyes, and submissive bearing, she was like a faithful dog who, despite all ill treatment, again and again returns to its master. Observing the old couple's behaviour, I reflected that they had probably been relating to each other in this way for forty or fifty years. Nonetheless, I had the impression that despite the husband's savagery the wife was, at bottom, no less tough than he was, and would probably outlive him for many a year.

When not observing the antics of the old couple I looked out of the window. It was certainly a very pleasant sight that met our eyes. Apart from having the blue waters of the Bay of Naples on the one side and Mount Vesuvius on the other, nearer at hand there were not only villas and farmhouses but also fields and market gardens. Once again I saw oranges and artichokes, as well as palm trees, umbrella pines, and cacti. What was more remarkable still, I saw beds of carnations blooming in the open air – at the beginning of November! For one born and brought up in the wintry regions of the North (which according to Goethe the Neapolitans thought of as having 'snow all the year round, wooden houses, great ignorance, but lots of money'), this was an extraordinary sight indeed. Goethe also quotes Pliny the Elder's 'extensive description' of Campania, on the coast of which Naples is situated.*

> In what terms to describe the coast of Campania taken by itself, with its blissful and heavenly loveliness, so as to manifest that there is one region, where Nature has been at work in her joyous mood! And then again all that invigorating healthfulness all the year round, the climate so temperate, the plains so fertile, the hills so sunny, the glades so secure, the groves so shady! Such wealth of various forests, the breezes from so many mountains, the great fertility of its corn and vines and olives, the glorious fleeces of its sheep, the sturdy necks of its bulls, the many lakes, the rich supply of rivers and springs, flowing over all its surface, its many seas and harbours, and the bosom of its lands offering on all sides a welcome to commerce, the country itself eagerly running out into the seas, as it were, to aid mankind.

2,000 years after Pliny and 200 years after Goethe much of the 'blissful and heavenly loveliness' still survived, but sadly marred (so far as the environs of Naples, at least, were concerned) by extensive urban development and, above all, by industrialization. Not that industrialization was very much in evidence along that part of the coast which we were now traversing. Though we passed through, or stopped at, several small towns, with their red-roofed houses and blocks of modern flats, the whole region was semi-rural and far from having lost its ancient fertility.

Half an hour after leaving Central Station we reached Pompeii, or rather the modest rural station of that name, and Prasannasiddhi and I stepped down from the train into the sun, which was already quite hot. A board announced in three or four languages the fact that here were the world-famous 'excavations'. But which way were we to go? On our emergence from the station we could see no signboard; but an

---

* The references are to J.W. Goethe, *Italian Journey*, Harmondsworth 1970, pp.184 and 322.

old woman who was passing by, seeing our perplexity, pointed us up the road with vigorous gestures that said, more plainly than any words, that the excavations were *there*. From the cheerful, friendly way in which she did this it was clear that she was glad that we had come to see Pompeii, glad that we were going to see the 'excavations', and that she hoped we would enjoy our visit. Before entering the site by the main gate, which was in fact situated only a hundred yards up the road, we turned aside at the shop-cum-restaurant next to the railway station and bought not the usual guidebook but a lavishly illustrated volume on Pompeii as it was 2,000 years ago. Besides maps and pictures of the existing monuments, together with much other useful informa-tion, this volume contained reconstructions of the streets and the houses, the temples and the villas, of the little town, which gave one a very good idea of what they had actually looked like before the terrible three days in 79 CE when Vesuvius erupted and covered the whole area from Herculaneum to Stabiae, a distance of about twelve miles, in a fifteen- to twenty-foot layer of pebbles, mud, and ashes. In visiting Pompeii I was concerned not so much to see the ruins as to obtain, with their help, a much more vivid impression of what it had been like to live and work in that idyllic corner of the Roman Empire all those centuries ago. Whether for this reason, or because of the pagan and Classical associations of the place, we entered the main gate and walked up the flights of wooden steps that led to the Forum with a good deal more excitement than we had felt on entering the churches of Naples. Before we reached the gate, however, I was recalled from my dreams of the past by the commercialism of the present. On the right-hand side of the road there was a string of little restaurants, ice cream parlours, and cold drink stalls. What struck me about them was the fact that each one displayed a sign that announced, in bold letters, 'FREE SEATS'. This was a reminder that in Italy it generally costs the tourist money to sit down. In the very first year of our travels together – and particularly in the course of our visit to Venice – Prasannasiddhi and I had discovered that one normally had one's drink or one's snack standing up at the bar. If one wanted to sit down there was an extra charge, which the proprietor of the establishment was usually very punctilious in exacting. Why did the same state of affairs not obtain at the entrance to Pompeii? Was it because there had been a dearth of tourists that year, or because of the keenness of local competition, or because it was All Saints' Day, or because of the natural generosity of the Southern Italian temperament? We did not know and since, for the time being at least, we had no need of a seat, free or otherwise, we did not greatly care.

The flights of wooden steps having been succeeded by a paved ramp, and this ramp having passed through a kind of vaulted tunnel in the wall, we found ourselves walking up a street that ran straight into the heart of the ancient city. On our right was the Basilica; before us, the Forum. All around were columns and half columns, some of the more intact of them still supporting sections of entablature, together with fragments of walls and arches. For a time we simply wandered round the empty spaces of the Basilica and the Forum, allowing ourselves to absorb impressions, and looked through the railings of the former grain market at the richly carved capitals, the fragments of sculpture, and all the other archaeological material that had been deposited there. Above our heads the sky was a flawless dome of azure, while the sun shone so brightly that the paved areas and the columns and half columns took on a dazzling whiteness. Standing on the steps of the Basilica and looking sideways down the Forum towards the Temple of Jupiter we could see above the ruins the familiar purple shape of Mount Vesuvius. This time I was not conscious of any smallness of scale – either because I was not expecting Pompeii to be bigger than it was or because, with only two or three parties of tourists about, both the Basilica and the Forum seemed quite spacious. When we had finished looking through the railings of the grain market we crossed over to the other side of the Forum, passing immediately in front of the Temple of Jupiter (that is, in front of what remained of it – I had already begun to see the city as it had been rather than as it was) and after taking a look at the Arch of Tiberius started on an exploration of the labyrinth of streets and alleys occupying the north-western quarter of the city – an exploration that lasted for the better part of two hours. Though they were not very wide, all the streets and alleys were paved with broad, flat stones that had been worn smooth by the tread of generations of feet. In some places deep grooves had been made in the roadway, presumably by the wheels of carts and chariots. During the earlier part of our exploration we seemed to be playing hide-and-seek with the tourist parties, each some twenty or thirty strong, which trailed along in the wake of their brazen-throated guides. Either we met them as we were going in at a villa or they met us as we were coming out. Prasannasiddhi was rather keen that we should attach ourselves to one of these parties, at least two of which consisted of Americans, and hear what the guide had to say; but I was doubtful of the utility of this, since I knew from past experience that professional guides were not necessarily the most reliable sources of information. However, our path crossed that of one or the other of the English-speaking parties so often that we could hardly avoid hearing what the guides were saying, and in this way were sometimes spared the trouble of consulting our book on Pompeii as it was 2,000 years ago.

Among the first places we visited were a bakery and the Forum Baths, said to be the smallest and most elegant of the public baths of Pompeii. On the paved floor of the bakery the solid conical bases of the mills used for grinding the corn were still standing, and with the help of the reconstruction in our book it was not difficult to imagine the whole work cycle of the bakery, from the arrival of the sacks of grain to the sale of the freshly-baked loaves over the wooden counter fronting the street. In the case of the Forum Baths the buildings were not only much larger but also much better preserved, and even without the help of the book it was possible to follow the entire bathing cycle, starting with the dressing room and progressing through the cold and the tepid baths to the final hot bath. I particularly admired the way in which the light was admitted through various circular and square openings in the domed and vaulted ceilings, thus producing on a small scale the same effect of diffuse lighting that I had observed in the Pantheon in Rome. What I did not admire, however, was the way in which 'counter-drawings' of people who had perished in the eruption of 79 CE were exhibited in glass cases in the dressing room, just as similar 'counter-drawings' were exhibited in the former grain market, as well as in the Pompeiian Galleries of the Archaeological Museum in Naples. These 'counter-drawings' were said to have been obtained by pouring plaster of Paris into the hollows left in the ash by the bodies of the victims, but some of them were so gruesomely realistic in appearance that I was unable to rid myself of the feeling that they were in reality not 'counter-drawings' at all but petrified corpses. If such were the case, it would have been more decent to have quietly interred the pathetic black objects than to have exposed them to the indifference or idle curiosity of the visiting public. But even granting them to be 'counter-drawings', it still was sufficiently painful to see these mute witnesses to the last agonies of men, women, and children who had perished in the eruption being exhibited in this casual and unfeeling manner.

Adjoining the Forum Baths there was a huge modern restaurant and cafeteria, and here Prasannasiddhi and I had our belated mid-morning coffee. On our way in we met, coming out, five or six diminutive Japanese tourists, each one of them loaded down with cameras. Inside we had the place practically to ourselves, though it was capable of seating three or four hundred people and at the height of the tourist season probably did so every hour of the day. Pompeii was clearly a major tourist attraction, and we were thankful that we had the opportunity of seeing it during the off season. We were still more thankful when, on calling in at the souvenir shop on our way out, we saw that in contrast to the restaurant it was full of people, all looking at the cheap – and not so cheap – reproductions of various Pompeiian artefacts. During the summer months the crush must have been terrific. The large reproductions of some of the better-known bronzes, such as the Dancing Faun, were of excellent quality, though it somehow lessened their effectiveness as works of art to see them standing in batches of a dozen or more on the well-stocked shelves. But we were not really interested in reproductions, however good. We wanted to see what was left of the real Pompeii, and after a few minutes we left the shop, without buying anything, to continue our exploration of the labyrinth of streets and alleys that lay within the triangle formed by the Forum Baths, the Herculaneum Gate, and the Vesuvius Gate.

Our exploration was not very systematic. We simply wandered along, occasionally consulting a map and from time to time bumping into one or another of the tourist parties. When we saw a building that looked as though it might be of special interest we went in. During the last two centuries hundreds of shops and houses had been uncovered, and it was not possible to explore all of even the best-known of them, many of which had been given fanciful names derived from the names of the supposed original owners or from a bronze or a mosaic – or in one case the surgical instruments – that had been found beneath the debris. At first whatever houses were uncovered were simply plundered and their contents transferred to various royal and private collections. Most of the treasures unearthed during this early period of excavation were acquired by the Bourbon rulers of Naples, from whose hands they had eventually passed – together with the Farnese Collection – into the keeping of the National Archaeological Museum, where we had seen them only two days previously. Many of the houses we entered had been stripped to the very walls, and now were no more than grass-grown shells, open to the sky, and in various stages of dilapidation. Only a patch of red on the walls or the glint of a white chip in the mud showed that they had once been adorned – even within the past two centuries – with frescoes and mosaics. As we wandered in silence through the deserted, crumbling rooms, into which the hot November sun penetrated with a strange poignancy, I was aware of the same atmosphere of not unpleasing melancholy that I had felt in the Cloister of the Poor Clares, except that here there was a note of wistfulness in the melancholy, as of regret for things that once had been and could not be again.

The houses that had been uncovered at a later, more scientific period of excavation had not been plundered and were, therefore, far from being grass-grown shells. Wall paintings and mosaics, at least, had been left *in situ* and helped to give one a good idea of the original appearance of the buildings and of what it must have felt like to live in them. This was particularly the case with the House of the Vettii, so called after the two brothers who owned it and who, according to our book on Pompeii as it was 2,000 years ago, had spent substantial sums of money not just to have the house decorated but – like the merchants they were – to show off their wealth. The paintings (in the so-called Fourth Style of Pompeiian wall decoration) covered the walls of practically every room. In the small atrium there was the genius of the paterfamilias between two household gods, with a huge serpent below; in the *oecus* to the right of the peristyle Ixion being tied to the wheel by Vulcan in the presence of an angry Juno and an imploring Nephele; in the large triclinium friezes of winged cupids imitating, against a black background, various adult occupations; in the *oecus* to the left of the peristyle the infant Hercules strangling the serpents and – a particularly vigorous work – Pentheus being slain by the Bacchantes, as well as architectural fantasies depicted as though seen through an open window – and so on. But although the paintings were of considerable merit, I was more interested in the general layout of the building and the feeling that this gave. The House of the Vettii was built along two adjoining sides of a rectangular peristyle which was about twice as long as it was broad and took up nearly half the total area. From a covered vestibule one passed into the atrium, in the centre of which there was a square pool, and from the atrium into the peristyle, which like the atrium was of course open to the sky. In the wing to the right of the atrium were situated the women's quarters (including the kitchen) and a large and a small triclinium or dining room, and in the wing to the left of the atrium three or four rooms the purpose of which was not clear. On entering the house from the street one therefore had an uninterrupted view right through the building to the peristyle, with its slender white Doric columns, its well-tended flower beds, and its strip of blue sky. The overall impression was one of both seclusion and openness, shade and sunlight, as well as of a richness and harmony which the warm reds and yellows and cool greens and blues of the wall paintings did much to enhance.

But beautiful as it was, the House of the Vettii had been meant not just to be looked at but to be lived in, and Prasannasiddhi and I were not altogether sorry to be looking round it in company with one of the tourist parties, which had arrived at about the same time that we ourselves had. This party was about twenty strong, and thus of about the same size as the 'extended family' that had occupied the building in the time of the two brothers, each of whom might be supposed to have had a wife and children of his own, apart from the slaves and workpeople and other dependants that they had in common. Even with twenty or more people wandering around, the place was therefore by no means crowded, though since the tourist party did not keep very much together Prasannasiddhi and I were inevitably caught up in bits and pieces of it from time to time. At one point, when we were exploring the women's quarters, we observed some nine or ten people filing through a door that had just been unlocked by a uniformed attendant. Following them, we found ourselves in a windowless cubicle in which there did not seem to be anything of particular interest – until we looked more closely at the small and rather undistinguished wall paintings. They were erotic paintings. On leaving the cubicle everyone dropped a few coins into the outstretched hand of the attendant, who thereupon locked the door until the next batch of tourists should come along. It was all rather absurd. The erotic paintings were not particularly obscene by modern standards (the elderly ladies and the children who had been with us in the cubicle had scrutinized them without change of expression and without comment) and considerably less obscene than the painting of Priapus in the vestibule, through which everyone had to pass in order to enter the house. Picture postcards of this Priapus, as well as of other erotic subjects, were in any case freely available at the National Archaeological Museum, as we had in fact discovered. The practice of keeping the door of the cubicle locked, and unlocking it only in return for a gratuity, was no doubt one that the attendants had inherited from Victorian times and which they had kept up for reasons of their own. Whether our present more relaxed attitude to what our parents and grandparents would have considered obscene is healthy or unhealthy it is difficult to say. Puritanism may well be harmful, but that does not necessarily mean that permissiveness is beneficial.

Owing to its fine state of preservation – not to mention the erotic paintings – the House of the Vettii was naturally part of the regular tourist itinerary, and on leaving it we saw a fresh party of tourists advancing down the Vicolo di Mercurio towards us. Turning in the opposite direction we soon lost ourselves in a more outlying part of the labyrinth and, having looked in at a few more houses, eventually emerged into the thoroughfare that led to the Herculaneum Gate. On passing through this gate we found ourselves in the Street of the Tombs and, as it seemed, in another world. Giant juniper trees, the dense green foliage of which stood out against the blue sky, mingled on either side of the road with smaller and darker Van Gogh cypresses to form a kind of irregular avenue, down the centre of which ran a road unevenly paved with broad, flat stones, from whose crevices grass sprouted. On either side of the road, which ran downhill, there was a raised footpath, almost completely overgrown with weeds, and beside the footpath an irregular stone wall. Above this wall, on either side, there rose at intervals the white shapes of the tombs. As we paced slowly down the silent and deserted avenue, I noticed that most of the tombs were in a fairly good state of preservation, though they had doubtless been rifled of their contents long ago. The tombs were of various types. Some were square and 'altar-shaped', while others were round, or built like temples or chapels or even like semicircular seats. Some tombs, again, were double-storeyed, the lower storey forming part of the massive wall beneath, or were actually built in the wall. The walls were also well provided with niches and memorial tablets, the bold Roman capitals of which were plainly visible from the road. How many sorts and conditions of people had been buried there in the course of the three or four centuries that Pompeii had flourished! There were men and women, magistrates and priestesses, merchants and military men. But though the road down which we were walking was dedicated to the dead rather than to the living it was not a melancholy place. What with the unbroken blue of the autumnal sky, and the clear golden glow in which the early afternoon sun steeped the green juniper trees and white tombs, the lichen-stained masonry of the walls and the grey paving-stones, the atmosphere was in fact one of philosophic calm and detachment, as though the dead had carried with them to the tomb some tincture of Stoicism. 'We were glad to accept life,' they seemed to be saying. 'Shall we not accept death with equal gladness, or at least with equanimity?'

At the far end of the Street of the Tombs, on the left-hand side of the road, there was situated (according to our map) the Villa of Diomedes, and it was towards this that we were directing our steps. On reaching the gate we found it locked and had to be content with a glimpse, through the railings, of extensive ruins amid which grew junipers, cypresses, and palm trees. Before one came to the Villa of Diomedes, however, there was a similar gate on the same side of the road, and this gate was unlocked. Within a minute I had slipped through it and was standing knee-deep in the coarse grass some ten or twelve paces from the wall (Prasannasiddhi, for some reason or other, remained outside in the road). According to the map I was standing on the very spot which had once been occupied by the Villa of Cicero, for the great Roman orator and moralist had owned a villa here in Pompeii as well as at various other points along the coast. So thick and tall was the grass, however, and so interwoven with brambles, that it was impossible for me to proceed even a step further, much less to explore the place. But I was quite content to remain where I was. I was quite content simply to stand there feeling the warmth of the sun and inhaling the fragrance of the grass. Earlier in the year I had been rereading the works of Cicero, especially his dialogue *On Friendship* and his essay *On Old Age*, and had even included a couple of volumes of selections in the books I had brought with me to Il Convento. Whether any of those works had been composed here in this secluded villa off the Street of the Tombs I did not know, but it was difficult to imagine a spot more conducive to literary work, and it was not without reluctance that I eventually returned to the road. When Prasanna-siddhi asked me what I had found through the gate I replied 'Not much,' and in the literal sense this was the truth. But metaphorically or imaginatively speaking I had found a great deal. In my mind's eye I had seen the villa as it was in the days of republican and imperial Rome. I had seen Cicero discussing philosophy with his friends over a cup of Falernian, and walking up and down one of the colonnades of the peristyle dictating to an amanuensis.

Since the Villa of Diomedes was closed it seemed more than likely that the Villa of the Mysteries, which was the most outlying of the villas, would be closed too, and we therefore decided to make our way back to the Forum. We made our way back to it by a very circuitous route, that took us through a more westerly quarter of the city, since we wanted to have a look at the Large Theatre, the more particularly since Prasannasiddhi had not had the opportunity of seeing a Classical theatre before. On the way we saw the House of the Bear and a number of other houses – more often than not through the railings of a locked gate. We also visited the spacious Stabian Baths, with their sports field and running track, and saw – again through the railings of a locked gate – the sacred enclosure wherein stood the Temple of Isis, which I recalled having seen on my earlier visit nineteen years ago. Though the small temple on the lofty podium was in a sadly ruinous condition, from the truncated columns and some fragments of architrave one could easily see that it had been Graeco-Roman rather than Egyptian in style. During the first century BCE and the first century CE the cult of Isis had spread throughout the Roman Empire, much as Buddhism has spread in the West in the course of the last hundred years. As we turned to go I reflected that the Temple of Isis had probably occupied a place in the religious life of Pompeii similar to that occupied by an FWBO centre in an English provincial town, say Brighton or Leeds, though obviously the analogy must not be pushed too far. Eventually we reached the Large Theatre, which had been built on the site of a natural slope, and sat down in the middle of the Pompeiian equivalent of 'the gods'. Below us the auditorium fell away in tier after semi-circular tier of stone seats to the horseshoe-shaped 'orchestra', beyond which was the stage and what was left of the monumental façade. On the whole the place was reasonably well preserved: further round to the right one could see the iron rings to which had been fastened the enormous canopy that covered the entire seating area. The Theatre had held 5,000 people, and Classical dramas had been performed there including, presumably, adaptations of the tragedies of Sophocles and Euripedes, as well as the comedies of Menander. Greece herself could hardly have provided a finer natural setting for the presentation of the sublime products of Attic genius. Behind the monumental façade rose the dense green masses of the umbrella pines and the 'black flames' of the cypresses, and beyond them the hills – blue with distance – that lay to the south-east of the city, in the opposite direction from Mount Vesuvius.

After we had sat there for a few minutes, absorbing the scene before us, we went and looked down at the ruins of the Samnite Palaestra and the Little Theatre and then made our way, through the covered corridor that ran behind the backing wall of the topmost tier of seats, to the remains of the Triangular Forum, with its ruined Doric Temple of

Hercules – Hercules being the mythical founder of Pompeii. From the Triangular Forum we walked down the Via dell'Abbandonza, where there was an abundance of recently excavated shops and houses. This brought us back to the point from which, some three or four hours earlier, we had set out on our exploration of the city, that is to say, back to the Forum and the Basilica. Having been on our feet for most of that time we were now feeling a little tired, and reluctantly concluded that we had perhaps seen as much of Pompeii as could profitably be seen in one day. After looking round the remains of the magnificent building which the priestess Aumachia, whose statue we had seen in the Archaeological Museum, had erected for the weavers of Pompeii, as well as round the more extensive remains of the Temple of Apollo, where a row of five Doric columns still supported a section of entablature, we therefore started slowly making for the exit. On the way we saw a refreshment kiosk, surrounded by white-painted chairs and tables, standing in a clearing among oleander bushes and stately umbrella pines. It was completely deserted, and looked so inviting that we decided to stop for a rest and a cold drink. Naturally, we had to pay for sitting down. Indeed, so expensive did our cold drinks and our packet of potato crisps turn out to be that we probably had to pay for looking at the view, as well as for the privilege of sitting out in the sun. But we did not really mind. So beautiful was the place, and so restful, that we felt that even if we *had* been charged for the 'extras' we had certainly got our money's worth.

On our emergence from the 'excavations' I was once more recalled from my dreams of the past – now considerably heightened by the experiences of the day – by the commercialism of the present. On either side of the path there was a row of souvenir stalls, behind which were stationed two stall-holders, one short, fat, and oleaginous, the other tall, thin, and desiccated. The stalls contained, for the most part, rather crude reproductions of Pompeiian artefacts, many of them made to look as though they had been buried for 2,000 years, or even longer; but there were also small cardboard boxes of Vesuvian mineral specimens (mica, covellite, olivine, and so on), and in these boxes I was definitely interested. Two out of the twelve different specimens that each box contained especially fascinated me, one of them being deep blue in colour, the other deep orange. Perceiving my interest the desiccated stall-holder came over to me and, after I had affected to hesitate for a while, reduced the price of a box by about a fifth 'just for me', saying that he could see I was English and that he had always been very fond of the English. Later on I had cause to remember that remark. A few days after Prasannasiddhi and I returned to Il Convento I noticed on the inside of the lid of my box, directly opposite the compartment in which rested the deep orange specimen, a faint trace of the same colour, and at once became suspicious. Though by no means a mineralogist, I knew that the colours of minerals – especially those that looked like semi-precious stones – did not usually rub off in this manner and by way of a test dropped the suspect specimen into a tumbler of warm water. Within half an hour all the orange 'crystals' dissolved, leaving only a small piece of ordinary lava. The same thing happened with the deep blue specimen. It was now obvious that orange and blue dye crystals of some kind had been stuck on to the pieces of lava in order to give the box as a whole a more attractive appearance (the other specimens were mostly brown or grey), and that I had been tricked. Though sorry to have lost my two most colourful specimens, I could not help laughing heartily at the deception, and at the rascality of the two stall-holders. Since there had been at least a dozen boxes of mineral specimens on sale, all with deep blue and deep orange specimens occupying the middle compartments, there must have been a small factory in the neighbourhood of Vesuvius engaged not only in producing the boxes themselves but also in faking at least some of their contents. At the time, however, I suspected nothing, for though I knew that artefacts could be faked I had not imagined that it would be worth anyone's while to fake mineral specimens. I was therefore well content with my purchase, and Prasannasiddhi and I marched to the little railway station with the consciousness of having brought our visit to Pompeii to a fitting conclusion.

At the station we had only a few minutes to wait before the train arrived and half an hour later we were climbing the stairs that led up to Central Station. I noticed that the train had been quite full, mainly with family parties who were apparently going into Naples to spend the evening with friends and relations and, perhaps, to visit the churches. As usual, everybody seemed rather short, rather stout, and rather drably dressed, the predominant colour of the crowd being dusty black, with just a touch of colour here and there. Immediately in front of us, as we went up the stairs, was a large family party that included two or three black-habited nuns, clearly present in their capacity as aunt or sister. From the station we walked straight to the hotel, which we reached somewhat past our siesta time. Since it was so late we decided not to visit any churches, as we usually did in the afternoon, but instead to have a rest and then go and eat at the corner restaurant at the usual hour. In any case, our excursion had left us with very strong impressions of the pagan and Classical civilization and culture of Pompeii, and we did not want to break the spell by exposing ourselves, so soon, to the very different atmosphere of the churches.

On our arrival at the corner restaurant we found it quite full, even our usual table by the window being already occupied. It had never been full at such an early hour before. Indeed, we had always had the place practically to ourselves. But today was a holiday, people had come out early, and in the restaurant itself a jovial – even festive – atmosphere prevailed. As would have been the case in India (though not in England), the customers were almost entirely of the male sex. Most of them seemed to come in small parties, and if a table was not big enough to accommodate everyone the waiters obligingly drew two or more tables together so that good fellowship should not be broken up. Several of the men present were in police or military uniform, and both they and all the other members of the different parties were clearly on very friendly terms with one another. Though the fact that the restaurant was so full, and the waiters therefore extremely busy, meant that we did not get served very quickly that evening, it was very pleasant to be sitting in the midst of so much camaraderie and mutual good will.

Back at the hotel a rather different kind of experience awaited us. Further along the corridor a party of three or four Africans was staying. They had arrived at about the same time as we had, but so far we had not seen or heard very much of them. On that evening of our third full day in Naples, however, when we were writing picture postcards to our friends in different parts of the world, we were made very much aware of their existence. In the adjoining room a violent quarrel suddenly erupted, with two or three hysterically angry voices shouting at one another in a way that was reminiscent of a disagreement between animals rather than human beings. What the quarrel was about it was impossible to tell, but it involved not only verbal exchanges but much violent slamming of doors and sudden rushes along the corridor and up and down the stairs. What was strange, in view of the seeming violence of the emotions that had been aroused, was the fact that no blows were exchanged. Despite the alarming volume of 'sound and fury' that was being emitted the quarrel was apparently of an entirely verbal and histrionic nature. As for the language in which it was conducted, this was a guttural tongue with which I was quite unfamiliar, though since one member of the party was called Antony and another Thomas, and since somebody kept shouting 'You very very no good!' I concluded that they were all Christians and had received a certain amount of Western education. After raging for about an hour the quarrel began to subside, but like a storm that has not exhausted its fury it kept breaking out afresh, and it was almost another hour before the last angry mutterings died away in the adjoining room. All this time Prasannasiddhi and I were steadily writing our picture postcards, and by the time the Africans had finished their quarrel we had written a couple of dozen between us. We then decided to call it a day and shortly afterwards retired.

Our last full day in Naples began (so far as sightseeing was concerned) with a visit to the Villa La Floridiana. This took us to a part of the city with which we were as yet unacquainted and which lay as far beyond the Royal Palace as the Royal Palace lay beyond the Cathedral. As usual we had recourse to the metro and after a fifteen-minute journey emerged from a station whose name I forget into surroundings with which we were completely unfamiliar and where we had some difficulty in getting our bearings. Eventually we set off in the opposite direction to that in which we had come, hoping to find a turning on our left that would take us away from the coast and towards the Villa La Floridiana. We must have walked for nearly a mile, passing luxury hotels that commanded a fine view of the Bay of Naples, but no turning on the left did we see. Eventually we came not to a turning but to a flight of stone steps. At the top of these steps, round a bend, we found another flight, and then another. What our map did not tell us was that that part of Naples was built on the side of a steep hill, and that although the route we were following was the shortest (apart from the funicular, which we should really have taken) it was also the most difficult. However, there was nothing for it but to continue, and up more and more flights of stone steps we therefore went. Though difficult, the route was not without its compensations. Flanking the steps, which seemed to be extremely ancient, were rows of low, stone-built houses. What was remarkable about these houses was that except in the few cases were modernity had crept in they had no windows, light being admitted through the open doorway, from which one could see deep into the interior of the dwelling. They were in fact more like caves than houses, though evidently quite snug (I had a glimpse of white tablecloths and pots of geraniums), and I was reminded of Goethe's description of the 'one-storey little houses constructed in a curious way without windows' which he had noticed when returning from an expedition to the mouth of the crater of Vesuvius.* Clearly part of the population of Naples still led a semi-troglodyte existence, and I was glad to have had an opportunity of seeing this for myself. After we had climbed ten or twelve flights of stone steps, however, my legs started to ache and my breath to come in gasps, and even cave dwellings lost something of their fascination. To make matters worse, the rain started falling, quite heavily. Though we were provided with an umbrella (the sky had been very grey when we left the hotel) it did not give us much protection, and we were relieved when the rain eased off after only a few minutes.

By this time we had decided to turn left on to the horizontal, leaving the now wet and slippery steps, which continued farther up the hillside, between more rows of cave dwellings. We had not taken more than a few steps in the new direction before noticing that we were in an area that differed from the rest of Naples – as far as we had seen it – not only geographically but, so to speak, sociologically. The streets were broad and well swept, and named after Italian composers. On either side rose luxurious villas and blocks of high-rise flats, interspersed with palm trees and flowering shrubs. There were few lines of washing to be seen, and even these fluttered furtively from the balconies of what were probably servants' quarters. We were, in fact, in the prosperous new suburb of Vomero, which might be described as the West Kensington or Hampstead of Naples, in contrast to the area around Central Station, which might be described as its Liverpool Street or Bethnal Green. Even the people were different. They were taller and better built, and the men wore well-tailored business suits. Before long (though not without having had to enquire our way more than once) we reached the Via Cimarosa, which eventually took us to the Via Luca Giordano (was he also a composer?), a busy thoroughfare that seemed to be the principal shopping centre of the area, being full of expensive shops, expensive cars, and expensive women. After walking several hundred yards down the street we came to a pair of massive bronze gates and, with something like a sigh of relief, exchanged the noise of the traffic for the comparative silence of the gardens of the Villa La Floridiana. A winding road led between green lawns and even greener trees in the direction of the house, and after a few minutes the white walls of the comparatively modest building could be seen

---

* *Italian Journey*, op. cit., p.195.

through the fine rain that was now falling. So shrouded in silence was the place that we at first thought it was closed; but it was open, or rather half open. Though this meant that only half the Villa La Floridiana's treasures (it was a museum of the minor arts) were accessible the full price of admission was being charged. From the way in which the man in the ticket office gave us this information it was evident that he more than half expected us to reject so bad a bargain in disgust; but since we had come a long way, and since half a museum was better than no museum at all, after hesitating a moment we paid our 4,000 lire apiece and spent the following hour looking round. We were not disappointed. The ten or twelve small rooms that were open contained ivories, Limoges enamels, Bohemian crystal, Murano glass, and Majolica ware of such uniformly high quality that almost every item was deserving of detailed examination. Some of the items were of Chinese and Japanese origin. One of the most impressive of these was a trumpet-shaped *famille noire* vase of the Kiang-hau dynasty, about five feet in height, that stood in the centre of a corner room.

When we came out the rain had stopped and the sunlight, piercing the dark foliage overhead, was falling in long golden shafts to the muddy ground. Taking advantage of a dry bench, I sat down for a few minutes while Prasannasiddhi wandered away among the trees. Not having sat down since we left the metro, I found it pleasant to rest for a while, and no less pleasant to look down the slope to the gardens at the rear of the Villa La Floridiana. In the middle of these gardens, at the bottom of a flight of steps that led, presumably, to the terrace at the back (or was it really the front?) of the building was a large circular pond.... On Prasannasiddhi's return we made our way back to the bronze gates and from there retraced our steps to the juncture of the Via Luca Giordano and the Via Cimarosa. Having spent the greater part of the morning finding and visiting a museum, we now had to start thinking of finding and visiting a church, except that today the church was a monastery and we would be visiting it not, as usual, after our siesta but before. The monastery in question was the Certosa di San Martino, and it was situated immediately below the Castel San Elmo, which occupied the highest part of the hill of that name. Since we had eaten nothing since the early morning, and moreover had another climb before us, we stopped at a rather stylish-looking bar for a hot drink and a pastry. Behind the counter was a smart young woman in a tight-fitting black silk dress (in all the other bars we had visited the servers had been men). Before handing us the pastries we had selected she enquired, with a smile and an upward motion of her black eyebrows, if we wanted them sprayed with the contents of a kind of scent-spray that she held in her beringed hand. Supposing the spray to contain a variety of syrup we responded affirmatively, and retired with our purchases to the only two seats in the bar. On sinking our teeth into the pastries, however, we discovered that they were impregnated with a scent that we were unable to identify. It was familiar yet at the same time unfamiliar. Eventually the truth dawned on us. The liquid with which our pastries had been sprayed was rum.

Refreshed by our snack, we continued up the Via Luca Giordano and, after climbing a broad flight of steps, made our way through a maze of streets and up several more flights of steps to the road that led, past the Castel San Elmo, to the Certosa di San Martino. On our arrival at the monastery gate we found several coaches parked in the front courtyard, which on one side was overlooked by the battlements of the Castel San Elmo and on the other itself overlooked the lower part of the city. Built in the fourteenth century, and enlarged and decorated in the sixteenth and seventeenth, the Certosa or Charterhouse (as Carthusian monasteries are called) was a monastery no longer. It was a museum, and judging by the comparatively large number of people about it was a major tourist attraction. Why this should be so was not immediately apparent. On passing through the gateway and crossing a small courtyard we found ourselves in a series of rather austere rooms, some of them panelled, containing glassware and china, an eighteenth-century coach, and, most interesting of all, some life-size wooden figures that apparently had formed part of a crib set. The *pièce de résistance*, however, was not inside but outside the building. This was an enormous balcony, a hundred feet long and thirty feet broad, from which one had an unobstructed view not only of the Bay of Naples but of practically the whole city, with Vesuvius brooding purple-grey in the distance. This was the famous view that had given rise to the saying 'See Naples and die,' and on account of which the former monastery was a major tourist attraction, and indeed one might have been content to die after seeing so splendid and soothing a panorama. At the time of our visit both the sky and the sea were a deep blue, while the houses and churches that filled the whole space between San Elmo and the Marina, as well as extending to the very slopes of Vesuvius, presented a brilliantly sunlit patchwork of white and apricot and red, interspersed with green. What was most remarkable, no sound at all ascended from the city to the balcony, so that sitting with my back against the wall I was aware only of the blueness of the sky and the warmth of the sun. On that balcony one was like the Gods on their hills in Tennyson's *The Lotos-Eaters*:

> For they lie beside their nectar, and the bolts are hurl'd
> Far below them in the valleys, and the clouds are lightly curl'd
> Round their golden houses, girdled with the gleaming world.

But though it was indeed a gleaming world that girdled the balcony, for a Buddhist reclining there could be only a respite, not a way of life.

When Prasannasiddhi returned from exploring the 'hanging garden' into which the balcony opened on the right-hand side, we made our way back through the cluster of rooms that constituted the nucleus of the museum and, after traversing a long and gloomy corridor, emerged into a sunlit cloister. Though of no great architectural significance, it was well suited to its purpose, and we were glad to spend a few minutes strolling round the ambulatory, the more especially since hardly anybody else was present. If I remember rightly, in a corner of the cloister-garth were four or five simple monastic graves, the head-stones of which were decorated with skulls. We were about to leave the place when Prasannasiddhi noticed, not far from the door, a short passage, and at the end of the passage a flight of stone steps. In a moment he was standing at the top of these steps and beckoning to me with subdued excitement. From the landing there a door opened into a range of enormous rooms, all panelled, carved, painted, and gilded to the highest possible degree. There was a chapter room, a sacristy, a treasury, and so on, one leading straight into the other. Above all, there was the church. Though the rooms through which we had already passed were a big enough surprise, especially since there had been nothing to indicate their existence, the church came as something of a revelation. We entered it from the apse behind the high altar, and were at once in a world of Neapolitan baroque fantasy that, in the sunshine that came streaming down through the windows of the clerestory and the still higher lights of the dome, was positively exhilarating. Though the frescoes were not of the first quality, and though the balustrade in front of the high altar – marble inlaid with semi-precious stones – was almost barbaric in its magnificence, the church as a whole produced an impression of elegance and gaiety such as we had encountered nowhere else in Naples – unless it was in the 'ornamental obelisks' that we had seen in the Piazza Jesù and else-where. Strange to say, the place was completely deserted, except that when we returned to the apse a decrepit attendant tottered out of the shadows and stared at us. I also noticed that the furnishings of the high altar were covered with dust.

With our visit to the Certosa di San Martino our sightseeing for the day was ended, and on leaving the monastery we walked back through Vomero to the funicular. This took us down to quite near the metro station from which we had emerged some four or five hours earlier, and from here we caught the train to Naples Central. We were very much aware of the fact that this was our last ride on the Naples metro, at least for the time being. Later we had our last siesta in the second-floor room overlooking the courtyard with the washing, wrote our last picture postcards, and took our last meal at the little corner restaurant, where we once again had the place practically to ourselves. After finishing our meal we walked through the Piazza Garibaldi to Central Station, where Prasannasiddhi bought stamps for our post-cards at a kiosk while I bought the latest issues of *Time* and *Newsweek* to read on the train the next day. As I was counting my change I noticed an elderly Italian of respectable, middle-class appearance buying two pornographic magazines – as their covers plainly revealed them to be – at the same newsagents. At a word from this customer, the man behind the counter ripped off the front covers and handed the maga-zines to him in a state of decent anonymity, whereupon he stuffed them into a pocket of his coat. From the way in which this was done I gained the impression that it was the regular procedure. Respectable middle-aged men wanted to be able to read their pornographic magazines without their fellow passengers – or perhaps their wives and children – knowing the nature of the material in which they were so deeply absorbed.

In the morning we rose a little earlier than usual and, having packed our bags, made our way down to the reception desk to pay our bill. While I was waiting for the man on duty to bring me my change I noticed hovering in the background two or three of the Africans whose violent quarrel had so disrupted the peace of our corridor two eve-nings previously. From the loudness of their voices I had imagined them to be enormously big men, with great barrel chests, but though by no means short they were in fact thin and weedy, and yellow rather than black in complexion. As I half-watched them a very large Ameri-can strode into the reception area and shook hands with the Africans with the rather exaggerated *bonhomie* which, as I knew from my Kalimpong days, characterized the Christian missionary's dealings with his converts. From the conversation that followed I gathered that the Africans were training for the ministry (or it may have been for the priesthood, if they were Roman Catholics) and that they were on vacation. Before I could learn more my change arrived, and Prasannasiddhi and I were on our way to Central Station, where we had breakfast in the glass-walled bar and cafeteria, thus reversing the order of our arrival. Since we had not been able to book seats on the through train to Grosseto (or rather, on the through train to Paris, which stopped at Grosseto), we boarded the Rome express and were soon deep in our *Time* and *Newsweek*. Rajneesh had, it appeared, publicly accused some of his closest associates of various criminal offences and the FBI was investigating. The headlines that we had seen in the newspapers of our fellow passengers on the way down were thus explained. In Rome we had only twenty minutes in which to change trains, but we experienced no difficulty and were soon once again on our way. At Grosseto the faithful Suvajra was there on the platform to meet us, this time without Buddhapalita, who was unwell.

After our four very full days in Naples we had a lot to assimilate, and though I had thoroughly enjoyed our little holiday I was not sorry to see the irregular orange mass of Il Convento rising before us as we drove up the hill and not sorry to be back in my spacious room with its view of the valley, the foothills, and the distant sea. The retreat still had four weeks to run, and I knew that I was going to be kept quite busy. Apart from having to edit a *Mitrata* and the transcript of my lecture on 'Authority and the Individual in the New Society', I would soon have to start taking my small discussion groups. I would also have to start writing this Letter. But I did not have to do any of these things immediately. Turning away from my desk, I made my way along the barrel-vaulted corridor, down the double flight of stone steps, and joined Prasannasiddhi in the dining room for a late lunch.

Urgyen Sangharakshita

Letter from Wales

Reflections on Sangharakshita's future role

Dear Dharmacharis and Dharmacharinis,

At present I am in Wales, staying at Tyddern Rydderch, midway between Vajraloka and Vajrakuta. With me is Paramartha. We arrived on 24 November, having spent the night at Stratford-upon-Avon after visiting my mother in Rayleigh earlier in the day. Before leaving Stratford we saw Shakespeare's birthplace and his memorial in the local church, besides visiting the Tropical Butterfly House – a type of tourist attraction I had not seen before and which seems to be growing in popularity.

During the three weeks that we have now been at Tyddern Rydderch we have been meditating, reading, and, of course, engaging in communication. We have also had a few outings, mainly to Caernarvon (via Snowdonia), Llangollen, Ruthin, Denbigh, St Asaph, and Rhyl – Paramartha not having had an opportunity of seeing this part of the country before. My main purpose in coming here, however (at least originally), was to have a rest and to try to see what would be the best use for me to make of the remaining years of my life. During my three months at Guhyaloka in the summer, taking part in the men's ordination retreat, I had become aware of a strong sense of dissatisfaction with the way I was functioning – a sense of dissatisfaction that had, in fact, been steadily growing for several years. In particular I did not want to function mainly as the head and, so to speak, administrator of the wbo and fwbo or to devote the greater part of my time and energy to organizational matters, as has been increasingly the case in recent years. If it was at all possible, I wanted to make a further creative contribution to the development of the Movement rather than to confine myself to helping with the running of the Movement as it already existed, though I did not know – and still do not know – what form that contribution might take, whether literary or non-literary.

My sense of dissatisfaction with the way in which I was functioning was strengthened by my contact with Paramartha, who also was taking part in the men's ordination retreat, in the course of which he was ordained. It had been arranged that after his ordination he should join the Order Office at Padmaloka, but before actually doing so he wanted to make sure that his duties would leave him sufficient time for study and meditation. I assured him that they would. Indeed, shortly after our return to Padmaloka I decided that, in view of his strong interest in study and meditation, he should have more time for these activities than originally envisaged and in fact started doing some study with him. As I became more deeply involved in this, as well as in my communication with Paramartha, I became aware that this was, broadly speaking, the kind of direction I wished to pursue.

Moreover, while at Guhyaloka I had decided to make certain changes with regard to the Order Office team/community. In the first place, I would involve myself with it in a more active manner, particularly by way of joining in the morning community meditation and leading a weekly study group. In the second, I would try to develop the Order Office team/community into something less like a group of Buddhist office workers and more like a real spiritual community – which might mean changing the name 'Order Office' into something more appropriate. On my return to Padmaloka I put these changes into effect, and by the time Paramartha and I left for Wales had achieved a measure of success, at least with regard to the first of them, i.e. my involving myself with the Order Office team/community in a more active manner.

Shortly before our departure I went to see my (official) doctor, since for some time past Dharmadhara had been a little concerned about my blood pressure. Unfortunately it transpired that this had now become quite dangerously high and I was immediately placed on daily medication. With his customary frankness (which I very much appreciated) Dharmadhara told me that my blood pressure was only slightly less than Dayasri's had been when she had her stroke and that, without medication, my life expectancy was not more than five years, possibly as little as one or two years.

With this sobering news I have come to Tyddern Rydderch to reflect on the future course of my life even more seriously than I should otherwise have done. Though it is not clear what might be the best use for me to make of the remaining years of my life, it is clear that I must withdraw from administrative and organizational responsibilities and that these must be taken over as soon as possible by Order members. It is also clear that I must avoid situations of stress, of which there have been far too many recently. Indeed, I may say that for reasons of which some of you will be aware the last two years have been by far the most difficult and painful of my whole life and that, if I am to survive and to make a further creative contribution to the Movement there must be a change in this state of affairs.

I have thought it proper to take you into my confidence in this manner, partly because I feel it is only right that you should be kept fully informed about all that concerns me, and partly in order to give each one of you an opportunity of reflecting on the nature of your own personal relation to me and to the Movement. I hope to be able to contribute a longer and more detailed letter about my current thinking to a future issue of *Shabda*.

Urgyen Sangharakshita

LETTER FROM NORFOLK

Tyddern Rydderch – Sukhavati – In the Footsteps of Ambedkar – the Order Office – Croydon Buddhist Centre and Aryatara – Brighton – Michelangelo: Life, Letters, and Poetry – Cecil Collins

Dear Dharmacharis and Dharmacharinis,

You may remember that I concluded my 'letter from Wales' with the hope that I would be able to contribute a longer and more detailed letter about my current thinking to a future issue of *Shabda*. This I am not yet in a position to do, but inasmuch as some of you have expressed the wish that I should write and give news of myself from time to time I thought that I would at least bring you up to date with regard to my movements during the last two months.

Before doing that, however, I would like to thank those of you who, in one way or another, have expressed your concern for my health and sympathy that the last two years of my life should have been so difficult and painful. I am glad to be able to tell you that, thanks to daily medication, my blood pressure is now much lower, though it seems that unless an alternative, possibly herbal, remedy can be found I shall have to continue with the medication indefinitely. At the same time, I must make it clear that, while I have already started withdrawing from some of my administrative and organizational responsibilities, the real reasons why the last two years of my life have been so difficult and painful have by no means been eliminated. I should also mention that shortly I shall be seeing a cardiologist and undergoing various tests, with a view to determining whether my high blood pressure is due simply to age and stress or whether other causative factors may not also be involved.

Now back to Wales. Paramartha and I left Tyddern Rydderch on 27 December, about a week after I had written my previous letter. Our last week in Wales was spent in much the same way as the previous three had been, that is to say, we meditated, read, and talked, as well as had another outing, this time to Conway Castle, where we were caught in a sudden heavy downpour, and to the Welsh Mountain Zoo, where we enjoyed warm sunshine and a wonderful view of Colwyn Bay. Though I was sorry to leave Tyddern Rydderch and would, in fact, have very much liked to spend a couple more weeks there (Hridaya, the owner, was coming on a family holiday, and we had to vacate the place), I was grateful for the opportunity of having a good rest and of renewing my acquaintance with Wales. (I have sometimes thought that Norfolk, London, and North Wales are the three points of the triangle of my life in Britain, as they are of the life of the hero of Watts-Dunton's *Aylwin*.)

On Monday, 27 December, therefore, Paramartha and I left Tyddern Rydderch at 8 o'clock in the morning and arrived at Sukhavati in good time for supper, having driven practically from one side of the country to the other in continuous brilliant sunshine and beneath cloudless blue skies. We would have arrived earlier, except that we made a short detour to St Albans (we had come down the M1), where we walked round the city centre and visited the Cathedral, a magnificent Romanesque structure of brick and flint and with the second longest nave in England. We spent two weeks at Sukhavati, staying in my flat and following much the same semi-retreat routine that we had followed in Wales. But before I say anything more about our stay in London let me tell you what books I read in Wales, since several of you have asked me about this and seem, in fact, particularly interested.

Not that there is really very much to tell. In fact, I read much less than I usually do, often being content simply to sit in front of the fire (stove) and reflect on things while Paramartha read, or got on with the cooking, or did yoga and/or prostrations. During the first week I read the greater part of Elisabeth Kübler-Ross's *On Death and Dying* and dipped into Glen H. Mullin's *Death and Dying: the Tibetan Tradition*, both of which I had been intending to read for some time and both of which are, I believe, quite popular in FWBO circles. Out of the nine Tibetan texts included in *Death and Dying* I was, I think, most impressed by 'Death and the Bodhisattva Trainings', a sermon delivered in Lhasa by the Thirteenth Dalai Lama on the occasion of the Great

Prayer Festival, and it occurred to me that this text could well be studied on ordination retreats in conjunction with the six element practice. Perhaps those of you who are responsible for conducting these retreats could give some thought to the matter. In subsequent weeks I read about half of Annemarie Schimmel's *Mystical Dimensions of Islam*, a scholarly work written with deep feeling for its subject, and the first third of David Snellgrove's *Indo-Tibetan Buddhism*, in which I found a certain amount of support for some of my own views. Though Snellgrove is not a Buddhist, and though he in some respects suffers from the usual scholarly myopia, his book is full of information not easily available elsewhere and repays careful study. My staple diet in Wales, however, so far as reading was concerned, was not so much Buddhist as Neoplatonic. I read many of the essays in *The Significance of Neoplatonism*, *Neoplatonism and Indian Thought*, and *The Structure of Being*, the first, second, and fourth volumes in the series 'Studies in Neoplatonism: Ancient and Modern', edited by R. Baine Harris, as well as the first volume of Dean Inge's *The Philosophy of Plotinus*. This notable work was, I think, the first book on Neoplatonism I ever read. At any rate, I read it when I was sixteen or seventeen (perhaps earlier), and nearly half a century later was glad to be able to recommend it to Paramartha. I also read ten of Plotinus' *Enneads*, David Melling's *Understanding Plato*, and a certain amount of poetry, mainly Homer and Milton.

(While I am still in Wales, so to speak, I would like to mention that shortly before leaving Tyddern Rydderch I visited Vajrakuta and spent some time with Kamalasila and other members of the Vajraloka chapter. As on my previous visit, I was greatly impressed by their evident emotional positivity and by the spirit of dedication in which they are working for the Vajraloka Meditation Centre. Apart from this, during my month in Wales I had no personal contact with anyone other than Paramartha.)

Though following much the same semi-retreat routine in my flat at Sukhavati as we had in Wales, Paramartha and I probably did proportionately more sightseeing. In the course of our two weeks in London we visited the British Museum, the Tate Gallery, and the Regent's Park Zoo, explored the Charing Cross Road bookshops, walked on Hampstead Heath (once again we had brilliant sunshine and cloudless blue skies), saw the paintings at Kenwood House, and looked round 'Keats' House', that is, round the house in which Keats lived for a while during the last two years of his life, where he wrote his 'Ode to a Nightingale' and other poems, and where we saw manuscripts, first editions, and locks of hair. On those days when we did not do any sightseeing we usually went for a walk in Victoria Park. We also saw a performance of *Richard II*, with Derek Jacobi in the title role.

On the evening of 6 January we joined members of the Sukhavati community in viewing *In the Footsteps of Ambedkar*, the TV documentary for the making of which I had gone to India in October. Since I had not seen the rough cuts, I had been looking forward to the showing of the film with a certain amount of apprehension. But I need not have worried. The photography was very fine, the music appropriate (though I gather not everyone would agree with me here), and there was nothing in my commentary that I would have preferred the director, Bob Mullen, to have left out. My only real criticism (though on a second viewing others might occur to me) was that towards the end of the film there was at times a certain lack of continuity between sequences. As you can imagine, seeing the film was for me a deeply moving experience. Not only did it bring back vivid memories of the sights and sounds of India, where I had spent twenty years of my life; it also brought back vivid memories of the love and devotion with which Order members, Mitras, and Friends alike had surrounded me from the beginning to the very end of my three-week visit – a visit which took me from Bombay to Poona, from Poona to Aurangabad, from Aurangabad to Wardha, and finally from Wardha (via Nagpur) back to Bombay. As I reflect on that love and devotion, I cannot but think that in this respect, as in others, we in the Movement in Britain have much to learn from our brothers and sisters in India.

Thus the time Paramartha and I spent in London passed both pleasantly and usefully. Except when we went into town, it also passed very quietly. During the earlier part of our stay, at least, there were very few people around in the Sukhavati community, and very few people around the Centre, many of them being away on retreat or else on holiday. The quietness suited me personally quite well (in the course of my stay I had 'interviews' with only three or four people, notably with Parami, who had a stylish new hairdo and was very much on form); but though it suited me quite well it seemed a great pity that more use had not been made of the Centre over the Christmas and New Year holiday period, the more especially since the former old fire station now looks very smart after the comprehensive refurbishment of its entire exterior. After all, facilities of this sort have taken a lot of time, money, and energy to create. Let us then make the best and fullest use of them that we possibly can.

In London I did even less reading than I had done in Wales – even allowing for the fact that I spent not four weeks there but only two. I did, however, read Devamitra's copy of Liz Hodgkinson's *Sex is Not Compulsory*, which I found in the flat, and was even more impressed by it than I was when it first came out. She puts the positive side of the case for celibacy extremely well, and I strongly recommend the book to those of you who have not yet read it. Those who *have* read it, but who have still not given serious consideration to the question of celibacy, should, I think, read it again. Before going to see the play I read *Richard II* (as did Paramartha), and dipped into Peter Fuller's *Theoria*, which Danavira had brought to my notice. The dipping showed the book to be of unusual interest, exploring as it did 'a fascinating web of connections between nature, science and faith from the early nineteenth century to the present day' (jacket blurb), and I looked forward to being able to read it more systematically on my return to Padmaloka.

The return in question took place on 9 January, when Paramartha and I once again had sunshine and blue skies for our journey. I returned with mixed feelings. On the one hand I was glad to be back at Padmaloka, which has been my 'home' for the last twelve or thirteen years, and glad to see Prasannasiddhi, Kovida, and other members of the community; but on the other hand I was sorry to be back at my desk, so to speak, and sorry to have to resume the administrative and organizational responsibilities from which, as I explained in 'Letter from Wales', it has become necessary for me to withdraw as soon as possible. Within a matter of days, therefore, my time was being divided between a greatly reduced routine of study, meditation, etc. with Paramartha and the work of the Order Office. In the latter I was greatly helped by the arrival of Kulananda, who joined the Order Office team on 10 January, having volunteered his services some time ago on hearing that I was badly in need of assistance. Since then he has proved his worth a dozen times a day and even though other 'senior and responsible' Order members will have to play their part (mainly, perhaps, through the Office of the FWBO) I already feel my responsibilities weighing on me a little less heavily than they did. My only regret is that Padmaloka's – and my own – gain should have been Cambridge's loss.

During my absence in Wales and London the Order Office was, I believe, less busy than usual, the more especially since Dharmadhara was away on a one month's solitary retreat. (He has now decided to leave the Order Office.)

Down at the 'other end' of Padmaloka (as members of the Order Office team generally call it) the Retreat Centre was busier than ever. In fact, it was making history. As those of you who have read the latest *Golden Drum* will know, in the course of a 'resoundingly successful' Winter Retreat in which seventy-five men took part, six men were ordained as members of the Western Buddhist Order by Subhuti and Suvajra. In the words of the *Golden Drum* report, 'These ordinations were especially significant, firstly because they were the first in the West not to be conducted by Sangharakshita, and secondly because none of the men involved were able to attend the more customary three-month ordination course, due to professional and/or family commitments.' For my part, I was not just relieved that I had been able to hand over another 'responsibility' but also overjoyed that the continuance of the Order was assured.

On 22 January Paramartha left Padmaloka for a month's solitary retreat at the White Cottage, near Wickmere, and four days later, on Thursday 26 January, Kulananda and I drove down to Croydon/Purley. Here we spent six days, our time being mainly divided between the Croydon Buddhist Centre and Aryatara. It was my first visit since April last year, when I had my Conversation with Kathleen Raine at Independent Arts, and of course my first since 'the revolution', as it has come to be called, and I was glad to be in personal contact with the members of the Croydon mandala again on their own ground. For their part, the members of the Croydon mandala were clearly glad to be in personal contact with me. My only regret was that two once familiar faces were no longer to be seen. In the course of my visit I had individual meetings (I don't like to call them interviews) with upwards of sixty order members, Mitras, and Friends, besides having dinner at Hockneys, and a discussion at Aryatara, with the men Order members 'collectively'. There was also time for a shopping expedition into the Croydon city centre with Kulananda and Manjunatha, for a quick visit to a bookshop or two, and for a stroll with Subhadra through one of the more affluent parts of Purley – a region of big houses and large, well-tended gardens. Subhadra had recently finished editing the transcript of my seminar on Dr Johnson's poem 'On the Death of Dr Robert Levett'. I was very pleased indeed that he had done this piece of work, the more especially since apart from the brief excerpts currently appearing in *Mitrata* no progress was being made with the editing of the transcripts of the seminars I have given from time to time or, for the matter of that, the editing of the transcripts of my lectures. Perhaps Order members of a literary bent will give the matter some attention. Before our stroll ended I asked Subhadra to edit two more transcripts, one of the seminar on Johnson's 'An Ode on Friendship', and the other of my lecture on 'The Heroic Ideal in Buddhism', a request to which he gladly acceded, adding only that since he was working full time in Hockneys it would not be possible for him to complete the assignment very quickly.

Nearly half-way through our stay, on Saturday, 28 January, Kulananda and I drove from Purley down to Brighton, where we spent about six hours. On the way we experienced not the snow that had been forecast but rain, through whose silver veils the countryside showed green and pleasant. It had been our original intention to refresh our respective memories of Brighton with a walk along the sea front, but parking space proved difficult to find, and we therefore turned round and made straight for the Brighton Buddhist Centre, where we were cordially welcomed by Yashodeva and where, as previously arranged, we had lunch with him and the other members of the Brighton men's chapter – minus Yashomitra, who only a few days earlier had left for a solitary retreat at Guhyaloka. After lunch Yashodeva showed us the two very beautiful thangkas that had recently been presented to the Centre by a friend. One of these depicted the mandala of Amitayus, while the other depicted a form of Refuge Tree with Vajradhara as the central figure. Surrounding the central figure were hundreds of other, much smaller figures, all outlined in gold on a black ground in what I believe is the Kham style. Having admired the thangkas, Kulananda and I set out for the second-hand bookshops, Yashodeva accompanying. Our way lay past the level (where the trees had been horribly devastated by the storm of October 1987) and the Royal Pavilion and through the famous Lanes, beyond which were the bookshops. We had time only for a quick exploration of three of them, including the biggest and best, where I was fortunate enough to discover a copy of *Rossetti's Poetical Works*, for which I knew Paramartha had been looking. From the third and last bookshop we took a taxi to Mitra Jane Evans's flat, where Kulananda and Yashodeva left me and where I had tea with Vidyasri and the two other, recently ordained, members of the Brighton women's chapter. It was a pleasant conclusion to my visit to Brighton. At 6 o'clock Kulananda and Yasho-deva came and collected me, and soon Kulananda and I were heading back to Croydon, where we had a late meal at Hockneys, followed by a quiet browse in the Centre bookshop which, the place being closed, we had all to ourselves. There was much that I could gladly have bought, but I decided to confine myself to *British Art Since 1900*.

Since so much of my time was spent seeing people, in the course of my visit to Croydon/Purley I was able to do very little reading. I did, however, manage to dip into two newly-acquired volumes, both of which I can highly recommend. The first of these was the World's Classics paperback *Michelangelo: Life, Letters, and Poetry*, translated and edited by George Bull with Peter Porter, which I bought at the other-wise rather disappointing Croydon Waterstone's in the course of my shopping expedition. The *Life* is by Michelangelo's pupil Ascanio Convivi, while two of the selected letters, and no less than nine, possibly eleven, of the selected poems (all sonnets), are addressed to Michelangelo's great friend Tommaso Cavalieri, regarding whom the editor writes:

> Michelangelo met this handsome young Roman nobleman for the
> first time in 1532, when he was 57, and Cavalieri probably in his early
> twenties. He was present at Michelangelo's death, and still a devoted
> friend, 32 years later.

I found this very moving, and reflected how few modern friendships last as long. The second volume was *Cecil Collins: The Quest for the Great Happiness*, by William Anderson. This was a gift from Gunabhadri, and by an odd coincidence she gave it to me on the very day that I bought a copy of the same book as a present for Prasannasiddhi, who has been interested in Cecil Collins for some time. (When we visited the exhibition 'A Paradise Lost: The Neo-Romantic Imagination in Britain 1935–55' together a couple of years ago Cecil Collins was the artist whose work impressed us most.) According to the publisher's blurb, Cecil Collins has been described as our most important metaphysical painter since William Blake.

> He is a visionary artist whose output, extending over the past sixty
> years, has been devoted to the expression of the inner realities of the
> soul. His central theme is the Great Happiness, the paradise we come
> from, for which we always yearn in our innermost being, and which
> is restored to us through the creative imagination. To an extent rare in

modern art his works lighten the spirit with qualities of joy and consolation, while opening up to us, through landscapes and archetypal figures, new depths in our own natures. Among the archetypal figures he portrays are the Eternal Bride, the Angel, and the figure for which he is most famous, the Fool, which for him symbolizes purity of consciousness.

By the time Kulananda and I returned to Padmaloka I was feeling quite tired. Indeed, I had felt quite tired on more than one occasion during my six-day visit – usually when I had had individual meetings with a number of people in fairly quick succession. Nevertheless, I was glad to have paid the visit and glad that I had been able to have such extensive personal contact with the members of the Croydon mandala. In particular, I was glad to see how seriously the Croydon Order members were taking the need for far-reaching changes (indeed, I had to warn them not to change too many things too quickly), and glad to see that, in making those changes, they could count on the continued loyal support of the Croydon Mitras and Friends. I therefore returned to Padmaloka considerably reassured, and for the next two or three weeks was engaged – with Kulananda's able assistance – in clearing my desk of the papers that had been accumulating there for the last year or more. I also went for walks with Prasannasiddhi, checked material for *Mitrata*, studied with the Order Office community, had individual meetings with a number of Order members (and others), especially in the course of the February National Order Weekend, and, finally, made one or two difficult and painful decisions. On Friday, 17 February, Kulananda and I left for Cambridge, where we spent one night, and where I addressed the Divinity School on 'The Real Nature of the Three Jewels', had dinner with the Cambridge men's chapter and tea with the women's chapter, and visited the Fitzwilliam Museum – mainly for the sake of the Pre-Raphaelites. On the morning of the day following our return to Padmaloka Kulananda and I drove up to Wickmere, where we collected Paramartha from White Cottage at the conclusion of his month's solitary retreat. Three days later Paramartha and I were in London.

Urgyen Sangharakshita

Letter from London

Sukhavati – London – Padmaloka – high blood pressure – The Sūtra of Wei Lang – precious and semi-precious stones – reflections on the future – accident at Rayleigh – WBO Day

Dear Dharmacharis and Dharmacharinis,

I am once again staying at my flat in Sukhavati, with Paramartha, and since my 'Letter from Norfolk' concluded with the statement 'Three days later Paramartha and I were in London' some of you may well be under the impression that I have been in London ever since. But such is not, in fact, the case, and my movements, over the past five or six weeks, have been rather more erratic then I had expected they would be. After spending six days in London, from Wednesday 22 February to Tuesday the 28th, Paramartha and I returned to Padmaloka for a week and then, on Tuesday 7 March, again drove down to London, where we have now spent just over five weeks.

The reason for our earlier, shorter visit was that Paramartha wanted to see his brother and sister-in-law before they left the country and that we both wanted to see the 'Last Romantics' exhibition before it closed. We also took the opportunity of seeing *Richard III*, with Derek Jacobi again in the title role, as well as Buñuel's *Simon of the Desert*, a forty-minute black-and-white surrealist film that had made a strong impression on me when I saw it seventeen or eighteen years ago and which I was keen that Paramartha should also see. We saw the film at the Scala, a cinema in Pentonville Road. In order to reach the auditorium we had to go up a flight of stairs and through a large, irregularly shaped room in one corner of which was a bar. The walls were covered with rather garish frescoes, while seated at the small tables, and propping up the bar, were a number of young people many of whom seemed to have come straight out of the late sixties. In a moment I was transported back to the time when Siddhiratna, Kevin Brooks, and I, then living together in a flat in Muswell Hill, used to go to the cinema quite regularly and when so many of our friends – including our friends in the FWBO – spoke in the kind of sixties-speak that Ananda (in his last reporting-in) attributes to Abhaya and which, he alleges, everyone except Aloka and Mangala have long since abandoned. Before going in to see *Simon of the Desert* Paramartha and I had a cup of coffee in a rather seedy café nearby. As we sat there I commented that I felt quite at home in such places – a remark that led to some reminiscences of my early life in Tooting.

Back at Padmaloka Paramartha attended the Regional Order Weekend while I cleared my desk of the last of the papers that – as I mentioned in my 'Letter From Norfolk' – had been accumulating there for the last year or more. It was at this juncture, I think, that I had a preview of *The Enlightened Englishman*, the first (in order of filming) of Bob Mullen's two documentaries about me, which was to be shown on Anglia TV in two weeks' time. The title was not of my choosing. In fact I had told Bob that I did not like it and asked him to change it, but in this as in so many other matters Bob went his own way. (In the course of the last six months Dharmadhara, Kulananda, and I – not to mention Lokamitra – have learned quite a lot about the way in which the makers of TV programmes like to do things.) Despite this minor irritant, however, I was pleased with the film and I believe that within the FWBO the general view is that it is more successful, if less ambitious, than *In the Footsteps of Ambedkar*. Paramartha and I also watched the video of the TBMSG's work in India that Mokshapriya has made for the Karuna Trust, as well as the video of one of Devamitra's recent meetings in Singapore. The former was clear in presentation and crisp in style. As for the latter, it was good to see with what confidence Devamitra communicated the Dharma as understood in the FWBO and how much he and his message were appreciated by our friends in the Far East. Besides watching these two videos we saw excerpts from the video of a rather crazy TV programme in which a visiting Martian (complete with antennae) interviewed various people, including A.J. Ayer, the Bishop of Woolwich, Jeffrey Archer, and myself and asked 'Why are we here?' In my case the interview took place in the main shrine-room of the London Buddhist Centre, and since I had only a couple of minutes in which to tell the Martian why we were on planet Earth, and what was the purpose of human existence, I was glad to have Chintamani's great golden Buddha behind me supplementing my inadequate words with his own silent communication. Thus in the course of a couple of days I saw more videos than I usually see in as many years, and was more than ever convinced that greater use should be made within the Movement of this very effective medium. I was also reminded that last year Mokshapriya had expressed a wish to make five videos of interviews with me and wondered what further thought, if any, he had given to the matter.

On the day before Paramartha and I again sped down the A11 to London I had the last of the tests which, as I mentioned in my 'Letter from Norfolk', were to determine whether my high blood pressure was due simply to age and stress or whether other causative factors might not also be involved. The other tests I had had some weeks earlier, when I saw the cardiologist. The results of all these tests were satisfactory, in that other (organic) factors were ruled out, though according to the cardiologist such factors accounted for only five per cent of cases of high blood pressure in men of my years. Did this mean, then, that my high blood pressure was definitely due to age and stress? It was not so simple. All that the cardiologist would say was that stress had *some bearing* on high blood pressure, the actual *cause* of high blood pressure being unknown. He also informed me that my blood pressure had not come down sufficiently for the medication to be reduced, so that at the time of writing I am on the same medication as before. Another piece of information was that blood pressure not only rises very quickly, often in a matter of seconds, but that it can rise in this way even if medication is being taken. From this I inferred (I am not sure if the cardiologist himself actually said as much) that it would not be enough for me to continue medication but that in addition I should, so far as possible, avoid situations of stress. The same piece of information served to confirm me in my determination to withdraw from administrative and organizational responsibilities, and it was partly because the Order Office tended to be the locus of such responsibilities that, for the second time this year, I left Padmaloka for London – for an indefinite period. I was sorry to leave Padmaloka, not only because spring was coming but because I had been involving myself in a more active manner in the Order Office team / community and because the latter had started to become more like a real spiritual community.

Since our return to London, Paramartha and I have been following much the same basic daily routine that we followed in Wales and which we have in fact followed – except when one of us was away – more or less continuously for the last eight-and-a-half months. Rising soon after 5.30, we meditate for two hours, usually from 6 until 8 o'clock, but occasionally a little later. After meditation comes breakfast, and after breakfast a walk in Victoria Park, the walk being shorter or longer according to the weather. Only very occasionally has the weather been so wet – or so wet and windy – that we have been unable to have a walk at all. During the last two or three weeks it has been a delight to see the pink of the ornamental cherries and the white and pink-and-white of the hawthorns, as well as the many different greens – some light, some dark – of the delicate new leaves that are in process of appearing on the branches of the various other trees. On the way back to Sukhavati we sometimes go to the Post Office or do a little shopping. The rest of the morning is devoted mainly to working on a revised version of Wong Mow Lam's translation of the *Sūtra of Wei Lang (Hui Neng)*. As you know, it was the reading of this work and the *Diamond Sūtra* at the age of sixteen or seventeen that made me realize that I was a Buddhist and that I had, in fact, always been a Buddhist, and my debt to it is incalculable. When the Brighton chapter gave me a copy of the original (1930) edition for my sixtieth birthday I therefore decided to produce a revised version of the work, and with Paramartha's help this is what I am now doing. In 1944 a revised edition was brought out by the late Christmas Humphreys, but it is not entirely satisfactory. In producing my own version I am also consulting the three English translations of *The Platform Scripture* (as the work is also known) that have appeared since Wong Mow Lam's pioneer effort, and moreover will be quoting from them alternative renderings of certain important passages, especially where such renderings throw additional light on the meaning of the text. I thus work with five different versions before me, and after comparing them dictate my own version to Paramartha, who takes it down on the word-processor. So far we have dealt with about half the text. In the spring of 1974 I conducted a seminar on *The Sūtra of Wei Lang (Hui Neng)*, while more recently Paramartha and I have explored it together and he has made notes of some of the more important points that emerged.

On some days we continue our editing work until lunch time, which is at 1 o'clock. Sometimes we finish early, in which case Paramartha spends the rest of the morning reading. Except on Sunday and

Monday, when we fend for ourselves, lunch is by courtesy of the Cherry Orchard. After lunch we talk for a while, after which Paramartha gets down to his more serious reading (Conze and Snell-grove as distinct from Dickens and Henry James), takes notes, writes (or tapes) letters, and does prostrations, while I either correct material for *Mitrata* or *Dhammamegha* or, more often than not, simply reflect. (I shall have something to say about the content of my reflections later on.) Dinner is at 6 o'clock, and is by courtesy of Sukhavati community. The evening passes in much the same way as the afternoon and by 10 o'clock we are usually in bed.

Such, then, is our basic daily routine in London. The routine is not, however, inflexible, being diversified by visits to exhibitions and to the cinema, as well as by outings of various other kinds. In the course of the last four or more weeks we have been to the Fourth International Contemporary Art Fair at Olympia, where we saw an amazing cross-section of contemporary Western painting and sculpture (much of it mediocre, but some quite interesting) and to the Eighth British Miner-alogy and Gem Fair at the Royal Horticultural Halls. As you will be aware from my *Travel Letters*, I have a (not very scientific) interest in minerals, especially in precious and semi-precious stones – an interest shared by Paramartha, who did Mineralogy for a year at university – and it was almost like a spiritual experience to see the striking shapes, and the extraordinarily beautiful colours, of some of the gemstones that, together with the minerals and fossils, were being exhibited. Even the names of many of the gemstones were unknown to me, while in some cases they were of colours I had not met with before. Seeing them was like being given a glimpse of a higher, archetypal world – a world which, being a world of beauty, was nearer to ultimate reality. (Inci-dentally, the exceptionally fine collection of precious and semi-precious stones which – as related in *Travel Letters* – I recollected occupying a mysterious corner on the top floor of the Glasgow Art Gallery and Museum had indeed been located there, so that my memory did *not* play me false on the occasion of my 1980 visit to that city. As I learned only some years later, the section of the museum containing the collection had been closed some time before my visit.)* Our visits to the cinema have taken us to widely separate parts of London (Hammersmith, Camden Town, Hampstead, and the West End), and in the course of the last four weeks or more we have seen

* This is a reference to *Travel Letters*, Windhorse 1985, p.145.

four films: *Caravaggio, Salaam Bombay, The Law of Desire,* and *The Moderns.* In all of these except the first, which was shot in the studio, though the action takes place in Rome and Malta, the background against which the story unfolds is the life of a great modern city – Bombay in the case of *Salaam Bombay,* Madrid in the case of *The Law of Desire,* and Paris (the artistic Paris of the twenties) in the case of *The Moderns.* In *Salaam Bombay,* indeed, which I probably enjoyed most (with *The Law of Desire* running it a close second, mainly on account of its photography), the story is closely interwoven with that life, so that at times it is difficult to separate the one from the other. Though I enjoyed the other two films also, *Caravaggio* was really a little too violent for my taste, while *The Moderns* was spoiled by a conventional 'happy ending' quite at variance with the characters of the 'hero' and 'heroine' (or was she in fact the villainess?) as established up to that point.

Besides being diversified by visits to exhibitions and the cinema, as well as by walks along the Embankment and through St James's Park and Green Park, our basic routine has been modified, in the course of the last week, by the fact that Paramartha has started attending yoga classes (he taught hatha yoga for a while when in Sydney) and also supporting one of the Monday evening men's study groups. There have also been a couple of actual interruptions to our routine, one of them being of a pleasant and the other of a painful nature. But before telling you about either of these perhaps I should, as promised, say something about the content of my reflections. As already indicated, while Paramartha reads and takes notes I, more often than not, simply reflect, with the result that during the last five weeks I have done less reading than at almost any comparable period in my life. In fact I have read only one book, Malcolm Lowry's *Under the Volcano,* which the French poet and critic Jean Mambrino, writing in *Temenos 9,* describes as 'a masterpiece in an absolute sense', adding that it was considered by all connoisseurs to be one of the most important novels of the twentieth century. The book was brought to my notice by Paramartha (he in fact gave me a copy), who had been impressed by the film based on it and thought it might be worth reading. (It certainly was worth reading, though I did not always agree with the author's own assessment of his work as given in the famous 20,000-word letter to his publisher.) While actually reading only one book I have, however, sampled or dipped into quite a few, including Christopher Hill's *A Turbulent, Seditious, and Factious People: John Bunyan and His Church*

1628–1968, which was a gift from Danavira and which left me wondering whether Danavira saw a parallel between myself and John Bunyan or between Bunyan's church and the FWBO. (I should also add that besides correcting material for *Mitrata* and *Dhammamegha*, when not simply reflecting I have been arranging some of my recent writings for publication in book form, making a selection from my unpublished poems for the same purpose, and choosing the poems for a poetry reading I shall be giving at the Croydon Buddhist Centre.)

The content of my reflections has been mainly the future course of my own life, but I must admit that this is no clearer to me now than it was in Wales four months ago, and that I am still living very much from day to day, or at least from week to week. Not that I have not had *ideas* about the future course of my life. Apart from ideas relating to projects of a (predictably) literary nature, one of the most persistent of these ideas is that of living – and 'working' – for a while in the United States. Indeed, there are times when the idea of living in the United States appeals to me quite strongly, and had I been ten or twelve years younger, and possessed of greater energy, I might well have established myself there already. As things are, however, the idea of living in the United States remains only an idea, even a dream, though I am still hoping it will be possible for me to carry out my long-cherished plan of paying a short visit to Aryaloka with Prasannasiddhi and to see, perhaps, something of New Mexico. (I have wanted to see New Mexico ever since reading D.H. Lawrence's *St Mawr* in the early seventies, and now that Roshi Philip Kapleau, who lives in semi-retirement in Santa Fé, has invited me to stay with him, I have an additional reason for going.) But although the future course of my life is no clearer to me now than it was four months ago, the necessity of my withdrawing from organizational responsibilities, and of these being taken over by Order members, has become clearer than ever. At the same time, it has become clearer that such a withdrawal is necessary not only for the sake of my health but in order to make it possible for me to make a further creative contribution to the Movement – whatever that contribution turns out to be.

That I shall be withdrawing from organizational responsibilities does not, of course, mean that I shall be withdrawing from *people*, even though my personal contacts with Order members, Mitras, and Friends may well be more selective than hitherto. In the course of the last five weeks I have, in fact, 'seen' very few people, and this state of affairs is likely to continue for some time. Moreover, contrary to my usual practice I have not been writing letters. Not counting picture postcards, and apart from my recent Letters to *Shabda*, since August I have written only two letters, one of them hardly more than a note. I would like to assure you all, however, that although I have not been writing letters, and have not felt like writing them, I continue to be glad to receive letters, and in recent months have indeed been greatly touched by the concern many of you have expressed for my health and well-being. (Letters at present 'on hold' for me at the Order Office I shall be seeing when Paramartha and I go up to Padmaloka in about two weeks' time.) But if I have not been writing letters I have been making more telephone calls than usual. Normally I prefer not to use Bell's little invention for purposes of personal communication (as distinct from using it for practical, business purposes), but since coming down to London I have been using it in this way to a limited extent, mainly as a means of keeping in touch with Prasannasiddhi.

The first of the two actual interruptions to our routine to occur was the painful one, and it took place on Wednesday, 29 March. Paramartha and I had returned from our walk in Victoria Park, and had just settled down to the editing of the *Sūtra of Wei Lang*, when there was a telephone call from the Order Office. There were two messages, one for me and one for Paramartha, and both messages were from the police. The first message was from the Rayleigh police. Would I contact them immediately. My mother had met with an accident, they had had to break into the bungalow, and she had been taken to hospital in an ambulance. The second message was from the Bethnal Green police. Our car, which was parked down a nearby side street, had been broken into, presumably during the night, and the car radio stolen. For most of the next hour I was on the telephone – to the Rayleigh police, to the Southend police, and to the Southend Hospital. Eventually I was able to reassure myself that my mother was alive and conscious, having fallen and fractured her arm in two places. After hurriedly partaking of an early lunch Paramartha and I therefore set out for Southend. Fortunately the car was undamaged, though the floor was strewn with broken glass and as unsightly bunch of coloured wires showed where the radio had been torn away from the dashboard. On our way out of London we encountered unusually heavy traffic (we also saw *five* funerals, which I hoped was not a bad omen), and it took us more than an hour and a half to reach Southend and find Southend Hospital.

As we entered the block in which the casualty department was located I met John, the elder of my two nephews, and his wife Tynia, who had only just arrived, and together we made our way to the reception desk, where a number of people – presumably friends and relations of accident victims – were anxiously making enquiries, and where we found David, my younger nephew. After a short wait John and I were allowed in to see my mother. We found her lying on a wheeled stretcher-bed, surrounded by all the apparatus of modern medical science and with a cheerful young woman doctor in attendance. Her arm was already in plaster, but she was very badly bruised and had a nasty gash in her leg and another on one side of her head, the hair of which was matted with dried blood. Despite her injuries she was in good spirits and even joked about her condition. It was all her own fault anyway, she declared. She had been very foolish. She had climbed up onto a stool in the conservatory in order to put up new curtains (she is in her ninety-third year), had lost her footing, and had fallen on to the stone steps leading down from the dining room. There she had lain, unable to move or to call for help, for twenty-four hours (or it may have been forty-eight – I have still not been able to find out which), until the arrival of her home help who, not getting any reply when she rang the front door bell, had called the police. While my mother was telling me all this the young woman doctor was looking for the x-rays that had been taken and which somebody had already mislaid. There was also a visit from the two ambulance men who had brought her in, and my mother broke off for a moment to thank them warmly for what they had done for her. They had been wonderful, she said. In fact, she seemed generally well pleased with the way in which she was being treated (except for not being allowed to eat or drink anything), and when I left her an hour or so later it was with the knowledge not only that she was in good hands but that she was perfectly content to be in them. My one fear (apart from the possibility that she might be more seriously injured than she actually was) had been that, never having been in hospital before, she might resist hospitalization and insist on going home. A week later I saw her again, with Paramartha. By this time she had been moved to Rochford Hospital, which was only five or six miles from Rayleigh and where she had a room to herself. She was already looking much better and had, in fact, made good progress towards recovery, as I knew from the telephone conversations I had been having with the ward sister. What was more, she was no less pleased with how she was being treated than she had been at Southend Hospital. Everything possible was being done for her, she declared. The doctors and nurses were kindness itself. She had only to express a wish, and it was granted. She would never be frightened of hospitals again. Her only complaint was that some of the staff tried to make her watch TV, whereas she would much rather talk to people.

The pleasant interruption to our routine took the form of a visit from Prasannasiddhi, who came down from Padmaloka for the FWBO and WBO Day celebrations on 8 and 9 April and who stayed with us at the flat. I did not attend the FWBO Day celebrations (though Paramartha did, for part of the time), but on WBO Day I went along to York Hall with Paramartha and Prasannasiddhi for Subhuti's and Parami's talks, arriving ten or fifteen minutes early in order to take a look at the various stalls. I was pleased to see the 'tree' representing the activities of the Croydon Buddhist Centre, which after the recent upheavals seemed to be flourishing vigorously. I was less pleased to see the relatively poor turnout of Order members. Where were all the Order members who *could* have been present? Did some Order members think the anniversary of the founding of the Order not worth celebrating? I also thought that the hall in which the celebrations were being held was less well decorated than last year, though I believe not everybody would agree with me here. Dissatisfaction with the turnout of Order members and with the decorations did not, however, prevent me from enjoying the two talks, even though some of the references to myself made me feel a little 'posthumous'. I particularly appreciated Subhuti's identification of career, ideology, and sexual relationships, plus factionalism, as the principal threats to the integrity of the Order. (Perhaps I should explain, in this connection, that when I originally spoke of 'having a career' as constituting a danger for Order members what I had in mind was not the ordinary 9 to 5 job – the drawbacks of which were obvious – so much as the full-time professional practice of one or other of the different 'alternative' therapies. If the former was the far enemy of the *dharmacarya* the latter was the near enemy, since it was far more easy for the practice of a therapy to become a substitute for practising the Dharma. The same could be said of social work and of the academic study of philosophy and comparative religion, as well as the academic study of Buddhism itself.) Though Prasannasiddhi had come down for the celebrations we were able to spend some time together, and on the evening of FWBO Day the three of us – Paramartha, Prasannasiddhi and me – went out together and had a pleasant meal at a nearby Indian restaurant.

Urgyen Sangharakshita

SECOND LETTER FROM LONDON

Operations – Guhyaloka – the Norfolk and Norwich Hospital – the Hampstead Buddhist Vihara – acupuncture with Mr Van Buren – headship of the Order and giving ordination – a prostatectomy – an out of body experience – a visit from Prasannasiddhi

Dear Dharmacharis and Dharmacharinis,

More than six weeks have passed since I wrote my 'Letter from London', and during that time quite a lot has happened. Besides continuing to pursue our programme of meditation, study, and personal communication, Paramartha and I have seen three art exhibitions and two plays, have visited the West London Buddhist Centre and had tea there with members of the local chapter, have been to see my mother in hospital again, have had an outing to the Isle of Dogs and Greenwich, have spent ten days at Padmaloka, have visited the Croydon Buddhist Centre (where we were royally entertained at Hockneys by members of the Croydon chapter and where I gave a poetry reading), and have dined with Silabhadra and Sanghapala at their community. I have also had meetings with Gunapala and Dipankara (both newly arrived from the antipodes), have sat for my portrait to Paramabodhi, and have done a fair amount of reading. Thus there is quite a lot that I could write about – quite a lot, in fact, that I would *like* to write about. Indeed, it would not be difficult for me to write at length about almost every one of the various activities in which I have engaged in the course of the last six weeks. But I am not going to do that. Instead, I am going to go back two-and-a-half years and tell you something about the operations I underwent in January and May 1987, as well as something about the events surrounding those operations.

There is a reason for my doing this. During my recent visit to Padmaloka I had a long talk with Dharmadhara, in the course of which I naturally told him about my mother's recent accident and about her experience of the modern hospital. Talk about my mother's accident led to reminiscences about my operations, with both of which Dharmadhara had been intimately associated. As we reminisced, and as Dharmadhara reminded me now of this incident and now of that, I realized that my recollection of the events surrounding the operations, and even of the operations themselves, had already begun to fade and that I ought, therefore, to tell you about them without further delay. A week or so earlier I had, in fact, told Paramartha that I was thinking of writing an account of the events connected with my operations and he had encouraged me to do so, the more especially since (as I indeed had remarked to him) very few of you had any definite knowledge of those events, even though they were, presumably, of interest to you and though – in the case of some of them at least – they very much concerned you as Order members.

The events in question began on Christmas Eve 1986, when I was in Spain. With Subhuti and others I had arrived at Guhyaloka earlier in the day, after completing a short and reasonably successful lecture tour of Valencia and Alicante, and since my arrival in the secret Valley I had done little more than admire the scenery and take a few photographs. That night it was quite cold, though the temperature had been in the eighties during the day, and I had to get up and pass urine some seven or eight times. This did not surprise me very much, as for the last few years I had been getting up for this purpose several times a night, and in any case I was aware that in the course of the day I had imbibed a greater quantity of fluids than usual – especially in the morning, before our little party left Alicante for the mountains. On the morning of Christmas Day, after breakfast, I started experiencing a sensation of discomfort and, I think, constriction, somewhere in the lower part of my abdomen. At first I thought it was due to indigestion, but it persisted, and since I had not urinated since getting up I thought that this might be the cause of the trouble. I therefore tried to urinate, but without success. This did not give me cause for concern, as I had urinated so much during the night, and I reverted to the theory that the discomfort I was experiencing was due to indigestion. However, in the course of the next hour or so the discomfort became more acute.

What was more, I now wanted to urinate but found I was unable to do so. At this point I realized that I was suffering from stoppage of urine and urgently needed to see a doctor. Since I was in no condition to make a car journey, especially in view of the bumpy state of the road, Subhuti drove off to Sella, the nearest village, to find a doctor and persuade him to return with him to Guhyaloka. During the time that he was away the sensation of discomfort not only turned into actual pain but started spreading from my abdomen to other parts of my body. I was therefore extremely relieved when Subhuti eventually returned with the doctor, a tall, handsome young Spaniard of the 'Castilian' type. Yes, I was suffering from stoppage of urine and a catheter would be needed. Unfortunately, due to an oversight the doctor had not brought a catheter with him. Subhuti therefore had to drive him all the way back to Sella, where they picked up both a catheter and a *practicante*, a kind of medical auxiliary who, under the Spanish system of medicine, apparently is responsible for the more practical side of medical treatment. While they were away the pain became well nigh unbearable. Neither sitting on the toilet seat nor lying down on the couch gave me any relief, and I spent most of the time pacing up and down the little sitting room of the bungalow with my hands clasped to my abdomen. Every now and then someone would put his head in at the door and ask if they could do anything for me. But there was nothing anyone could do, and through the pain I was aware of people's distress at my suffering and their feelings of frustration and impotence at not being able to help. Philip Veale (now Arthadarshin) was, I remember, particularly affected in this way. After a time I started blacking out intermittently, while besides the actual pain I started experiencing a variety of rather odd sensations, including pins-and-needles in the extremities. I felt, in fact, extremely ill, and it seemed quite possible that I should die.

At last I heard voices outside, then footsteps on the veranda. Subhuti was back. He had brought the doctor with him again, the doctor had brought the *practicante*, and the *practicante* had brought the catheter. Within minutes the *practicante* – a Catalan as short and stocky as the doctor was tall and slim – had set to work, and in the course of fifteen or twenty seconds I passed from a state of extreme suffering to a state of relief of suffering so great as to be positively blissful. So great, indeed, was the relief as the accumulated urine was drawn off that I believe I actually laughed aloud. For once it seemed entirely feasible that the bliss of Nirvāṇa should consist simply in the cessation of

suffering. When I related my experience to Dharmadhara at Padmaloka some weeks later he became very excited. Yes, yes, he exclaimed,
he had seen stoppages of urine relieved in that way dozens of times!
The relief was tremendous – and almost instantaneous. To be able to
relieve suffering in such a way – in any way – was the greatest and
most rewarding experience of a doctor's life. That was why he himself
had become a doctor: simply in order to relieve suffering. (I am of
course paraphrasing Dharmadhara's sentiments, but they were certainly very fine and noble, and not only moved me deeply but also
gave me a further insight into his character and enabled me to appreciate the very real connection that, for him, exists between Buddhism
and medicine – between being a Buddhist and being a doctor.) I also
told Dharmadhara I was well aware that, had I been a Tibetan lama,
and had I suffered a stoppage of urine in Tibet, traditional Tibetan
medicine would have been unable to help me and I should have died
in agony. Dharmadhara could not but agree. Despite being open to
criticism in some respects, modern scientific medicine was not without
its advantages. – But to return to Guhyaloka. We were not in a position
to offer the doctor and the *practicante* the traditional Christmas drink,
and I believe they declined tea and coffee, but we thanked them
warmly for the trouble they had taken. Subhuti afterwards told me
that he had found the doctor in the middle of his Christmas lunch but
that he had needed no persuasion at all to come out to Guhyaloka.
Indeed, he had been quite interested to see the place and to hear what
we were trying to do there. Moreover, Subhuti added, both doctor and
practicante had absolutely refused to accept any remuneration for their
services. It was Christmas Day, they had declared, and on that day
their services were free.

The afternoon passed uneventfully, and apart from enjoying the
experience of being free from pain I spent most of my time taking a
few more photographs and getting used to wearing – and operating –
the catheter. Before his departure the doctor had told me to keep the
catheter in for twenty-four hours and then to go and see the *practicante*.
Stoppage of urine was quite common in men of my age and was often
only temporary. If by any chance the stoppage continued the *practicante* would fit me with a permanent catheter and I would have to see
my own doctor on my return to England. I was still absorbing the
implications of this last statement when a visitor was announced. It
was Devaraja, who was then travelling in Spain (I believe with Chintamani) and paying a flying visit to Guhyaloka. I was glad to see him,

Sangharakshita relaxing at Guhyaloka

though with his usual considerateness he did not stay very long. In
fact he stayed only long enough to express his concern, and to present
me with a handsome earthenware teapot of local manufacture. At 6
o'clock I sat down to a quite elaborate Christmas dinner with Subhuti,
Indrabodhi, and the other members of the Guhyaloka community-
cum-building-team, who had been struggling manfully to create the
facilities for the first of the Guhyaloka ordination retreats, now due to
begin in four months' time. We sat down to our meal in the smoky and
congested room that was then the community's kitchen and dining
room but had once been the garage and was eventually to become my
study. (Earlier this year it was re-roofed, the floor tiled, and other
improvements carried out.) Despite the good fare that had been provided the atmosphere of the occasion was gloomy rather than conviv-
ial, and though I was not feeling particularly well I did my best to
enliven the proceedings by talking about my life in Kalimpong and
relating humorous anecdotes about some of the people I had known
there and in the neighbouring state of Sikkim. In this I was assisted by
Crispin Balfour, who besides being acquainted with the area knew
some of the people I had known and had anecdotes of his own to
relate. By the time I retired to my room for the night the atmosphere
was distinctly brighter. The gloominess had been due not only to my

own unfortunate experience, which had left people badly shaken, but also, apparently, to the fact that not long before my arrival one of the gesso huts that were being built had collapsed, thus precipitating a crisis of confidence within the building team that had not yet been resolved. Some weeks later I heard that a bizarre tale had been circulating at Guhyaloka. With whom it originated I do not know, but it was to the effect that the Valley was a place of ill omen. Had not the gesso hut collapsed, against all expectations, and had not Bhante been taken seriously ill within hours of his arrival and nearly died? Moreover, the tale went on, Bhante's unfortunate experience at Guhyaloka had turned him against the place, and he would not be coming again. As soon as I heard this tale I contradicted it in the most emphatic terms. My unfortunate experience at Guhyaloka had not in the least affected my attitude to the Valley, I declared. I still thought it one of the most beautiful and inspiring places I had ever seen, and I still intended to spend as much time there as possible. As it happened, I spent three months there in 1987 and three months in 1988, and would have liked to spend longer. At no time did I feel that the Valley was other than a place of the utmost good omen. Indeed, I marvelled that it had been possible for a tale such as I had heard to have circulated even for a minute.

Twenty-four hours after its insertion I took the catheter out (with, I believe, a little help from Subhuti) and found that the stoppage of urine was continuing. At about 3 o'clock Subhuti therefore drove me down to Sella, proceeding very slowly and negotiating the numerous bumps and potholes – not to mention the bends – with the greatest care. (On second thoughts, it *may* not have been Subhuti who did the actual driving but somebody else.) It was, of course, Boxing Day, and little knots of men were lounging in the sunlit streets, while a gang of boys played noisy games outside the church. After making a few enquiries we managed to locate the *practicante's* house, which was situated in one of the more elevated parts of the village and which, though of sufficiently traditional appearance on the outside, was almost offensively modern within. From the way in which it was furnished and decorated Subhuti and I formed the impression that a *practicante* was well paid and that he and his family enjoyed quite a high standard of living. The *practicante* himself greeted us cordially, and before many minutes had passed I had been fitted with a 'permanent' catheter, that is to say, one of more durable make and with a tap instead of a plug, several yards of plastic tubing and a plastic bag. For various reasons the fitting of the second catheter was a more painful business than that of the first, and for half an hour or so afterwards I felt sick and dizzy. However, Boxing Day was Boxing Day, just as Christmas Day was Christmas Day, and as we left the *practicante's* house I was glad to see that Subhuti was having no difficulty in persuading him to accept the usual remuneration plus, I think, a little extra.

That night and the following morning I did some hard thinking. I was not due to return to England for another week, and despite my condition the idea of spending a week at Guhyaloka, as originally planned, appealed to me strongly. Nonetheless, I was well aware that an operation was now inevitable, and though both the doctor and the *practicante* had assured me that it would be perfectly all right for me to stay on in Spain for another week, I reasoned that if an operation was necessary then the sooner arrangements for it were made the better and the sooner, therefore, I ought to return to England. Having come to this conclusion I asked Subhuti to go and change my ticket and book me on to the earliest return flight he could. Willing as ever, Subhuti at once set off for Alicante airport, returning four or five hours later having found a seat for me on a plane leaving the following day, which was a Sunday. He had also telephoned the Order Office, informed them of the time of my arrival, and asked Dharmadhara to make an appointment for me with my own doctor. Subhuti had, in fact, spoken to Dharmadhara a couple of days earlier, when Dharmadhara had emphasized the importance of my taking antibiotics as a precaution against infection. The Spanish doctor had, in fact, already prescribed them, and since I was bleeding from the constant friction of the catheter I could well understand the need for such a precaution.

On Sunday 28 December, therefore, I returned to England in rather less happy circumstances than I had left it a week or so earlier, having been seen off by a worried – but, at the same time, somewhat relieved – Subhuti. At Heathrow I was met by Dharmadhara and the ever faithful Kovida and driven straight up to Padmaloka. The following day I saw Dr Sattar, the tall, affable Bangladeshi who had been my GP since 1979, and after I had told him what had happened at Guhyaloka he examined me. Though taking only a few minutes the examination was unpleasant and slightly painful (I was grateful to Dharmadhara for having warned me in advance what to expect) and revealed that I was, as suspected, suffering from enlargement of the prostate gland. Dr Sattar therefore arranged for me to see Mr Green, the consultant urologist, whom he described as 'a very nice man' and whom I saw at the Norfolk and Norwich Hospital a few days later. This was the first time I had had the opportunity of observing the workings of a big modern hospital, and as I sat in the reception area of the out-patients department waiting to see Mr Green I looked about me with interest. Everything seemed well organized. Indeed, it was evident that a great deal of thought had gone into the planning of the hospital itself and into the co-ordination of its various activities. Moreover, the place was spacious and well appointed and, as I remarked to Dharmadhara, who accompanied me, looked more like the offices of a modern business than like a hospital. Thus by the time I entered Mr Green's consulting room I had formed a favourable impression of at least some aspects of a modern hospital. The middle-aged, quietly-spoken urologist himself was indeed a very nice man. He examined me, confirmed that I had an enlarged – a greatly enlarged – prostate gland, and explained, in the nicest possible way, that an operation would be necessary. For my part, I told him that this was no more than I had expected, and that I would like him to perform the operation and to accept me as a private patient. Matters were accordingly settled between us. Before agreeing to accept me as a private patient Mr Green enquired if I had medical insurance and, on learning that I did not have it (I do have it now, though) conscientiously pointed out that, so far as the actual medical treatment was concerned, it would make no difference whether I had the operation as a private patient or on the NHS. However, as I was anxious to have a room to myself and to be able to see people whenever I wished I assured him that I definitely wanted to be a private patient. He therefore promised to find me a 'private' bed, either at the Norfolk and Norwich itself or at the BUPA hospital, and to inform me as soon as arrangements for my admission had been made. Before leaving the hospital I had an x-ray and an electrocardiogram, and gave four separate blood samples. As there was a long queue, and as the nurses were very busy, Dharmadhara took the blood samples himself, and I was grateful for his gentle touch. Meanwhile, Mr Green must have been moving fast, for on our return to Padmaloka I found that his secretary had already telephoned and left a message. A bed was available at the Norfolk and Norwich, in the Ingham Ward, and I should admit myself that Sunday by midday.

At 11 o'clock on Sunday, 4 January 1987, I accordingly left Padmaloka for the hospital with Prasannasiddhi, Dharmadhara, and Kovida. Snow had recently fallen and fields and houses were blanketed in whiteness. Besides clothes and a little cash I took with me only a copy of *The Lotus of the Wonderful Law* and the small sandalwood Buddha-image Prasannasiddhi had given me at the time of his (private) ordination in 1982. On our arrival at the Ingham Ward, which was situated on the top floor of a modern ten-storey block, I checked in and was at once shown to my room. Prasannasiddhi and the others saw me settled in and then said goodbye, leaving me to my reflections. It was only a week since my return from Spain, and during that time things had happened quickly. But though things had happened quickly – more quickly than one might have thought possible – they did not happen so quickly that I was unable to deal with certain matters of vital importance to the future of the Order, and it is about these matters that I must tell you before giving an account of my nine days in hospital and the first of my two operations.

As I have already mentioned, even before returning to England I was well aware that an operation was inevitable, and being aware of this I was also aware that an operation could go wrong – that the surgeon's knife might slip or the anaesthetic be wrongly administered. I was aware, in short, that I could die, as people sometimes did even when undergoing dental treatment. In view of this fact – the fact that I could die, either during the operation or as a result of it – I concluded that I ought to do two things. In the first place, I ought to leave the Order some indication of my wishes regarding the headship of the Order and the giving of the Dharmachari/Dharmacharini ordination; in the second, I ought to try and find out how likely it really was that I should die during or as a result of the operation. That I should try to find out how likely it really was that I should die during or as a result of the operation might seem rather strange, but there was a reason for this. In order to make that reason clear I shall have to go back to the beginning of 1965, when I was living at the Hampstead Buddhist Vihara and, of course, giving lectures there. After one such lecture I was approached by a young woman. She was a nurse, she said, but she also had a kind of second sight that enabled her to 'see' when someone was suffering from cancer. She was sorry to have to tell me that I had cancer of the stomach, and that I should see a doctor as soon as possible. Her words naturally gave me quite a nasty shock, especially as she obviously believed what she said and was deeply concerned for me. I therefore consulted with Maurice and Ruth Walshe (Maurice was the chairman of the English Sangha Trust, which owned the Vihara), both of whom strongly advised me to go not to an 'orthodox' medical practitioner but to an acupuncturist. The acupuncturist they recommended was Mr Van Buren, from whom Ruth herself had been receiving treatment for (I believe) several years. To Mr Van Buren I accordingly went. He could find no trace of cancer but said I needed treatment for my heart. He would give me a 'little prick' then and I could come for the 'big prick' in June or July, summer being the best time for the treatment of heart conditions. Five or six months later, therefore, I paid him a second visit and he gave me the 'big prick' in the middle phalange of the third finger of my left hand. The instant he gave me it a wave of energy rushed up my arm, hitting my brain and knocking me right out of the body. I found myself located, as it seemed, fifteen or twenty feet above my own head, a little to the right. I felt quite unperturbed, as though what had happened was the most natural thing in the world. Moreover, even though I was out of the body I still had a body – a body that was in all respects identical with my ordinary physical body. (Presumably this was the *manomayakāya* or 'mind-made body' of Buddhist tradition.) Looking down with the eyes of this body, I could see Mr Van Buren frantically massaging my legs. When I 'came to' my heart was beating faster than usual, I felt slightly sick, and I was bathed in perspiration. I also had a feeling of physical well-being such as I had never experienced before. This feeling lasted for several days. Before I left him Mr Van Buren told me that for thirty or thirty-five minutes I had been technically dead. With this statement I was not in a position either to agree or disagree, since while looking down at myself, so to speak, I had had no awareness at all of the passing of time. So far as I was concerned, the experience could have lasted two minutes or it could have lasted two hours.

Years later I learned, from friends who were studying acupuncture under Mr Van Buren, that mine had come to be regarded as a classic case, even being mentioned in the text-books. The lesson Mr Van Buren was said to have derived from his experience with me, or mine with him, was that one had to be very careful when treating people who had done a lot of meditation. The lesson I myself derived, or thought I derived, was that the connection between my mind (or 'soul') and my body was quite tenuous and could easily be disrupted. This led me to think that were I to be given an anaesthetic – as was bound to be the case if I had an operation – the anaesthetic could well have much the same effect on me as Mr Van Buren's little silver needle. Under anaesthetic I might have another 'out of the body' experience and be technically dead for thirty or thirty-five minutes or even longer. More than that. Under anaesthetic I might not just have another 'out of the body' experience but might *remain* out of the body and not come back.

In other words, instead of being just technically dead for thirty or thirty-five minutes I might actually die, which I did not want to do just yet since I felt I still had work to do. This, then, was the reason for my concluding that I ought to try and find out how likely it really was that I should die during or as a result of the operation. It was because of the 'out of the body' experience I had had with Mr Van Buren back in 1965 and the lesson I had, as I thought, derived from that experience. As soon as I knew that I would definitely be having an operation, therefore, I decided to discuss the whole matter with the two doctors with whom I was most intimately connected. With their help, I thought, I might be able to find out exactly what degree of likelihood there was of my dying under anaesthetic and what precautions – other then the usual medical ones – could be taken against such an eventuality.

The two doctors with whom I was most intimately connected were Dharmadhara and Virabhadra. Dharmadhara was, of course, a member of the Order Office team/community, while Virabhadra lived in Norwich and worked at the Norfolk and Norwich Hospital, in the Obstetrics and Gynaecology Department. A few days before I entered hospital the three of us met in my study after lunch and spent the best part of the afternoon discussing the different aspects of my experience with Mr Van Buren and trying to ascertain what had actually happened. The upshot of the discussion, which was both comprehensive and thorough, was that Mr Van Buren was mistaken in thinking that for thirty or thirty-five minutes I had been technically dead. At the time of death there might well be an 'out of the body' experience, but it did not follow from this that an 'out of the body' experience constituted an experience of death. The two doctors were moreover at a loss to understand how, in the circumstances, Mr Van Buren could possibly have known that I was really dead and not simply unconscious. Because Mr Van Buren was mistaken in thinking I was dead, technically or in any other sense, I had no reason to think that the connection between my mind and my body was quite tenuous and could easily be disrupted and no reason, therefore, to think that under anaesthetic I might not just have another 'out of the body' experience but might remain out of the body and not come back. There was, in fact, no particular likelihood that I should die under anaesthetic, and consequently no question of my taking precautions against such an eventuality. But why had I had an 'out of the body' experience at all when being given acupuncture? The explanation was, it seemed, quite simple. My body had experienced the insertion of the needle as an act of

aggression and had reacted accordingly. Adrenaline had been released
into the bloodstream and this had had the effect of rendering me
'unconscious'. It also accounted for the faster beating of the heart and
the other symptoms I had experienced on 'coming to', as well as for
the feeling of enhanced physical well-being.

The knowledge that the connection between my mind and my body
was *not* quite tenuous and could *not* easily be disrupted naturally came
as something of a relief to me. It did not, however, really come as a
surprise. As I remarked to Dharmadhara and Virabhadra at the beginning of our discussion, my actual feeling was that the connection
between my mind and my body was, if anything, all too solid. The
lesson I had derived from my (supposed) experience with Mr Van
Buren had been derived by way of logic rather than by way of emotion.
But though the connection between my mind and my body was in
truth neither tenuous nor to be easily disrupted, and though there was
no particular likelihood of my dying under anaesthetic, this did not
mean that there was no likelihood at all that I should die during or as
a result of the operation I was about to undergo. A prostatectomy was
in any case a serious matter. As Mr Green bluntly told me, the day after
I entered hospital, 'Make no mistake about it. This is major surgery.' It
was because a prostatectomy was a serious matter, and I might die, that
I concluded that I ought to leave the Order some indication of my
wishes regarding the headship of the Order and the giving of the
Dharmachari/Dharmacharini ordination. Since I was not in a position
to write anything myself I decided to take a 'senior and responsible'
Order member into my confidence and get him to draft a letter in
accordance with my instructions. Normally I would have taken
Subhuti into my confidence and entrusted the responsibility to him;
but Subhuti was in Spain, and I therefore turned to Nagabodhi, then
a member of the Order Office community, who readily put aside his
own work in order to help. In the course of two or three days we met
a number of times, Nagabodhi made notes on his conversations with
me, collated and wrote up these notes (on his Amstrad, of course),
submitted the result to me for my approval, rewrote where necessary,
and eventually produced a 1,200-word document entitled 'Ordination
into the Western Buddhist Order' – the question of the headship of the
Order having been subsumed under that of the ordination process.
This document being finalized, Nagabodhi made half a dozen copies
of it. Five of these copies were placed in envelopes and the sealed
envelopes addressed to five (I *think* it was five) 'senior and responsible'

Order members. The envelopes were to be opened only in the event of my death. This means that the contents of 'Ordination into the Western Buddhist Order' are known only to myself and Nagabodhi, who is of course pledged to confidentiality. I may, however, say that progress had already been made towards the implementation of at least some of the provisions contained in this document, and that all the provisions should be implemented in the course of the next few years, possibly after being modified as a result of further reflection.

Thus from the time of my return to England on Sunday, 29 December, to the time of my entering hospital on Sunday, 4 January, I was quite busy. What with consultations with Dr Sattar and Mr Green, discussions with Dharmadhara and Virabhadra, and conversations with Nagabodhi, I in fact had very little time for anything else, though I believe I saw a few people and wrote a few letters. I also telephoned John, my elder nephew, and after telling him I was about to have an operation asked him not to say anything to my mother until it was all over. Even then, I added, he would have to be careful what he said. As we both knew, on such occasions my mother was quite capable of making herself ill from worry. Having dealt with all these matters, after Prasannasiddhi and the others had said goodbye I felt that I could concentrate on adjusting to my new surroundings and getting used to the unfamiliar routine with a clear conscience. The first thing I did was to go and look out of the window. Since my room was situated on the tenth floor and faced south-west, I could see practically the whole of that quarter of Norwich, as well as something of the countryside beyond, though the difference between urban and rural tended to be obscured by the ubiquitous whiteness of the snow. I was not allowed to look out of the window for long. There were various papers to be signed, while at 12.30 began the serving of lunch and therewith the routine by which I was to be gently borne along for the next nine days. Contrary to my expectations, I had no difficulty obtaining vegetarian food. In fact I there were three different menus: non-vegetarian, vegetarian, and vegan. After lunch the tea trolley came rattling round, dispensing not only tea and coffee but every other kind of beverage. It came around again in the afternoon, and yet again after supper. It came round, in fact, at two-hour intervals throughout the day. In between there were visits from the nurses, in a variety of uniforms and wearing different badges, telephone calls to and from Padmaloka (I had a bedside telephone), a visit from the ward sister, more papers for signing and, of course, a visit from Mr Green.

Mr Green's visit took place shortly after my arrival, and was only a courtesy call, so to speak. He may also have looked in on me again that evening. In any case, our final consultation did not take place until the following day. Mr Green was at pains to explain to me, with the help of a diagram, exactly what needed to be done. (Contrary to what I had been led to believe, throughout my stay in hospital I found both doctors and nurses willing to clarify things for me and to answer questions.) He also explained that there were two different ways of performing a prostatectomy, one proceeding via the urethra and the other by means of an incision in the wall of the abdomen. This I already knew, as Dharmadhara had gone into the matter with me in some detail. Dharmadhara had also advised me that in my final consultation with Mr Green I should express a definite preference for the first way of performing the operation, since the surgery involved would be less drastic and require only a local anaesthetic. When I expressed my preference, however, I encountered a certain amount of resistance from Mr Green. I therefore pressed the point, even going so far as to suggest that it might be desirable to have a second opinion. This suggestion shook Mr Green's professional composure. In fact it definitely riled him, and he informed me, with some asperity, that he was president of the Urological Section of the British Medical Association and that he very much doubted if any urologist could be found to disagree with his opinion. I therefore assured him that I had every confidence in his judgement and fully appreciated that the final decision in the matter must rest with him. However, I had made my point, and having recovered his composure Mr Green assured me that even though the prostate gland was greatly enlarged he would do his best to perform the operation via the urethra and would resort to the other way of performing it only if this was really necessary. When Dharmadhara came to see me a few hours later I recounted the conversation to him and he declared himself well satisfied with its outcome. Mr Green would surely keep his word, he told me, and would make a genuine effort to operate via the urethra.

Besides my final consultation with Mr Green, there were also visits from the anaesthetist and the cardiologist, as well as from the haematologist. This last visit was made necessary by the fact that, in response to Mr Green's enquiries about my medical history, I had mentioned that in 1949 – thirty-eight years earlier – I had suffered a slight attack of jaundice. Taking no chances, Mr Green had ordered a blood test. The result of the test was negative. I did not have jaundice. When I commented to Dharmadhara on Mr Green's extreme caution he explained that it was fully justified. Jaundice could linger for many years, and had I still been infected I could have passed on the infection to Mr Green and his colleagues at the time of having my operation, with the result that the entire staff of the operating theatre would have been out of action for several weeks and unable to perform any operations in case they, in their turn, should infect the patients being operated on.

My operation took place on Tuesday, 6 January 1987, the day after my final consultation with Mr Green. I was not allowed to have any breakfast that morning or even, I believe, anything to drink. Shortly after 8 o'clock Mr Green looked in on me in the course of his rounds, as did the ward sister. There was also an unexpected visit from the hospital barber, a short, unwholesome-looking young man who entered my room with a cry of 'Gotta do the pubes, yer know!' The 'pubes' having been done, I took a bath, changed into the standard white theatre gown, and got back into bed. (The theatre gown had tapes down the back that it was impossible to do up oneself. Would my medical friends please explain the reason for this ridiculous garment?) When I was settled in bed a nurse came and gave me a pill. In fact she not only gave me the pill but stayed until I had swallowed it down. It was a sedative, she said (later I learned that it was actually a sleeping pill), and would take effect in an hour or less. This meant that I had an hour or less in which to make my final preparations for the operation and, possibly, for death. After repeating the Refuges and Precepts to myself, and reciting a few mantras, I took up my copy of *The Lotus of the Wonderful Law* (Soothill's partial translation of Kumarajiva's Chinese translation of the *Saddharma-puṇḍarīka Sūtra*) and turned first to Chapter V, 'Parable of the Rain', and then to Chapter XIV, 'The Serene Life. The Four Spheres'. Both these chapters I read carefully, as I had done many times before. I then closed my eyes and did an Order mettā-bhāvanā, passing from West to East and directing my thoughts to Order members in the United Kingdom, Sweden, Finland, Germany, India.... By the time I reached New Zealand the sedative was taking effect and the last Order members of whom I had any consciousness were, I believe, Udaya and Ratnaketu.

The next thing I knew was that the bed on which I was lying was being wheeled through the open double doors of my room and along the corridors of the Ingham Ward to the lift by two male orderlies. I was in a peaceful, dreamy state and observed what was going on as though from a distance and as though it did not really concern me.

Besides the two orderlies there was a nurse in the lift with me, I noticed, and as the lift descended to the basement the journey assumed something of the character of an archetypal Descent into Hades. In the basement there was a change of tempo. The orderlies were pushing my bed along a corridor at tremendous speed, which in reality could hardly have been the case. The bed was positively hurtling along. Other beds were hurtling along on either side of it, like cars on a busy road. There was also a lot of noise and confusion, and a lot of bright lights. (Virabhadra later confirmed that my impressions were not entirely subjective.) Beds were, in fact, coming from all directions and converging on a sort of crossroads. At the crossroads there seemed to be a kind of sentinel, or Guardian of the Gates, and there was a lot of checking and ticking off on lists before one was allowed through. (Perhaps I should mention that on the day of my admission a plastic identity bracelet had been fastened round my wrist.) Somewhere beyond the crossroads, or on the other side of the Gates, I encountered the anaesthetist. Despite the white coat and white surgical mask he was now wearing I recognized him immediately. On the occasion of his visit the previous day we had had a pleasant, friendly chat; but I had nonetheless formed the impression that beneath the surface affability there lurked a dangerous – even a 'diabolical' – element. (Virabhadra, who sometimes worked with him, subsequently confirmed that this was indeed the case, adding that his colleague possessed a savage temper which he was capable of unleashing on anyone who failed to meet his own exacting standards of professional competence.) Now, as we met for the second time, the 'diabolical' element was nearer the surface. In fact it had risen above the surface, and the expression in the eyes that gleamed at me from above the surgical mask was one of positively Mephistophelean menace and mockery. By this time I was sitting on the edge of the bed, though I have no recollection of how I got there, and being given a spinal injection. Moreover, the white-clad figure and I were talking. We were talking about India, he afterwards told Virabhadra, though of this too I have no recollection. The last thing I remember is being transferred from the bed on which I was (once again) lying to another, much narrower bed. After that all is darkness.

Faintly etched on the darkness, however, there is what I take to be an 'out of the body' experience. I am located at a distance of some six or eight feet from the end of the operating table, but on a slightly higher level, and I am looking up the length of my body, from the feet to the head. My knees are drawn up, I observe, and my feet are resting in a kind of stirrups. When I told Dharmadhara about the experience some months later he informed me that for a prostatectomy the knees are drawn up and the feet placed in stirrups exactly in the way I described. Since I had not known this, I was inclined to think that I had had a second 'out of the body' experience, though this time the experience was less vivid and seemingly did not last so long. What was more, whereas at the time of my first experience I had seen not only my own body but also Mr Van Buren, on this occasion I had seen only my own (prostrate) body.

When I 'came to' after the operation it was to find myself back in my room, in bed, and wearing not a surgical gown but my own pyjamas. It was also to find that I had various plastic and/or metal appliances attached to different parts of my anatomy. There was a saline or intravenous drip (out of the corner of my eye I could see a pair of bright red bottles), a wound drain, the three-channel irrigation catheter that had replaced the 'permanent' catheter I had been wearing for the last ten days, and the metal disc which, by means of a wire threaded through the abdominal wall, anchored the irrigation catheter and prevented it from slipping out. None of these details registered immediately, of course, any more than the fact of my having a visitor registered immediately. The visitor wore a white coat, and above the white coat I could make out the chubby-cheeked, blue-chinned visage of Virabhadra, who had taken time off from his work of delivering babies in order to come and see me. (He had, in fact, already seen me in the recovery room immediately after the operation.) We exchanged a few words, but I have no recollection of what was said, and Virabhadra afterwards remarked that at the time I had not fully regained consciousness. In the course of the next few days he came to see me a number of times, and I was always glad of his cheerful, friendly presence. Later that afternoon I also had a visit from Suvajra and Padmaraja, whom I had asked to stay at Padmaloka while I was having my operation and to visit me as soon as possible afterwards. Why I asked Suvajra to do this requires no explanation. In Padmaraja's case I suspected that in his heart of hearts he had begun to drift away from me and from the Movement and hoped that, if such was indeed the case, a demonstration of affection and confidence on my part would help reverse the process. As you all know, it did not help very much. Padmaraja's drift away from me and from the Movement continued, and eventually led to his resigning from the Order. At this stage, however, I little thought that things would come to such a pass, and when he and Suvajra came to see me I was genuinely glad to see them both. We must have talked, but again I have no recollection of what was said, though I remember both visitors being quite affected by the sight of me. Suvajra afterwards said that he had thought I looked very relieved. I do not recall experiencing any feeling of relief. My predominant feeling at the time was one of extreme weakness, to which was joined a sensation of stiffness and soreness in the lower abdomen where, as I discovered later, I had fifteen stitches, Mr Green having found it impossible to perform the operation via the urethra.

My last visitor of the day, apart from Mr Green and the nurses, was Dharmadhara, who came just as I was finishing my first meal for twenty-four hours and who sat with me for an hour or more. If Suvajra thought I looked very relieved Dharmadhara thought – and said – that I looked quite pink, the pinkness being due to the blood transfusion I was being given.

From Dharmadhara I also learned how Mr Green had tried to perform the operation via the urethra and how in the end, the prostate gland being so greatly enlarged, he had had to make an incision in the wall of the abdomen instead. (Dharmadhara himself had been told this by Virabhadra, who I believe telephoned him immediately after the operation to let him know all was well with me.) Because of the need for the more drastic surgery I had been given a general anaesthetic on top of the local one, and Dharmadhara warned me that this might affect my memory a little. Whether it actually did affect it I cannot say. Certainly my memory is not as good as it was a few years ago, but this may be no more than one of the natural consequences of old age. In any case, the knowledge that the anaesthetic *might* have affected my memory has probably made me more conscious of any failure to recollect a name or a date than I would otherwise have been. Was it not Dr Johnson who once remarked that if a young men forgets his hat no one thinks anything of it, whereas if an old man forgets *his* people shake their heads and say, 'Ah, his memory is going'?

What with all the plastic and/or metal appliances that were attached to me I did not find it easy to turn over, and after Dharmadhara had left and I had settled down for the night I could not help wondering if I would get any sleep. But I need not have worried. With the help of a couple of pain-killers I passed a reasonably comfortable night, sleeping – or rather dozing – intermittently until about 5 o'clock. In fact I was bothered less by the drip and other appliances than by the light shining in through the little observation window in the door, the curtain of which had been drawn back so that the night nurse could take a look at me from time to time without disturbing me. With the coming of morning there began my first day in the hospital as a 'post-op' and the first stage in the long process of my recovery from the prostatectomy. Lights were turned on, the day nurses came on duty (I could hear them talking and laughing round the nurses' station, as it was called), breakfast was served, and the tea trolley came rattling round. Soon nurses were bustling in and out of my room taking my temperature and my pulse, giving me antibiotics and other medication, changing my sheets and pillow-cases, and replacing the grey papier-mâché bottle that hung by the side of my bed. At 8 o'clock I had a visit from Mr Green, who was making his first round of the day (he made at least three a day) and who, one of the nurses told me, was accustomed to start earlier than the other doctors. Having enquired how I had slept, he examined my wound, studied the contents of the wound drain and the blood clots that were slowly moving along the transparent plastic tube of the catheter together with the urine, and scrutinized my temperature chart. Apparently all was going as expected. Before leaving he commented on the quantity of flowers – and get-well cards – that had already arrived for me.

Indeed in the course of the week, as more and more flowers and pot plants arrived, he got into the habit of joking with me about them and asking if I had opened a florist's shop. He did not, however, comment on the presence of the sandalwood Buddha-image, which I had placed on top of the television set, around which most of the flowers and get well cards were arranged. Shortly after Mr Green's visit the newspaper-and-magazine trolley came round, as it did every morning, and I bought a newspaper. To my surprise I found I was unable to do more than read the headlines. I simply did not have the energy. I also discovered that I did not have the energy even to think. If I read or thought for more than a few minutes I felt dreadfully tired and had difficulty staying awake. It was the first time I had had such an experience, and when I *was* able to read and to think properly – which was not for a few more days – I found myself with food for reflection. Was thought indeed dependent on physical energy, and if so to what extent? Were mental energy and physical energy separate and distinct, or were they complementary aspects or manifestations of a more fundamental neutral energy that was itself neither mental nor material?

Later in the day a fresh dressing was applied to my wound and I was given a bladder irrigation – so far as I remember by two different nurses. Both the dressings and the irrigations continued until I left hospital the following week, the bladder irrigations – which were meant to reduce the risk of infection – being repeated twice or even thrice a day. I also had a few more visitors. Who the visitors were I no longer recollect, but they must have included Kovida and Nagabodhi, both of whom certainly came to see me in the days immediately following my operation, as did several Order members from Norwich. It was while two of these visitors were with me that Mr Green unexpectedly put his head in at the door to tell me that he had just received the pathologists report. The prostate gland was benign. I did not have cancer. This was good news indeed, for although neither Dharmadhara nor Mr Green had dwelt on the subject I knew there was a possibility of the prostate being malign, and it was a relief to know that this was definitely not the case. I also appreciated Mr Green's thoughtfulness in communicating the pathologist's findings to me as soon as he himself had been informed of them.

Though I had visitors almost every afternoon and evening, and though Mr Green came to see me at least three times a day, I naturally saw – and heard – more of the nurses than of anyone else. There were upwards of twenty of them altogether, though they were not all on duty at the same time (they followed a complicated shift system that I never succeeded in fathoming), and they included nurses from other wards – even from other hospitals – who were replacing regular Ingham Ward nurses who had gone down with the flu. With one exception they were all vigorous and cheerful, and with one exception they were all female. In the latter case the exception was a young man, hardly more than a boy, who was a nursing auxiliary and whom I saw only once. He had nothing to do, and the other (female) nurses ignored him completely. Since the nurses were always busy I did not often have an opportunity of talking to them. The only time this was really possible, in fact, was when they were either changing the dressing on my wound or giving me a bladder irrigation, and on such occasions they seemed glad of a little chat. Two of them, aged twenty-five and sixty-two respectively, expressed interest in Buddhism and meditation and asked me a number of questions. With the older woman I was indeed able to have quite a long talk, mainly because I was bleeding that day and needed bandaging. At one point I asked her what it was that had kept her working as a nurse all these years. She replied simply,

'The money.' She had taken up nursing shortly after the war and had intended to give it up after getting married, but her husband had never earned enough to keep them all so she had had to carry on. Though it was the money that kept her working she was clearly an excellent nurse, and I marvelled that such dedication could, in a sense, be purchased. I was reminded of Housman's 'Epitaph on an Army of Mercenaries.' *They* 'saved the sum of things for pay.' *She*, it seemed, helped to relieve suffering, and even to save life, just in order to balance the family budget.

But if the sixty-two-year-old staff nurse was working for the money, the two much younger ward sisters were obviously committed to nursing as a career. Besides being vigorous and cheerful, they were women of more than average competence and force of character and as such stood out from the rest of the nursing staff. Different as the ward sisters and the other nurses were from each other in certain respects, however, they were all alike in that they dearly loved a good gossip, especially at the beginning and end of a shift (the two ward sisters were never, of course, on duty at the same time). Since my room was only a few yards from the nurses' station, round which they usually gathered, I could not but hear what they were saying, especially if the door of my room had been left ajar. Matters professional excepted, conversation seemed to be confined to three – and only three – topics: holidays, husbands-and-children (usually in connection with illness), and clothes – in that order. The topic of holidays was, in fact, by far the most popular of the three, and generated tremendous interest and enthusiasm. This may have been because the nurses worked very hard and their holidays meant a lot to them, or it may have been because it was January and the summer holiday brochures had already started appearing in the colour supplements of the Sunday newspapers. I also noticed that the nurses hardly ever complained or grumbled about anything. The only complaint I myself ever heard from a nurse was in connection with some medicines she had ordered. In the old days – which I gathered had ended a few months earlier – all you had to do was to pop downstairs to the pharmacy and tell the man there what you wanted. He would get it for you immediately. Now you had to fill in a form and order the medicines through a computer. More often than not the medicines took two days to arrive; sometimes they were the wrong medicines, and sometimes you got double or treble the quantity for which you had asked. She for one, the complainant concluded, would be glad to go back to the old system, but she very much doubted if this would be possible. Progress was, it seemed, irreversible.

On my second or third day as a 'post-op' I had a visit from Prasanna-siddhi. He had not been able to visit me before as his mother, whom he had not seen for six or seven years, had recently arrived in England. She had in fact arrived at Heathrow from New Zealand on the very day that I had arrived there from Spain. Not having seen her for so long Prasannasiddhi naturally wanted to spend as much time with her as possible, and it was only because her three weeks in England included a few days in Norwich that he had been able to see me into hospital the previous Sunday and was now able to visit me after my operation. I was very glad to see him, though I could not help wishing that it had been possible for him to come earlier. With him he brought his mother, a slim, still attractive woman of fifty who resembled Prasannasiddhi in little more than her fresh, blonde looks and who was, I gathered, keen to meet the founder of the FWBO and the person with whom her son spent so much of his time. At any rate, she fixed me with a penetrating stare, in which I read a certain amount of puzzlement, and we had a short and unremarkable conversation which may or may not have fallen below her expectations. The fact was that I was feeling rather tired at the time and though glad to see her did not find it easy to talk to someone I had not met before. Since she worked in an Auckland hospital as a ward hostess she knew all about prostatectomies and told Prasannasiddhi that he should lay in a good stock of underpants for me since I was sure to bleed a lot after coming out of hospital and would need many changes. Prasanna-siddhi was, of course, his usual pleasant, imperturbable self and looked very smart in the expensive new overcoat his mother had bought him. Some time later, when we were both back at Padmaloka, he told me that she thought him very much improved. Apparently he used to argue with her a lot. On her arrival from New Zealand, however, he had resolved to argue with her as little as possible, to comply with all her wishes, and to do whatever he could to make her stay in England pleasant and worthwhile.

By the time of Prasannasiddhi's visit I had already started shedding the various plastic and/or metal appliances that were attached to me. The first to go was the saline or intravenous drip. Then went the wound drain. The last to go was the three-channel irrigation catheter, after which the fifteen stitches were taken out (a tedious and some-what painful process), half of them being taken out the day before I left hospital and half on the morning of my departure itself. At the same time that I was gradually shedding the appliances I was also engaged in the difficult and painful task of forcing myself to walk despite the wound and stitches in my lower abdomen, for there was the danger that unless I started walking the tissues would contract and leave me with a permanent stoop. So difficult and painful was it for me to walk, indeed, that for a day or two I could not even get out of bed without assistance, but I persevered and before long was slowly making my way round the ward, all the time doing my best to maintain an upright posture. As I passed along the corridor I looked into the rooms of the other private patients, most of whom had their door ajar. Young or old, male or female, without exception they were all watching television, the raucous sound of the more popular programmes being sometimes audible at a considerable distance. I was the only person in the ward who did not watch television – and watch it for the greater part of the day. In fact I did not watch it even once, and was not tempted to watch it. The only use I had for the television set in the corner of my room was as a makeshift 'altar' for my sandalwood Buddha-image.

My favourite time for making my slow progress round the ward was late evening, when the day staff had gone off duty, when the last visitors had left (some patients received visits from noisy family parties), and when doors were closed, the volume of television sets turned down, and corridor lights dimmed. At this time a peculiar silence would reign in the ward, a silence not unlike that of a graveyard or a cremation ground – a silence which, not surprisingly, I found conducive to serious thought and even to meditation. On most evenings, however, I would pause at the nurses' station and exchange a few words with the night nurse who, more often than not, would be glad to relieve the tedium of her vigil with a little chat. At 9.30 the silence would be broken by the distant rattle of the tea trolley, coming round on its last journey of the day, while at 10 o'clock – when I was in bed – a gentle chink-chink of bottles outside my door would announce the arrival of the medicine trolley.

On the first two nights after my operation I took a couple of pain-killers, but from the third night onwards I discontinued them, taking only the antibiotics and other prescribed medication (the pain-killers were optional). The reason I discontinued the pain-killers was that I did not want to become dependent on them, preferring to put up with a little discomfort instead. As it happened, apart from the soreness in my lower abdomen I experienced no pain whatever – except when trying to stand upright and walk. I certainly experienced no internal pain, despite the major surgery I had undergone. The relative pain-lessness of the whole business was, in fact, one of the things that most surprised me about my operation.

Once the medicine trolley had completed its round, silence would again reign in the ward. After reading for a few minutes I would switch off the bedside lamp, so that the room was in darkness except for the light that came in through the little observation window in the door. From the third or fourth night onwards it came in less brightly, for the curtain on the door was no longer drawn back so that the night nurse could look at me from time to time without disturbing me. This I took to mean that I was now considered to be out of danger – if indeed I had ever really been in danger – and that the nurses were not required to monitor my condition as closely as before. In the course of the nine days I spent in hospital the way in which the nurses treated me passed, I noticed, through three distinct phases, each lasting for three days; though whether the progression happened naturally and, as it were, unconsciously, or whether they had actually been trained to vary their behaviour towards patients in this way, I was unable to tell. During the first phase they kept a very close eye on me, and came at once when the light outside my door started flashing; during the second they gave me much less attention, at times ignoring the light for several minutes; while during the third phase, discarding their professional manner, they treated me in normal, friendly fashion and not like a patient at all.

As it became obvious that my recovery was proceeding according to plan ('My patients *always* proceed according to plan,' said Mr Green, a trifle pompously I thought, when I questioned him one morning), I started feeling a little restless. For the four or five days immediately following my operation I was quite content to be in hospital, realizing that it was the best place for me. But as my energy started to return, as one appliance after another was removed, and as with each day that passed I made my way round the ward a little less painfully, I began to find the confinement to a single small room and a short stretch of corridor rather irksome. Nor was that all. I started looking forward to the day when I would be able to leave hospital and get back to Padmaloka. Indeed, by the end of the week I was longing to be back and started pressing Mr Green to fix the date for my discharge. At first he was understandably reluctant to do this, but after I had pressed him on two or three consecutive visits he told me that provided my recovery continued to proceed according to plan I would probably be able to leave hospital on Tuesday, 6 January. This I took to mean that I would almost certainly be leaving hospital on that date, and accordingly started counting the days and the hours to my release with an increasingly keen sense of anticipation. Those last days and hours did not pass any more quickly for my counting them, of course, though their tedium was considerably relieved by the visits I continued to receive from Dharmadhara and other friends. There were also a few unexpected visits. One of these was from the hospital chaplain, a tall figure in a dog collar who, on the antepenultimate day of my incarceration, breezed into my room with a cheery, 'Holy communion? No? Right-ho!' and was out again before I had time to utter a word.

At last the day of my release came, though I could not be sure that it had come until Mr Green had visited me in the course of his morning round. For the last two days both my pulse and my temperature had been quite erratic, and the urologist had pursed his lips and raised his eyebrows each time he perused the chart at the foot of my bed, while the attendant ward sister studiously refrained from comment. On the morning of Tuesday, 6 January, however, both pulse and temperature were normal, and after keeping me in suspense for a few minutes Mr Green decided that I could leave at midday. After shaking hands with him, and thanking him warmly for what he had done for me, I therefore finished packing my suitcase, transferred my vases of flowers to the nurses' station (the potted plants I decided to take with me), and sat down to wait for Dharmadhara and Bodhiraja to come and collect me. They came at 12.30, and a few minutes later, having said goodbye to the nurses and having safely negotiated the icy pavement outside the back entrance of the hospital, I was in the car and on my way back to Padmaloka. While I was in hospital there had been several very heavy falls of snow, and progress along the slushy roads was difficult. Dharmadhara and Bodhiraja had, in fact, taken the precaution of bringing Matthew Bouic and a couple of shovels with them in case a way had to be cleared through the snow. On leaving the main road, and taking the turning to Surlingham, I saw that there were snowdrifts six feet high on either side of the road and that the hedges had completely disappeared.

At exactly 1 o'clock the car came to a halt outside the familiar portico; I disengaged myself from the front seat, and slowly climbed the stairs to my study. I was glad to be back: glad to sit in my armchair, glad to contemplate my books, my images, my little collection of semi-precious stones and even my filing cabinet. Above all, perhaps, I was glad to be once more surrounded by the members of the Padmaloka community, though Prasannasiddhi was still with his mother and would not be back for another week. But if it was good to be back, it also felt quite strange. Only a week earlier I had been face to face with the possibility that I might not see Padmaloka or the members of the community again. Yet here I was, back in the old familiar surroundings and looking at them, perhaps, with fresh eyes. It was indeed not surprising that besides being glad to be back I should, at the same time, feel it to be quite strange. It was also not surprising that I should feel both relief and gratitude – relief that the operation was over and gratitude to all those who had assisted in the process of my recovery. In particular I felt grateful to the nurses of Ingham Ward. Before leaving the Norfolk and Norwich I had, in fact, asked Dharmadhara to buy me the biggest and most expensive tin of biscuits he could find, as well as a greetings card. Shortly after my arrival at Padmaloka I signed the card and gave it to Dharmadhara to deliver to Ingham Ward personally, together with the biscuits. This pleasant duty done, I lay back in my armchair and allowed myself to enjoy the feeling that I was 'home' again at last and that I could, in all probability, look forward to making a full recovery.

Urgyen Sangharakshita

THIRD LETTER FROM LONDON

London – Sukhavati – daily routine with Paramartha – mother in hospital – the 'Camera Portraits' exhibition – poetry reading at the London Buddhist Centre

Dear Dharmacharis and Dharmacharinis,

It is 7 o'clock on a wet and windy evening in East London. Paramartha is in his room taping a letter to a friend, while I am in the study (the scene is, of course, our newly-decorated flat at Sukhavati) listening to the roar of the wind and to the soft hissing of the gas fire and thinking that I have not communicated with you through the pages of *Shabda* for several months. Looking through my files I find that the concluding instalment of my 'Second Letter from London' appeared in the November 1989 issue. As you may remember, in this Letter I dealt with the events which, beginning on Christmas Eve 1986, culminated twelve days later in my having a prostatectomy. My '(First) Letter from London', which appeared in the May and June issues of *Shabda*, was concerned with the events of the three months from the last week of February to the second week of April, the events of the six weeks immediately following being briefly mentioned in the opening paragraph of my 'Second Letter from London'. This means that for the last nine months you have had no news (no news through the pages of *Shabda*, that is) of where I have been and what I have been doing. For reasons that I expect you can imagine, it is not possible for me now to go back and give you even a moderately full account of the events of these months. Once again literature has been unable to keep up with life. In this Letter I shall therefore first tell you what I have been doing since my return to London three weeks ago and then give you a summary of my life since May last year.

Paramartha and I left for London on Tuesday, 2 January 1990, immediately after lunch, having spent the ten days of the Christmas recess at Padmaloka with Kulananda and Mangala (Prasannasiddhi and Kovida were away on a Performing Arts Retreat, though they returned in time for Prasannasiddhi and me to spend an agreeable hour together). On the eve of our departure Paramartha and I performed a special puja and have since decided to perform a puja every month, so far as possible on the full moon day. On the Tuesday morning I went and saw Dr Sattar, my Bangladeshi GP, and had my blood pressure taken. Systole was up but diastole was down (or it may have been the other way round), but since it was the more important of the two factors that was down my blood pressure could be said to be a little lower, which was reassuring news. Before leaving the surgery I gave a blood sample for a routine test, and in consequence felt sick and a little weak until Paramartha and I were well on our way to London. The journey was uneventful, with no delays, and we were back at Sukhavati and re-ensconced in the flat in what I think was record time. During the first week we did not go out at all, except to Victoria Park for our usual walk, and concentrated on getting settled in and resuming our routine of study (or reading), meditation, and communication. In this connection I should perhaps mention that communication now includes a daily session of 'reporting-in' to each other on our thoughts and feelings during the day. These sessions usually take place in the evening, just before we go to bed, and normally last for about half an hour, though they have been known to go on for an hour or more. Since starting them two or three months ago we have found the sessions helpful in maintaining continuity of communication and, in fact, more or less continuous rapport between us. Besides his routine with me Paramartha has his own programme of extra meditation and/or prostrations, hatha yoga, and drawing, though he does not do all of these on a daily basis. He also attends a weekly drawing class at the Sir John Cass School of Art and a weekly class for trainee yoga teachers at the Iyengar Institute, supports the new Monday evening city meditation course, and takes part in the meetings of the Sukhavati chapter. When occupied neither with our routine nor with his own programme he spends time with his friends, and of course there are occasions when both routine and programme are diversified by an outing of some kind – as when we visited my mother in hospital and

Mrs Wiltshire, Sangharakshita's mother, aged 92

went to see the 'Camera Portraits' exhibition at the National Portrait Gallery.

The visit to my mother took place exactly a week after our return to London and some three weeks after Prasannasiddhi and I spent the afternoon with her at her home in Rayleigh. She was then quite well, having made a good recovery from her accident last March, though still being without the full use of her left arm. Shortly before Christmas, however, she complained of pains in her chest and these eventually became so severe that my nephew John sent for an ambulance and had her taken to hospital. Several anxious days followed. According to John, who kept in touch with me by phone (I was of course at Padmaloka, recovering from the flu), my mother talked of wanting to die, which was so unlike her that we both felt quite alarmed. Though I am not, I think, attached to my mother (as distinct from being very fond of her) the prospect of her death fell like a black shadow across my heart and I waited for John's bulletins with a mixture of dread and resignation. Fortunately our worst fears were not realized. By the end of the week her condition had improved, and when Paramartha and I visited her in Rochford Hospital we found her as bright and lively as ever. Though out of bed, she was not yet walking (she started the following day) and I thought she looked thinner and older. She told me she had had two heart attacks, one before and one after her admission to hospital, and that after being admitted there she had slept for four days. Nothing was said about her having wanted to die, and I left feeling that she had regained her will to live and would once again pull through.

The 'Camera Portraits' exhibition, which we saw ten days later, was billed as a celebration of photography's one-hundred-and-fiftieth anniversary. Consisting of photographic portraits taken over the past one-hundred-and-fifty years, it was described as 'a survey of stylistic and technical developments that featured politicians and personalities [are politicians, then, not personalities?] from Florence Nightingale and Palmerston to Thatcher and the Beatles.' Though interesting, it could not be compared to the much bigger 'Art of Photography' exhibition which Paramartha and I saw at the Royal Academy in the autumn. Besides being more limited in scope, it was full of old favourites like Julia Cameron's portrait of Herschel and portraits of Queen Victoria with John Brown and with her Indian servant (all the exhibits were drawn from the National Portrait Gallery's own holdings), and it was noticeable that the nearer one came to the present day the less sensitive the portraits were and the less 'atmospheric'. Commercialism seemed increasingly to take over. Moreover, the photographs, which were mostly small and very small, were not only hung close together but provided with lengthy captions in small print that were difficult to read. The result was that the movement of viewers round the exhibition was extremely slow, with small pile-ups in front of some portraits.

As if visiting my mother in hospital and going to see the 'Camera Portraits' exhibition was not enough, an element of diversification was also provided by the poetry reading I gave at the London Buddhist Centre on Friday, 12 January, and repeated three days later at the Croydon Buddhist Centre. In fact the Croydon poetry reading may be said to have qualified as an outing. Under the heading of 'Friendship: A Selection of Poems Ancient and Modern' I read twenty-seven poems and parts of poems, from extracts from the *Epic of Gilgamesh* and the *Iliad* to Edward Thomas's *The Sun Used to Shine* and Christmas Humphreys' *The Pilot*, through poetic gems such as Walt Whitman's 'I saw in Louisiana a Live-Oak Growing', Shakespeare's 'Sonnet 30', and an apologue from Jalal Ad-din Rumi's *Masnavi*. The poems were arranged in five sections: Friendship in the Heroic Age, Rejoicing in Friendship, Remembering Friends, Friendship in War, and Higher Dimensions. Between the third and fourth sections there was a musical interlude (on cassette), consisting of the so-called 'Friendship Duet' from Bizet's *The Pearl Fishers* sung by Jussi Bjoerling and Robert Merrill. The reason for my giving the readings was that I wanted to emphasize (yet again) the crucial importance of friendship in human life, and especially in spiritual life, but did not, at the same time, want to deliver a lecture on the subject or even an informal talk. Friendship was a sentiment, and what I wanted to do was not simply to convey ideas about friendship, however correct those ideas might be, but rather to communicate something of the sentiment of friendship itself. Reading poems actually expressive of friendship seemed a good way of doing this. Whether I succeeded in kindling in the hearts of my audience a spark of the flame that burned so brightly in the hearts of my twenty-three poets I do not know, but at the London and the Croydon centres alike the reading obviously evoked an emotional response of some kind. After the poetry came the prose, the reading being followed, on both occasions, by a book launch, the book in question being *The Taste of Freedom*, an edited transcript of my three lectures 'The Taste of Freedom', 'The Path of Regular Steps and the Path of Irregular Steps', and 'Enlightenment as Experience and as non-Experience'. The actual launching was done by Nagabodhi, in his usual masterly fashion, and afterwards I had the satisfaction of signing a goodly number of copies, as well as of greeting the many old friends who brought them to me for signature – friends whom I had not seen, perhaps, for a long time. Naturally I was glad to have 'The Taste of Freedom' and its companions in print at last, and hope that other tape-recorded lectures of mine – of which there must be about 150 – can be transcribed and edited and brought out in the same way.

On the morning of Wednesday, 10 January, two days before my first poetry reading, I was interviewed for the BBC's (Saturday morning) *Prayer for the Day* programme. I did not, of course, conclude the interview by offering up the usual prayer, as the young man who was interviewing me knew perfectly well that there was no place for petitionary prayer in Buddhism. Instead, I read Vipassi's 'free "translation" or paraphrase' of the *Karanīyamettā-sutta*, which appeared in the December 1989 issue of *Shabda*. Shortly afterwards Dharmapriya arrived at the flat, by prior arrangement, and Paramartha and I had the pleasure of taking him out to lunch at a nearby Indian restaurant. Conversation naturally turned to FWBO Germany, and to Essen, which Paramartha and I had visited the previous autumn and about which I shall have something to say in the second half of this Letter. No less naturally, perhaps inevitably, it also turned to the recent political developments in Eastern Europe and the opportunities that these might provide for the expansion of the FWBO. Would it not be possible, for instance, to open a centre in Berlin? After the meal I returned to Sukhavati, while Dharmapriya and Paramartha went off together for a (presumably yogic) session of their own elsewhere. Dharmapriya was not the only Order member whom I saw during this period. Earlier I had seen Vidyavati and Tejamitra, and subsequently I saw Devamitra and Dharmaruci, besides seeing a couple of Mitras and sitting to Alison Harper again for my portrait. Paramartha and I also had Moksaraja staying with us at the flat one weekend. He had recently returned from Germany, and presented me with a piece of the Berlin Wall. As well as seeing Order members and Mitras personally I talked with some by telephone and sent picture postcards to others. During the last three weeks my output of picture postcards has in fact steadily increased. Of course I would prefer to reply to each and every letter I receive with a proper letter of my own, but at present this is not possible. Nonetheless I appreciate hearing from people, especially from Order members, and hope that the fact that you do not always get a reply (letters from Order members received at Padmaloka are in any case acknowledged in *Shabda*) will not discourage you from writing again. Letters from Order members, as well as your letters and reportings-in to *Shabda*, form one of my most important links with the Order and the Movement and I should be sorry to see that link weakened.

My reading during the last three weeks has been mainly Neo-platonic. Immediately after my return I read the second volume of Dean Inge's *The Philosophy of Plotinus* (a very readable introduction to a rather difficult subject), the first volume of which I had read more than a year earlier. This was followed by Porphyry's *Launching-Points to the Realm of Mind* (as the translator called it), a translation of the *Pros ta noeta aphorismoi*, some sections of which I read in conjunction with the corresponding passages of the *Enneads*. While I was thus engaged Paramartha continued working his way through the two bulky volumes of the transcript of my seminar on Chih-i's *Dhyana for Beginners*, as well as through Mircea Eliade's no less bulky *Shamanism*. I have also read Plato's *Euthyphro*, Robert Bly's *A Little Book on the Shadow* (Paramartha and I listened one evening to the tape of his lecture on 'The Naïve Man'), and Paul Bowles's Morocco-based novel *Let It Come Down*, the last being a present from Moksaraja. Most recently, I have been reading Paul Williams's *Mahāyāna Buddhism*, a thoughtful and (on the whole) well-informed study that I would like to recommend as a useful supplement to *A Survey of Buddhism*, more particularly to Chapter 3.
Urgyen Sangharakshita

LETTER FROM SPAIN

Guhyaloka – Order Convention at Stonyhurst – Essen – Cologne – Aachen – Handel's Julius Caesar – 'The Cave' – exhibitions, concerts, plays, and films – Lenore Friedman's Meetings with Remarkable Women – Buddhism in Australia – mother's death and funeral – James Hillman – My Relation to the Order – the death of Dhardo Rimpoche – Burghley House – Sheffield – Castleton – York – Rievaulx – books, films, and plays – questions and answers at the London Buddhist Centre – life at Guhyaloka with Paramartha – The Life of Milarepa – an article on Anagarika Dharmapala – an official birthday

Dear Dharmacharis and Dharmacharinis,

When I started writing my last Letter I was in London. It was a wet and windy evening and I was sitting in my study listening to the roar of the wind and the soft hissing of the gas fire. That was five months ago. Now I am in Spain, at Guhyaloka. It is a warm, bright morning, and I am sitting on the veranda of my bungalow looking out at a prospect of holly oaks, green Canadian pines, and smooth grey cliff and listening to the twittering of the small brown birds that dart in and out of the trees and bushes. Paramartha is sitting a few feet away from me reading.

We arrived here on the afternoon of Tuesday, 3 July, having been seen off at Heathrow by Kovida and met at Alicante airport by Sumitra and Baladitya. After an absence of two years it was good to be back in Spain and good to recognize familiar landmarks as we drove along the coast and up through Sella into the mountains. As we approached the magic Valley, and passed between the rocks that stand as though sentinel on either side of the road, the landscape seemed even more beautiful than I remembered it. On our arrival at the bungalow we were warmly greeted by Subhuti, Padmavajra, and Mokshapriya, all very colourful in their blue robes, who after giving us tea and seeing us settled in quietly withdrew to the retreat centre further up the Valley. Later our supper was brought down by two more shaven-headed, blue-robed figures. After that we simply sat out on the veranda, drinking in the scene. I could hardly believe that we really were back, and that I was actually sitting and looking out across the Valley, just as I had done two years ago.

Now it is Monday, 6 August, and we have been here for practically five weeks. For five weeks we have bathed ourselves in the peace of Guhyaloka – a peace that has been broken only by the occasional flight of planes overhead and a fire that, for an anxious day and night, threatened to spread from the next valley into our own. For five weeks we have.... But I must not anticipate. Before I can give you an account of our life here there are a few loose ends to be tied up; or rather, there are apologies to be made for loose ends *not* tied up. You may recall that I never finished my last Letter, that is, my 'Third Letter from London', the first instalment of which appeared in the March issue of *Shabda*. In this instalment I told you what I had been doing since my return to London with Paramartha three weeks earlier, on Tuesday, 2 January 1990, after we had spent the ten days of the Christmas recess at Padmaloka. The promised second instalment was to have given you a summary of my life since May 1989 and would thus have covered the nine months from that time to the time of writing. As it happened, literature was not only unable to keep up with life but fell so far behind that in the end it gave up the attempt in despair. The second instalment was never written, and my 'Third Letter from London' remained unfinished. Nor have I communicated with you all through the pages of *Shabda* since. Now that I have been at Guhyaloka for five weeks, however, it occurs to me that I should start writing to you again. But how should I proceed? Should I finish writing my 'Third Letter from London' or should I write an entirely new 'Letter from Spain'? After thinking the matter over for a day or two, and discussing it with Paramartha, I have decided to adopt the second course. Finishing my 'Third Letter from London' is really out of the question. News that was then nine months old is now fifteen months old, and much having faded from my memory it would in any case be difficult for me to give you even the promised summary of my life from May 1989 down to the writing of my last (unfinished) Letter. An entirely new 'Letter from Spain' it will therefore have to be, though in the course of it I hope to be able to mention at least some of the more important events of the last year or so, besides giving you an account of our life here in the magic Valley. This Letter will, in fact, consist of three parts. The first part will deal with the past, i.e. the last year or so, the second with the present, i.e. the last five weeks, and the third – though I shall not be venturing any predictions – with the coming eighteen months. In all three parts I shall be as brief as possible, since I want not only to start writing this Letter but to finish it, so that in the next issue of *Shabda* there will be a *complete* Letter from me for you all to read.

PART 1

As I look back, there are two events in the second half of last year that stand out for me above the rest: the Order Convention at Stonyhurst, and my visit to Essen.

Stonyhurst was, I discovered, in Lancashire. Paramartha, Prasanna-siddhi, and I travelled up from Padmaloka together by road, my two companions sharing the driving between them. *En route* we did a little sightseeing, stopping first at Peterborough Cathedral, with its tomb of Catherine of Aragon and its memories of Mary Queen of Scots, and then at Hardwick Hall, built in the reign of Elizabeth by the formidable Bess of Hardwick and described by a contemporary poet as 'more window than wall'. Once we had skirted the massive conurbation of Greater Manchester it did not take us long to get into Lancashire, which I had never really visited before (as distinct from passing through Preston by road or rail), and which was, I discovered, indeed a green and pleasant land, with gently undulating hills, lush pasturage, and picturesque old-world villages. On our arrival at Stonyhurst College we were conducted through a perfect maze of corridors to the secluded suite of rooms which Mangala had reserved for us in a remote corner of the huge complex. As we soon realized, our quarters were in fact the College infirmary.

Apart from attending the evening lectures, and talking to the different Dharmacharis (and later the different Dharmacharinis) whom I invited to join me at my table each day for lunch or dinner, I did not take a very active or a very prominent part in the proceedings of the Convention or meet many people. On most days I went for a walk with Paramartha after lunch and on most days I read, wrote letters, and wandered in the extensive grounds. The name of Stonyhurst, the famous Jesuit college where Gerard Manley Hopkins had once taught and which was probably the model for Gormenghast, had long been familiar to me, and I found it intriguing that this bastion of British Roman Catholicism should now be playing host to a gathering of committed Buddhists. There were not many Jesuits about, most of them presumably being away on holiday, and only occasionally did one encounter an elderly figure in clerical black shuffling along the gloomy corridors. But though there were not many Jesuits about, Roman Catholicism was very much in evidence in the form of crucifixes, pietas, statues of the Virgin Mary (there was one with a broken finger at the entrance to the infirmary), and religious paintings and engravings of all kinds, from saints and martyrs to views of Rome. Some of you, I know, were not very happy to be surrounded by these reminders of Christianity, at least at the beginning. Personally they did not bother me. In fact I felt quite at home in the vast building, or at least in that corner of it that I shared with Paramartha and Prasannasiddhi. Living at Stonyhurst was for me rather like living in a shabby, third-rate museum, the contents of which were of little more than historical or even antiquarian interest, so that I could photograph (for instance) a baroque Mary Magdalen bursting out of the shrubbery with hands theatrically clasped with much the same feeling that I would have photographed a classical Greek Aphrodite or Roman Ceres.

Now that a whole year has passed since I was at Stonyhurst it is difficult to say what for me constituted the highlights of the Convention. I certainly appreciated the lectures, especially Subhuti's 'Going for Refuge and Spiritual Friendship', Padmavajra's 'Going for Refuge in India', and Nagabodhi's 'Signs of the Times' (though all the lectures were worth hearing), and was glad that on this occasion the different lectures had – more or less – a common theme, instead of being on a variety of topics as on the previous Convention. I also appreciated being able to share a meal with Vimalakirti, Chandrabodhi, and Chandrasila, who had already been to see me in London and whose presence at the Convention served to emphasize the international and intercontinental character of the Order. India and England occupy an equal place in my affections and I was no less delighted to see the first Indian Order members in England than I had been delighted, twelve years ago, to see the first English Order members in India. From now onwards may we see more and more of one another and may the bonds of friendship grow ever stronger throughout the whole Order!

Finally, I greatly appreciated the kindness and generosity with which I was showered when, on the last evening of the Convention, Nagabodhi presented me with the card (created by Shuddhavajra) that everybody had signed, together with an envelope containing a sum of money.

Essen is hardly a name to conjure with, or at least it was not until Dharmapriya and Dhammaloka established FWBO Germany there. Essen was part of the Ruhr, the industrial heartland of West Germany, one associated it with coal mines and steel works and black smoke, and had there not been an FWBO centre there it is unlikely that I should ever have visited the place. Yet visit it I did. Shortly after the Convention, and having spent a few days in London, Paramartha and I flew from Norwich to Amsterdam where, the Rijksmuseum and the Van Gogh Museum both being closed, we visited Rembrandt's house and a not very interesting museum of modern art whose name I forget. Shanti-pada, who had met us at the airport, then drove us up to Essen. It was a pleasant journey, mainly by motorway, though once – having lost our way – we had to cross a small river by ferry. At the border there was a minimum of formalities. Indeed, apart from having to show our passports there were no formalities at all, even in the case of Paramartha, who of course carried a non-EEC passport. By evening we were in Essen, and after a meal at an Indian restaurant Shantipada drove us to a building in a quiet street and the flat that was to be our home for the next week. Dharmapriya, who occupied one of the flats above, was there to greet us, there was a letter on the kitchen table from Dhammaloka, who was unavoidably absent, and before long we had settled in.

The week that followed was busy without being hectic and full without being rushed. Paramartha and I had most mornings to ourselves. Rising at 6.30, we practised t'ai chi chu'an, meditated, had breakfast, and then went for a walk in the nearby Schlosspark, with its winding paths, its lake, its many trees, and its white-walled, partially moated castle. On the way home we usually strolled through the old part of the town, past the market place and the ancient cathedral, and through the cemetery. With its well-tended graves, its gravelled paths, its abundance of colourful flowers, its red lamps, and its groups of dark cypresses, the latter was indeed a marvel of beauty and order. Back at the flat we usually talked and studied for the rest of the morning. Lunch was a social occasion. At my suggestion, four or five different Mitras and Friends were invited to join us for this meal each day, which gave me the opportunity of meeting them on a comparatively informal basis, besides enabling me to see a little more of the Order members (including Gunavati from Finland), at least one of whom was always present. At lunch, as also at dinner, when the same arrangement was followed, conversation generally led to discussion and discussion to a sort of impromptu seminar in the course of which I found myself speaking on a number of different topics, from Theravāda 'vipassana' meditation to my own childhood, and from the FWBO triad of centre, community, and co-op to the question of Buddhist schools. In this way I got to know some thirty or forty different people from Essen and other parts of West Germany, from Holland, and from Belgium. After lunch I saw people individually, and in the course of the week received three requests for ordination.

There were also visits to the spacious and well-equipped Centre, which Dharmapriya took us to see on our first full day in Essen, where I was given a reception four days later, and where Paramartha attended a hatha yoga day retreat led by Dharmapriya.

About fifty people attended the reception, though such were the dimensions of the room in which it was held that there was no overcrowding. Dharmapriya made a speech, and I was presented with a magnificently illustrated volume on Cologne Cathedral. We then all adjourned to the shrine-room, where I led a sevenfold puja. I led it, by request, in English. At first I was reluctant to do this, as it seemed ridiculous to have an English puja in Germany, which has its own splendid language and literature, and consented only when I was assured that everybody would be perfectly happy for the puja to be in English. In English it therefore was. I led in English, and they all followed me in English, and a very positive atmosphere prevailed. Many of those present had, of course, recited the sevenfold puja in English when on retreat at Padmaloka or Taraloka. Even so, I appreciated the clear and confident manner in which they followed me. So clearly and confidently did they follow, that I could easily have imagined that I was leading a puja at one of our major English centres. I also appreciated everybody's broadmindedness in being willing to celebrate the sevenfold puja in what to them was, after all, a foreign language, and I secretly resolved that *next* time I visited Essen I would lead at least one puja *in German*, even if this meant my reciting it parrot fashion without actually understanding the precise meaning of the words.

Both before and after the reception and puja, as well as in between, I talked with various Mitras and Friends, some of whom – the shyer ones – were led up to me by Dharmapriya or Dhammaloka and some of whom came and introduced themselves. In this way I got to know quite a few more people. Some of those present I had, of course, already met at the flat over a meal. As I chatted now with this person and now with that, and as I let my gaze wander round the room, I could not help noticing how bright and intelligent everybody looked. I also noticed that the average age was lower than that of the people nowadays attending our centres in England. This augured well for the future of the FWBO in Essen. Indeed, by the time the reception ended I was convinced that with such dedicated Order members, such a fine centre, and such promising Mitras and Friends, the FWBO's future was assured not only in Essen but in Germany.

Essen is only about forty miles from Cologne, and it was perhaps inevitable that Paramartha and I should spend a day in the 'German Rome', as it was known in the Middle Ages, which despite Coleridge's epigram I had long wanted to see and which the ever-hospitable Dharmapriya and Dhammaloka were delighted to show us. On our arrival there we headed straight for the Cathedral, the massive bulk of which towered blackly against the clear blue sky, and were soon inside admiring its treasures. These included the gold-covered and gem-encrusted shrine of the Three Kings (which gave me an idea of what the shrine of Thomas à Becket must have looked like before it was plundered by Henry VIII), the great stained-glass windows, the Stephen Lochner altarpiece, and – my own favourite – the huge wooden figure of St Christopher. After having coffee and cream cakes at one of the hundreds of tables set out to one side of the Cathedral square (Cologne is famous for its cakes), we made our way to the adjacent Romano-German Museum, which was on the whole of archaeological rather than artistic interest. There followed lunch, which we had on the terrace of one of the many restaurants overlooking the Rhine. Though it was early September the weather was perfect, with the sun blazing down from a sky of cloudless blue, and even though there was not much of vegetarian interest on the menu we thoroughly enjoyed the meal and one another's company and were almost sorry to have to resume our sightseeing. We were not sorry for long. At the Wallraf-Richarz Museum (actually an art gallery), where we spent the remainder of the afternoon, there was a staggering wealth of medieval and late medieval paintings of the Cologne school to be seen, as well as paintings belonging to other periods and other schools. The work of some of the old Northern masters, both the known and the unknown ones, was of an extraordinary refinement and emotional sensitivity, and I could have spent many more hours imbibing its unique quality.

Paramartha and I also spent a day in Aachen, this time with Shanti-pada. It was not my first visit to Charlemagne's northern capital, which had been for a while the centre of Western culture and learning. I had visited it with Subhuti and two Mitras (now Order members) in 1981, when *en route* to Italy and the first Tuscany Men's Ordination Retreat, but I was glad to see the quaint old place again. As before, I walked round the tenth-century octagonal cathedral, the eighth- to ninth-century original of which is said to have been designed on the model of San Vitale in Ravenna, looked into the ornate Gothic choir, and admired the famous bronze chandelier and such antique marble and granite columns as had survived Napoleon's lust for loot. We also visited the town hall, which I had not had time to see before. A Gothic structure erected on the ruins of Charlemagne's palace in the four-teenth century, this contained the magnificent coronation hall of the emperors, in which thirty-five German kings and eleven queens had banqueted after the coronation ceremony in the Cathedral.

We also saw something of Düsseldorf, which we visited one evening with the resident Order members and a Mitra and where we attended a performance of Handel's *Julius Caesar* (sung in German), the only opera that happened to be on in the area that week. (Though a lover of Handel, I had rather hoped for either *Parsifal* or *Fidelio*.) Unfortu-nately, as I thought, the production was of the avant-garde type. The cast wandered on to the stage in ordinary dress and picked up their costumes from around a camp fire; an enormous golden falcon, in itself rather splendid, hopped about enfolding people in its wings; there was a lot of elaborate 'business' with a pair of outsize curtains which at crucial moments in the action collapsed on to the heads of the princi-pals; and from time to time there would descend great triangles, spirals, eagles, and grilles of variously coloured neon lights. The music was, of course, very enjoyable, though the young English tenor(!) who sang the title role was not nearly so good as Janet Baker, whom I had heard in the same role some years previously in London. The three female singers, one of whom took a male part, were all very good, especially the elderly mezzo-soprano who sang – and acted – the part of Cornelia, Pompey's widow.

All too soon our week in Essen was over. There was a farewell meal with the resident Order members at a restaurant, and the following morning Dharmapriya drove us to Amsterdam, where we visited the Rijksmuseum and the Van Gogh Museum and where I realized that, except for a handful of paintings, I did not really like Van Gogh. Dharmapriya then drove us to the airport, where I bought a watch, and soon Paramartha and I were above the clouds and heading back to Norwich, taking with us many pleasant memories of Essen and FWBO Germany.

The next three or four months saw a certain amount of toing and froing between London and Norwich and, in Paramartha's case, between London and North Wales. Following our return from Germany I spent two weeks at Padmaloka while Paramartha was away at Vajraloka attending the Meditation Teachers' Retreat, Level One. During this time I recorded the whole of my book *Human Enlightenment* for Dharmachakra Tapes, as well as recording as much of my translation of the *Dhammapada* as I have so far completed. I also paid a visit to Cambridge, which of course meant visiting Windhorse Trading and the Cambridge bookshops. By the end of September Paramartha and I were back in London and once more living at the flat, which thanks to Danavira's initiative and the generosity of the London Buddhist Centre, the Cherry Orchard, Windhorse Typesetters, and other friends had been redecorated in our absence. Apart from attending the Men's National Order Weekend there in early November, we did not see Padmaloka again until the beginning of the Christmas recess. For the first half of December, however, Paramartha was away at Vajraloka attending the Meditation Teachers' Retreat, Level Two, and Prasanna-siddhi came down from Padmaloka and looked after me in his absence.

Despite the toing and froing during this period, whenever Paramartha and I were in London – and we were in London for the greater part of the time – we got on with our customary routine of study (or reading), meditation, and communication, and Paramartha, in addition to his own hatha yoga and prostrations, started attending a weekly life drawing class and a weekly class for trainee yoga teachers. On the literary front (and I use the hackneyed expression advisedly, since writing continues to be a struggle), I completed my new revised version of the Wong Mow Lam translation of *The Sūtra of Wei Lang*, though I have yet to write the introduction and notes, Paramartha started editing the transcript of my seminar on the *Meghiya Sutta*, and I wrote a short story. The short story was the first I had written for seventeen years. Entitled 'The Cave', and about 10,000 words long, it is set in India at the time of the Buddha. The Buddha in fact appears in it, as does Ānanda. Paramartha has read it, and pronounced it 'all right', but I am not sure whether to publish it or not. Probably I will keep it by me until I have a few more such stories, perhaps set in other

Sangharakshita in Cologne

periods, and then bring them all out together in book form along with 'The Artist's Dream'.

Paramartha and I also kept up our interest in the arts, and continued to visit exhibitions, attend concerts, and see plays and films whenever we conveniently could. Among the exhibitions we saw that autumn were 'A Hundred Years of Russian Art' at the Barbican and exhibitions of the work of Miró and the contemporary Cornish artist Uglo at the Whitechapel Gallery. Miró's bold and colourful work impressed me greatly, not least on account of his evident awareness of what he was doing, and I immediately bought and read Ronald Penrose's excellent book on the artist. On 14 November we attended the Nehru Centenary Concert at the Royal Festival Hall. The concert, which started forty minutes late, was attended mainly by prosperous-looking Indians in dark business suits and colourful saris (the hall was by no means full, though) and featured the famous sarod-player Ali Akbar Khan who, in partnership with a young Bengali tabla-player, gave a dazzling performance which sent shock after shock of delight through the audience and drew the traditional 'wahwahs!' from aficionados. A few weeks later I attended two more concerts, this time with Prasannasiddhi. Both concerts were held in the Purcell Room of the South Bank Centre and both were devoted to Ancient Music. One of them, given by the Dufay Collective, was devoted to thirteenth-century music from the court of Alfonso the Wise of Castile and Léon, and featured such extraordinary instruments as the vielle, the rebec, the shawm, the whistle, the oud, and the saz. Half the items were songs dealing with the miracles of the Virgin Mary. It was at about this time – I have no diary and am writing from memory – that I heard Beethoven's Eighth and Ninth Symphonies with Oliver Katz, a German Mitra living at Aryatara and working in Hockneys, with whom I later visited an interesting if rather idiosyncratic exhibition of the work of six 'ethnic' British artists at the Hayward Gallery. One of the six artists was David Medulla, who in 'the old days' used to call in at Sakura and who would, I think, have become involved with the FWBO had not Emile Boin (Upaya) in effect discouraged his visits. (Emile was terrified lest our nascent spiritual movement should be 'taken over by the hippies', of whom David Medulla then certainly appeared to be one.)

Films seem to belong to a world of their own, and though I can recollect the titles of quite a few of the films Paramartha and I have seen during the last twelve months I cannot always remember whether we saw them during the latter half of last year or the earlier part of this (Paramartha cannot remember either). I shall therefore deal with all of them together later on in this Letter. I do, however, remember our seeing Strindberg's *Master Olaf* towards the end of the year in the gloomily appropriate setting of Hawksmoor's Christ Church, Spitalfields, now unused for religious purposes and beginning to show signs of neglect.

At this point it occurs to me that I have said nothing about my reading. I should have mentioned it immediately after telling you how, on our return to London, Paramartha and I got on with our customary routine, and before telling you about my literary activities. But better late than never. Before I move on to our Christmas recess at Padmaloka let me, therefore, give you a brief account of my reading, both Buddhist and non-Buddhist, during the latter half of last year. My Buddhist reading was rather limited, at least in respect of new publications, being more or less confined to two books. Lenore Friedman's *Meetings with Remarkable Women*, subtitled *Buddhist Teachers in America*, consisted of interviews with seventeen women 'from various spiritual traditions and backgrounds'. Some of the women interviewed were more remarkable than others but between them they showed what a variety of role models are already available to Buddhist women in the West. I also found it interesting that they were so little beholden to feminism. *Buddhism in Australia* (unfortunately I cannot recall the name of the author) is a frank and dispassionate – and highly readable – account of the progress of the Dharma in Australia during the last hundred years. It explodes the myth that the eccentric Sister Dhamma-dinna (whom I met in India) was the founder of Australian Buddhism and shows how extensive has been the influence of Buddhism, and of Far Eastern Buddhist culture, on Australian writers and artists. The author also refers to D.H. Lawrence's visit to Australia and to his novel *Kangaroo*, and makes the interesting suggestion that Kangaroo, the charismatic leader of the Diggers, stands in part for Buddhist values – values against which Lawrence is reacting. Altogether *Buddhism in Australia* is a fascinating book. It is a much better book, on the whole, than its American counterpart *How the Swans Came to the Lake*, possibly because the author has less to fear from his country's libel laws, and I have asked Nagabodhi to have it reviewed in *Golden Drum*.

My non-Buddhist reading was much more extensive and consisted mainly of modern American fiction and of biography. The former included F. Scott Fitzgerald's *Tender is the Night*; Sinclair Lewis's *Elmer Gantry*; Carson McCullers's *The Heart is a Lonely Hunter, The Ballad of the Sad Café*, and *The Member of the Wedding*; Truman Capote's *Other Voices, Other Rooms*, and various short stories; Paul Bowles's *A Hundred Camels in the Courtyard*; Edmund White's *A Boy's Own Story* and *The Beautiful Room is Empty*; and Paul Auster's *New York Trilogy* – all of which, except the last, I thoroughly enjoyed. I also read two non-American works of fiction, namely, Malcolm Lowry's *Under the Volcano* (recommended by Paramartha) and George Gissing's *Born in Exile* – Gissing being an old favourite of mine. In addition I started reading Henry James's *The Spoils of Poynton*, which I had read once before, many years ago, but was obliged to desist after eight or nine chapters as I found the story *too exciting*. Among the biographies were *The Kindness of Strangers* and *An Invisible Spectator*, devoted respectively to the lives of Tennessee

Williams and Paul Bowles, *Capote: A Biography*, and a life of Father Ronald Knox found, not surprisingly, in our sitting room at Stonyhurst. Besides these more or less 'straight' biographies there were also biographical-cum-critical studies of Carson McCullers, Lionel Trilling, and Simone Weil. The rest of my non-Buddhist reading was of a rather miscellaneous character, including as it did Peter Fuller's *Theoria*, Simone Weil's *The Need for Roots* and other writings, three of Shakespeare's historical plays, Shakespeare and Fletcher's *The Two Noble Kinsmen*, and Adrien Henri's *For Beauty Douglas*, his collected poems, which I picked up at the Anarchist Bookshop in Whitechapel. At intervals I also dipped into Milton, Spenser, Herrick, Roy Campbell, and other old favourites of mine among the English poets.

When Paramartha and I drove up to Padmaloka shortly before Christmas I was already beginning to suffer from a kind of flu and after our arrival went down with it properly for six or seven days. Fortunately the Order Office was not very busy at the time and I could rest and read until I felt well enough to start going through my mail and attending to administrative matters. There were also talks with Subhuti and a meeting with Lokamitra, then in England for a few weeks. Paramartha, having recently come off the Meditation Teachers' Retreat, Level Two, spent much of his time doing extra meditation. Then on the morning of 2 January 1990 we drove down to London, as related in my unfinished 'Third Letter from London'. A week later we went to see my mother, who was then in Rochford Hospital, having been taken there on Christmas Day after complaining of severe pains in her chest. Though she had had two heart attacks, and looked thinner and older, she was bright and lively as ever, and I left her feeling, again as related in my 'Third Letter from London', that she had recovered her will to live and would pull through. On the evening of 29 January, however, I had a telephone call from my nephew John. He and his wife Tynia had just been to see my mother, as they did practically every evening. She was in full possession of her senses, but every now and then she would 'drift away'. John thought she did not have much longer to live, perhaps no more than two or three weeks. I told him I would try to see her the following week.

At breakfast the following morning, however, I suddenly had a strong feeling that I should see my mother that very day. Paramartha and I had planned to spend the day out somewhere, but when I told him about my feeling and suggested that, as a compromise, we should visit Southend, have lunch there, and then go to see my mother in

Rochford Hospital, he at once agreed. By 11 o'clock we were in Southend and walking along the deserted sea front towards Leigh-on-Sea, where my Auntie Lil, my mother's second eldest sister, used to live, and where my mother herself had lived for a while after her second marriage. It was a cold, wintry day. The sky was the colour of lead, and the sea the colour of lead mixed with silver. As we walked, the wind drove the icy rain into our faces. Somewhere under the cliff we found a café that was open and had a coffee and a piece of cake, then walked on for another mile or so before turning round and finding our way back into Southend by an upper road. There were no vegetarian restaurants in Southend, it seemed, but eventually we located an Italian restaurant in the new shopping precinct and made our meal there. We then drove straight to Rochford Hospital, which was only five or six miles away. As we made our way along the last of the corridors I cast a quick glance into the room my mother had occupied at the time of our last visit, three weeks earlier, but her corner was empty and the bed stripped down and I had a premonition that something had happened. Going up to the nurses' station I enquired of the nurse on duty where I could find Mrs Wiltshire. She looked at me for a moment, rather suspiciously I thought, and asked, 'Who are you?' 'I'm her son,' I replied. At once her expression changed and I knew what was coming. 'I'm awfully sorry,' she said, after a pause, 'but she died early this morning.'

After ascertaining that my mother had died between 1.15 and 1.30, that there had been nobody with her at the time, and that to all appearances she had died peacefully, in her sleep, I asked if it would be possible for me to see my mother. The nurse looked doubtful but said she would telephone and find out. We were then shown into a little sitting room and given tea. Paramartha and I talked, as I came to terms with the situation, and I was glad of his emotional support. I also tried to telephone John, but without success. After fifteen or twenty minutes I was told that I could now see my mother, the nurse handed us over to a junior nurse, and the junior nurse, having conducted us through half a mile of corridors, in turn handed us over to two orderlies, one of whom led us out of the back of the hospital and into a small brick building – not the mortuary, as I had at first supposed, but the mortuary chapel.

My mother lay swathed in white sheets and with her feet towards the altar, on which stood a plain cross – not a crucifix – and two vases of flowers. Her eyes were closed and her face had a waxen look, and though it was very much my mother at the same time it was somehow not my mother at all. Drawing up the two chairs, we positioned ourselves on either side of the bier, opposite my mother's head, so that we were facing each other across her. I took my rosary from my pocket. Actually I never take it with me when I go out, but on this one day I had for some reason slipped it into my pocket as we left the flat. Paramartha, with a little smile, also took his rosary from his pocket, and for the next fifteen or twenty minutes we meditated and recited the Vajrasattva mantra. As we did so, we were aware of something – it could not be called a consciousness, it could not be called a soul – as it were hovering above my mother's chest between us. At the end of the fifteen or twenty minutes, mindful of the fact that the two orderlies were waiting for us outside, we took a last look at my mother and left the chapel. Before we left Paramartha, at my request, took a couple of photographs of my mother with my new Pentax Zoom 90 which, for some reason, I had also brought with me, and which I had not previously used.

On leaving the hospital we drove through the rain to Rayleigh. Here I called on my mother's next door neighbour Jean, a white-haired smiling woman of about sixty who for many years had been a good friend to my mother. I did not know if she had heard of my mother's death and thought that I should find out and, if necessary, inform her. As I rang the bell, I glanced across the fence at my mother's bungalow.

The place was in darkness, and looked dreadfully deserted. As it happened, Jean had heard of my mother's death, but was glad to see me, and after we had talked for ten or fifteen minutes – I refused her offer of tea, as Paramartha was waiting in the car – we parted with mutual expressions of warm good will. The next call was on John and Tynia, who lived about a mile away, having moved to Rayleigh a few months earlier. We found them sad but calm, though one of their two grown-up sons, who was working out in the garage when we arrived, was apparently too upset to come into the house and talk. The hospital had informed them of my mother's death around breakfast time; John had telephoned me at Sukhavati, but I had already left, and he had been told that I was out for the day. Naturally we talked about my mother, who of course was John's grandmother and who in fact had brought him up, and whom Tynia had regarded less as a grandmother-in-law than as a mother, her own mother having died when she was quite young. Among other things, they told me that on their leaving her the previous evening she had given them a smile of particular sweetness – a smile they now understood had been one of farewell. While we were talking, and drinking cups of tea, their twelve-year-old daughter Anna came home from school and had to be told the news. She was quite upset, having been very devoted to her great-grand-mother. After shedding a few tears in the kitchen she came into the sitting room and quietly sat down beside me on the sofa, resting her head on my shoulder, and I put my arm round her.

The funeral took place nine days later, on Thursday, 8 February. Paramartha was unable to accompany me, as he had a prior engage-ment, so Prasannasiddhi came down from Norwich the night before and drove me to it. We left Bethnal Green at 9 o'clock, having first collected the wreath – pink and white roses – from the florist's (I was surprised how expensive wreaths were) and were in Rayleigh by 10.30. The funeral cortège left from my mother's bungalow at 12.00, with my sister and her husband and me, together with the officiating clergy-man, in the first car, immediately behind the hearse. About twenty people were gathered in the very new chapel of the crematorium (John, as executor, had decided on a C of E service). Most of the women wore black, I noticed, but John and his sons wore only black ties, while I did not make even that concession to solemnity. Business being quite brisk at the crematorium that day, we had been allotted only twenty minutes (originally it had been twenty-five), and were warned that we should on no account exceed our time. The clergyman, a dignified elderly man with silver-grey hair, conducted the service quite well, in the sense that he read and spoke clearly and confidently and with a certain amount of feeling. He had to sing the hymns virtually by himself, however, and no one seemed to know the responses, scarcely so much as an 'amen' being heard from the congregation. (I did not join in on principle.) The language of the much abbreviated service was densely theological, as was the clergyman's five-minute address, and though the majority of those present probably considered them-selves Christians I am sure it was Greek and Hebrew to them. It would certainly have been totally meaningless to my mother, whose sympa-thies were definitely Buddhist rather than Christian, and I was all the more glad that there were at least four Buddhists present at her funeral, Prasannasiddhi and I having been joined by Padmasuri and Jayaprabha, who had driven down from Cambridge for the occasion. I was also glad that I was able to say a few words about my mother. Indeed I had insisted on doing this. I spoke of her as a woman of unfailing kindness who was, at the same time, firm in her adherence to principle and never afraid to speak her mind. As I spoke, I rested my right hand on her coffin, as if to emphasize the closeness of our connection. The clergyman then continued the service, the coffin disappeared from sight, the clergyman concluded the service, and we all filed out into the sunshine, a shaft of which had illuminated my mother's coffin during the ceremony.

After the funeral we all drove back to the bungalow for tea and sandwiches, and such of Tynia's relations as I had not already met were introduced to me. Before long I noticed that all the younger members of the family had drifted from the sitting room to the kitchen, where they were apparently gathered round Prasannasiddhi. At any rate, I could hear his voice and the words 'Open University' and 'retreat'. As it was now 2.30, I suggested to Prasannasiddhi and the two Dharmacharinis that the four of us should drive into the town centre and have lunch there. Unfortunately, Thursday is early closing day in Rayleigh, but eventually we found at the rear of a baker's and confectioner's a self-service restaurant that was open and had a moderately good meal together, as well as a much better talk. Prasannasiddhi, who had met my mother a number of times and was aware of the nature of her religious sympathies, had some strong things to say about the absurdity and inappropriateness of the funeral service and the general irrelevance of Christianity.

Between the day of my mother's death and the day of her funeral came the February National Order Weekend. On the Saturday morning I had a question-and-answer session in London with the women Order members, towards the end of which I spoke about my mother, and in the afternoon Paramartha and I drove up to Padmaloka for the Men's Order Weekend, where I chaired Subhuti's challenging talk 'Have We Friendship in the Order?' and underlined some of the points he had so brilliantly made. A lightly edited transcript of the talk is, I am glad to say, being made available to Order members. It was also in February, I think, that Paramartha and I saw the 'Joseph Wright of Derby 1734—1797' exhibition at the Tate Gallery and 'The Last Romantics' exhibition at the Barbican, besides visiting Brighton for me to give the third reading of my selection of poems on the theme of friendship. The first of the two exhibitions was a little disappointing, even though a handful of paintings were outstanding, but in the second there was much to interest and impress. I particularly liked Glyn Philpot's *Melampus*, depicting the youthful prophet with the centaur Chiron, though there were quite a number of other paintings that appealed to me strongly. The Brighton reading of my selection of poems on the theme of friendship took place at the Royal Pavilion in what the organizers thought was the King William IV Room, but which was certainly not the King William IV Room in which I had delivered a series of four lectures some years before. King William IV Room or not, however, the place was packed, and my reading evoked, I thought, a somewhat livelier response than it had done at either the London Buddhist Centre or the Croydon Buddhist Centre. The following morning, having enjoyed the warm hospitality of Amitayus, Paramartha and I went for a walk along the sea front. The weather was bright but cold, and after a while we turned back and headed for the town centre. Paramartha had not been to Brighton before, and I had the pleasure of taking him to see the Royal Pavilion, where we admired the splendid chinoiseries of the Banqueting Room and the Music Room, as well as the more restrained taste of the other apartments, and to the nearby Brighton Art Gallery, the main hall of which was unfortunately closed. We also visited a few second-hand bookshops.

On the second weekend in February Paramartha attended, with Vasumitra, a seminar conducted by James Hillman, formerly Director of Studies at the Jung Institute in Zurich and now calling himself an 'imaginal psychologist'. The seminar, entitled 'Towards an Aesthetic Ecology of Soul', was described as 'an exploration of the relationship between the animal and the human worlds', the principal field of enquiry being 'how the delicate ecosystem of the external world is mirrored in the human soul, especially in the form of both natural and animal images in dreams.' Paramartha was interested in attending the seminar partly on account of his interest in Shamanism and partly because he had had a number of dreams in which animals appeared (we had been telling each other our dreams for more than a year). For my part, having come across Hillman's *Archetypal Psychology* a few years back I was interested in knowing more about the man and his ideas and therefore encouraged Paramartha to go on the seminar. Besides encouraging him to go on it, I suggested that he should take notes and buy whatever literature was available. This he faithfully did, with the result that for the next three or four months James Hillman's books formed an important part of our reading and his ideas on psyche or soul a frequent topic of discussion between us.

March saw me working on my rather cumbersomely entitled paper on 'My Relation to the Order and the Order's Relation to the Buddhist World' and thus fulfilling, or trying to fulfil, the promise I had made, towards the end of *The History of My Going for Refuge*, to share with the Order some of my current thinking on this topic. Originally I was going to finish my 'Third Letter from London', the first part of which had been written towards the end of January, but eventually decided to write the paper first. It was as well that I did so decide. The paper became far longer than I had expected and I was able to complete only the first section, on 'My Relation to the Order', in time for 140 of you to hear me read it at our Order Anniversary celebrations on 8 April. During the time that I was working on the paper the only real interruption, so far as I remember (and in itself it was not an interruption at all), was when Paramartha and I went up to Manchester for the fourth reading of my selection of poems on the theme of friendship. The reading took place at the neo-Gothic Town Hall, in the richly decorated Mayor's Parlour, and was followed by a sort of regional launching of my book *The Taste of Freedom*, which Nagabodhi had already launched in East London and in Croydon and which, again rising magnificently to the occasion, he now launched in Manchester. On the morning of the reading Paramartha and I spent a couple of hours at the Lady Lever Art Gallery, Port Sunlight, with Ratnaguna and Aryasingha (I had visited the gallery once before, mainly on account of the Pre-Raphaelites); and the following day, shortly before we left for London, I had morning coffee with Kalyanaprabha, Vidyavati, and Jayadevi at Kalyanaprabha's little terraced house.

'Young or old, strong or weak, we may die at any moment, as my mother's recent death served to remind me (if indeed I needed a reminder), and as some of you will have been reminded yourselves by recent bereavements of your own.' When the first section of my paper was nearly finished, and only hours after I had written the foregoing sentence, I learned of Dhardo Rimpoche's death. The news came as a surprise to me, not to say a shock, even though I knew that Rimpoche had been taken ill a few weeks earlier, shortly after his return from Nepal. Since it was a Sunday, Paramartha was due to attend his chapter meeting, but I asked him to stay with me instead. He readily agreed, and we spent the evening talking about Rimpoche. Despite the fact that I had always felt spiritually in touch with him, and continued to feel in touch, it seemed strange that I would never see my teacher in the flesh again. Paramartha, like many others, had looked forward to meeting Dhardo Rimpoche personally one day and was sorry that this would not now be possible. Within a matter of hours the news of Rimpoche's death had spread throughout the Movement, and at a number of centres and communities special pujas and meditations were held. Pujas, meditations, and readings from the *Perfection of Wisdom in 8,000 Lines* were also held a week later, on the day of Rimpoche's funeral. I did not take part in any of them, but that morning Paramartha and I had a puja, meditation, and reading of our own in the flat. As Order members started returning from India, and as letters arrived, I was able to get a clearer and fuller picture of the events preceding Dhardo Rimpoche's death, from his merit-making pilgrimage to the holy places of Nepal to his return to Kalimpong, his collapse from a stroke, his seeming recovery, and his final instructions to Jampel Khalden, his secretary, concerning his funeral, the recognition of his tulku-successor, and the future of his school. But since you are already apprised of these events, having read Suvajra's account of them in his articles in *Shabda* and *Golden Drum*, I shall say nothing about them in this Letter.

For the same reason I shall say very little about the FWBO and WBO Day celebrations on 7 and 8 April respectively, reports of which you will also have seen. The celebrations were held, of course, at Manchester Town Hall, definitely the most pleasing and appropriate surroundings in which they have so far taken place. On FWBO Day I attended the afternoon seminar on the FWBO triad of urban 'Buddhist Centre', single-sex residential community, and team-based 'Right Livelihood' businesses, and was glad that the importance of these three basic institutions of our Movement was again being stressed. I was less glad, however, to see that there were fewer people taking part in the celebrations than one might have expected. That evening Paramartha and I had a very enjoyable meal at a vegetarian restaurant with Ratnabandhu, Jinaraja, and Moksaraja – all cronies of Paramartha's. We sat a long time over our coffee, and Paramartha tells me that I reminisced at some length about the early days of the Movement. The next day, being Order Day, I attended Kamalashila's serious and striking talk on 'The Death of the Order' in the morning and in the afternoon, after lunch, read my paper, or half-paper, on 'My Relation to the Order'. The paper was well received, and in the course of the next few months – especially after the publication of the paper in booklet form – many of you wrote to me expressing your appreciation of the candour with which I had shared with you my current thinking as regards my relation to the Order – my relation to *you*. Those of you who did write expressed, in particular, your appreciation of the fact that I had actually said, in so many words, that you were important to me, both individually and collectively, that I was interested in your progress, that whatever concerned you concerned me, that I was always glad to hear from you, that I was not too busy to take notice of you, however many of you there were, and that I cared for you. At first I was rather surprised that these words of mine should have been so greatly appreciated. (Some of you had even shed tears on hearing me say that you were important to me.) I had assumed that Order members knew very well that they were important to me, and that I cared for them, and that there was no real need for me to spell it all out. On reflection, however, I realized that this was not necessarily always the case. I could not take it for granted that my feelings were known to you. Whether in the case of a friend, a teacher, or a pupil, one's positive feelings had to be *expressed,* and they had to be expressed frequently, fully, and unmistakably.

So far as Paramartha and I were concerned April was *not* the cruellest month. Apart from attending the FWBO and WBO celebrations in Manchester (not to mention my poetry reading there) we spent three or four days on retreat at Padmaloka and an equivalent period on holiday in the Peak District. The retreat was a special study retreat which, with Paramartha supporting me, I led for four German Mitras who had asked for ordination, the four Mitras being Oliver Katz, whom I had known for a couple of years and who regularly spent time with me, Werner Kierski and Robert Lusch, whom Paramartha and I had met in Germany, and Wolfgang Schröder, who some time previously had had lunch with us in London. We studied chapter 3 of *The Sūtra of Golden Light*, 'On Confession', besides listening to the tape of my lecture 'The Spiritual Significance of Confession'. It was the first study retreat I had led for some time (as well as leading the actual study I led all the pujas and meditations) and I had decided to hold it for two reasons. In the first place, I wanted to see what it would be like to lead a retreat again; in the second, I wanted to have more contact with the four German Mitras who, as first fruits of Dhammaloka and Dharmapriya's labours, would surely be playing an important part in the development of the FWBO in Germany.

The morning after the retreat Paramartha and I drove to Sheffield, stopping *en route* to see Burghley House, seat of the descendants of the elder son of Queen Elizabeth's great minister William Cecil, Lord Burghley. The place was of enormous size, and with the rest of a small party we were led through room after room crammed with paintings, some of them very fine and of great historic interest (I particularly noticed Cranach's portrait of Luther), as well as with tapestries, antique furniture, porcelain, and silverware. On the walls of one spacious apartment, known as the Olympus Room, there were frescoes depicting Mount Olympus, the gods and goddesses all being drawn life-size. Frescoes also covered the walls of a vast landing and stairwell. These frescoes depicted, in lurid fashion, the Mouth of Hell, the aperture in question being formed by the open jaws of an enormous cat. What delighted me most, however, among the treasures of Burghley House, was a collection of several hundred Chinese (and I think Japanese) snuff bottles, many of them exquisitely carved from semi-precious stones. Before leaving we had lunch in the restaurant, through whose windows one looked across a small flagstoned courtyard, complete with fountain, and up at the rows of ornamental Jacobean chimney-stacks.

In Sheffield we stayed at the Windhorse Publications community with Nagabodhi, Shantavira, and Chris Pauling. It was my first visit to Sheffield, as it was also Paramartha's (apart from when we had stopped by at the community for lunch on our way to the Manchester poetry reading), and I was glad to see that the FWBO had begun to take root in this Northern industrial city, with its associations with John Ruskin and Edward Carpenter. Each morning we meditated with the community, had breakfast, and then went out for the day. Five minutes after leaving the house (Nagabodhi had *not* exaggerated) we would be amid the green hills of the Peak District. On our first day we went on a long walk (long for me, if not for Paramartha) in the hills above Ladybower Reservoir and then drove on to Castleton. Here we visited an eighteenth-century lead mine, in which more than 200 men had lost their lives. Having bought our tickets and passed through the turnstile, we descended a flight of eighty-five stone steps, all rather steep and slippery, the air becoming colder and colder as we went. At the bottom of the steps there was a barge, not unlike that in which Charon plies his dismal trade. In this barge, together with some twenty other souls, we slowly bumped and banged our way along half a mile of dimly lit underground canal, the dank walls of which were no more than eight feet apart and the ceiling so low that we had to keep our heads down. After what seemed a very long time we emerged into a gloomy cavern and disembarked. The cavern, in which we spent about twenty minutes, was funnel-shaped and about eighty feet high. Stalactites hung from the roof and rudimentary stalagmites were in process of formation here and there on the floor. In one corner, behind a barrier, there was a deep shaft, from the bottom of which came the muffled roar of rushing waters. The return journey seemed to take less time than the outward one, and soon we were ascending the eighty-five steps, had passed through a door, and found ourselves among the toys and trinkets of a souvenir shop.

On subsequent days, the weather being usually fine, we visited – or drove through – Bakewell, Buxton, Hathersage, Edale, and more than a score of other towns and hamlets. We sampled home-made cakes in quiet, charmingly old-fashioned tearooms, lunched at crowded restaurants in busy town centres, pored over the fascinating – sometimes wildly miscellaneous – contents of little local museums (including a Blue John museum), wandered round arts-and-crafts shops, and bought picture postcards. In the spa town of Buxton we spent an hour or so at the Micrarium (the only one in the world), where we studied the movements of larvae, marvelled at the formation of crystals in polarized light, and admired the colouring of a section of peacock feather or butterfly's wing. Driving further afield than usual, we also visited Chatsworth House; but we arrived late, it was raining, and we did not go inside. (We had seen the gardens on the way back from Stonyhurst, with Prasannasiddhi, when the three of us had also visited Southwell Minster, the wonderful stone carvings of which I had long wanted to see.) One day, varying our programme, we took the bus into Sheffield's very modern city centre, where we visited the Ruskin Gallery and saw, among other things, some of Ruskin's own drawings and his mineralogical collection.

Returning to Crookesmoor at the end of the day's outing, we had dinner with Nagabodhi and the other members of the community, and a discussion usually ensued. Since his removal to Sheffield more than a year earlier I had missed Nagabodhi's presence at Padmaloka and was glad of the opportunity of experiencing his warmth and good humour again. (He very kindly gave up his own room to me, while Paramartha slept among the potted plants of Terry Williams's old room.) One evening, however, after dinner with Shantavira (Nagabodhi had gone down to London), Paramartha and I went into the city centre and saw the *film* of a *stage performance* of *The Magic Flute*. Though we enjoyed the music, we agreed that this kind of hybrid was not very satisfactory and did little justice to either art-form. In the stage performance, moreover, the Egyptian setting had been changed to a Gothic one (which meant that the words of Sarastro's great invocation 'O Isis and Osiris' had to be altered), and the archetypal significance of the whole opera greatly diminished. On another evening we had dinner with Advayachitta and Punyamala, who lived only a few hundred yards from the Windhorse Publications community. It was an excellent meal, and Paramartha and I voted Punyamala one of the best cooks in the Movement, perhaps the very best. Marriage was not without its compensations, it seemed, at least for men. After dinner the four of us adjourned to the sitting room, where we talked about ... well, about the sort of things that Order members usually talk about over their coffee after a good meal.

From Sheffield we drove up to the city of York, which once upon a time was, for a few years, effectively the capital of the Roman Empire. The place was bigger than I had remembered it, and extremely crowded. We were unable to get into the Minster, as a special service was in progress, and instead visited the nearby art gallery, which was unexpectedly extensive and contained a number of fine paintings, mainly of the English and Scottish schools. A whole room was devoted to the work of William Etty, who was born in the city, and a statue of whom stood in the forecourt of the building. Many of his paintings were rather stiff and awkward, falling considerably below the level of his finest work. By far the best of them, I thought, was a small life study of a male nude executed with quite exceptional sensitivity. Returning to the Minster, we found the special service still in progress (it was running more than an hour late, we were told) and therefore visited the archaeological museum down among the foundations of the great building and went and had lunch. We also visited St William's College and tried to get into the Viking Centre, desisting when we saw the enormous length of the queue. Eventually we succeeded in gaining admission to the Minster, edging our way through the crowds that were now pouring out to the sound of some very thunderous organ music. Once inside, we saw the rose window, the series of beautiful lancet windows known as the Five Sisters, the chapter-house, and various monuments and tombs. I enjoyed the visit much less than my previous visit a few years ago. The presence of so many people for what was more like a public meeting than a religious service had had a distinctly disturbing effect on the atmosphere.

Having spent more time in York than we had intended, we left the city rather late and drove straight to Rievaulx, some forty miles further north. For several years I had wanted to see the ruins of Rievaulx Abbey, once the biggest Cistercian monastery in Britain, and we were not sure if it would still be open. It was open, though we did not arrive until 5 o'clock and had only an hour in which to explore the very extensive remains of the church, the cloisters, and the various domestic buildings. The Abbey was situated in a deep wooded valley, and already the mists were rising, providing a silvery backdrop to the massive piers and lofty pointed arches of the ruined but still very impressive nave of the church. It was here that St Aelred had lived and taught, here (perhaps) that he had composed his *Spiritual Friendship*, and I renewed my resolve that I would one day lead a study retreat on this beautiful Christian classic. In fact I conceived the idea (which I communicated to Paramartha) of holding the retreat in Yorkshire and combining study of the text with excursions to Rievaulx and other monastic sites, of which there were many in the area.

Rievaulx being the northernmost point of our journey, after seeing the ruins we turned round and headed south-east, towards Hull. On the way we visited Beverley Minster, or, rather, saw it from the outside as it was closed. After having dinner at a rather good, and rather expensive, Indian restaurant in Hull, we drove across the newly completed Humber Bridge, the great curves of which loomed up at us out of the mist. Further on we found a bed-and-breakfast establishment in a quiet side street and there spent the night. The following morning we drove, as we had driven the previous evening, through a part of the country that was new to me. It was very attractive, and seemed thinly populated. At one point we had to stop to allow a procession of bicyclists in Edwardian costume to cross. Among the ancient machines that had been wheeled out that bright Sunday morning were a number of penny-farthings, their riders perched atop the gigantic front wheels in very precarious fashion. Later in the morning we entered Boston, eventually finding our way to St Botolph's, the 290ft west tower of which is commonly known as Boston Stump. Like Beverley Minster it was closed, and we had to be content with viewing it from the outside.

By the time we reached King's Lynn I was on more familiar ground. Indeed, we were now in West Norfolk. It being Sunday, all the shops were closed, and the place presented a dreary, desolate appearance. In the vast, empty shopping mall we found a large restaurant open and decided to have lunch there. We were the only customers. I distinguished myself by sending the food back – a thing I had never done before and which English people do far too infrequently. We had ordered vegetable raviolis but when they came we found they contained meat. In the end, after profuse apologies from the manageress, we got what we wanted. Perhaps because we were tired after our long drive, perhaps because we were aware that we were not far from home and that our brief holiday was almost ended, we lingered over our coffee. All too soon, however, we were on the road again; the landmarks grew more and more familiar, and we arrived at Padmaloka in time for afternoon tea.

Two days later I was back in harness, so to speak, reading six poems from *Conquering New Worlds* for a series of five short BBC television programmes in celebration of Wesak. The following day Paramartha and I drove down to London, where before long I was giving another (public) poetry reading and participating in the launching of another book. The occasion was Buddha Day (Wesak), the venue the colourfully decorated London Buddhist Centre shrine-room. This time I read not a selection of poems on friendship but poems of my own on the theme of Wesak; the book that was being launched was not *The Taste of Freedom* but *New Currents in Western Buddhism*, and the person doing the launching was not Nagabodhi but Ratnaketu, who having heard me give the lectures on which the book was based was in a position to reminisce. I had given them in Auckland in 1979, he recalled – one of them on that very day. They were 'Tantric' lectures (New Zealand was a 'Tantric' country), and they had had an electrifying effect. People had been stunned.... Whether on account of Ratnaketu's heartfelt words, or for some other reason, people queued up afterwards to buy the book and I had to sign a record number of copies.

My reading during this whole period, that is, the period from the end of January to the end of June, followed much the same pattern as in the preceding six months. (I have written about my reading for the month of January in the 'Third Letter from London'.) Once again my Buddhist reading was rather limited, at least in respect of new publications, though I dipped into quite a number of the latter and in some cases made a mental note to read them later on. Michael Aris's *Hidden Treasures and Secret Lives*, a study of Pemalingpa (1450–1521), the controversial Bhutanese terton, and the Sixth Dalai Lama (1683–1706), was one of the most fascinating and well-written books on Buddhism that I had come across in years. It made me realize, yet again, how few authors of books on Buddhism can actually write. No less fascinating and readable, though translated from the Japanese, was *The Love of the Samurai: A Thousand Years of Japanese Homosexuality*, by Tsuneo Watanabe and Jun'ichi Iwata. So far as I know, this is the first book to have appeared in the English language on Buddhism and homosexuality, and it will be interesting to see if it is followed by similar studies of homosexuality among Sinhalese monks and in Tibetan monastic colleges, or even in Thai and Burmese nunneries. *Feminine Ground*, edited by Janice Wills, was a collection of essays by leading female writers on Tibet 'covering such topics as Tibetan nuns and nunneries, the meaning of Dakini, and Yeshe Tsogyal as female role model.' I found the essay on the Dakini interesting, though it said nothing new.

Modern American fiction and biography continued to make up a large part of my non-Buddhist reading, though not such a large part as they did last year. The former included William Faulkner's *Intruder in the Dust*, Willa Cather's *Death Comes to the Archbishop*, and Paul Bowles's *Collected Stories*, besides Truman Capote's *The Grass Harp* and *The Muses Are Heard* – both beautifully written and the latter (actually reportage rather than fiction) of particular interest in view of recent developments in the Soviet Union. I also read some modern English fiction: A.J. Ackerley's *We Think the World of You* (recommended by Mangala), a study of jealousy, human and canine, and Francis King's *A Domestic Animal*, a story of homosexual infatuation. The biographies, or rather autobiographies, consisted of W.H. Davies's classic *The Auto-biography of a Super-Tramp*, together with its sequel, the title of which I forget, and Elia Kazan's substantial and highly readable *A Life*. The rest of my non-Buddhist reading was again of a rather miscellaneous character, including as it did David Newcome's *The Two Classes of Men* (i.e. the Platonists and the Aristotelians), Robert H. Hopake's *Jung, Jungians, and Homosexuality* (required reading, I think, for all homosexuals – and perhaps all heterosexuals – in the Movement), James Hillman's *Re-Visioning Psychology* and *Suicide and the Soul*, a book on the psychology of romantic love which I found on Prasannasiddhi's desk on one of my visits to Padmaloka, Plato's *Euthyphro, Phaedo*, and *Phaedrus*, Porphyry's *Launching Points to the Realm of Mind* (read for the third time), Proclus' *Elements of Theology*, Marsilio Ficino's *Commentary on Plato's Symposium on Love*, and Benjamin Whichcote's *Aphorisms*, as well as W.H. Davies's *Collected Poems*, Patrice de la Tour du Pin's *The Dedicated Life in Poetry*, and *Sculpting in Time: Reflections on the Cinema*, by Andrei Tarkovsky, perhaps best known in Britain as the director of *Solaris*, the Russian space odyssey.

Which brings me to the subject of films. During the latter half of last year and the earlier part of this, Paramartha and I saw about a dozen films, the most memorable of which for me were *Jesus of Montreal*, *Lawrence of Arabia* (the original, uncut version), and perhaps *Yeelen* ('Light'), a subtitled African film dealing with witchcraft and father–son rivalry against a background of tribal life. Among the other films were *Henry V* (*not* the Olivier version), *Paris by Night* (an ambitious English civil servant murders to protect her career), *The American Friend* (skulduggery in the international art trade), *The Moderns* (expatriate Americans in the Paris of the twenties), *Torch Song Trilogy* (the life of a not-so-young New York drag queen), *The Navigator* (men from a plague-stricken medieval English village bore through the earth to twentieth-century Auckland), and *McCabe and Mrs Miller* (sentiment and violence in a Canadian pioneering town). Artistic merits apart, these films showed, between them, human life as lived at different periods of history, in various parts of the world, and on a number of different social and cultural levels. They not only increased one's knowledge but enlarged one's sympathies. This capacity to enlarge our sympathies is one of the most valuable features of the film, and the fact that film has this capacity is one of the reasons why I go to see films.

The film and the stage play are, of course, two very different art forms, and seeing them two very different experiences. Nonetheless it is possible to appreciate both, and during the earlier part of the year Paramartha and I saw nearly as many plays as films. The first play we saw was, I think, Webster's *The Duchess of Malfi*, which I had read in my teens, never imagining that I would ever see it actually performed. We went to see it with Vasumitra, and after the performance the three of us went round to the stage door to meet Harriet Walters, an old friend of Vasumitra's, who had taken the title role, and whom I had met once before. We also met Vasumitra's brother, who at very short notice had taken the leading male part. Subsequently we saw Chekhov's *The Cherry Orchard* at the Aldwych, Ibsen's *The Wild Duck* at the Phoenix, and Rowe's *The Tragedy of Jane Shore* – which I had also never imagined I would ever see performed – at a fringe theatre above a pub in Kentish Town, not far from the house (the ex-Suvrata's) in which our poetry group used to meet in 'the old days'. Finally, not much more than a week before leaving England, we saw Arthur Miller's *The Crucible* at the Royal National Theatre and Tennessee Williams's *A Streetcar Named Desire* at a fringe theatre in a very seedy, run-down part of North Clapham, not far from where I was born. Despite the rather equivocal sets, *The Crucible* came across as a very powerful play, and I felt at the end that the audience was applauding the play's 'message' as much as the actors' performance. As for *A Streetcar Named Desire*, since it was a fringe production I had consulted Jayamati, a former theatre director, before Paramartha and I went to see it. Was it true, I asked, that *Streetcar* was such an effective play that it communicated itself even through the most amateur performance? Jayamati replied that such was indeed the case, adding that the cast seemed to consist of senior drama students and that they would be sure to give an energetic performance. That they certainly did, and though the acting could have been more refined Paramartha and I not only enjoyed the play but came away as much impressed by Tennessee Williams's genius as we had been by Arthur Miller's.

All this time, except when we were out of London, Paramartha and I continued to follow our customary routine. In fact we each added to it. Paramartha supported Vasumitra's six-week city meditation course, then led two successive courses of his own. For my part, from mid-May I held a series of six Sunday evening question-and-answer meetings for all Order members within the East London region. These meetings, which temporarily superseded chapter meetings (though some chapters met for 'business' in the afternoon), took place in the shrine-room of the London Buddhist Centre, and I shall have something to say about them shortly. On most Saturday mornings in April, May, and June I sat for my portrait to Alison Harper, a Glaswegian Mitra connected with the London Buddhist Centre who had had exhibitions of her work in Glasgow and London. At the beginning of May Paramartha and I attended the Men's National Order Weekend, where I saw a few people, as indeed I had been doing every week in London. The two of us also watched the video of Dhardo Rimpoche's funeral and cremation, shot by someone who apparently had been a student of mine in Kalimpong. Watching the video was for me a moving experience, as I believe it also was for Paramartha.

There were two reasons for my holding the question-and-answer meetings. I wanted to have personal contact with Order members in the region 'collectively', and I wanted to ascertain the depth of their understanding of the Dharma. As already mentioned, the meetings took place in the shrine-room of the London Buddhist Centre. I led a sevenfold puja and a meditation (Paramartha had pointed out that there were new Order members who had never meditated with me); we adjourned to the reception area for tea; then having had tea we returned to the shrine-room and the questions and answers began. I had asked for questions to be pre-submitted in writing, and in the course of the six weeks I received some three dozen questions from twelve or thirteen Dharmacharis and one Dharmacharini. The questions related to such topics as Dzog-chen 'staring', idealism, visualization practice, jealousy, homosexuals as community members, awareness and negative emotions, marriage and the single-sex principle, 'questioning' Bhante's teaching, meditation and psychotherapy, the 'criteria' for Mitraship, and the education of children, and with some of these topics I chose to deal at length. One of the topics with which I so dealt was that of idealism, since I was dismayed to find that for many Order members in the region – and probably for many Mitras and Friends too – 'idealism' had become something of a dirty word. At the end of the six weeks I concluded that most Order members needed to study more and to reflect more on what they studied, i.e. needed more *śrutamayī-prajñā* and *cintamayī-prajñā* – not to mention more *bhāvanāmayī-prajñā*. Nonetheless, I was pleased with the meetings and with the happy and harmonious atmosphere that prevailed. At our final meeting I was presented with a rosary consisting of forty-nine lapis lazuli beads, one for each Order member in the region, plus a larger amber 'master' bead presumably representing myself.

Paramartha attended all the meetings except the last. Shortly before the last meeting he left for Leeds, to spend a few days with Jinaraja, and shortly after it Kulananda came and drove me up to Padmaloka, where I spent the rest of the week attending to administrative matters and making final arrangements for the journey to Spain. On the evening of Monday, 2 July, Paramartha having rejoined me at Padmaloka, Kovida drove my much-valued friend and myself down to London and the following morning drove us to Heathrow and saw us off.

PART 2

Now we are in Spain, at Guhyaloka, and as I observed at the beginning of this Letter we have been here for practically five weeks. Indeed, some days having passed since I started writing to you we have in fact been here for more than five weeks. For more than five weeks we have not stirred out of the magic Valley, though once or twice we have climbed up to the end of the Valley – a forty-minute walk from the bungalow – and looked eastward down through the haze at the distant white villas of the coastal plain and at the dark blue waters of the Mediterranean. For more than five weeks we have rested our eyes on the vivid green of pine and arbutus, and on the greyer green of holly oak or ilex, as well as on the mingled greens and greys and browns of rock rose, gorse, rosemary, fennel, lavender, and thyme. For more than five weeks we have breathed the healthful aromatic air of the Valley,

and felt its soft breezes on our cheek. For more than five weeks we
have enjoyed clear blue skies and hot sunshine, with only the occasional spell of cloudy or misty weather. For more than five weeks we
have heard few sounds other than the chirruping of birds, the sighing
of the wind, and the cracking of pine cones with, at night, the hooting
of the owls, the howling of the foxes, and the incessant chirr-chirr-chirr
of the cicadas. For more than five weeks we have, in fact, lived in a
kind of Buddha- or Bodhisattva-land, and I have more than once been
reminded of the description of Avalokiteshvara's abode in the *Ārya-
tārābhaṭṭārikānāmaṣṭottaraśatakastotra*.

1. The beautiful and delightful Potalaka is resplendent with various
   minerals,
   Covered with manifold trees and creepers, resounding with the
   sound of many birds,
2. And with murmur of waterfalls, thronged with wild beasts of many
   kinds;
   Many species of flowers grow everywhere,
3. And it is furnished with many savoury fruits; one hears there the
   humming of the bees,
   And the sweet songs of the Kinnaras; throngs of elephants
4. Frequent it by hosts of accomplished Holders of the magical lore,
   Gandharvas and sages free from passion....

Guhyaloka is certainly beautiful and delightful, and though it is not
exactly resplendent with various minerals it has grey limestone cliffs
on either side, as well as having the Lion's Head and other curious rock
formations. There are no waterfalls, but there are springs, and while
the Valley may not be thronged with wild beasts, herds of boar have
been known to come foraging for acorns. So far we have not heard the
song of the Kinnaras, though perhaps we would if we listened hard
enough; but we have heard the occasional threefold shout of 'Sadhu!'
from the retreat centre higher up the Valley. Throngs of elephants
certainly do not frequent Guhyaloka, though a black cat frequents the
bungalow and demands food and attention, neither are there any
hosts of accomplished Holders of the magical lore, Gandharvas, and
sages free from passion, though we have two or three people meditating in the solitary retreat huts. All the same, Guhyaloka *is* a kind of
Buddha- or Bodhisattva-land, and I am more glad to be here than I can
express.

Our day begins at dawn, though dawn comes rather late to Guhya-loka, partly on account of the mountains and partly because Spain does not observe Summer Time. I give Paramartha a call, and after he has done yoga for ten or twelve minutes we have a drink. While having our drink we tell each other our dreams, or as much of them as we can remember. Once I told Lokamitra that in at least one out of every three dreams I had I was in India, and this pattern still persists. In one out of every three dreams I am either visiting Kalimpong, or staying with bhikshus or lamas, or talking to Buddhist villagers. I even speak Hindi in these dreams, sometimes noticing (in the dream itself) that I am not so fluent as I used to be. In one dream somebody spoke to me in Marathi and I understood him. Having told each other our dreams, we make our way to the shrine-room, which stands amid pine trees about fifty yards up the path from the bungalow. Ten foot square, and like the bungalow painted white, with yellow doors and windows, it was formerly the generator shed; but last year I had the floor tiled, the roof repaired, and a door and windows put in, and now it serves us in the office of a shrine-room. Sitting inside, I can easily imagine that I am sitting in a sadhu's *kuti* somewhere in the Himalayas and that were I to step outside the door I should see the snow peaks. (Actually from the shrine-room steps there is a very fine view down through the Valley and over range upon range of mauve-blue mountains, while at night we can see the lights of Alicante twinkling fifteen or twenty miles away.) Usually we do a double meditation, with a few minutes' break at the end of the first session for us to stretch our limbs.

After meditation comes breakfast, which like all our meals we have on the veranda, and it is only towards the end of the meal that

> ... *down the cliffs afar*
> *Hyperion's march [we] spy, and glittering shafts of war.*

Only towards the end of breakfast does the sun rise above the mountains and, shooting his beams through the Valley, by degrees flood the veranda with golden light as we sit absorbed in our respective books. So far my reading has been mainly classical and Buddhist. First I read Plotinus' *Fourth Ennead*, dealing mainly with Soul or *psyche*, together with *Ennead V*, treatises 1–3, which are respectively entitled 'On the Three Primary Hypostases', 'On the Origin and Order of the Beings Which Come After the First', and 'On the Knowing Hypostases and That Which is Beyond'. As I read them, I marked those passages in which the teaching of the great Neoplatonist philosopher appeared to be similar to, or in harmony with, that of Buddhism. Between treatises I read Aeschylus' *Prometheus Bound*, in Philip Vellacott's (Penguin) translation, Charles Boer's superb new version of the *Homeric Hymns*, and Book Six of Virgil's *Aeneid* as translated by C. Day Lewis. Aeschylus was the first Greek dramatist I read, in Gilbert Murray's translation. I must have been twelve or thirteen (at the most) and I have never forgotten the impression made upon me by the Watchman's great opening speech in the *Agamemnon* or the arrival of the Oceanides in *Prometheus Bound*. From the Swinburnian rhythms of Gilbert Murray to the Poundian simplicities of Charles Boer is a big step. Nonetheless his sensitive and evocative renderings of the Homeric Hymns delighted me more than almost any other translations of poetry I have ever read, and I strongly recommend them to all lovers of poetry and lovers of the Greek myths. Reading them here in the magic Valley, it was as though Dionysus and Hermes were living presences who might at any moment emerge from the undergrowth or materialize out of the blue air.

My Buddhist reading has consisted mainly of Lobsang P. Lhalungpa's new translation of *The Life of Milarepa*, some suttas and Jataka stories, and Conze's *Buddhist Texts Through the Ages*. I read the *Jetsün-Kahbum* for the first time in 1946, when I was in Singapore and still in the army. I read it, of course, in the Dawa-Samdup / Evans-Wentz version, published as *Tibet's Great Yogi Milarepa*, and forty-four years later it was interesting to compare the new translation with the old. Though Lhalungpa's version may well be more accurate, the Dawa-Samdup / Evans-Wentz version is, frankly, more literary and goes more to the heart, especially in the case of the songs. Compare, for instance, their respective renderings of Milarepa's 'Song of what would constitute my Satisfactions' (Dawa-Samdup / Evans-Wentz) and 'Song on Fulfilment of My Aim' (Lhalungpa). I quote only the first two verses. The old version gives us:

My happiness unknown unto my relatives,
My sorrowing unknown unto my enemies –
Could thus I die, amid this Solitude,
Contented would I be, I the devotee.

My growing old unknown unto my betrothed,
My falling ill unknown unto my sister –
Could thus I die, amid this Solitude,
Contented would I be, I the devotee.

Whereas the new version gives us:

My happiness unknown to my relatives,
My misery unknown to my enemies,
If I could die in solitude,
The aim of this yogin will be fulfilled.

My growing old unknown to my friends,
My growing sick unknown to my sister,
If I could die in solitude,
The aim of this yogin will be fulfilled.

Lobsang P. Lhalungpa's translation of the text is preceded by an interesting Introduction in which he characterizes nirvāṇa (the lower case initial letter is his) as 'a subjective state of freedom', as compared to the Dharmakāya, which is thought of as 'expressing itself (in roughly equivalent Western terms, as "emanating") through all levels of cosmic reality, including both the material world and the realms of subtle reality.' The Dharmakāya is 'not only a "subjective" state (as in Hīnayāna Buddhism), but an ontological reality – *the* ontological reality' – a statement which is no doubt in need of further elucidation.

Since our arrival here I have also read James Hillman's *The Dream and the Underworld* and Knut Hamsun's *Mysteries* (a present from Ratnadharini), and have started rereading Hillman's *Re-Visioning Psychology*. As for Paramartha, while I have been immersed in Plotinus and Milarepa he has been no less immersed in the *Laṅkāvatāra Sūtra* and Suzuki's *Studies in the Laṅkāvatāra Sūtra*, with *Anna Karenina* and *Mysteries* for lighter reading.

At 11 o'clock we stop for a drink (we tend to drink more camomile tea than anything else) and perhaps discuss points arising out of the morning's reading. Paramartha then goes and does yoga for an hour and a half while I write up my dreams of the previous night, or continue to read, or write postcards or even the occasional letter. The room in which Paramartha does yoga was originally the garage. When I came out here in December 1986 (the time my prostate trouble started) it had been turned into the building team's kitchen and dining room; subsequently it became my study, and now, the floor having been tiled last year and the roof made watertight, it functions as Paramartha's yoga studio.

When he has finished doing yoga Paramartha prepares a light salad lunch (we are being provisioned by the retreat support team, consisting of Dharmabandhu, Sumitra, and Baladitya) and after lunch we sit out in the little clearing in front of the bungalow, or lie on the bungalow's flat roof, and sunbathe for an hour or more (we started with twenty minutes). Paramartha is now a beautiful golden brown, while I am probably browner than I have ever been in my life (in India, of course, one does *not* sunbathe). During the earlier part of the sun- bathing I read to Paramartha from the Romantic poets. Since I would rather read than listen, while he would rather listen than read, this arrangement suits us both. On one occasion, however, he read Rilke's 'The Spanish Trilogy' to me and on another Walt Whitman's 'Song of the Open Road'. At 3.30 we have a cup of tea and talk, sometimes discussing the poems I have read, after which Paramartha does prostrations for forty or forty-five minutes in the shrine-room while I read or write or wash the dishes. We then go down to the shower. This is situated in the lowest part of the Valley, almost directly below the bungalow. The quickest way of getting there is to plunge straight down the hillside, through the pine trees, following the precipitous little paths, which in a number of places are overgrown by bushes – some of them very thorny. Paramartha and I went this way only once, on the day after our arrival. Since then we have preferred to go the long way round, following first the main track through the Valley, then the much narrower track that branches off from it and leads directly to a small clearing that apparently was once an orchard. To one side of the clearing, amid the bushes and grasses, and with three or four enormous rock formations towering above it like so many drunken church steeples, stands the primitive open-air shower, consisting of no more than a few feet of piping. In a matter of seconds Paramartha and I have stripped and are standing beneath our respective nozzles. Very often the water is warm, even hot, the sun having been beating down on the supply pipe for some hours. The clearing is very quiet, even peaceful, and it feels wonderful to be in direct contact with all four elements at once: with water – the water in which we take our shower; with fire – the bright, hot sunshine; with air – the breeze that blows across the clearing; with earth – the earth, or at least the duckboard, beneath our feet....

From the shower we sometimes walk down to the lower spring, which is situated just within the boundary of Guhyaloka. To reach it one leaves the main track and follows a little path that eventually loses itself among the long grasses of a neglected apple orchard. At the far end of the orchard, flanked by brambles and overhung by massive rock formations, is the spring. Three spouts project from the rough cement, and from the spouts water pours into a stone trough, not unlike an old-fashioned English horse trough, running thence into a narrow channel that carries it far down the Valley. What with the silence, and the comparative gloom, the spring is

A savage place! as holy and enchanted
As e'er beneath a waning moon was haunted
By woman wailing for her demon-lover!

Except that it is wild rather than savage, and whether beneath a waning or a waxing moon, it is easier to imagine it as being haunted by the nymphs and satyrs of classical myth and legend than by the demon lovers of Gothic romance. (The only demons that are known to haunt the place are the campers who leave plastic containers and other rubbish behind them.) In the course of my last two visits to the magic Valley, in connection with the 1987 and 1988 Guhyaloka ordination retreats, the spring was a favourite spot of mine, and Prasanna-siddhi and I often came here. On both these visits I felt as though the Valley was situated not in Spain at all but in Greece, and in Ancient Greece at that, and sitting in the shade of the spring it was not difficult for me to imagine that the latter was haunted not by nymphs and satyrs, even, but by the Muses themselves. Indeed, I planned to write a long narrative poem on the subject of Orpheus, a poem that would begin with my falling asleep at the spring and having a vision of Calliope, the Muse of epic poetry and mother of Orpheus.

On this present visit I feel as though the Valley is situated in India rather than in Greece, and that I am living in one of the sacred mountains of South India (the Potalaka is traditionally located somewhere in the South), in a cave on the slopes of one of which I indeed once stayed for six weeks, more than forty years ago. This feeling of being in India is enhanced by the fact that we spend the greater part of our day out of doors, that we wear a minimum of clothing, and that much of our time is devoted to study and meditation and (in Param-artha's case) to yoga and prostrations. It has also been enhanced by the fact that I have written an article about someone who spent the greater part of his life in India. I shall tell you about this article later on.

By the time we get back to the bungalow after our shower it is 5.15 or 5.30, depending on whether or not we have visited the spring. Paramartha does yoga for fifteen or twenty minutes, after which we have our evening meal. This is brought down from the retreat centre by two blue-robed, shaven-headed figures whom we do not always recognize immediately and with whose 'virginal new names' we have to familiarize ourselves. The blue-robed figures are, of course, newly ordained members of the Western Buddhist Order, Subhuti and Suvajra having ordained fifteen men about a month before Paramartha and I arrived in the Valley. Apart from when they bring down our meal I have had no personal contact with the new Order members, though Paramartha has been for walks with four or five of them. I have, however, seen Suvajra, and I am hoping to see Subhuti before he leaves for Valencia at the end of the retreat. Suvajra had just returned from the UK, having spent two weeks there with his mother while she was undergoing medical treatment, and he came down to the bungalow with a magnificent present in the form of the thirty-two volumes of the Handy Volume Issue of the *Encyclopaedia Britannica* (eleventh edition). After the meal we generally read until it is time for us to report-in to each other, which we do over a drink. Paramartha then meditates, and if I am not too tired I join him. On our emerging from the shrine-room there is sometimes a moon in the sky and if it is a clear night, as it usually is, the floor of heaven will be 'thick inlaid with patines of bright gold.'

The article to which I referred was on Anagarika Dharmapala. A few weeks before leaving England I had a visit from Venerable Vajiranana, a Sinhalese monk, at present incumbent of the Chiswick Vihara, who was one of the two Theravāda bhikshus present on the occasion of the first ordinations into the WBO. He came with a message, he said. The message was from the Trustees of the Maha Bodhi Society of Ceylon. Next year they would be celebrating their centenary, and in this connection were planning to bring out a special souvenir volume. Would I contribute an article on Anagarika Dharmapala? Having reflected for a moment I agreed, and after we had reminisced about common friends now dead Venerable Vajiranana departed well pleased with the success of his mission. Two weeks after the arrival of Paramartha and myself at Guhyaloka, therefore, I set to work. Dharmapala was, of course, the founder of the Maha Bodhi Society and resuscitator of Bodh-Gaya, and had led a very busy life, as I well knew from the writing of my *Anagarika Dharmapala: A Biographical Sketch* in 1952. Thinking that there would be more than enough people to write about his material achievements I decided to concentrate on the spiritual dimension of the man, as exemplified by his recognition that the Buddha was the only refuge, his aspiration to ethical and spiritual perfection, his inclination to the mystic, ascetic life, his devotion to meditation, his observance of the *brahmacarya* vow, his adoption of the homeless life, and his gift for friendship. Though the subject was familiar to me, and though I reread my *Biographical Sketch* (as did Paramartha), I did not find the article easy to write. In fact I was working on it for three weeks. During that time I was quite immersed in my material, and talked to Paramartha at length not only about Dharmapala and the Maha Bodhi Society but about people I had known in India and about the kind of life I had led there. I became very aware that in India, even now, the individual spiritual life has a traditional underpinning that is almost entirely lacking in the West. I also became more aware of the intensity of Dharmapala's idealism and reflected, rather ruefully, on the fact that there were Order members for whom 'idealism' had become something of a dirty word. I even wondered if my own youthful idealism might not have become a little tarnished by its prolonged exposure to the hateful materialism, cynicism, scepticism, and indifferentism of the West and resolved that after my return to England in September I would be more than ever on my guard against such a possibility.

Which brings me to the future.

PART 3

In four or five weeks' time Paramartha and I will be going to Madrid, mainly for the sake of the Prado, and from Madrid to Toledo, Seville, Cordoba, Granada, and other places, taking in all about two weeks. On 20 September we fly to Heathrow, where we will be met by Kovida or Prasannasiddhi and be driven straight up to Padmaloka. Two days later I shall give a reading of my selection of poems on friendship at the Norwich Buddhist Centre and a week after that, on Sunday, 30 September, I shall have my official birthday, the 'loves that be' having informed me that my having an official birthday on that date would be more convenient than my having the real one on 26 August. Where and how I shall have my official birthday I do not know, nor do I know whether I am to have an official birthday every year from now on; but I am sure that the loves that be have matters well in hand and that many pleasant surprises are in store for me. I must admit, though, that I am rather hoping for an official birthday cake and an official launching of at least two or three official new publications.

On or about 11 November I shall be going to the United States for three weeks, with Prasannasiddhi, and Paramartha to Nepal and India for a month, with Jinaraja. I shall be staying at Aryaloka, and look forward to meeting our many American friends, some of whom I have already met in England. After rejoining forces, Paramartha and I will again be in London, where I hope to finish writing the first part of my second volume of memoirs, as well as to write papers or prepare talks for the first anniversary of Dhardo Rimpoche's death, for FWBO and/or WBO Day, and for the Order Convention. Towards the end of the year, all being well, I shall go to India for a couple of months with Paramartha, visiting Bombay, Poona, Nagpur, Agra, Delhi, and, perhaps, the Punjab. This may well be my last major Indian tour. By the time I get back to England it will be eighteen months from the time of my writing this Letter, and it is hardly necessary for me to look further ahead. In any case, in telling you about my plans for the future I am not venturing any predictions, as I have already said. Plans are only provisional. I may not live long enough even to go to Madrid. Nonetheless, I hope I live long enough to see you all again, whether in England, or the United States, or India, or wherever else you happen to be.

So much, then, for the past, the present, and the future. So much for the last year or so, for the last five weeks and more, and for the next eighteen months. I am glad that I have been able to finish this Letter and that in the next issue of *Shabda* there will be a complete Letter from me for you all to read. Though I have tried to be brief, it has turned out to be considerably longer than I had expected. Even so, much has been omitted. I have said nothing about Vanessa Redgrave's amazing performance in Martin Sherman's *A Madhouse in Goa*, which Paramartha and I saw in June last year; nothing about my sixty-fourth birthday 'party' at Padmaloka, when the Order Office community presented me with an 'Indian lotus tree' tea-and-dinner service for use at the Sukhavati flat, and nothing about the visit Paramartha and I paid to Canterbury and Herne Bay in March or April. I have also said much less than I would have liked about the books that I have read. And of course I have said very little about my more personal thoughts and reflections. Nonetheless, I hope this 'Letter from Spain' will be of interest to you. I am glad I could write to you from the magic Valley – glad and grateful. I am grateful to all those whose generosity, five years ago, made the purchase of Guhyaloka possible. I am grateful to Subhuti for masterminding the project. I am grateful to Dharmabandhu and the other members of the support team for provisioning

Paramartha and me, and for rendering a dozen other services. I am grateful to the newly ordained Order members for cooking for us each day. Finally, I am grateful to Paramartha for giving me his companionship in the magic Valley and for being, here as elsewhere, what only a friend can be.

Urgyen Sangharakshita

Fourth Letter from London

Sixty-fifth birthday – journey to Madrid – Puerta del Sol – the Prado – the paintings in Museo del Prado – Monasterio de San Lorenzo del Escorial – Palace of Philip II – Museum of the Royal Academy of Fine Arts – Toledo – the church of Santo Tomé – El Greco's The Burial of Count Orgaz – Toledo Cathedral – Museo de Santa Cruz and El Grecos – El Greco's house – Tránsito Synagogue – Monastery of San Juan de los Reyes – train to Cordoba – Cordoba – the Mezquita – the statue of Averroës – eating in Cordoba – Alcázar de los Reyes Cristianos, or 'Alcázar of the Christian Monarchs' – Seville – Cathedral of Santa Maria de la Sede – Torre del Oro – statue of the poet Bécquer – Palacio Español – Museo de Bellas Artes – Don Juan – Granada – the Alhambra – the Alcazaba – Casa Real – the palace gardens of the Generalife – Royal Chapel – Granada Cathedral – Paseo de los Tristes – Convento de San Jeronimo – Hospital de San Juan de Dios – the Cartuja – journey to Murcia – Murcia Cathedral Museum – Murcia Cathedral – zoo – Alicante – Villajoyosa – Sella – reflections on Spain and the Spanish

Dear Dharmacharis and Dharmacharinis,

The dateline is Sukhavati, Thursday, 28 September. Paramartha and I have been back at the flat for three days, back in England for a week, and more than seven weeks have passed since, sitting on the veranda of my bungalow at Guhyaloka, I started writing my 'Letter from Spain'. It is 8 o'clock on a mild, cloudy evening. Paramartha has gone to see a friend, while I am sitting in the study listening once again to the soft hissing of the gas fire and thinking, this time, that I ought to tell you about our two-week sightseeing tour of six or seven Spanish cities before impressions start to fade or become obscured by subsequent impressions. But first I must tell you how we spent the four-and-a-half weeks after I started writing my 'Letter from Spain' and before we exchanged the quiet and seclusion of the magic Valley for the noise and relative congestion of the tourist trail.

Not that there is really much to tell. We continued to follow the same daily routine as during the first five weeks, the principal difference being that I now spent more time writing (writing my 'Letter from Spain', that is) and less time reading, though even so I managed to read Ellmann's *Yeats: The Man and the Masks* and most of the essays and articles in Kathleen Raine's *Defending Ancient Springs*. There was also a change of weather; for a few days it was cold and cloudy, with a little rain, and we were unable to go down to the shower. As the time for our tour approached we started dipping into travel books about Spain, while Paramartha also read a couple of volumes on Spanish history, besides keeping up with his study of the *'White Lotus of the True Law' Sūtra* – on which he had started after finishing the *Laṅkāvatāra* – and of the *Survey*. I felt quite exhilarated by the prospect of seeing more of Spain and visiting such places as Toledo, Cordoba, and Granada, hitherto familiar to me only from books, and visions of gilded retables, Moorish arches, and lofty steeples started to rise before my mind's eye. Paramartha, who had visited Toledo and Granada before, was rather more phlegmatic. I did, however, read him a few of Longfellow's poems on Spanish themes, that neglected bard having been added to the (Romantic) poets from whom I read to Parmartha after lunch along with Milton, Dryden, Gray, Campbell, and Tennyson. One of the poems was 'Torquemada', a narrative poem in which a pious Catholic father not only denounces his two heretical daughters to the Inquisition but actually brings the fuel for their burning and sets light to it with his own hand. Torquemada, the Grand Inquisitor, commends his piety. He is a true son of the Church. Another poem, a poem of reminiscence whose title I have forgotten, consisted of a series of romantic pen-pictures of places in Spain that Longfellow himself had visited – among them places that we too were hoping to see.

A week before we set out on our travels, on Sunday, 26 August, I had my sixty-fifth birthday. This was my actual birthday, as distinct from the official birthday which I shall be having here in London in a few days' time. Since it was only my actual birthday I had not expected the day to be marked by any particular observance, but in the event this was not quite the case. As I wrote to Prasannasiddhi five days later:

'Not much has happened since I last wrote to you. I have written a long letter to *Shabda* and had my sixty-fifth birthday, and that is about all. Five or six more cards did reach me before 26 August, and on the morning of the day itself there was a home-made card (with cherubs) and a poem from Paramartha. Later on a little procession, headed by Dharmavira, came down from the retreat centre bearing, respectively, cards, a cake, a bunch of flowers, and a basket of fruit. Paramartha also managed to get hold of some low-alcohol lager. So I had quite a good birthday, and am wondering what the 'official' celebration on 30 August will be like. No doubt you will give me a hint of what to expect.' As it happened, Prasannasiddhi was not in a position to give me any such hint. Neither he nor anyone in the Order Office seemed to know what form my official birthday was to take. All I know is that I am to arrive at the City University, Northampton Square, at 3 o'clock, though I gather that Subhuti will give a talk and Nagabodhi launch two new publications. Oh yes, I am also to read a few of my poems!

Two days after I had written to Prasannasiddhi, on Monday, 3 September, exactly two calendar months after our arrival in Spain, Dharmavira collected Paramartha and me from the bungalow and drove us to Benidorm. We left Guhyaloka at 7.15, when day had not yet fully dawned in the magic Valley. On our way down to Sella I noticed that the road had been widened during the last two years and a further section of it surfaced. This made the trip between Guhyaloka and Sella less difficult for vehicle and passengers alike, not to mention the driver. It also meant that the Guhyaloka community was less likely to be cut off by landslides after heavy rain. But I could not help wondering whether this increased accessibility would not result in Guhyaloka losing something of the isolation and the seclusion that were among its greatest assets. At Finistrat, an overgrown, touristified village between Sella and Benidorm, we stopped for breakfast at a bar known to Dharmavira. However, the place had only just opened, the floor was covered with cigarette ends and other litter, and all we could get was coffee and yesterday's croissants. It was a rather sordid start to what I had hoped would be a romantic journey. Half an hour later we were in Benidorm, which seemed to have sprouted a hundred more pink and biscuit-coloured high-rise buildings since I was last there. After the three of us had had a second breakfast, Paramartha and I wandered round a vast, surrealistically-modern shopping precinct looking for an English newspaper or news magazine. A day or two earlier Paramartha had bumped into Vajrananda, then newly arrived in the Valley to do building work, and from him learned of the invasion of Kuwait a month ago, and we wanted to catch up with what had been happening in the world. After a brief search we found a copy of the current edition of *Time* and an hour or so later, having already said goodbye to Dharmavira, we boarded the No.1 Benidorm–Madrid coach. We did not board it without incident. Dharmavira had bought our tickets two days before, but apparently there had been a double booking (bookings were all computerized) and there was much talking and gesticulating and scratching of heads and consulting of passenger lists before we could enter the vehicle. On this occasion, at least, the fact that neither of us spoke any Spanish was perhaps an advantage; we simply stood there without saying anything until the hubbub subsided and we were allowed to get on board and take our seats.

But though there may have been a double booking, Spanish motor transport was punctual, and at 10 o'clock the coach nosed its way through the traffic and was soon on the motorway and heading south. Paramartha immersed himself in *Time*, while I was content simply to observe the rapidly changing landscape. Having by-passed Alicante, we swung inland and before long were in the neighbourhood of Novelda, a small town that I had visited with Subhuti and where we have a few Friends, including Xavi Alongia, our Spanish publisher. It was a region of brown, scarred hills and unsightly industrialization the bleak monotony of which was relieved only by the occasional vineyard or still more occasional crenellated hilltop fort. Once we passed a white-walled columbarium from which rose the black spires of cypresses. There was very little traffic on the road. At 11.30, an hour and a half after our leaving Benidorm, a signboard indicated that we had left the province of Valencia and were entering that of Castilla-La Mancha. La Mancha! We were in Don Quixote country, for was not the Knight of the Rueful Countenance surnamed de la Mancha, and had not he and his faithful Sancho Panza traversed on horse and mule respectively the vast steppes over which I was now moving so quickly and so comfortably? Comfortably, that is, except for the cacophony that was assaulting our ears from the TV loudspeakers and which the imaginative Don himself could not have mistaken for music. At 11.40, when we had passed fields of maize and blackened sunflowers, came what I believe the Northamericans (as the Spanish insist on calling them) term a comfort stop. Paramartha and I got out and comforted ourselves. Thereafter we passed through a flattish, empty region the soil of which showed first red then orange. After a while wood-covered hills appeared, and there was an increase of traffic. Suddenly a fort rose up on the right, towering above the village at its foot. Nearby were cave dwellings, as well as holes in the rock that could well have been dwellings once upon a time. From then onwards the terrain was quite flat. Occasional groves of pine were succeeded by vineyards (the vines, I noticed, were not supported on trellises as in Valencia); then came umbrella pines, such as I had seen lining the road between Pisa and Grosseto, as well as poplars and olives. On the top of a solitary hill stood four whitewashed windmills; not much remained of their sails, as though they had got the worst of an encounter with the valiant Don Quixote. At 2.30 we passed through a town where there was a signpost pointing to Toboso and an advertisement for Dulcinea chocolates. The country after that had a more prosperous look, with whitewashed farmsteads nestling at intervals amidst extensive vineyards. Gradually the traffic became more dense; there were houses, small factories, hoardings.... Eventually, strung out along the distant skyline, appeared the high-rise buildings that betokened Madrid. It was strange to see a great capital city rising up 'like an exhalation' in the midst of nowhere.

Shortly after 5 o'clock we descended from the coach into the heat and exhaust fumes of the crowded bus station. We had been on the road for seven hours instead of for the five that Dharmavira had been informed the journey would take. Our first concern was to get our bearings. This we did with the help of a map and the barman in the bar where we stopped for a drink, and before long we had dived into the nearest Metro station and were on our way to the Puerta del Sol, considered the theoretical centre of Madrid and indeed of Spain, where Paramartha had stayed on his previous visit and which was only three stations up the line. The train was quite full, the passengers being mostly short and dark and apparently on their way home from work (Paramartha has just suggested that they may have been going *to* work, Spanish working hours being different from our own). On our emerging into the sunlight of the Plaza Puerta del Sol the first thing I saw was a group of elderly women selling lottery tickets. We were to see – *and* hear – these sellers of lottery tickets, both male and female, wherever we went in Spain; most of them were blind, the blind apparently having a virtual monopoly of the business. From the Plaza we combed the adjacent streets for a suitable hostel and eventually settled on one quite near the Plaza itself called the Maria del Mar, where we secured a reasonably quiet room on the third floor, overlooking the street.

Having unpacked our holdalls – we had decided to travel light – and had a short rest we sallied forth and, after an expensive glass of mineral water in a flashy bar that we decided not to patronize again, went in search of the vegetarian restaurant we had been told was situated 'behind the Prado'. On the way we bought a guide to Madrid and the surrounding area with a map which, as it turned out, was not particularly helpful. Since our information regarding the vegetarian restaurant was not very precise we had great difficulty finding the place; in fact, we trudged up and down the shabby streets 'behind the Prado' for nearly an hour before coming across it, and when we did so it was not due to open for another hour, at 8.30. We therefore retired to a nearby bar and passed the time drinking coffee and talking. In the event Biotica, as the restaurant was called, proved a great disappointment. The food was of the most basic 'vegetarian' type conceivable: boiled rice, boiled vegetables, and boiled lentils without any seasoning – though I *did* enjoy the iced beetroot soup with which my own meal started. So far as vegetarianism was concerned Madrid seemed to be living in the Dark Ages. Having walked back to the hostel we reported-in to each other and, despite the noise from the street below, eventually slept.

Our first full day in Madrid was devoted mainly to the Prado. Indeed it was in order to see the Prado – in Paramartha's case to see it for the second time – that we were in Madrid at all. But first came breakfast, which we had in an old-fashioned (i.e. relatively quiet and roomy) bar Paramartha had discovered on his previous visit where one could sit in the window and watch the passers-by. The breakfast consisted of *churros*, a kind of fritter, and hot chocolate (one dipped the *churros* in the chocolate, which was very thick and very sweet), washed down by tea in my case and black coffee in Paramartha's. Thus refreshed, we proceeded up the Calle de San Jerónimo to the Paseo del Prado, on the way passing or seeing in the distance a number of fine buildings that – with the broad boulevards and magnificent fountains – gave the impression that Madrid was a real capital city and that *here* was its actual centre. On our arrival at the Museo del Prado itself we found the place not very crowded and spent some four hours wandering from room to room, with a coffee break half-way through in the cafeteria, where we also had lunch afterwards. Some of the rooms were closed, but even so there was plenty for us to see and we managed to view paintings by all the artists (all the artists represented in the Prado, that is) in whose work one or both of us were particularly interested:

El Greco, Zurbarán, Velasquez, Goya, Botticelli, Titian, Tintoretto, Poussin, Lorrain, and Bosch. The individual painting before which we spent most time was undoubtedly Velasquez's *Las Meninas*, to which no reproduction does anything like justice, though we also lingered over such masterpieces as Bosch's *The Garden of Earthly Delights* and El Greco's *The Baptism of Christ* and *The Resurrection of Christ*. Rubens I am afraid we neglected, Goya proved on the whole disappointing, while as for Picasso's *Guernica*, exhibited in a separate section behind a bullet-proof screen, neither of us felt the least inclination to see it (I had in any case seen it in New York in 1970). Some of the paintings we saw were of interest to us as much on account of their subject matter as for their purely artistic qualities. Such were Berruguete's *Auto da Fe*, depicting St Dominic presiding over the burning of two heretics, the saint seated aloft and the heretics bound naked to stakes below; Brueghel's *The Triumph of Death*, described by one guidebook as 'one of the most frightening pictures ever painted', and the three (out of an original series of four) panels by Botticelli illustrating the story of Nastagio degli Onesti from the *Decameron*, Dryden's vigorous poetical version of which I had read to Paramartha during one of our sun-bathing sessions a few weeks earlier. But it is quite impossible for me to give a proper account of what we saw or even of our impressions of what we saw (Paramartha might in any case give a different account). Having had our rather late lunch and bought a few picture postcards we left the Prado a little dazed by our exposure to so much great art and feeling that we had a lot to reflect on and assimilate.

The process of reflection and assimilation started quite soon. On a sort of traffic island not far from the Prado we found a kiosk-type bar with a 'garden', and in this 'garden', where two workmen were fast asleep on chairs, we had afternoon tea and discussed some of the paintings we had seen. Among these was *Las Meninas*, which had made a strong impression on both of us. Tea and discussion over, we walked back to the hostel, where we rested and read *The European*, *Time*, and *Newsweek*. At 6.30 we went out again. This time our objective was Booksellers SA, the English bookshop, about which I had read in *The Rough Guide*. To get to it we had to take the Metro to Iglesia and then walk for a couple of miles through a busy, rather upmarket area. Booksellers SA proved almost as great a disappointment as Biotica. I had hoped to find English versions of Spanish classics, but all that was available was a translation of Calderón's *La Vida Sueño*, or 'Life is a Dream', which I had long wanted to read, and for this I was sufficiently grateful. Retracing our steps, we spent some time at a pavement café over a drink and then had a vegetarian pizza at a pizzeria near the Metro station (pizzerias were to be our salvation in more than one Spanish city). Like practically all the bars and restaurants we patronized on our tour, the place was extremely noisy – so noisy we could hardly hear ourselves speak. Moreover, there was only one waiter for about twenty tables, and the pace at which he was having to work was clearly doing his nerves no good. Whenever he had a spare second he took a drag at a cigarette or gulped down a mouthful of wine. Our pizzas were up to standard, however, and I had my first *horchata*, a milky drink made from tigernuts that I rather liked (Paramartha was not so keen on it). From Iglesia we walked all the way back to Puerta del Sol and our hostel where, on passing through the lounge to get to our room (the place was a bit warren-like), we found the ten-year-old son of the establishment still curled up in front of the TV set, where he seemed to spend most of his time.

Anyone who knows anything at all about English history must have heard about the Spanish Armada, most of those who know about the Spanish Armada have probably heard of Philip II, and most of those who know about Philip II have probably heard of the Escorial, the monastery-palace-mausoleum built by that monarch in the latter half of the sixteenth century. Paramartha and I spent the best part of our second full day in Madrid visiting the Escorial. Leaving the Maria del Mar at 8.30, we walked to the Estacion de Atocha, which Paramartha knew from his previous visit. On our arrival there we received a shock. The station was in process of demolition, all that was left of the enormous structure being an empty shell surrounded by several acres of rubble. Fortunately the rather modernistic new station had been built not far from the old and we reached it just in time to catch the train. The journey lasted for more than an hour, and took us through a dozen little stations, all either new or renovated. At first the country was wooded, but after a few miles it became more arid and in the distance the sierras appeared. Shortly before reaching our destination we saw on the hillside a few miles away an enormous cross. Somehow it had a sinister look, and I realized that here was the Valle de los Caidos or 'Valley of the Fallen', and that the cross surmounted the huge underground basilica containing the remains of 'the heroes and martyrs of the Civil War' (thus the guidebook) – and of General Franco.

El Escorial was, we found, not only the name of the railway station but also of the town that had sprung up on the slope below the monastery-palace-mausoleum, which was situated on a spur of the Sierra de Guadarrama. Outside the station we caught the shuttle bus, which took us up to the centre of the town by a series of hairpin bends, depositing us a few hundred yards from the 'Monasterio de San Lorenzo del Escorial', to give Philip II's creation its full name. Whether on account of the altitude, or the smart new villas, or the beautiful flowering trees and shrubs, or tourism both native and foreign, there was a light-hearted, holiday atmosphere about the little town that was quite exhilarating. There was nothing light-hearted about the Escorial itself, however. Though certainly impressive, the enormous granite building, with its spire-crowned corner towers and 680-foot west façade, was severe almost to the point of bleakness, it indeed having been described as looking more like a prison than a palace. The interior was hardly less severe than the exterior, the vast courtyards and lofty, vaulted corridors through which we passed being adorned only with a few gigantic statues and some rather poor frescoes. Perhaps the most attractive part of the complex was the library, which we visited first. The frescoes on the barrel vault and between the windows represented the seven Liberal Arts, as well as various poets and philosophers, while down the middle of the apartment ran a series of showcases containing, among other treasures, some splendidly executed Arabic manuscripts, an illuminated bible the lettering of which was entirely in gold, and St Teresa's personal diary. As for the carved and gilded bookshelves, with their Doric columns, I noticed that the thousands of huge volumes they contained all had their gilt edges turned *outwards*, so that the sides of the apartment appeared to be lined with gleaming gold. We also visited the huge domed basilica at the rear of the complex, the octagonal crypt containing the black-and-brown marble tombs of several dozen Spanish monarchs in niches round the wall (kings on the left, queens on the right), and the eighteenth-century Royal Palace, which according to *The Rough Guide* was 'stuffed with treasures' but which we found to consist of a range of poorly furnished rooms decorated with even poorer frescoes (or was it tapestries?).

The apartments in which we spent most time were the sacristy and the chapter rooms, for it was here that most of the Escorial's paintings were to be found. These included works by El Greco, Ribera, Zurbarán, Velasquez, Titian, and Bosch. The first painting we saw, and the one that probably impressed me most, was El Greco's *The Martyrdom of St Maurice*, which the artist painted for Philip II but which the king did not like. Among the other paintings by El Greco were the highly contrasted *St Peter* and *St Ildefonso* – each a striking representation of its subject. Rather to our astonishment, we came across Bosch's *The Garden of Earthly Delights*, which we had already seen in the Prado, though whether it was a copy and, if so, whether it was from the hand of the Dutch master himself, was not clear. (In the course of our tour we were to discover that quite a few well known paintings had as it were duplicated themselves, some of them several times – rather like holy relics.) There were also a number of paintings by Titian, most of them quite dark compared with those in the Prado, which had prob-ably been cleaned. The rest of the Escorial's collection was contained in the suite of comparatively small rooms that comprised the Palace of Philip II, to which there was a staircase from the (Bourbon) Royal Palace. It was here that the Catholic monarch had planned the dispatch of the invincible Armada, here that he had received news of its defeat, and here that he had died. His chair, his canopied bed, and his desk, were still preserved *in situ*. The paintings themselves were all small, as befitted the dimensions of the rooms, but of the finest quality, and included works by Titian and Bosch. After looking at them in a less leisurely fashion than I would have liked (this was a part of the Escorial that one had to see in convoy) I cast a quick look out of the window at the courtyard below, where there was a very green formal garden with mazes and flower beds. How many times, I reflected, must King Philip have risen from his desk, walked to the window, and looked down at that garden! On the other hand, he may have been quite indifferent to nature. One did not know.

Feeling a little tired after being on our feet for so long and seeing so much, we had a drink in a wainscoted recess in the rather gloomy, tunnel-like cafeteria and left the Escorial to go in search of lunch. This we eventually found in a quiet, rather upmarket pizzeria, and after a leisurely meal we walked to the bus stop and took the shuttle down to the station. The train was delayed, however, and we did not reach Atocha until 4.30 – an hour later than we had expected. Our plan was to visit the Museum of America, as I was keen to see its collection of pre-Columbian art. Having had a wash and brush-up at our hostel we therefore took the Metro to Moncloa, which was six stations up the line and as far out on the system as we had been. According to the guide-book, 'Madrid displays a majestic suburban character in this particular area.' I could see what the writer meant. We were on the edge of the University City, huge government buildings were very much in evi-dence, and there was a 100-foot high Arco de la Victoria or 'Victory

Arch' which had been erected in homage to the Spanish Army in 1956 and which, the guidebook assured us, was 'very impressive'. Having taken what we thought was a short cut through West Park, and having passed beneath some *really* impressive trees, we found ourselves opposite the Museum of America. Unfortunately, we were on the wrong side of the road, which apparently had been widened and along which the traffic was hurtling at an alarming rate. Eventually we managed to cross, and after climbing up a grassy bank, walking across a rather elegant bridge, and making our way up a winding road, we found ourselves outside the museum. It was closed. In fact it was closed for restoration, as the heaps of sand and cement sufficiently attested, and apparently had been closed for four or five months. Indeed the whole surrounding area seemed to be undergoing a facelift.

Retracing our steps across the bridge and traversing the Plaza de la Moncloa we walked down a busy commercial street lined with orange trees to the Plaza de España and from there to the Plaza Mayor. On the way we passed the monument to Cervantes, which despite its size was dwarfed by the adjacent skyscrapers. Our idea was to have dinner at one of the restaurants in the Plaza Mayor before returning to the Maria del Mar for the night, but though we walked twice round the arcades surrounding the magnificent seventeenth-century square, where heretics had been burned, we were unable to find a single restaurant with a vegetarian option on its menu. In the end we contented ourselves with a toasted sandwich at a bar in a nearby lane. Here we witnessed an amusing yet, at the same time, saddening incident. An elderly woman sitting with her husband at a nearby table, just within the row of potted plants that marked off the bar's frontage, had a little dog at her feet. When a middle-aged man passed by with an Alsatian on a lead the little dog started yapping furiously. The Alsatian responded with a louder, deeper bark and did its best to get at the little dog, who yapped more furiously than ever, thus further exciting the Alsatian. The little dog's owner shouted to the owner of the Alsatian to take his dog away, while the owner of the Alsatian shouted to the woman to stop *her* dog yapping. Within minutes a violent altercation had arisen and the two respectable-looking people were hurling abuse at each other while their respective dogs, now thoroughly aroused, showed every sign of wanting to get at each other's throats. Eventually the middle-aged man dragged his Alsatian away, hurling a parting insult at the elderly woman over his shoulder as he did so, and the fracas subsided. The woman's husband, I observed, took no part in the dispute, and indeed seemed not to notice it. The five Japanese tourists at the next table were quite alarmed, however, and some of them vacated their seats until the Alsatian had been dragged away. I wondered what they thought of the manners of Europeans.

The following day we spent the morning – our last morning in Madrid – visiting the Museum of the Royal Academy of Fine Arts, which occupied a Churrigueresque building not far from the Plaza Puerta del Sol. The collection was a very mixed one, containing not only paintings by a variety of artists, mainly Spanish and Italian, but also some very choice Chinese and Ancient Egyptian *objets d'art*. What drew my eyes most was El Greco's *St Jerome* (this may not have been the painting's full title) and Zurbarán's full-length portraits of five white-robed monks of the Merced order, an order I had not heard of before. Perhaps the most famous painting in the collection, and the only one from it to feature in our guide to Madrid, was Goya's *The Burial of the Sardine*; but much as I relished its satire I liked it rather less than I did some of the paintings by Ribera, Cano, Carreño, Callejo, and other Spanish artists whose work I was beginning to appreciate. The most striking object in the Museum, however, and one that it was difficult to miss, since its *disjecta membra* were scattered among a number of rooms, was an extremely realistic polychrome *Massacre of the Innocents* by the sculptor José Gines. So realistic was it that it was hardly possible to view the savage, brutal features of the Roman soldiers or the demented expressions of the bereaved mothers without a shudder. The Chinese *objets d'art* consisted mainly of carvings in jade and cloisonné ware – the latter items being all in bird form. All the Ancient Egyptian *objets d'art*, on the other hand, were in the form of cats and cat-headed divinities. Who had been responsible for assembling *this* part of the Museum's collection, I wondered.

Having packed our holdalls and paid the bill for our three nights at the Maria del Mar, we took the Metro to the bus station and caught the 12 o'clock coach to Toledo. It was an uneventful journey, lasting not much more than an hour, at the end of which time we found ourselves in Toledo bus station – and a long way from the centre of the city. As *The Rough Guide* warned, many towns in Spain still had no main bus station, so that buses left from a variety of places, and where a new bus terminal *had* been built it was often on the outer fringes of town. The truth of these words was brought home to us as, in the hot midday sun, we toiled up the road that led to the heart of the old walled city which, like Siena, was situated on a hill and overlooked a river. Only later did we learn there was a local bus we could have taken. The heart of the old walled city was the Plaza de Zocodover, and into this we emerged about three-quarters of an hour after leaving the terminal. On one side of the plaza there was a row of restaurants and bars, the white tables and blue umbrellas of which extended out into the square itself. At one of these tables we sat and had a low alcohol lager and a toasted sandwich, and Paramartha recalled his previous visit. We then went in search of a hostel. Our search took us through streets lined with souvenir shops where one could buy anything from a damascened paper knife to a full suit of armour, up and down narrow, precipitous lanes, and into blind alleys and deserted squares, but no suitable hostel could we find. Eventually, when we had crossed from one side of the city to the other, and had almost decided to retrace our steps and start all over again, we saw in what turned out to be the medieval Jewish quarter a red-tiled, biscuit-coloured building with the sign 'Hotel Pintor El Greco'. Though it looked a little expensive (by our standards), we decided to see if they had a room; they did have, and we took it – and did not regret it. As soon as we had unpacked and had a shower we were out again. Our first stop was the church of Santo Tomé, which was less than half a mile away and which we had already passed on our way down to the hotel. In the church there was a chapel, and in the chapel, above the altar, was El Greco's *The Burial of Count Orgaz*, probably his most famous painting and the one that the guidebooks invariably described as his masterpiece. The chapel had only just opened, and there were not many people standing before the painting, so that we could see it without much difficulty. In fact after a while we were able to sit on the bench immediately in front of it and study it at our leisure. It was certainly a wonderful painting. As one critic has written:

> Every head [of the gentlemen and priests] is a masterpiece, every
> hand a proof of incomparable draughtsmanship. Moreover, the
> varied expressions (resignation, acceptance of the divine will, hope,
> curiosity, unspoken opinions of the virtues of the dead man, etc.) all
> show the painter's wealth of psychic perception, his gift for
> understanding and representing human beings, which was as great
> as his ability to show the diverse degrees of participation in Glory,
> and his genius for depicting the divine beings by idealizing
> traditional types.[*]

[*] See also 'A Note on The Burial of Count Orgaz', in Sangharakshita, *The Priceless Jewel*, Windhorse, Glasgow 1993.

Later on I remembered the first time I saw a reproduction of *The Burial of Count Orgaz*. It was in 1940, in Torquay, and I saw it in the window of a bookshop. Not long afterwards I read about the artist in the pages of Sacheverell Sitwell and Aldous Huxley and included descriptions of some of his paintings in the novel I wrote in 1943, shortly before being conscripted.

Our second stop was the Cathedral. As we entered, some rather gentle Bach was coming from the loudspeakers, creating a peaceful and contemplative atmosphere. Massive Gothic cluster pillars rose through the gloom, which here and there was pierced by the unearthly radiance of the stained-glass windows. We wandered in and out of the vast spaces between the cluster pillars, the four rows of which divided the nave into five aisles, making no attempt to 'do' everything. Before long we were looking through the wrought-iron screen at the high altar and at the elaborately carved and gilded reredos that rose tier upon tier behind it almost to the roof. The reredos was said to contain a synopsis of the entire New Testament, culminating in a Calvary at the summit, and we indeed could pick out individual scenes from the Gospels; but I noticed that the carvings were covered with dust, which dulled the brightness of the gilding and gave an impression of neglect and decay. We also looked at the carved wooden stalls of the *coro* or choir, which in an English cathedral would have been situated in the presbytery but which here, as (I think) in all Spanish cathedrals, occupied the centre of the nave. Behind the high altar rose the famous 'Transparente', a Churrigueresque fantasy in marble, bronze, and alabaster that, towering from floor to ceiling, was lit from above by a window cut in the vault. It was fortunate that it was *behind* the high altar, and thus invisible from the nave, the Gothic harmonies of which would have been ruined by the intrusion of so alien a style. On the wall beside one of the nave doors was a huge, ancient fresco of St Christopher, not unlike the one we had seen in Cologne Cathedral, while high on the wall of one of the apse chapels a very unecumenical Santiago, or St James as he is known in England, was slaughtering Muslims. Off the apse there was a plateresque doorway, on passing through which we found ourselves in the rather magnificent six-teenth-century chapter room. The coffered ceiling was richly gilt, the walls brilliant with frescoes, while below the frescoes, in separate panels, were depicted the archbishops of Toledo from the earliest times down to the present day. Except for the more recent, one of whom sported a white eighteenth-century wig, all the archbishops wore jewel-studded mitres and carried gold ceremonial crosses.

The Cathedral's greatest treasures, from the artistic point of view, were in the sacristy, in the first room of which, above the altar, was El Greco's *El Espolio*, or 'The Stripping of Christ'. So strong was the impression made by the central figure in the blood-red garment, on which one of the surrounding figures had already laid hands, that it was difficult to pay much attention to the other paintings, even though these included such masterpieces as Goya's *The Arrest of Christ* (also known as *The Kiss of Judas*), Giovanni Bellini's *The Burial of Christ*, a *Crucifixion* by Titian, Raphael's *The Baptism of Christ*, Velasquez's *Portrait of Cardinal Borja*, and Caravaggio's *St John the Baptist*, as well as El Greco's own *St Peter in Tears* and a series of 'portraits' of the Apostles. Besides paintings, the sacristy contained illuminated manuscripts, including the three-volume *Bible of St Louis*, and an extensive collection of vestments and tapestries. The greens, pinks, and other hues of the vestments, in particular, were of extraordinary beauty, no doubt because only dyes of natural origin had been used. Before leaving the Cathedral we paid a visit to the treasury, where we saw the Cathedral's lesser treasures of gold and silver. Chief among these was a nine-foot-high silver-gilt processional monstrance in the form of a kind of Gothic shrine. The gold with which it was covered was thought to be the first gold brought by Columbus from the New World, and I could not but wonder at what cost in innocent blood it had been obtained.

Toledo lies within a loop of the River Tagus, which surrounds it on two of its three sides. On these two sides there are steep cliffs and, meandering along the top of the cliffs, a relatively quiet road. Having seen the Cathedral, Paramartha and I wandered down to this road and by its means found our way back to the hotel. *En route* I took a few photographs (it was the first real photographic opportunity I had had since our departure from Guhyaloka), being especially pleased with the rocky hills on the other side of the river, the little arcaded structure on the opposite bank, and the white-toothed 'comb' across the river itself that indicated the presence of a weir. At the hotel we rested until it was time to go out for dinner (in Spain, we had already learned, restaurants did not open until 8.00 or 8.30 and it was no use looking for a meal before then). Our destination was the Plaza de Zocodover, but we took a roundabout route, not exactly getting lost, yet not bothering if we were slightly off course. Our way lay through cobbled streets down which the occasional car rumbled with a sound like thunder, the sound usually being heard before the car itself appeared. Streets narrowed into lanes, lanes into alleys only a few feet wide. Blank walls rose twenty and thirty feet on either hand, their eaves almost touching. We seemed to be in a labyrinth – a labyrinth of biscuit-coloured stone; in a maze, a warren. At one point we came upon a whole block of ancient buildings in process of demolition. I hoped this did not mean that the area was to be 'developed'. Eventually, not without having had to enquire the way once or twice, we reached the Plaza de Zocodover, the restaurants of which proved to be no kinder to the vegetarian than those of the Plaza Mayor had been. Fortunately there was an Italian restaurant nearby and here, when it opened, we had a meal and a good talk.

In the morning Paramartha did some yoga, after which we had breakfast in the Plaza de Zocodover and then went to see the Museo de Santa Cruz. This very rich collection, containing not only paintings and sculptures but tapestries, ceramics, silverware, and items of historical interest, occupied a huge building the ground-plan of which was in the form of a Greek cross. The interior of the building, with its intersecting two-storeyed aisles with coffered ceilings, was one of the noblest I had ever seen. What was its original function? Could it have been a cathedral, as suggested by the form of its ground plan – not immediately recognizable as a Greek cross – and by its rather spectacular dimensions? Or was it originally a palace, as suggested by the plateresque staircase and the balcony that, on the first floor, surrounded the central well of the building and from which a king or a prince might have looked down on the crowd of courtiers below? Later I discovered that it had been built, in the first decades of the sixteenth century, as a hospital and a foundling home. So noble was the interior on account of its size, its harmonious proportions, and the propriety of its embellishments, that I gave it hardly less attention than I gave the exhibits themselves – that is, until we came to the museum's El Grecos, which were kept together in one arm of the cross on the upper floor. Here architecture was forgotten. One had eyes only for the wealth of visionary art that the room contained. One had eyes only for *The Immaculate Conception*, in which the figure of the Virgin was caught in 'a wonderful spiral of angels and seraphim' the starting-point of which was a bouquet of pink roses and white lilies; for *The Coronation of the Virgin*, with its group of upward-gazing saints; for *St Joseph and the Infant Christ*, in which the two figures wandered barefoot through the world – a 'world' represented by a panoramic view of Toledo – as three angels descended with a wreath and flowers; for the glowing *St John the Baptist* and *St John the Evangelist*; for the strongly expressive *St Peter* and *St Andrew*, and for a number of other works marked by the same visionary quality. Having seen the main collection, we strolled round the beautiful Renaissance courtyard, in which there were various objects of archaeological interest, Roman, Visigothic, and Arab. Adjoining the courtyard was a suite of rooms. Here we found in progress an exhibition of photographs of Peru, by two different photographers, one apparently working in the twenties and thirties, the other contemporary, and spent half an hour looking round and learning something about this whilom part of the Spanish Empire.

By this time I was feeling a little tired. We therefore returned to the Plaza de Zocodover for a drink and a snack. Paramartha then went and enquired about the times of buses to Cordoba, as we wanted to leave for that city the following day. Definite information was not available, however, and we therefore took the local bus down to the terminal and made enquiries there – just to make sure. There were no buses to Cordoba. We would have to take the train. Returning once more to the Plaza de Zocodover, we accordingly went along to the RENFE city booking office (or was it a travel agency?) and bought tickets *not* for Cordoba but for Aránjuez, where we would have to change and buy tickets for the remainder of our journey. We then walked back to the hotel. As we passed the Cathedral, I noticed hanging high up on the walls of the building several sets of chains. These, I discovered, were supposedly the chains of former prisoners of the Moors. We were to see such chains in other Spanish cities. Back at the hotel we wrote picture postcards to our friends for an hour or so and then, at 4 o'clock, set out for El Greco's House, the Tránsito Synagogue, and the Museum of Visigothic Art. While it has not been proved that El Greco lived in the house that now bears his name, he is known to have lived in the old Jewish quarter, where it is situated, and since he must have lived somewhere he may well have lived in this particular building. Whether he lived in it or not, Paramartha and I were glad to look round the rambling old place with its patio, its low ceilings, its windows .adorned with grilles (it was strange to be on the *inside* of them for once), its creaking floors, and its tiled kitchen, and glad to see there and in the adjoining museum a number of El Greco's paintings, including *St Bernardino*, the famous *Map of Toledo*, and a second series of 'portraits' of the Apostles, the models for which are said to have been patients from a nearby lunatic asylum (could El Greco have thought that *religion* to madness 'sure is near allied'?).

The Tránsito Synagogue was just down the road from El Greco's House, so to speak, and was one of the three synagogues surviving in Spain from the Middle Ages, the others being in Toledo itself and in Cordoba. Built in the fourteenth century in Mujedar style, it had survived by becoming first an archive and then a church. One wall was covered with beautiful lace-like plasterwork incorporating coats-of-arms and Hebraic inscriptions and pierced by arched lattice windows. There was also a polychrome coffered ceiling and a women's gallery, corresponding to the matroneum in early Christian (and Eastern Orthodox) churches, for in Judaism as in Early Christianity it was not considered proper for men and women to sit (or rather stand) together for public worship. Our third objective, the Museum of Visigothic Art, was situated in a different part of the city, not far from its geographic centre. At least we thought it was situated there. Having looked round some souvenir shops and had a drink we walked in the direction of the Plaza de Zocodover until we came to a crossroads and a sign that said 'Museo Visigotico'. The sign pointed up a very steep and narrow lane. Up this lane we accordingly went, only to find that it terminated in a perfect maze of streets and squares with no further indication of the direction we should take. Old ladies dressed in black and sitting on doorsteps fluttering fans assured us that the museum was just round the corner, young men seemed not to have heard of it and indeed to be quite stupefied by the idea of there being any such place, while an elderly man was positive that it lay in a direction exactly opposite to the one from which we had just come. In the end, when we had combed the area for more than half an hour and had more than once found ourselves back at the sign that said 'Museo Visigotico', we decided to call it a day and go and see something else instead.

The 'something else' turned out to be the Monastery of San Juan de los Reyes, a building in the late Gothic 'Isabelline' style situated at the western end of the city. We spent some time strolling round the cloisters, above the entrance to which a recumbent human skeleton had been carved. The upper floor of the cloisters had a beautiful coffered ceiling, while through the traceried windows of its arcades we had a fine view of the pinnacles and waterspouts opposite, the latter being carved in all sorts of fantastic human and animal shapes. Since there was no access to the interior of the church from the cloisters we went outside and walked round to the doorway. Here we found thirty or forty people gathered for a wedding and waiting in the sun for the arrival of the bride. She arrived after a few minutes, in bridal white, and disappeared into the church on her father's arm. The throng followed them in. There was no question of our being able to look round the church while the ceremony was in progress. We there-fore started making our way back to the Plaza de Zocodover and to our vegetarian-friendly Italian restaurant. As we left the precincts of the Monastery of San Juan de los Reyes we saw on our right, on a strip of lawn bordering a crenellated building that appeared to be a palace, a rather new-looking white marble statue. This turned out to be a statue of Queen Isabella who, in conjunction with her husband King Ferdinand, had founded the monastery, it having been the original intention of the Catholic Monarchs to be buried in the place. When we reported-in that night, having had dinner and walked back to the hotel, I commented on the fact that we had so far seen only two priests in Toledo, one old and one young, even though Toledo was an archi-episcopal city and its archbishop Primate of Spain. In Madrid we had not seen a single priest – unless they were all wearing mufti! Back in Borrow's day Spain had swarmed with clerics of every description, and in books about Spain written even thirty or forty years ago priests, monks, and nuns were very much in evidence. What had happened? Had there been a decline of religious faith, or a drop in the number of vocations?

Toledo railway station was the most attractive railway station I had seen. The booking hall was adorned with wooden grilles like those of a cathedral, with wrought-iron work, and with colourful tiles. Along the platform hung baskets of geraniums. The whole place was im-maculate, and in England would undoubtedly have won the 'best kept station' award. Paramartha and I arrived there at about 8.30 a.m., having taken a taxi from the hotel to the Plaza de Zocodover and the local bus from the Plaza to the station, and after a brief wait caught the train to Aránjuez. The journey took only half an hour. The country through which we passed was comparatively green; there were fields of maize and other crops, and plenty of trees and plenty of water. Aránjuez itself was a peaceful place – except for the bar, from the noise of which we escaped on to the spacious platform as soon as Paramartha had got our drinks. In the bar we had seen a bright-looking five-year-old boy playing pinball. Though so tiny that he had to stand on a chair to operate the machine, he played with intense concentration and complete self-confidence, every now and then shouting to his mother to give him more money to put in the slot. As we sipped our drinks I remarked that today's youngsters seemed to take very readily not only to games like pinball but also to such things as pocket calculators and computers (not to mention TV), which were unknown in my own day, and this led to a discussion between us. Aránjuez was of course famous for its palace and gardens, but although these were quite close at hand we decided against visiting them and continued talking until it was time to cross to the platform at which our train was due to arrive. As we were waiting there an old wooden steam train chugged in at the platform we had just left, which was the main platform, and was welcomed with some rather spirited songs by a troupe of girl singers and musicians dressed in medieval 'page boy' costume. Evidently the train was a tourist attraction. A few minutes later, at 11.20, our own train arrived. Since it came from Madrid it was already quite full, and it was fortunate that we had not just tickets but seat reservations. Even so, we found that our seats, though indeed next to each other, were on different sides of the gangway, and that while one seat faced the engine the other did not.

The country through which we passed was at first quite flat; in fact it looked like a desert, especially when the flatness started corrugating into sand hills. After a while vineyards appeared, and towns dominated by their churches. The towns had Arabic, or partly Arabic, names … Alcazar de San Juan … Manzanares … Santa Cruz de Mudela.… When we had been in our seats for nearly two hours Paramartha and I got up and made our way, through about a dozen carriages, to the buffet car at the rear end of the train and there had a drink and – the sandwiches all being non-vegetarian – a piece of cake.

On our way we passed through a carriage that had been converted into a crèche. Here about a dozen small children were happily playing with the brightly-coloured rocking horses and other toys that had been provided for their amusement. Three young women attendants kept an eye on them. I thought the crèche a very good idea. It was obviously far better to have the children playing there than to have them becoming bored and fractious and annoying other passengers. On our return to our seats I read a monograph entitled *The Burial of the Count of Orgaz: Message and Technique* which I had bought at the Museo de Santa Cruz. Though it was well illustrated, and made a few interesting points, it was written in a style that was at times grandiloquent to the point of absurdity and reminded me, more than once, of the attempts of some Indian authors writing in English to be 'literary'. There was, moreover, an Introduction by a friend of the author that was one of the most vigorous pieces of backscratching I had encountered for a long time and in which she (as I thought it must be) wrote of the two of them as being 'radically Toledian souls, made of Ceramics and sword, of marzipan and olive tree.' This probably sounded quite well in the Spanish in which it was, I imagine, originally written, or at least conceived. But in English it did not sound at all right. In between paragraphs I contemplated the unprepossessing features of the stout, middle-aged woman sitting opposite, or, more often, gazed out of the window. We were now passing through quite hilly country, where there was plenty of pine and ilex, though it saddened me to see how ruthlessly the new roads that were under construction were cutting their giant swathes through the living green. Presently came tunnels, rock formations with vertical strata, olive trees, and more towns with Arabic or partly Arabic names ... Linares – Baeza ... Andujar ... Montoro.... By this time the country had become less hilly and more fertile; there were olive groves and fields of sunflowers and – no doubt the reason for the area's fertility – numerous irrigation channels. At one point I saw a man riding on a donkey – the first donkey I had as yet seen in Spain. Thereafter came a muddy river, willow trees, and beds of reeds. Between Andujar and Montoro, however, there were only olive trees to be seen (through the haze), while the sky, which for some time had been overcast, started to clear. After Montoro the trees were larger, and I saw a few cows. At 4.20, when the sky was a little clearer, we entered Cordoba.

Cordoba! I had expected to enter it through orange groves, or at least through suburbs resplendent with white-walled villas surrounded by oleanders. Instead we entered it through an unsightly industrial area, got down on to a crowded platform, and before long were having a drink in a bar dominated by a corner TV set that was blasting out an unbelievably noisy and melodramatic film. Spanish television, I reflected, must be among the worst in the world. While I was thus reflecting, a man came into the bar and started embracing everyone in the most enthusiastic fashion. At first I thought it must be an old Spanish custom (the embrace-ees were all male), or that perhaps the man had a lot of friends, but after a few minutes I realized from some of the reactions he was getting that he was either mad or drunk. In the circumstances we felt no inclination to linger over our drinks, and leaving the station made our way along the Avenida del Gran Capitan in the direction of the Mezquita. On the way one of the handles of my holdall broke, and I was left feeling a little like Milarepa when his cooking-pot broke. From the Avenida del Gran Capitan we eventually penetrated into a network of lanes with whitewashed walls and wrought-iron grilles. In one of the lanes, on a plinth set in the middle of a tiny cobbled court, was a statue of Maimonides, the twelfth-century Jewish philosopher, who had been born in Cordoba. Evidently we were in the Judería or old Jewish quarter, that is, the quarter occupied by the Jews before their expulsion from Spain by Ferdinand and Isabella in 1492. The lane debouched into a little 'square' into which debouched other lanes with whitewashed walls and wrought-iron grilles. There were souvenir shops and bars and quite a few tourists, many of them English (or at least English-speaking) and German. There were also hotels and hostels and at one of these, the Hotel Seneca (Seneca had also been born in Cordoba), we tried to get a room. (I must admit that with my long-standing love of Seneca I rather liked the idea of staying at a hotel named after him.) Unfortunately, no room was available, but a boy was detailed to show us the way to a sister establishment about five minutes walk away. At this establishment, which was called the Alcázar, we accordingly settled in – in a tiny ground-floor room whose only window looked out on to the patio.

Fifteen or twenty minutes later we were in the Mezquita, the great mosque that was said to be the second largest mosque in the world, only that of Mecca being bigger. A forest of columns rose through the gloom. The columns, which were mainly of lustrous green and red marble, were not very big, and supported on their Corinthian capitals not only their own horseshoe arches but also rectangular pillars that, in their turn, supported a second row of round arches high above the first. Both upper and lower arches were striped with alternate bands of white and red which, as we wandered in and out of the aisles, gave an impression of opening fans. Columns and arches also gave an impression of the rising and falling waters of a fountain, the eye not being carried up indefinitely, as in a Gothic cathedral, but carried up and then brought gently down, so that the overall emphasis of the building was as much horizontal as perpendicular. Once the eye had been brought down, and so to speak returned to earth, it was not directed anywhere in particular but left free to wander among the columns and down the aisles as it pleased. If it was directed anywhere at all it was directed towards the golden glow that could be seen dawning through the columns at the far end of one of the rows of aisles like the newly risen sun through the trees of a forest. This golden glow was the highly decorated mihrab, the niche showing the direction of Mecca. We had not been long in the Mezquita before we became aware that the view down some of the aisles was blocked and that there was, in fact, an alien presence at the very heart of the building. This alien presence was the 'mainly Plateresque' Catholic cathedral which, in the sixteenth century, had been forcibly inserted into the Mezquita, and to make room for which sixty-three of its nine hundred-odd columns had been sacrificed. Besides blocking the view, and destroying the architectural unity of the place, the Cathedral was in itself of little artistic merit, especially as compared with the mosque by which it was surrounded and out of which it tried to burst, though I would not go so far as to describe it as being 'of colossal ugliness', as one writer has done. The view was not just blocked by the Cathedral, however. The sides of the Mezquita, open originally to the skies of Andalusia, had been walled up to allow the construction of a whole series of chapels, so that the rows of interior columns no longer appeared to be an extension of the rows of orange trees in the Patio de los Naranjos, or 'Court of the Orange Trees', as a result of which the sense of continuity between the works of men and the works of Nature was lost.

From the Mezquita we wandered down to the river, on the way passing a rank of horse-drawn carriages, and walked some distance along the embankment. The light was beginning to fade, and the scene that presented itself to our eyes was a peaceful one. Across the Guadalquivir lay the old Roman bridge (at least the foundations were Roman), with its dozen or more round arches; nearer at hand, between the river and the embankment, were reed beds and a tangle of trees and bushes. There was also a giant Arab waterwheel, its gaunt frame silhouetted blackly against the pale blue sky. At one point we descended a flight of steps and walked a few dozen yards along the actual river bank, but so overpowering was the stench that we were forced to retreat. Soon afterwards, having walked along the embankment for a couple of miles, we began retracing our steps and eventually ended our day with a meal in the quiet, at first quite empty, patio of a quasi-Italian restaurant. It was on this occasion, I think, that I first tasted gazpacho, an ice-cold soup to which I took an instant liking and which I thereafter had whenever I could (Paramartha did not take to it to the same extent, but has recently been thinking of making some).

The next day we had breakfast in a small bar which, though not far from the Mezquita and therefore within the main tourist area, was very much of the traditional type. Sides of bacon and strings of onions hung from the rafters, while in place of chairs there were a few low wooden stools. At the end of the counter, however, stood a very untraditional TV set. Since we were so much within its range I could hardly ignore what it was showing. Strange to say, at that particular moment it was showing a bearded and turbaned man in Islamic costume rolling his eyes with every appearance of astonishment and even of terror. Could it be a programme about the Middle East? Stranger still, the bearded and turbaned man had his eyes fixed on what was obviously a Hindu temple. Perhaps it was a programme about communal problems in India. Strangest of all, dancing down the steps of the temple came the figure of the god Shiva, waving his eight arms simultaneously and looking like a gigantic spider. The scene was made even more weird by the fact that the programme was in black and white with only a sitar on the soundtrack, so that it was difficult to know what was going on. I was still speculating on the nature of the programme, and wondering what could be the significance of our chancing to see it that Sunday morning in a place like Cordoba, when Paramartha cut my reveries short by remarking, 'It's an old black-and-white movie of *Sinbad the Sailor*.' Shortly afterwards we were again in the more genuinely Islamic surroundings of the Mezquita. Happening to skirt the fortress-like wall of the place, we had noticed that one of the side doors was open and had slipped inside. There were not many people about, and since it was early in the day there was more natural light in the building than there had been previously. We took the opportunity of taking a closer look at the arabesques surrounding the arch of the mihrab, with their rich golds and greens, reds and blues. We also craned our necks to see the octagonal cupola between the mihrab and the kiblah, the row of columns that preceded the mihrab and whose ornate double arches were boldly scalloped. From the glittering splendours of the mihrab we turned to the chapels, of which there must have been about fifty, including a large one dedicated to St Teresa. They were all locked, and peering through the bars we could make out dusty tombs and altars, faded polychrome statues, and darkened paintings. The cathedral had a more cared for look. Sitting in the nave for a few minutes, we looked at the carvings in marble and in wood, as well as up into the ovoid dome – three times as high above our heads as the cupola between the kiblah and the mihrab.

The rest of the morning we spent visiting two of the town's principal museums and its sole remaining medieval synagogue. The first of the two museums was the Museum of Fine Arts, which we eventually found in the Plaza del Potro, so named from the colt which – with the help of some stylized scrollwork – reared up on its hind legs above the basin of the fountain, and famous for having been mentioned by Cervantes in *Don Quixote*. The writer himself, it seems, had once lodged at the *posada* or inn across the way. But our business was with the museum, which contained paintings of the Cordoba school from the fifteenth to the seventeenth century. Holders of British passports were admitted free of charge, which makes me all the more sorry that I am unable to recollect any of the paintings we saw, though I could probably call some of them to mind with the help of an illustrated catalogue.

The Bullfighting Museum we came across quite by accident, not having known of its existence before. Exhibits included posters, mounted bulls' heads, costumes, and a plaster cast of the tomb of Manolete, the famous *torero* being depicted lying on his deathbed, hands clasped as though in prayer, and looking for all the world like a deceased archbishop. As might have been expected, the synagogue was located on one side of the same little cobbled court in which stood the statue of Maimonides (actually the philosopher was seated, one hand resting on the book in his lap). Though much smaller than the Tránsito Synagogue, it had a women's gallery and some elaborate stuccowork round an arched niche.

Between the Bullfighting Museum and the synagogue we passed the statue of Averroës, the great twelfth-century Islamic philosopher, who like Seneca had been born in Cordoba and whose attempts to reconcile Aristotelian philosophy with the Islamic religion had profoundly influenced Christian scholasticism. He too was seated and his hand too was resting on a book, but in his case the book was upright on his knee and his hand rested on the top of it. His nose, I observed, was slightly chipped, though the statue was a recent one (as late as 1968 James A. Mitchener was complaining that there was no memorial to Averroës in Cordoba). Was the chip simply the result of vandalism, or was it an expression of actual anti-Muslim feeling on the part of Spanish Catholics? Averroës had in any case been one of the *bêtes noires* of the medieval Church (in art he was sometimes represented being trampled on by St Thomas Aquinas), and in view of Spain's long history of conflict between Cross and Crescent it would not have been surprising if some anti-Muslim feeling should have persisted or some Spanish Catholics been outraged by the sight of a statue of the great infidel philosopher. But I did not allow thoughts of this kind to occupy me for long. As I contemplated the philosopher's rather aquiline features, I recalled the occasion when, as an old man, he had made the acquaintance of the great Sufi master Ibn 'Arabī, then only twenty years old. The meeting, arranged by Ibn 'Arabī's father, had taken place here in Cordoba, in Averroës' own house. Years later, when he had migrated from his native Murcia to the Middle East, Ibn 'Arabī wrote an account of this meeting, at which there had been a mysterious exchange between the youthful mystic and the aged philosopher. The exchange had centred on the question of the relation between mystical illumination and speculative thought, and according to Ibn 'Arabī it had left Averroës pale and trembling.

The biggest difficulty Paramartha and I experienced on our tour was in connection with food. Spain simply did not cater for the vegetarian. In Cordoba, however, we were more fortunate than usual. Besides the quasi-Italian restaurant where we had eaten the night before there was, we discovered, a self-service cafeteria where pasta was available and here, having visited the two museums and the synagogue and the statue of Averroës, we decided to have lunch. We did not decide to have it there without a certain amount of discussion between us. After all, the words 'self-service cafeteria' had all sorts of connotations. But we need not have worried. The place was quiet and secluded, being well away from the street, and having chosen the dishes we wanted we carried our trays to one of the heavy wooden tables in the spacious cobbled patio, which at that time of day was deserted (we ate much earlier than the Spanish, and earlier than most foreign tourists). Rows of potted shrubs stood against the high whitewashed walls, on which there hung dozens of flowerpots filled with creepers and other plants, some of them in bloom. There were also fan palms in huge earthenware jardinières. Altogether the patio was a delightful place. There was only one drawback – only one serpent in this Andalusian Eden – perhaps on the same principles on which it provided a few vegetarian dishes the cafeteria did not provide either tea or coffee. Having had our meal, we therefore wandered off in search of a bar. Not that bars were difficult to find (on the contrary!), but we wanted one that was reasonably quiet and where we could sit outside. Our wanderings took us through the greater part of the Judería, where there were more whitewashed walls, more cobbled patios, and more hanging flowerpots (such flowerpots seemed to be a regular feature of Cordoban houses, even of Cordoban life). Eventually we found a small bar with a single row of tables on the narrow pavement outside and sat there in the brilliant sunshine. Paramartha read *Life is a Dream*. I wrote postcards. After an hour or so we became aware that the bar was closing, presumably for the midday siesta, and accordingly adjourned to the Plaza de Juda Levi, a square midway between the Hotel Seneca and our own hotel, and to a table beneath the orange trees. Here we were not a little troubled by the dreadful racket made by passing scooters (we had been troubled by them when wandering through the Judería). According to a famous poem by Machado the city in which we were now staying was *'Romana y mora, Córdoba callada'*, and I could not but think that if many more scooters were allowed on its streets – and in its lanes – it might still be 'Roman and Moorish' but it would certainly not be *'silent* Cordoba' any more.

Every Spanish city of any pretensions has, it seems, an Alcázar or Moorish fortified palace, and Cordoba was no exception. Having sat a while in the Plaza de Juda Levi, and had yet another drink (Cordoba was even hotter than Toledo and we often felt thirsty) we walked the few hundred yards to the great iron gates of the Alcázar de los Reyes Cristianos, or 'Alcázar of the Christian Monarchs'. The Christian Monarchs in question were, I assumed, Ferdinand and Isabella, more usually known as the Reyes Catolicos or 'Catholic Monarchs'. Not that they had founded the Alcázar. They had only set up court there for a while (according to one guidebook. According to another they had 'rebuilt it a little to the west'). It had been built a couple of hundred years before their time on the site of an older Arab castle. We spent a pleasant two hours wandering over the palace, from the towers of which we had a view of the Guadalquivir and its Roman bridge. There were also some fine Moorish-style apartments, all marble columns, scalloped arches, and colourful tiles, some wonderfully cool and quiet baths, and a little museum containing Roman mosaics and a sarcophagus. But perhaps the most beautiful part of the Alcázar was the gardens, where there were lily-ponds and fountains, rows of clipped orange trees and junipers, and Moorish pavilions that contemplated their own reflections in green water, and where I had my second real photographic opportunity since our departure from Guhyaloka. There was only one discordant note. This was a twenties-style stone figure of a nude female who, lying on her stomach and with her legs in the air, looked down the principal avenue of the gardens. Men were having their photographs taken with their hand on her buttocks, and there came into my mind a line from one of the poet Iqbal's scornful indictments of Indian and European (as opposed to Islamic) civilization: 'The Female sits astride their quivering nerves'.

After two hours at the Alcázar we were ready for a drink, and accordingly 'stopped by' at the Plaza de Juda Levi. (In the course of our tour we must have patronized between fifty and sixty bars, some of them more than once.) Paramartha thought the new waiter rather abrupt in his manner. I thought that probably it was just his friendly disposition. Even the closest friends could, it seemed, sometimes have different perceptions of one and the same person or situation, and we discussed the point for a while. Having discussed it, we made our way to the Mezquita and to the Court of the Orange Trees. Paramartha sat down on the edge of the stone parapet and started sketching. I wandered about looking for photographic opportunities. Each of the orange trees, I noticed, stood in a circular sunk bed of its own and all the beds were connected by irrigation channels. Here and there among the orange trees stood a few date palms, their stately heads rising clear of the tops of their glossy companions. Before I could take any photographs, however, or Paramartha finish his sketch, it was 7 o'clock and, apparently, closing time. Attendants were doing their best to clear the court of visitors and two or three young Spanish women who had just arrived were protesting vigorously. Hoping we would not be too early we went along to the self-service cafeteria, this time without any discussion, and had dinner. Once again we had the place to ourselves, except for a party of four Chinese (or perhaps Japanese) girls and an English couple who came in when we were half-way through our meal. There was also some taped guitar music. But of course no hot beverages. It was therefore back to the Plaza de Juda Levi, where we had not only tea (in my case) and black coffee (in Paramartha's) but also a pink liquid called sangria which we had seen people drinking in a number of places and which we wanted to try. It turned out to be a kind of punch, rather sweet and fruity, and neither of us took to it very much.

That night it was very hot – so hot that Paramartha had difficulty sleeping and rose late. Instead of going out for breakfast to a bar we had it, such as it was (coffee and magdalenas), in the little patio of the hostel which, like all self-respecting Cordoban patios, had flowerpots full of creepers and other plants hanging from its whitewashed walls. Being now somewhat familiar with the layout of the city, we took the shortest route to the railway station, on our way passing the statue of Averroës and, a few hundred yards further on, the statue of Seneca, which was situated outside the Puerta de Almodova and which we had not seen before. The grand old Roman philosopher (or moralist, as some would say) stood on a plinth of about the same height as himself; he wore a toga, and looked down at the rose garden below with an expression of grave benignity. On our arrival at the railway station we discovered that, despite the printed timetable, there was no 10.20 train to Seville – in fact no train to Seville at all for three or four hours. There was, however, a 10.20 coach. Hastily retracing our steps to the bus stop, which we had already passed, we had just time enough to buy tickets in the shabby little office and board the coach before the driver climbed into his seat and we were off. A week had passed since our departure from Guhyaloka; our tour was half over, and we were about to penetrate deeper into Andalusia and the South. If in old Cordoba the traditional silence of the place was threatened by scooters in the modern city it had long since been destroyed by motor vehicles of every kind, and there was heavy traffic to be negotiated before we could reach the highway. Once we were clear of the traffic, however, our way lay through bare brown hills, round the sides of which the road made long curves. From bare brown hills we emerged into a brown – and red – plain where I saw a few olive trees and a man ploughing with a wooden plough and a single horse. Thereafter we passed through three or four small towns, at each of which the coach stopped to put people down and take them up. When we had been on the road a couple of hours we climbed up into the mountains. Big trees appeared, and a building that looked like a Cartuja or Carthusian monastery. Half an hour later, at about 12.45, we were in Seville.

The capital of Andalusia was a big, bustling city that, to judge by the enormous construction projects that were in progress, was in a fever of preparation for Expo 92, the fair that would celebrate the five-hundredth anniversary of Columbus's 'discovery' of the New World. It was also more cosmopolitan than I had expected, and as I sat in the bus station guarding our modest luggage while Paramartha went to get us a drink I could almost have fancied myself in Bombay. There was the same litter underfoot, the same brown faces, the same hawkers of foodstuffs, the same child beggars, the same smells. On leaving the bus station we found ourselves crossing road after busy road and heading (so we hoped) in the direction of a bank and the Tourist Information Centre. Having located these, and cashed travellers cheques in the one and obtained a map of the city from the other, we went in search of accommodation. Our search took us past the

Cathedral, with its famous bell tower, originally the minaret of a converted and subsequently demolished mosque, and into the maze of alleyways and squares that made up the medieval Jewish quarter. Here, in a hostel with the name of 'Good Sleep', we at length found an upstairs room overlooking the patio which, as we had already discovered, was hung about not only with flowerpots but with birdcages containing a variety of colourful small birds. There was even an aquarium with terrapin. Not wanting the promised 'good sleep' just then we had a shower and went straight out and soon were seated beneath a blue-and-white umbrella in a little square half-way between our hostel and the Cathedral. On one side of the square was a gallery named after John Fulton, the American artist and matador. On another, against a background of brilliant blue sky, the upper storeys of the beautiful Giralda – as the Cathedral's bell tower was known – could be seen above the intervening buildings. It was extremely hot. As Paramartha and I were having our snack a young man appeared from among the white-painted chairs and tables and, with many cheerful smiles, insisted on polishing Paramartha's boots (my own shoes had canvas uppers, and as such were beyond his ministrations). Paramartha remarked that in Granada we would be sure to encounter many of these importunate shoe-shine boys who, like their Indian counterparts, would polish one's footwear quite regardless of whether or not one wanted it polished or even whether it needed polishing. Having spent the best part of three minutes on Paramartha's boots, in the course of which he informed us that he had a wife and three children, this Sevillian representative of the tribe asked an outrageous sum for his services – a sum which my good-natured friend smilingly paid. It was now time for us to see the Cathedral. As we left the square I saw standing on the corner a slim young man; he was naked to the waist, and appeared to be doing something. Paramartha, in some respects more streetwise than myself, afterwards told me that he had been giving himself a fix.

The Cathedral of Santa Maria de la Sede, Seville, is the biggest Gothic church in the world, and the vast interior must have made a strong impression on me when we entered the nave that afternoon from the Patio de los Naranjos or 'Court of the Orange Trees'. Lofty multiple pillars and soaring arches apart, however, my only distinct recollection of our visit is of Paramartha and myself gazing through the wrought-iron grille of the Capilla Mayor at the 75-foot Gothic retable, the yellow gold – Mexican gold – of which gleamed through the semi-darkness in a way that, curiously, made me think of the Golden Fleece. There also are vague recollections of unlit side chapels, time-darkened paintings, reliquaries with mouldering bones, embroidered vestments, and an imposing monument to Columbus which, I subsequently discovered, had been brought from Havana when Cuba achieved independence, and which now stood awkwardly just inside one of the doorways. Perhaps my memories of the interior of the Cathedral were so indistinct because of the even stronger impression made on me by the exterior of the building, in particular by the Giralda, which reminded me of the minaret of the Koutoubia mosque in Marrakesh (a picture of which I had seen in an illustrated Koran) and which with the possible exception of Giotto's Tower in Florence must be the most beautiful tower in the Western world. (While Giotto's Tower lacks the spire the artist-architect had originally planned, the Giralda, on the contrary, possesses four stages that were not part of the twelfth-century minaret but which were added 300 years later. In both cases the result is one of extreme beauty – a beauty perhaps beyond the original architect's intention.)

Emerging from the gloom of the Cathedral into the sunlight, we walked up a busy road in the direction of the Museum of Fine Arts. Half-way there we discovered it was closed. Having had a drink seated at a table on the pavement outside a bar (it was very noisy), we therefore plunged into the adjacent side streets and made our way down to the river, which was, of course, the same Guadalquivir that we had seen flowing past Cordoba. Here, however, there was a broad embankment that seemed to extend for miles in either direction. There were date palms (I had already noticed that there were far more of these stately trees in Seville than in Cordoba) and horse-drawn carriages. What with the blue sky, the sunshine, and the sense of spaciousness, I felt quite exhilarated as we stepped out along the bottom tier of the embankment in the direction of the parks and gardens which, as we knew from our map, were situated beside the river a mile or two further up. On our way we passed the so-called Torre del Oro or 'Tower of Gold', a handsome, twelve-sided Moorish structure only the lantern of which lived up to its name. (According to one account it had once been decorated with gilded tiles; according to another, it had served as a repository for the gold brought back to Seville from the Americas.) Inside the Torre del Oro there was a small naval museum, but this we were unable to visit as the place was closed for restoration – no doubt in preparation for Expo 92. Round about lay heaps of sand and cement, and workmen were passing in and out of the open door. Further on there were pedal-boats for hire, and gaily painted craft that dashed up and down the river as if in holiday mood. Shortly before reaching the parks and gardens we found ourselves in front of a very grand building that looked as though it was a palace or museum. Since the door was open we walked in, and for the next ten minutes wandered in and out of the vast empty rooms and up and down broad flights of marble steps without encountering anyone and without seeing any sign of life other than a desk with a few papers on it. Only on our way out did we pass a nondescript person in a dark coat who took no more notice of us than if he had been a ghost, and we left the building no wiser about its history and present function than when we entered.

The parks and gardens were, we found, quite extensive, and after passing through the main gates, where horse-drawn carriages stood waiting to be hired, and walking some distance down a leafy avenue, we saw on our left a path that led to a clearing in which was a garden – a circular garden with stone seats disposed at the four quarters. The garden was, it transpired, a memorial garden. In the centre rose an enormous tree of a species I did not recognize, and up against the rough bark, and as it were incorporated with the tree, was a white marble pedestal surmounted by the white marble bust of a handsome, youngish man of sensitive, melancholy appearance. What was stranger still, on the white marble platform that surrounded the tree was a life-size bronze group of three women; all the women wore crinolines, and all were sitting in attitudes expressive of extreme grief. Between the bronze group and the white marble pedestal was a bronze Cupid who, so far as I remember, was in the act of shooting an arrow at the heart of the white marble bust. Rising from the seat from which we had been surveying this unusual – and really quite beautiful – monument I approached nearer and learned from a plaque that the garden commemorated the poet Bécquer (1836–70), whose name I had not heard before. Walking round to the other side of the tree I saw a second bronze Cupid; he was lying on his side with, it seemed, broken wings; one hand was raised and clutched at the side of the pedestal, and there was a knife sticking in his back. After our return to Padmaloka I discovered that Gustavo Adolfo Bécquer had been born in Seville and that he was best known for a series of lyrics which, according to one authority, lamented 'the impossibility of fulfilling erotic passion,' while according to another they described 'his struggle for perfect expression, his joy in love and his anguish in betrayal.'

Evidently the second bronze Cupid, with the knife in his back, represented love betrayed. But who were the three grief-stricken women in crinolines? Were they female relations? Or the objects of his 'erotic passion'? Or the appropriate Muses? I still do not know.

The memorial garden was surrounded by date palms and other trees, both tropical and non-tropical, and having left it and started heading in the direction of the Maria Luisa Park Paramartha and I found ourselves following a narrow path through what was almost jungle. So dense was the vegetation on either side, and to such an extent did fronds and branches interlace above our heads, that the sunlight came through only in thin pencils and there was an agreeable change from glare to shade, from heat to coolness. After a few minutes the trees thinned out, jungle gave way to parkland, and dotted here and there we saw a number of imposing buildings. Along the far side of the park there was a highway, up and down which the heavy traffic roared at an unconscionable speed, and on the other side of the highway – as we shortly discovered – there lay the vast, crescent-shaped mass of the Palacio Español or 'Spanish Palace', built in 1929 as the centrepiece of the ill-fated Spanish-American fair. Here plenty of photographic opportunities awaited me, and I made my way round the semicircular courtyard of the arcaded palace happily taking pictures of the colourful tile-work scenes illustrative of the history of the different provinces of Spain while Paramartha wandered on ahead, eventually seating himself on some steps and gazing thoughtfully at the waters of the little ornamental canal. When I had caught up with him, and we had crossed one of the bridges over the canal, we completed our circuit of the courtyard and made our way to the adjacent picnic area, where there were hundreds of pure white pigeons, some of them fluttering and cooing round the people feeding them and even perching on their heads and shoulders. I had seen pigeons of this kind in Valencia and other parts of Spain but never in such numbers. On leaving the picnic area we skirted around the back of the Palacio Español, the dimensions of which were even more impressive when the building was viewed from the rear, and started heading back towards the old city, having agreed that we had probably done enough sightseeing for the present. On the way we stopped for a drink, sitting out on the pavement beside a busy road in the cold cement shadow of what seemed to be a kind of flyover. The neighbourhood had a bleak, rather run-down look. As we neared the Cathedral, and were about to enter the Barrio Santa Cruz, as the medieval Jewish quarter was called, it occurred to us that perhaps we ought to make enquiries about coach services to Granada. This we accordingly did, having made our way to the bus station by a sordid street that was pervaded by the sickening stench of urine. Once again I could almost have fancied myself in Bombay.

Back at the 'Good Sleep' Paramartha sat out on the balcony and read while I lay down and perused the section of our guidebook dealing with Seville and Cordoba. At 7.30, the time at which the restaurants started opening, we went out in search of our evening meal. Restaurants with a vegetarian option other than toasted sandwich were not easily come by in Seville, but eventually we located one not far from the hostel and spent the next couple of hours at a table in the square that it shared with two rival establishments. While we were talking I noticed an elderly Indian couple standing outside a shop across the way. They were the first Indians I had seen in Spain. The woman wore a bright red sari; the man appeared to be blind. This was not the only reminder of India that I received that evening. The 'Good Sleep' was situated in a narrow alleyway, on one side of which there was a high wall. As we made our way up the alleyway after our meal I became aware of a familiar scent. It was the scent of jasmine. I had been aware of the scent in parts of old Cordoba, but here it was stronger and sweeter. Looking up I saw the creeper with its white stars hanging over the top of the wall and remarked to Paramartha that some Indian Muslims were so fond of the scent of jasmine that they went for their evening walk with a jasmine flower stuffed up each nostril – a practice which my friend seemed to think rather excessive. That night we were kept awake by the (English) occupants of the neighbouring rooms, who banged on doors and conducted loud, drunken conversations on the landing outside until about 2 o'clock. As often before, I wondered what it was that made men and women behave with so little consideration for other people. A shower, breakfast in the square where Paramartha had had his boots polished, and a brief visit to the John Fulton gallery, were the order of the day for us when – a little later than usual – we rose the following morning. In the gallery we saw a number of paintings by Fulton, most of them depicting bulls. The paintings were not of a very high standard; or rather, they were of no standard at all. We also saw pottering around the gallery a large, elderly man who seemed to be its proprietor. Was this the artist-matador himself, I wondered, or was it an admirer who had established the gallery in his memory? The rest of the morning we spent in the Alcázar, which like the Alcázar of Cordoba possessed extensive gardens. Much of the fortress-palace itself was closed, but we were able to see at least some of the splendid Moorish-style apartments, which were even more impressive than those in the Alcázar of Cordoba. The gardens of the Alcázar were, I thought, less beautiful than their Cordoban counterpart, though being less well tended they were also much ranker in their growth and I was glad to be surrounded by such an abundance of vegetation. After seeing the Alcázar we discovered that the Provincial Archaeological Museum, which we had thought was closed on Tuesdays, was in fact open – but only until 1 o'clock. Since it was now almost 12 o'clock and the museum was situated at the far end of the Maria Luisa Park we took a taxi there, only to find on our arrival that the museum was open until 2 o'clock. We were therefore able to look round it in more leisurely fashion than we had expected. It contained a substantial and well-arranged collection of prehistoric finds, as well as finds from the Iberian period and from Roman classical times. Apart from fragments of statuary and some gold jewellery there was little that was of artistic interest, and I soon became tired of flints and potsherds. As we left the museum we learned from the woman in the ticket office that the Museo de Bellas Artes, or 'Museum of Fine Arts', which we also wanted to visit, was only open until 3 o'clock. We therefore took another taxi, though not before we had noticed, directly opposite the Archaeological Museum, a fairy-like structure with Moorish doors and windows, and painted pastel pink, blue, and yellow, that seemed to belong to some opium-inspired dream of the Arabian Nights. As I learned later on, it was 'a mix of 1920s art deco and mock Mujedar', had been built for the Spanish-American fair, and was now the Museum of Popular Arts.

The Museum of Fine Arts was housed in the former monastery of the Merced order, an early seventeenth-century building with a baroque façade and beautiful inner courtyards. (Since my previous mention of the Merced order, in connection with Zurbarán's white-robed monks, I have discovered that it was an order devoted to the work of ransoming Christian captives from the Moors.) The paintings in the museum were very much in keeping with the hushed and solemn character of the building, most of them being by Spanish artists and on religious themes. There was only one outstanding non-religious painting. This was El Greco's portrait of his son Jorge Manuel, also known as *Portrait of a Painter*. Otherwise the paintings were predominantly of a religious, i.e. Catholic and Counter-Reformation, character, and included

Zurbarán's *Apotheosis of St Thomas Aquinas* (his largest canvas) and *St Hugo in the Carthusian Refectory* (the aged saint, attended by a young page, has come to reprove the brethren for unlawfully dining upon flesh meat), Valdés Leal's dramatic *Temptation of St Jerome* and *Defeat of the Saracens at Assisi*, and Murillo's *Adoration of the Shepherds, Immaculate Conception of the Franciscans*, and *St Thomas of Villanueva Distributing Alms*. Murillo in fact came as something of a revelation. As seen at the Royal Academy's 'Spanish Paintings of the Golden Age' exhibition, some years ago, he had seemed vastly inferior to Velasquez – an impression not even a visit to the Prado had entirely dispelled. But now, viewing the Museum's over twenty paintings from his hand, I thought him very little inferior to Velasquez.

Besides being the birthplace of Velasquez and Murillo, Pacheco and Góngora, Seville was the birthplace of Don Juan, that is to say, of Don Miguel Manara, the seventeenth-century nobleman who was the original of Byron's and Mozart's hero or hero-villain. Paramartha and I did not have time to visit his tomb, or to see the hospital which he (i.e. the real 'Don Juan') had founded after his conversion and for whose chapel he had commissioned a series of twelve paintings by Murillo, but shortly after leaving the Museum of Fine Arts we did happen to see a character who might have been a latter-day incarnation of the celebrated Don. We were having a drink at a pavement café in a noisy side street half-way between the Museum of Fine Arts and the Cathedral. Contributing to the din with his constant revving up was a swarthy-visaged man on a scooter almost immediately opposite to where we were sitting. He wore a silk shirt with the buttons undone, so that one could see the gold chain on his hairy chest (he also wore a gold bracelet), tight-fitting trousers of some shiny material, and black patent-leather shoes without socks. His smooth black hair, which was beginning to recede at the temples, gleamed with brilliantine, he had a thinly pencilled moustache, while the smile at the four or five scantily clad young women – one of them also on a scooter – with whom he was talking had the dazzling brilliance of an advertisement for toothpaste. From his lined face and slight bulge at the waist I judged him to be in his middle thirties or even older. Who was he? The playboy son of a wealthy family? A pimp? A pusher? Or was he, perhaps, simply the neighbourhood Romeo or local Don Juan? According to James A. Michener, in 1962 a newspaper had asked its readers whether Don Juan still existed in Spain. It was generally agreed that he was hanging on, especially in small towns, where men took seriously their obligation to be lady-killers. 'He exists in every Spanish man. We all dream that we are brave, honourable and death to ladies.' That was twenty-eight years ago. What had happened to Don Juan in the meantime? Had he ceased to exist, even as a myth? Or was he, perhaps, still alive and well – at least in Seville?

Since it was too early for supper, and since we did not feel like returning to the hostel, we made our way to the gardens adjoining the Maria Luisa Park and sat down on a bench in one of the broad, tree-shaded walks. Here we drank a bottle of mineral water and got into a long conversation which, at one point, became rather animated. While we were talking the evening promenaders began to appear and I noticed, as I had noticed earlier, that even apart from their undoubted dash of Moorish or Negro blood the people of Seville were not of a single homogeneous stock but comprised quite a variety of physical types. This was not surprising. Seville was a port; for two centuries it had been the centre of Spanish colonial trade. Where there are ports there will be prostitution, where there is prostitution there will be miscegenation, and where there is miscegenation there will be a variety of physical types – as I had years ago observed was the case with Bombay. When we had finished both the mineral water and our conversation we walked back through the fading light to the Barrio Santa Cruz and to the square where we had eaten the previous night. Here, over our meal, we had another long conversation, about meditation, particularly the practice of visualization, and about the spiritual life.

Rising at 7.20 the next morning and settling our bill in the aviary-patio, we left the hostel in time to have breakfast at the bus station before catching the 8.30 coach to Granada. Though lasting for more than four hours, the journey was quite pleasant – or perhaps we were becoming used to long-distance coach travel. First came brown hills on which grew olive trees and a few vines, then a series of prosperous-looking whitewashed townships. After we had stopped at one of these for ten minutes the mountains began to loom in the distance – rather like thunderclouds on the horizon – and at 11.50 we passed the handful of white cubes scattered at the foot of a mountain with twin peaks that was Archidona. Beyond was olive country; I saw a man driving a herd of goats, and at 12.50 we arrived in Granada. At first sight, at least, the city of the Alhambra looked more prosperous than Seville, which had, as I learned subsequently, the highest rate of unemployment in Spain. After a drink at the bus station bar, where two bright-eyed, very ragged small girls came begging at our table, we caught a taxi up to the Puerta Real, one of the city's two principal squares. On account of the traffic system the driver had to make a detour that took us through an extremely crowded, upmarket shopping district. As in Cordoba and Seville, it seemed one could get to the ancient monuments only by first traversing a thriving modern city of whose existence one had not, perhaps, been aware when planning one's itinerary and which was certainly not mentioned in the travel brochures. From the Puerta Real we wandered along a busy road, up and down various side streets, and through a couple of squares, without being able to find either the Tourist Information Centre – which was somewhere in the area – or a suitable hostel. Eventually we found at the end of a blind alley a modest hotel with an English-speaking proprietress and were soon installed in a quiet back room on the fourth floor, overlooking another alley. A wash was all that we required before setting out for the Alhambra. On the way we had a drink at a pavement café screened by glossy-leaved orange trees and bought some picture postcards, an illustrated guide to the Alhambra and the Generalife, and a copy of Washington Irving's *Tales of the Alhambra* at one of the souvenir shops facing on to the Plaza Nueva. The rest of the approach to the Alhambra was longer and steeper than I had expected, leading as it did to a massive Renaissance gateway and from the gateway to a broad cobbled track that climbed up the hillside through some fine trees. The trees were very big and very old, and so little sunlight filtered through their branches that it felt quite chilly. At the top of the hill, beyond the huge Renaissance terrace-fountain, was the main entrance to the Alhambra. Since it was nearly 4 o'clock we did not go in but decided to wait until the morning, when there would in any case be fewer people about and we would have more time. Instead, we went across to the Manuel de Falla Centre, a very new, very modern building set on the hillside in the midst of a semi-tropical garden. A conference was in progress; there were display boards, and fifty or sixty conventionally dressed men and women standing about in small groups talking animatedly. They were not talking about music. It was some kind of ecological conference, and they were talking about pesticides. Edging through the throng, we made our way downstairs to the spacious bar, which was deserted except for two men arguing very earnestly (in English) about the use of pesticides in Third World countries. Here we had a drink and looked out through the picture windows at the view. It was very hazy.

On the way back we located, in the warren of streets between the Plaza Nueva and Gran Via Colon (the city's principal thoroughfare), a cafeteria-restaurant with a vegetarian option. It was of course closed, but we managed to find out when it would be open and decided to come back later and have our evening meal there. By this time we were both ready for another drink, which we accordingly had at a deserted pavement café in the pedestrianized shopping street off which was the alley where our hotel was situated. Opposite the pavement café was a photographic studio, the windows of which were filled with portrait studies and wedding pictures, all heavily framed and obviously touched up. This led Paramartha to reminisce about the days when he had worked in a photographic studio. Thousands of photographs must have passed through his hands, all of them so incredibly banal that he had developed a positive dislike for photography. While he was speaking I experienced a twinge of toothache. I had been troubled by toothache at Guhyaloka for a couple of days, after losing a filling; it now seemed to be returning, and I experienced further twinges while we were resting in our room at the hotel, when we went out, and during the earlier part of our meal at La Riviera, as the cafeteria-restaurant was called. The dining room of this latter establishment was small and – when no one was playing one-armed bandits in the adjoining bar – unusually quiet, while the (vegetarian) meal itself was reasonably good and the service the best we had so far encountered in Spain, the waiter being an elderly man who spoke a little English and made helpful suggestions. We therefore felt well satisfied as we left La Riviera and made our way through the crowded streets towards the square on the far side of the Cathedral and our last drink of the day. In order to reach the square we had to pass through a passageway that ran alongside the Capilla Real or 'Royal Chapel', which was conterminous with one side of the Cathedral. On our left, opposite the Capilla Real, was a strangely-painted building; the door stood open, light streamed forth, and an art exhibition seemed to be in progress. Paramartha and I stepped inside. A poster said something about (I think) 'Magic-Imagien'. Whatever that might have been intended to convey, the paintings were, for the most part, sufficiently fantastic, not to say surreal, and *very* colourful, and we spent a good half-hour looking round. On the way out we saw a magnificently decorated mihrab or prayer niche. The early fourteenth-century building was, in fact, a former Islamic college that was now used for the occasional exhibition.

The greater part of the square in which we had our last drink was taken up by phalanxes of round white tables, as well as by trees, kiosks, benches, and a monumental fountain. Most of the tables were occupied, either by couples or by family parties; a few of the older women wore black. From further down the square came the sound of flamenco, or at least of a guitar and some rather throaty singing. Beggars wandered in and out of the tables, a blind man hawked lottery tickets in extraordinarily stentorian tones, and children screamed. There was even what appeared to be a madman wandering about. Having found an unoccupied table on the edge of one of the phalanxes we ordered our drinks, surveyed the scene, and talked. In this way an hour or more passed. We then returned to the hotel, where we reported-in as usual and Paramartha read for a while.

That night I slept reasonably well. I would have slept better, though, had it not been for the noise made by the street-cleaning vehicles, which woke me up at 4 o'clock with their rumbling and clattering and kept me awake for some time. In the morning, having risen a little later than usual, we had breakfast in the square where we had been the previous evening, which at that hour of the day was practically deserted. Breakfast consisted of coffee and *churros*. In Madrid the *churros* or fritters had come in two-inch rings, but here they came in sticks a foot long. They also came in three sheets of thick white wrapping paper, the idea apparently being that as they lay on the table in front of one the paper would soak up the excess oil. The paper was, in fact, indispensable, since the *churros* were deep-fried and served with the oil still dripping from them. They were, however, delicious – much better, I thought, than the ones we had had in Madrid – and after a second cup of coffee we felt ready to set out for the Alhambra hill. It was our first full day in Granada, and we planned to spend the greater part of it visiting the fortress-palace of the Moorish kings, in the construction of which Moorish art reached, it was said, 'a spectacular and serene climax.' The walk there seemed to take less time than it had done the previous day, and within forty minutes of leaving the square we had reached the top of the hill and were standing on the threshold of the Puerta de la Justicia or 'Gateway of Justice', as the enormous keyhole-shaped main entrance to the Alhambra was called. Passing through the gateway, above the inner arch of which there was a niche with life-size figures of the Virgin and Child, we emerged into the Alcazaba, the military fortress on the western extremity of the hill. This was the oldest part of the complex, and had originally contained a whole 'government city' of mansions, smaller houses, baths, schools, mosques, barracks, and gardens. All that now remained – apart from the massive circumvallations – were various gateways, courts, and towers, the loftiest of the towers being the five-storeyed Torre del Homenaje or Keep, from the sunlit top of which we had a panoramic view of the Sierra Nevada, as well as being able to see the thickly wooded slopes of the Alhambra hill itself immediately below and the trees and houses in the middle distance. As we were exploring the Alcazaba, the simple grandeur of which reminded me of the Moghul forts of northern India, the place was invaded – there is no other word for it – by three or four large tour groups, each led by an English- or German- or Spanish-speaking guide. Paramartha and I soon escaped into a narrow, delightfully cool garden just inside the ramparts, thence making our way to the Palace of Charles V, a rather heavy Renaissance-style building on the front of which were bas-reliefs depicting the emperor's victories. Though not without a grim sort of dignity, the building was as much out of place in the Alhambra complex as Cordoba Cathedral was in the Great Mosque into whose fabric it had been so rudely inserted. Inside the palace there was a circular two-storeyed colonnaded courtyard which once had served as a bull-ring.

Round the corner from the Palace of Charles V was the entrance to the Casa Real or 'Royal Palace'. Here we had to wait in the sun for half an hour or more, during which time the queue behind us lengthened – and widened – at an alarming rate. Eventually we were allowed in, and found ourselves in the series of tiled and stuccoed rooms that made up the Palacio Mexuar, as the administrative department was called, the first of the three areas into which the Casa Real was divided. We also found ourselves with what seemed like several thousand other people, all progressing, with or without a guide, from hall to court and from court to hall, from the Mexuar to the Diwân and from the Diwân to the Harem. So many people were there, indeed, that at times we were afforded no more than a glimpse of slender columns and scalloped arches, or of richly tiled dados and bands of Arabic script. At other times, however, we were afforded more than a glimpse, as when we saw the Hall of Kings, or Hall of Justice, with its unique series of paintings on leather, and the Hall of the Two Sisters (the sisters in question being two huge slabs of marble in the floor), where we gazed up into a stalactite dome of over 5,000 'honeycomb cells' – a dome which, seen as it were in two-dimensional terms, had the appearance of a multi-pointed golden star. The Patio de los Leones or 'Court of the

The Alhambra

Lions', so called from the twelve archaic lions of its central fountain, had long been familiar to me from photographs and engravings, and I particularly wanted to see it and, perhaps, take a few photographs. In the event this was possible only to a very limited extent. Paramartha and I indeed saw the Court of the Lions, but only when the delicate marble columns supporting the surrounding arcades could hardly be seen for people, and I indeed took a few photographs, but for the most part only of those portions of the arcades that were visible above the heads of the crowd. The least congested part of the Casa Real was the cool and spacious Royal Baths, which were lit by stars and rosettes pierced in the tunnel vaulting and where we were able to admire the colourful glazed tilework at our leisure. Such tilework was in fact one of the principal glories of the Alhambra, and I never tired of looking at its rich colours and intricate designs. Unfortunately, light conditions in the baths were not favourable to photography, and for photographic opportunities I had to wait until, having seen the last of the rooms comprising the Harem, we had left the Casa Real and were wandering in the Partal Gardens, where vistas of ornamental ponds and beds of roses, palm trees, and giant junipers, greeted us at every turn, and where one could not but recall that the word paradise originally meant a park or garden.

But even the Partal Gardens were by no means free from tour groups, and commenting on the fact to Paramartha half an hour later, when we were having a drink and a snack in a smoky bar near the Palace of Charles V, I remarked that I had not expected to find the Alhambra quite so crowded. Paramartha replied that when he had visited the place in April 1988, prior to attending the ordination retreat at Guhyaloka, it had been even more crowded. September was apparently one of the Alhambra's *less* busy months. This was cold comfort, and I quoted to my friend Aldous Huxley's quip that a beauty spot that becomes popular soon ceases to be a beauty spot and becomes a Blackpool. Was the Alhambra about to turn into the Andalusian Blackpool, then? Not staying for an answer, we decided to see the palace gardens of the Generalife, which would no doubt be less crowded than the Alhambra proper, and accordingly retraced our steps to the Torre del Agua or 'Water Tower', near which the entrance to the Generalife was situated. The gardens of the Generalife (the name itself was a corruption of an Arabic phrase meaning 'Architect's Garden') were even more beautiful than those we had seen earlier on. Their central feature was a canal, several hundred yards in length, on either side of which were flower beds and low hedges and gravelled paths enclosed by dark green walls of clipped juniper. The canal ran right up to the little fourteenth-century summer palace of the Kings of Granada, the last few sections of it being flanked at intervals by inward-falling fountains which, meeting in the middle of the canal, formed a glittering double arcade. Though the gardens were not exactly crowded, there were more people about than we had expected, and when we came to explore the little summer palace we found it so congested that there was hardly room to move. This was even more the case when we came to the pavilion behind the palace, and to the Camino de los Cascadas, a staircase with water flowing down its stone balustrades. Here there were not only people but tour groups, and not only tour groups but tour group guides. So great was the crush round one of the pavilions that, giving up hope of being able to see the inside of it, we turned away and started retracing our steps. As we did so I heard one of the guides loudly assuring his flock that wherever one went in the Alhambra there was the sound of water. I could not help thinking that if only he would stop talking we might be able to hear that sound.

On the way down from the Puerta de las Granadas (as the Renaissance gateway to the Alhambra avenues was called) to the Plaza Nueva we visited some of the rather tawdry souvenir shops that lay between there and the Plaza Nueva and I bought a Picasso T-shirt for Prasannasiddhi. Appropriately enough, it showed the well-known drawing of two hands – the hands of two different people – holding the same bunch of flowers. We then had a drink in the Plaza Nueva. Inevitably, conversation turned to the Alhambra and to the fact that it had been so dreadfully crowded. Our visit had, it seemed, taken place none too early in the day. On leaving the Puerta de la Justicia we had seen what looked like a couple of hundred tour coaches lined up in the parking bays and more coaches were arriving every minute. Back at the hotel we had a short rest and I read the previous day's *Times* while Paramartha read the latest *Time* magazine. At 4 o'clock we went out and made our way to the square near the Cathedral. It was Thursday, 13 September; in exactly one week's time we would be flying back to England, and over our afternoon tea we naturally adverted to the subject. Soon Spain would be a thousand miles away, and Madrid and Toledo, Cordoba and Seville, as well as Granada itself, no more than a memory, albeit a pleasant memory. But a week was a long time, not only in politics but in other fields of human activity. Tomorrow we would be having another full day in Granada; today itself was not yet ended, and there was much to be seen in the immediate vicinity. Having finished our tea we therefore went and saw first the Royal Chapel and then, passing through a communicating door, the Cathedral. The early fifteenth-century Royal Chapel, which had been built as a funerary chapel, contained the elaborate marble tomb of Ferdinand and Isabella, complete with life-size recumbent effigies of the Catholic Monarchs, and the no less elaborate tomb of their daughter Joanna the Mad and her husband Philip the Handsome, also complete with life-size recumbent effigies (Paramartha thought that Philip did not deserve his sobriquet). Between the tombs and the high altar was a splendid wrought-iron screen, said to be the most beautiful in Spain. Below the chapel, at the bottom of a short flight of stone steps, was a tiny crypt in which rested the plain lead sarcophagi of the four monarchs and other members of the royal family. In the opinion of Joanna's son, the future Emperor Charles V, the unadorned crypt was 'too small a room for so great a glory', and he accordingly had built the Royal Chapel and commissioned the tombs. The glory in question was, apparently, that of having conquered Granada, expelled the Moors, introduced the Inquisition, persecuted the Jews, and burned heretics and relapsed Christian converts at the stake. The sacristy of the chapel contained a small but important collection of medieval Flemish paintings, including exceptionally fine works by Memling, Bouts, and van der Weyden, together with Ferdinand's sword and Isabella's iron crown, as well as kneeling polychrome figures of the Catholic Monarchs, both extremely lifelike. There was also Botticelli's *Christ on the Mount of Olives*, in which the crimson-clad figure of Christ, framed by realistically depicted branches of olive trees, knelt to receive the cup of his Passion from the hands of the descending angel. Separating him from his sleeping disciples was a fence of suggestively sharpened wooden stakes.

'For all its stark Renaissance bulk, Granada's Cathedral ... is a disappointment.' Thus *The Rough Guide*. I certainly did not find it a disappointment when we entered it from the Royal Chapel, neither, I think, did Paramartha. In fact I was agreeably surprised, even delighted. Despite the enormous size of the place the predominant impression was one of lightness, even grace, an impression that was heightened by the fact that the prevailing colours were white and gold. Perhaps I was mistaken, but there seemed to be a touch of the rococo about the interior of the Cathedral, and for a moment I was reminded of the chapel of Certosa di San Martino in Naples. There was no *coro*

(I believe it had been removed), which meant that one's view was less obstructed than it usually is in a Spanish cathedral, so that what with the mighty compound pillars of the four-aisled nave, and those of the ambulatory and the rotunda within which the high altar was situated, there were some truly marvellous vistas.

Though we must have visited the sacristy of the Cathedral I have no recollection of our so doing. I do, however, recollect our going from the Cathedral to 'La Riviera' and my having *arranza de Cubana*, a dish consisting of mixed rice and banana topped with a kind of tomato sauce (Paramartha stuck to the pasta dish we had had the previous evening). After our meal we had tea in one of the squares and walked up to the Paseo de los Tristes, a sort of promenade overlooking the River Darro. In order to get there we had to go up a narrow cobbled track lined on one side with ancient, shabby houses with wrought-iron balconies and window grilles and wooden casements projecting irregularly from the upper storeys (on the other side of the track was the gorge down which flowed the polluted waters of the Darro). From the track a succession of alleyways, each no more than a few feet wide, climbed up the hillside into the heart of the Albaicin, as the old Moorish quarter was called. Most of the alleyways were deserted, but once or twice a dark, gypsy-like face could be seen peering from a doorway. Arrived at the Paseo, we saw on the other side of the River Darro the tree-clad slopes of the Alhambra hill and, rising out of the mass of living green, the pinkish-grey walls and towers of the ancient fortress-palace. For a few minutes we sat there in the fading light, silent, then made our way down the darkening track to the last drink of the day, the hotel, and our reporting-in.

In the course of our second full day in Granada we did even more walking than usual, and concentrated on Christian rather than on Moorish monuments. The day began, after breakfast, with a second visit to the Paseo de los Tristes, the principal reason for the visit being that I wanted to take some panoramic shots of the Alhambra hill, the light the previous evening not having been sufficient for this purpose. Now the newly risen sun shone directly on to the crenellated walls and towers, turning them from pinkish-grey to pale apricot-gold, and I was able to take photographs both from the Paseo itself and from the garden of a charming old mansion that I discovered a little higher up, a mansion that was now denominated the Archivo Historico de Cividad Granada. When I had taken my photographs, and we were making our way back down the Carrera del Darro, as the narrow cobbled track was called, we saw that one of the ancient shabby houses was in fact a Renaissance mansion and that it was in this mansion that the Archaeological Museum was housed. There was not much to see. According to *The Rough Guide* the museum was 'surprisingly mundane'. It did, however, contain a replica of a 'dama' of the same type as the famous 'dama de Elche', the mysterious half-length statue that may have represented – scholarly opinions differ – a queen, a sacred prostitute, or a Carthaginian divinity. We also saw, further down the track, that the ground floor of one of the houses was an antique shop, or rather, the dusty depository of an extraordinarily varied collection of Iberiana (as one might say), both ancient and modern, Christian and non-Christian. The elderly proprietor encouraged us, in the most friendly way, to have a good look round, but made no attempt to sell us anything. Instead, he showed us how to tell the difference between genuine Roman glassware (or was it pottery?) and modern fakes, of both of which he had plenty of examples. There were a lot of things I would have liked to buy, but apart from the expense there was the question of how I would transport them to England and where I would house them (some of them were quite large). Perhaps I shall have to start a museum at Padmaloka, in the same way that I have started a library. Having lingered a while in the antique shop we had a drink in one of the squares and then went to see the Convento de San Jerónimo. It was deserted except for two elderly nuns who seemed to be the caretakers (I was reminded of the deserted monasteries of Mystra, where only nuns remained to light lamps before the icons), and we were able to wander about the fine old Renaissance building undisturbed. We particularly admired the vast two-storeyed cloister, the broad arches of which were supported by thick round pillars with elaborately carved capitals. The garth or courtyard of the cloister was planted with orange trees, the glossy green foliage and golden fruit of which made a welcome contrast with the rather sombre hues of the surrounding stonework. As part of the convent (or monastery, as we would say in England), there was a huge church. Here, as in the Cathedral, the prevailing colours were white and gold, and I was more than ever reminded of the chapel of the Certosa di San Martino. Round the corner, as it were, from the Convento de San Jerónimo, was the Hospital de San Juan de Dios. The hospital's baroque church was closed, but we were able to see something of the hospital itself, which was still in use, and to admire the splendid tiled Renaissance courtyard. (At this point I should perhaps explain that 'San Jerónimo' was none other than my old friend St Jerome, in whose name an order was established that had many monasteries in Spain, and that San Juan de Dios or 'St John of God' was the founder of the Hospitaller Order of St John of God, an order of nursing brothers.) From the hospital we made our way to a bar where, as so often in non-vegetarian Spain, lunch had to take the form of a snack. We then returned to the hotel, where I read *Time* magazine while Paramartha went and did some sketching in the vicinity of the Cathedral.

At 4 o'clock, Paramartha having returned from his sketching and had a doze, we left the hotel and set out for the Cartuja or Carthusian monastery, which was situated on the northern outskirts of the city, two or three miles from the Cathedral. On the way we had tea and looked in at the church of St John of God, where a service was in progress. The single-aisled church was illuminated only by the candles on the high altar, the blaze of which lit up the extraordinarily ornate reredos that filled the entire back wall, causing the gold with which it was covered to glitter. Very few people were present, most of them women. What effect did all this splendour have on them, I wondered. Did it heighten their sense of devotion? Or were they so used to it that it failed to register? While I was still asking myself these questions, the road grew progressively steeper, and after a thirty- or forty-minute walk we found ourselves at the foot of the acclivity on which stood the Cartuja, described as 'perhaps the grandest and most outrageously decorated of all the country's lavish Carthusian monasteries.' Grand it indeed was, and more frequented than the Convento de San Jerónimo, there even being café-bars and souvenir shops in the court-yard. The grandest part of the monastery, not unnaturally, was the church, which was of 'staggering wealth' and which, with its extensive use of coloured marble, reminded me of the Jesù in Rome. Either in the church or the sacristy there was a fine polychrome statue of St Bruno, the founder of the Carthusian order. Clad in voluminous white robes, the saint's right hand rested on his breast, while his left held up a human skull, at which he was gazing intently. Much less grand than the church, but more beautiful, was the cloister, which with its slender columns, its flower beds, and its central fountain, as well as its few orange trees, looked much more like the courtyard of a Moorish mansion than the cloister of a Counter-Reformation Christian monas-tery. The most interesting part of the place, however, was the refectory, on the walls of which hung huge paintings depicting the history of the Carthusian order. One of these showed the awful moment when a much respected canon of Cologne Cathedral came back to life during his own obsequies to declare that he had been damned – an incident which, according to Carthusian legend, had precipitated the future St Bruno's resolve to abandon all worldly vanities. Other paintings showed the trial and execution of the English Carthusians who in the reign of Henry VIII suffered the supreme penalty for refusing to recognize the king as head of the national church. It was impossible not to admire the heroic spirit of the monks, even though one *did* wish they had laid down their lives in a better cause than that of papal supremacy. Who the artist was I do not know, but the paintings were quite well executed, with some regard for authenticity as to costume, and it was in any case interesting to see an episode from the history of Protestant England through Spanish Catholic eyes. Indeed, it came as something of a shock to see the Protestant English government behaving, so far as Continental Catholics were concerned, in the same brutal fashion that the authorities of the pagan Roman Empire had behaved in the days of the early Church. The actual execution of the English Carthusians was depicted with gruesome realism, as were similar episodes in the history of the Carthusian order, and Paramartha wondered why such paintings were hung in the refectory, of all places. It was enough to put anyone off their food! But perhaps that was the idea, I suggested. Not that the monks were to be put off their food to such a degree that they could not eat. They were to be put off it only to the extent that they ate for the sake of sensual indulgence rather than to sustain life. There were parallels in Buddhist monastic praxis. As we walked round the cloister we noticed that a number of its flagstones were, in fact, the tombstones of seventeeth- and eighteenth-century monks, as the inscriptions on them testified, and Paramartha wondered what they were doing there. I said I thought the monks had asked to be buried in the cloister out of humility, since they would there be daily trodden underfoot, besides which they would be giving the living brethren a constant reminder of the inevitability of death. Outside in the courtyard we continued the conversation over a cold drink, sitting on a bench beneath a tree through whose branches we could see the statue of St Bruno in a niche above the portico. From the monastic life itself we turned to people's attitude towards monasticism and to the conflict between the spiritual and the mundane. By this time it was quite late in the afternoon, and we wanted to make our travel arrangements for the following day. This entailed a long walk to the RENFE station, then a taxi ride to the bus station, where we booked seats on the 2 o'clock coach to Murcia. From the bus station we walked all the way back to the hotel, reported-in, and had a long talk about spiritual life, spiritual communities, etc.

That night my sleep was disturbed not by the street-cleaning vehicles but by the shrieking of what seemed to be a horde of drunken females a couple of hours after we had gone to bed. Over breakfast, which as usual consisted of *churros*, we continued our conversation of the previous evening and again talked about the conflict between the spiritual and the mundane. We then paid a second visit to the Cathedral, where a festival of some kind was being celebrated. Apart from the priests and the choirboys there were only a couple of dozen people present, all gathered in front of the high altar and all singing lustily. Paramartha and I wandered round the place, which at that hour of the day was comparatively well lit, and looked at the age-darkened paintings. By the time we had finished the celebration had ended, everyone was processing out through the doorway, and we followed in their wake. Two or three of the cassocked and surpliced choirboys, I noticed, had stayed behind to extinguish the candles. Outside the Cathedral we were pestered by gypsy women who tried to thrust flowers into our hands (it was not the first time we had encountered them), but shaking them off we went and had a drink and talked about the rival claims of friendship and sex. At noon, having packed our bags and paid our bill, we walked from the hotel to the bus station down a busy street lined with rather upmarket shops. On the way we had a snack and bought a few simple souvenirs. Paramartha bought a little crimson starfish, while I bought three mineral specimens, one of them a piece of *eritrina*, a mineral I had not heard of before.

The coach, which was quite full, left on time, and at once we were passing through hilly, almost mountainous country where there was an abundance of pine and olive. Within the hour, however, we had descended to the plains. On either side lay fields and orchards, as well as sandstone ridges in which caves could be seen. Shortly before entering Guadix we passed a number of big roadside stalls, all selling pottery, mainly blue-and-white and brown and presumably of local origin. In Guadix itself, which we reached at 3 o'clock, the coach halted for a few minutes, and we had a fine view of the baroque façade of the Cathedral. An hour later, having passed through yellow plains and more mountains, we reached Baza, a small town surrounded by extensive olive gardens. Between Guadix and Baza there were many cave dwellings, some of them not so much cave dwellings as cottages that had been built out from, and extended back into, the hillside, and which were even equipped with electricity. Hundreds of people must have lived in them, and no doubt we saw only a small proportion of those that existed in the area. By this time the sky had become overcast and there was a little rain. At Valez Rubio, which we reached at 5 o'clock, we got out and stretched our legs for a few minutes. After Valez Rubio came Lorca and Totana, with olive gardens and vineyards, and at 7 o'clock we reached Murcia. Our first thought was to find accommodation. We therefore started walking in the direction of the city centre, or what we believed was the direction of the city centre, but it took us a long time to get there (Murcia turned out to be far bigger than we had expected), and at one point we started feeling we were going round in circles. According to *The Rough Guide, hostales* were scattered all across the old town, but though we looked down every street and alley all we found were two four-star hotels. To make matters worse, it was raining heavily, and we were both quite wet. Paramartha therefore left me in a small, brightly lit bar while he went and had a further look round on his own. Forty minutes later he returned, without having met with any success and very wet. Moreover, despite a good sense of direction he had not found it easy to locate the bar in which I was waiting, Murcia being even more maze-like in character than the other cities we had visited. It was now 9 o'clock, and having had no lunch we were feeling rather hungry. We therefore had a pizza in a pizzeria which, though crowded and rather noisy, was at least warm and dry. While we were waiting to be served Paramartha went and bought a map of the city and one of the waiters not only pointed out where we now were but indicated the district in which the hostels were to be found. Having finished our pizzas (I had the misfortune to break a tooth on mine) we made our way to the river, crossed over by the Old Bridge, and found ourselves in a busy, rather down-market area with a lot of night life. Even here hostels were not exactly thick on the ground, and after we had wandered round for a while, and Paramartha had checked prices at two or three seedy-looking establishments, we found a back room on the third or fourth floor of a small *pension* on the approach road to the Old Bridge.

Though our room was reasonably quiet when we moved in, it did not remain quiet for long. TV blasted at full volume from open windows on all sides, as though everybody wanted to assure everybody else in the neighbourhood that they *had* TV; there was a constant revving up of lorries immediately below, as well as the sound of car horns, often inordinately prolonged. In the *pension* itself there was a frequent slamming of doors. We were therefore a long time getting off to sleep and rose late. In the bar where we had breakfast there was the usual difficulty over tea, the barman being apparently quite unfamiliar with the fact that tea was made with *hot* water and that one could put milk in it. The main object of our interest that morning was, of course, the Cathedral, but it being Sunday a service was in progress and we could not enter. We accordingly looked round the Cathedral Museum. This contained a small but interesting collection of paintings and polychrome sculptures, as well as a Roman sarcophagus called 'of the Muses', ecclesiastical vestments, and gold and silver sacred vessels. The most striking of the polychrome sculptures was a life-size figure of St Jerome undergoing penance by Salzillo. As in a number of paintings of the subject I had seen, the bearded, half-naked saint was on his knees; in his left hand he held a crucifix, which he regarded with an anguished expression, while the fingers of his outstretched right hand were clenched round the stone with which he was about to smite his breast. On a rock or tree stump in front of him rested a human skull and a book, the open pages of which supported the saint's left arm; beneath his feet, or rather beneath his knees, reposed his faithful lion; on the ground nearby lay another book and a somewhat battered red cardinal's hat. Perhaps the finest of the paintings was an altarpiece by Bernabe de Modena, a fourteenth-century Italian artist who I thought probably belonged to the Sienese School. In an adjacent room we also saw the incredibly elaborate, multi-tiered seventeenth-century *custodia* or processional monstrance, about seven feet in height and described by *The Rough Guide* as '606 kilos of gold and silver twirling like a musical box on its revolving stand.' It did not twirl for us, but perhaps there was a slot for the insertion of coins that we had failed to notice.

By the time we had finished looking round the Cathedral Museum and admiring the *custodia* the service was over and we were able to enter the Cathedral itself, which was basically Gothic and exhibited all the usual features of a Spanish cathedral, including a *coro* with a wrought-iron screen. There was one feature, however, that we had not seen anywhere before. This was an image of the Virgin Mary *without* the Child. The image moreover was surrounded by *ex votos* in the form of eyes, hands, feet, and other limbs all realistically modelled in wax, and I was reminded of similar *ex votos* I had seen in the archaeological museum at Epidaurus and in the chapel dedicated to St Anthony of Padua in Padua Cathedral. The Catholic Christian practice was, it seemed, a direct continuation of the classical pagan one. As we were leaving the Cathedral I saw, crouching on the ground just inside the porch, a strange figure. Clad entirely in rusty black, and with bowed head covered so that her face could not be seen, she crouched there with one hand outstretched in what appeared to be a mute appeal for alms. Yet she did not seem to be an ordinary beggar, and I had the peculiar impression that she was engaged in expiating some dreadful crime. Whatever the truth of the matter, as I passed I dropped a coin into the half open hand. Subsequently Paramartha told me that he too had given her some money and that she had raised her head and looked not so much at him as through him (she had not raised her head for me) and that he had had an impression of extreme suffering. He had also had the impression that notwithstanding her passive and suppliant posture she was possessed of intense energy and that it was the energy of hate. From the Cathedral we walked across to the church of the Dominicans and looked round the entrance to the nunnery. An elderly nun who happened to be peering through the grille gave Paramartha a very suspicious look. It was evident that she had a deep distrust of men, especially young and handsome ones, and with Don Juan perhaps still at large in Spain no doubt even elderly nuns could not be too careful. At all events, both the door of the church and the door of the nunnery remained firmly shut, and having perused the notices we went and had a drink in a bar and then wandered round for an hour or more looking for a museum or church that was open. But it was Sunday and nothing was open – least of all, it seemed, the churches. All that was open, if that is the right word, was the Moorish-style casino, which had once been a rather grand place, but which was now dusty and dilapidated, with faded velvet drapes and tarnished mirrors, and with two or three elderly gentlemen being silently waited upon by even more elderly waiters. After a quick look round we resumed our wanderings and eventually had lunch, or what in non-vegetarian Murcia had to do duty for lunch, and then returned to the *pension*. Here we stayed only long enough to consult our map and to decide that we might as well go and sit for a while in the park, which was situated on the other side of the river, the Cathedral side, little more than half a mile away. Paramartha would sketch while I would take photographs or contemplate the trees.

When we had passed an hour or so in this manner we shook the dust of the park from our feet (there was more dust than grass) and made our way to the bus station. Tomorrow we would be leaving for

Alicante, and we wanted to book seats on the express coach. Unfortunately, the ticket window for the Murcia–Alicante service was closed, though other ticket windows were open and people were queuing up at them. In one of the queues there was a dwarf, a little woman in a green coat hardly three feet tall, and I was reminded of the portraits of dwarfs by Velasquez that we had seen in the Prado, particularly those of 'El Primo' and Sebastian de Morra, both of which revealed the artist's extraordinary power of psychological penetration. Though our ticket window was closed, the bus station bar was open, and we accordingly had a drink and talked about our forthcoming return to England. I would have preferred, I said, to spend two more weeks at Guhyaloka rather than the two days that were all we would be having before catching the plane back to Heathrow, since this would have given us more time to assimilate the experiences of the last two weeks. Paramartha was inclined to agree. Having talked for a while in this vein we returned to the park, at the far end of which we now discovered a small zoo. Incredible as it may sound, the enclosures containing the camels and horses were situated directly underneath a busy flyover. The camels seemed to be not in the least bothered by all the noise, but the horses, sensitive creatures at the best of times, were, I thought, quite disturbed by it. Other enclosures contained zebras, peacocks, deer, wild pigs, wallabies, pelicans, and emus. Though I have always liked to see animals, I am not sure that I like to see them in cages, or even in enclosures, especially in the case of such beasts as the big cats who, in the wild, are accustomed to having plenty of living space. Back in the park Paramartha did some more sketching and I took a few more photographs, after which we went and made another attempt to book seats on the early morning express coach and had another drink in the bus station bar. This time it was tea *with* milk for me and coffee *without* milk for Paramartha, though when my friend went up to the bar he did not find it easy to make the barmen understand these outlandish requirements. When the peseta did drop smirks of derision appeared on their faces and they started ridiculing Paramartha among themselves in a rather unpleasant manner. It pained me to see my good-natured friend being made the object of this uncivilized behaviour, and by the time he returned to our table with the beverages in question I was having some rather critical thoughts about cultural chauvinism. That people belonging to different cultures should have different manners and customs was only natural. It was also natural that those belonging to one culture should sometimes be surprised, even amused, by the manners and customs of those belonging to another. But ridiculing someone on this account, or treating him with contempt, was a different matter altogether. It was a sign of low intelligence and narrow sympathies. In fact it was a sign of ethnocentricity which, one might say, was group egocentricity. Sipping my glass of lukewarm tea (*with* milk) in the frowzy bar I shared these thoughts with Paramartha, who apparently was quite unperturbed by the barmen's behaviour, and I believe a discussion ensued. On leaving the bus station we found it was raining, and it was therefore not long before we took shelter in another bar. Here we talked about Titian, and I commented that I thought his women, though beautiful, lacked character in the sense in which Pope uses the term in the famous line 'Most women have no characters at all.' (Pope was, of course, quoting his friend Martha Blount.) In fact the beauty of Titian's women consisted in this very lack of (individual) character, i.e. consisted in their generic nature. Paramartha was not sure that he agreed with this. We continued the discussion some time later, having had our evening meal in a noisy pizzeria and having finished reporting-in. On this occasion I said that I thought Titian 'idealized' his women, in the sense of subduing the individual to the generic, and that their beauty was therefore ideal rather than real. Now that it was clearer what I had meant by 'lack of character' Paramartha agreed.

The following morning we caught the express coach and, rather to our surprise, reached Alicante at 10 o'clock, after travelling – non-stop – for no more than an hour. We had not realized the journey would be so brief. Had we done so, we would have left Murcia a little later, after seeing the Museo Salzillo, which did not open until 10 o'clock. But no matter. Before our departure Paramartha had bought me a few picture postcards of the museum's collection, which consisted entirely of figures carried in Murcia's famous Holy Week procession. These figures had been carved in the eighteenth century by Francisco Salzillo, who I suspected was of Neapolitan origin, and though superbly executed were of such cloying sentimentality as to be quite ridiculous. No less ridiculous, in a different kind of way, was the Arnold Schwarzenegger video that the bus company put on to beguile the tedium of the journey. It was dubbed in Russian, with Spanish subtitles, and in it the redoubtable Arnold was transmogrified into a Red Army colonel who had (apparently) come to the United States to collect a criminal. So ridiculous were the muscle-man's adventures that one could not help following them, and I looked out of the window only as we by-passed

Elche and the famous palm forest. A man on the other side of the aisle seemed to take it all very seriously, however, leaning forward in his seat with open mouth and shining eyes, especially when Arnold knocked someone down an elevator shaft or through a window, as he quite frequently did. Nonetheless, he seemed not to mind when, on our coming to a halt in the Alicante bus station, the video was suddenly switched off and his hero disappeared from the screen in the middle of a particularly exciting episode.

The first thing Paramartha and I did on descending from the coach was to find a *consigna* and leave our modest luggage there. We were then free to wander around Alicante until it was time to catch the 2 o'clock coach to Villajoyosa. Both of us had been in the lively port city before, myself three or four times, and we had no difficulty in negotiating the busy shopping district where I bought a new holdall, and finding our way down to the sea front, where we had a drink in or outside three different bars. The weather was, in fact, distinctly sultry, even though the brightness of the sunshine was from time to time veiled by a shower of rain. Though it was mid-September, the sandy beaches were still quite crowded, mostly with elderly people who did not look their best in bathing costumes, and from one of the bars we saw three or four men putting the finishing touches to a truly magnificent sand castle, Spanish style, complete with crenellated battlements, drawbridge, corner turrets, and red-and-yellow Catalan flags. We had hoped that the Museum of Twentieth Century (Spanish) Art would be open, but since it was a Monday the place was closed, and we therefore strolled along the narrow back streets in the direction of the city centre until we came upon a first-floor pizzeria. Here we had lunch. It was a quiet place, with only two or three other customers, and we had a leisurely meal before returning to the bus station and retrieving our luggage from the *consigna*. On reaching the outskirts of Alicante our coach was slowed down for half an hour by very heavy traffic, so that the journey to Villajoyosa took over an hour, and I had plenty of time in which to study the now familiar landmarks on either side of the coastal road, especially a biscuit-coloured luxury hotel that looked as though it had been designed and built by a mad Aztec. In Villajoyosa we had a drink at a pavement café situated on a busy main road and talked about the need for inspiration in the Order, or rather I held forth on the subject while Paramartha listened, after which we took a taxi to Sella. Within minutes it became apparent that the driver was not sure where we wanted to go. 'Sella!' Sella!' we vociferated, pointing in the desired direction, as he went round in a circle. Eventually I happened to pronounce the name of our destination quite forcibly, whereupon his face lit up with a smile of understanding. 'Oh you mean *Sella!*' he exclaimed, pronouncing the name more forcibly still, and at once started heading inland.

It was good to be in the hills again, good to see the olive gardens and carob trees on either side of the winding road; good to see in the distance the serrated ridge behind which was the magic Valley. Sella had not yet arisen from its siesta, and the narrow, sun-drenched streets were deserted. Paramartha and I sat on the back veranda of the Bar Maria, which since I was last there had been extended out over the hillside, and was now very spacious indeed. It too was deserted. I noticed that a pumpkin plant had climbed up from the kitchen garden below and that the pale green tendrils had extended themselves right along the veranda railing. This reminded me of the pumpkins I had grown in Kalimpong, at the Triyana Vardhana Vihara, and I started reminiscing about them and about the other crops I had grown there: maize, rye, bananas, cauliflower, beans, and bitter gourd. I spoke about my 110 orange trees and my bamboo grove, both of which had been a useful source of income. Before long we were discussing the possibility of the Guhyaloka community growing its own vegetables. I had been quite disappointed, I said, when the kitchen garden at Padmaloka was grassed over. It might indeed be cheaper to buy vegetables, but economy should not be the only consideration.

We had now been in the Bar Maria an hour and it was 5 o'clock, the time at which we had arranged to meet Dharmavira there. At 5.05 we heard a vehicle draw up outside. 'That sounds like a small Scotsman,' I remarked. Sure enough, a couple of minutes later Dharmavira appeared, looking red-faced and healthy. On the way up to Guhyaloka I enquired how he and the other members of the community had been faring, at the same time gazing out at the ever-changing landscape. Almond orchards and pine forests appeared, and soon I saw on the skyline the pinnacles of grey rock that guarded the entrance to the magic Valley. That night, after supper, Paramartha and I sat out on the veranda of the bungalow and talked about Freud, particularly about his theory that without a degree of instinctual repression there could be no civilization – a theory with which I was inclined to agree. Having reported-in, we retired early. We were glad to be back, glad to be again permeated by the deep stillness of the Valley, and slept soundly.

The next two days – the last that we would be spending at Guhyaloka for the time being – were occupied mainly with preparations for our departure, though we managed to go down to the shower and I saw Dharmabandhu and one or two other members of the building team. On the morning of Thursday, 20 September, we locked the door of the bungalow and handed the key to Dharmavira, who then drove us down to Sella and from Sella to Alicante airport. In the airport the three of us had lunch together in the restaurant, after which Paramartha and I went through to the departure lounge. Three hours later, after an uneventful flight, we were being met at Heathrow by Kovida and driven straight up to Padmaloka, stopping on the way only to eat at a Little Chef. Two days later, on Saturday, 22 September, I gave my poetry reading on the theme of friendship at the Norwich Centre, and on the following Monday Paramartha and I drove down to London. On Thursday, 28 September, when we had been back in England for a week, and I sat down at my desk at 8 o'clock on a mild, cloudy evening and started writing this Letter, as I wanted to give you an account of our Spanish tour before impressions started to fade. For one reason and another, the account has taken me longer to write than I had expected, but the work is now done, and it only remains for me to share with you a few miscellaneous observations. I would like, however, to remind you that these observations relate to what fell beneath my personal notice in the course of a tour that lasted for only two weeks and was confined to the south-east quarter of Spain, and they are not to be regarded as being generalizations about Spain or the Spanish people.

One of the first things that struck me was the extent of the distances Paramartha and I had to cover even though, as I have just mentioned, our travels were confined to one particular corner of the country. Moreover, it was possible to go for as much as a hundred miles and see virtually no sign of human habitation. Wild animals were non-existent and domesticated ones a rarity. As for wild birds, there were even fewer about than in trigger-happy Italy, possibly for the same reason (though the entire absence of hedges must also have played a part), and in the whole course of our tour the only members of the feathered tribe that I saw in the countryside were three crows, all foraging together in a field, and a solitary hawk. In the cities there were few dogs and even fewer cats, and I was glad to see that dogs were not allowed to foul the footpaths in the way that they do in Britain. All the cities we visited were, in fact, remarkably free from rubbish and litter of every kind. The only exception was Murcia. I also noticed that there were no signs of vandalism – no wrecked telephone booths or smashed street lamps – and very little in the way of graffiti. Though *The Rough Guide* warned that bag snatching was common in Seville, neither there nor in any other place did we see the slightest evidence of petty crime and felt perfectly safe wherever we went, even at night. This happy state of affairs may well have been due to the Guardia Civil, which is said to enjoy – in those parts of Spain which we did not visit, as in those we did – much of its old prestige and authority.

Though our ignorance of Spanish precluded any closer contact with the local people, in such dealings as we did have with them Paramartha and I found them polite and helpful almost without exception. I particularly appreciated the fact that, when we entered a souvenir shop, no attempt was made to hassle us and we were left to look around as we pleased. The only time we were ever hassled was when the blowsy gypsy women of Granada attempted to thrust their wilted flowers into our hands. But though they were polite and helpful, and though they did not hassle us, the people we encountered, or among whom we found ourselves, all had what I, for one, regarded as a serious fault. Whether Madrilenian or Toledan, Cordoban or Sevillian, Granadian or Murcian, they all were extremely noisy. It was not that they talked loudly, which they undoubtedly did. They seemed to want to make as much noise as possible. As James A. Michener wrote more than twenty years ago:

> I doubt if there is any country in Europe which has the unremitting
> noise quotient of Spain.... Anyone who has a television set must play
> it at top volume to let his neighbours know he has it. Anyone who
> has a motorcycle must run it open-throttle to impress those who
> aren't so lucky. And now a family down the alley, who had neither TV
> nor motorcycle, showed the world what they did have by playing
> their radio full-blast.... How I got to sleep I don't know....

Michener's experience was very much our own, except that since his day the noise quotient of Spain must have reached new levels. In those parts of the country which Paramartha and I visited, at least, the concept of noise pollution seemed to be unknown.

From what I have written about our tour it will be obvious to you that Paramartha and I saw quite a lot. But there was a lot that we did not see. Indeed, there were certain things we had no particular wish to see. Among these were buildings and monuments of a military character, so that we did not go to see the Valle de los Caidos or 'Valley of the Fallen', near the Escorial, or the Alcazar of Toledo, which had sustained a famous siege during the Civil War. But though we did not go to see them, buildings and monuments of a military character were much in evidence, and I formed the impression that the army occupied quite a prominent place in people's consciousness, even if not in their actual lives. It could hardly have been otherwise. The Civil War, in which a million Spaniards had been killed, mainly by other Spaniards, had ended only fifty-one years ago. Men of my own generation had fought in that war, and not a few of the stooping, grey-haired pensioners I saw in the streets, and on trains and coaches, must have had blood on their hands. In the seven or eight cities we visited the material damage done by the Civil War seemed to have been made good (though the doorway of at least one government building in Toledo *was* still surrounded by bullet-marks), but I had little doubt that the minds of older people, at least, were still scarred by memories of the conflict. Indeed, there were times when, watching the crowds milling in the squares and other public places I wondered what passions might yet smoulder beneath the surface.

Nonetheless, the majority of the people we saw had not only taken no part in the Civil War but had not even been born then. They were no older than my own children and grandchildren might have been, and in the course of their lives they had seen many changes, especially during the last fifteen years. Spain, including those parts of it to which our travels were confined, had become more like the rest of Western Europe. Tradition was in retreat. Nowhere was this more evident than in the field of dress. In none of the places we visited did I see anyone wearing regional costume (unless one counts the girl singers and musicians we saw on the platform of Aránjuez station), though books on Spain published no more than thirty or forty years ago were full of pictures of men and women in this or that colourful local dress. Young people, especially, looked just like their counterparts in England and Germany – and North America. Even the gypsy women who tried to force their flowers on us wore, for the most part, soiled jeans and open-neck shirts. In the south-east, much of the old Spain seemed to have disappeared, or to be in process of disappearing, and I found myself paraphrasing Yeats' well known lines and murmuring:

Romantic Spain is dead and gone.
It's with young Lorca in the grave.

Nor was that all. Not only was Romantic Spain dead, but maggots were already beginning to swarm in the corpse. On the eve of World War I an American traveller, the author William Dean Howells, could write,

> In Seville the law of the mantilla is rigorously enforced. If a woman drives [i.e. drives a carriage], she may wear a hat; but if she walks she must wear a mantilla under pain of being pointed at by the finger of scorn.

In contemporary Seville, as in all the other places Paramartha and I visited, not only was the law of the mantilla not enforced but a woman could, it seemed, appear in public without quite a number of articles of clothing hitherto deemed indispensable without being pointed at by the finger of scorn. The fact was that in reacting against one extreme, the extreme of prudery, a number of women, including some older women, had gone to the opposite extreme, that of shamelessness. In the field of female dress, as in other fields, a middle way was needed: a middle way between puritanism and hedonism. Ultimately, of course, a middle way was needed between dogmatic theism and equally dogmatic materialism. Perhaps Buddhism, in the form of the FWBO, could help at least some Spaniards find that middle way.

Urgyen Sangharakshita

LETTER FROM NEW ZEALAND

A summary of visits to the United States, Australia, and New Zealand

Dear Dharmacharis and Dharmacharinis,

Paramartha and I arrived in New Zealand on Monday, 25 November, and as we are now half-way through our tour I thought I would give you a brief account of our programme so far.

In the course of the last three-and-a-half months we have visited eight FWBO centres in four countries (the United States, Canada, Australia, and New Zealand) and stayed in seven men's communities, besides which I have taken part in three book launches, given one poetry reading, and conducted altogether twelve Mitra ceremonies. There have also been receptions to attend and people to see.

The highlight of our visit to the United States was our road trip with Manjuvajra, in the course of which we drove through eight states (Montana, Wyoming, Colorado, New Mexico, Arizona, Utah, Nevada, and California) and covered, in the course of two weeks, nearly 5,000 miles. Manjuvajra did all the driving and was an excellent companion and guide. We visited Yellowstone National Park, Monument Valley, Yosemite, the Grand Canyon, and Death Valley, and saw bison, elk, moose, and coyote in their natural habitat. In Boulder, Colorado, where we spent three nights, we renewed contact with Bill Douglas, an old Friend of the FWBO, and enjoyed a very worthwhile exchange with Reginald A. Ray, the author of *Buddhist Saints in India*. In Denver we were entertained to dinner by Anagarika Martha Dharmapali, an old correspondent of mine, and ten or twelve members of her group, and afterwards had an interesting discussion with them. Our experience of New Mexico was somewhat marred by rain, but we spent a couple of hours in Taos (touristy and very commercial) and in Santa Fé, as well as visiting the D.H. Lawrence Ranch and Memorial Chapel. We also saw the notorious 'obscene' Lawrence paintings, now languishing in a corner of a hotel in Taos, the proprietor of which, an expatriate Greek, has offered to give them to Britain if the British government agrees to restore the Elgin Marbles to Greece. Also in Colorado, we spent a night at the Chrestona Zen Center, where Roshi Richard Baker has established his headquarters, but could not meet the Roshi himself as he was in Germany. The centre is situated on the edge of 'UFO Valley', where we met an elderly eccentric, the proprietor of a rock-shop, who was also selling a book on the mysterious events alleged to have taken place there.

In San Francisco I renewed contact with Reb Anderson and Norman Fischer, ex-abbot and abbot respectively of the San Francisco Zen Center, as well as meeting, for the second time, the very friendly and welcoming people who run Dharma Publishing, who entertained us royally both there and at the Nyingma Center.

From San Francisco Manjuvajra drove us up the coast to Seattle, and from there Aryadaka drove us up across the US–Canada border to Vancouver. In the course of the former journey we passed through avenues of magnificent redwoods, some of them of enormous height and girth. In Seattle we visited the Japanese Pure Land temple, where Manjuvajra and I renewed our acquaintance with the minister, Don Castro.

After visiting Vancouver, we flew from Seattle to Los Angeles via San Francisco, and from Los Angeles to Sydney – a fourteen-hour flight. At Los Angeles there occurred the only hitch we have so far experienced: our evening flight was cancelled and we were obliged to spend the night at a hotel, continuing our journey the following day.

In Sydney and Katoomba, and again in Melbourne, we received the same warm welcome that we had received in the United States and Canada, and in these places too I saw many people individually, as I am now doing in New Zealand.

My overall impression of the FWBO centres I have visited is that they are flourishing, though not all are free from difficulties. Some, indeed, are flourishing to a greater extent than I had been led to expect. Everywhere Paramartha and I have been shown great kindness, have been well looked after, and have not neglected the local art galleries and second-hand bookshops. Speaking for myself, what I have enjoyed most, apart from the personal contact with Order members, Mitras, and Friends, has been the opportunity of seeing – in some cases for the second time – so many areas of great natural beauty, both in North America and Australia. Now that I am in New Zealand I look forward to seeing some of the beauties of both Islands. All being well, the week after next Paramartha and I will be travelling down the east coast of the North Island to Wellington, there to see the last FWBO centre of our present trip, and from Wellington we shall be flying down to the South Island. There is much more that I could write, but to do justice to all the experiences, thoughts, and human communication of the last three-and-a-half months would require a small volume, and I must ask you to be satisfied with these few notes.

Urgyen Sangharakshita

Nine Days in South Island, New Zealand

Wellington – Invercargill – the journey from Invercargill to Picton – the journey from Te Anau to Milford – Milford Sound – the Japanese – Mararoa Lakes – thoughts on reading Lloyd Geering's Tomorrow's God – Te Anau – Queenstown – Arrowtown – Bungee Bridge – Wanaka – Lake Hawea – valley of the Haast River – Haast – the journey from Haast to Hokitika – Fox Glacier and Franz Josef Glacier – reflections on saying goodbye to friends and teachers thirty years ago and the return to England – Terry Delamare – 400 miles through Shantytown, Punakaiki, Buller Gorge, to Murchison – Murchison Museum – Nelson – Wellington to Auckland – Wanganui River Road – Hiruharama (Jerusalem) – Mount Ruapehu – Mount Egmont – reflections on urbanization

Dear Dharmacharis and Dharmacharinis,

Nine days in my own case, that is, Paramartha having already spent two weeks in Invercargill with his parents when I arrived there from Wellington. In Wellington I had passed the time happily enough, seeing Order members, Mitras, and Friends individually, visiting second-hand bookshops, and reading. There were also outings to various bays and beaches, in the course of one of which I was taken to a nearby national park and given a glimpse of the glories of the New Zealand bush. Paramartha and I had spent four days motoring from Auckland to Wellington, travelling along the coastal road to Ohope, from Ohope to East Cape, and from East Cape to Napier, in this way seeing quite a lot of the North Island. We saw the Bay of Plenty, Poverty Bay (famous in New Zealand history as the place where Captain Cook landed) and Hawke Bay, visited Whakatane, Gisborne, Hastings, and a number of smaller towns (some of them very small indeed), drove through two limestone gorges, and spent a morning on the windswept shores of an inland lake, high up in the mountains. Now I was to see something of the South Island, and see it in the company of Paramartha. Having flown from Wellington to Christchurch, where I transferred to a small propeller plane, I landed at Invercargill on the afternoon of Wednesday, 1 January 1977, and was met at the airport by my friend, who drove me to his parents' home via the city centre.

Invercargill is the southernmost city of mainland New Zealand. It has a population of 48,000, and as I saw as my plane landed it is laid out in rectangular style, with a number of parks and other green spaces. It is also Paramartha's birthplace. I noticed, though, that the former Damon Peterson had no particular fondness for his home town, which he had left when he was eighteen, had visited only rarely thereafter, and had not seen for the last nine or ten years. Nevertheless, in the course of my two days in Invercargill he drove me round the place and showed me the house where he had grown up, the Roman Catholic primary school and college he had attended, and the Roman Catholic Basilica where he and his family had worshipped, the imposing dome of which was visible from most parts of the city. We also visited the museum, whose most interesting exhibit, at least to me, was not a dead one but a live one. This was Henry, the museum's male tuatara, who at the time of our visit fortunately happened to be giving *darshan*. The tuatara is not, as one might have supposed, a kind of lizard, but the only living representative of the mighty dinosaur family, which for 400,000,000 years dominated the earth.

There were also excursions to places of interest further afield. The first of these was to Bluff, the port for Invercargill and Southland, some twenty miles away, where we walked for a mile or more along the cliff-top path, looking down every now and then through gaps in the bushes at the rocks below, on one of which a seal was lying. The sky was overcast that morning and there was a light mist, but we were able to make out the shape of Stewart Island in the distance. Apart from a few scattered islets, beyond Stewart Island there was nothing but ocean until one reached the frozen wastes of Antarctica. Our other excursion was to Curio Bay and Porpoise Bay, which were situated about thirty miles to the east of Invercargill. According to the road atlas Curio Bay was a place of historical interest, but I do not remember in what the interest consisted. There was little doubt, though, that it was a popular place for camping and barbecues and a few ancient caravans could be seen parked among the huge New Zealand flax bushes. In fact it had recently featured in the news, having been the site of New Year's Eve celebrations at which a young man was stabbed by a member of a rival gang. As Paramartha and I made our way down to the wide swathe of sandy beach we saw that the fire brigade had cordoned off the area where the murdered man's body had lain. Not far away, the sea had deposited among the rocks masses upon masses of seaweed, the rubbery brown ribbons of which were of a length and thickness I had not seen before.

Much as I enjoyed these excursions I could not ignore the fact that the region through which we passed had, on the whole, a wild and desolate air, so that it was not surprising that Paramartha should have left when he did, the more especially as Invercargill, where everything seemed to shut down after 6 o'clock, had little to offer a young man who enjoyed poetry and had begun to think about life. Indeed, during my two days in Invercargill I felt as though I was living at the very edge of the inhabited world, even at the very edge of civilization, and could easily imagine someone thinking that if he was not careful he might slip off and fall into a kind of void. Hence perhaps the urge, on the part of so many New Zealanders, not just to leave Invercargill, not just to leave the South Island, but to leave New Zealand itself and travel to the ancient centres of civilization and culture in both Europe and Asia. Hence perhaps the willingness, in the past, of so many young men to look upon life in the armed forces, whether as conscript or volunteer, as the doorway to a wider experience of the world.

Between excursions, and in the evenings, I talked with Paramartha's parents, who, having heard, as they said, a lot about me, had greeted me cordially on my arrival at their home and made me very welcome. At one point the family photograph album was brought out, and I was able to follow Paramartha's development from a rather fat-faced baby to an unusually good-looking sixteen- or seventeen-year-old. It was interesting to see the gradual emergence not only of the features with which I was familiar but also the *expression*.

Though the previous day the sky had been overcast, and there had been a little rain, on the morning of our departure from Invercargill the sunshine could hardly have been brighter or the heavens more ethereally blue. Before us lay seven days of travel through the wonderland that was the western side of the South Island and I felt quite exhilarated. As for Paramartha, though fond of his parents he was not

Paramartha

sorry to be leaving Invercargill after his two-week sojourn there, his memories of the place being inseparable from the feelings of dullness and boredom he had experienced in it as a teenager. In respect of interest and variety the next seven days in fact rivalled the fortnight Paramartha and I had spent, three months earlier, driving with Manju-vajra from Missoula to San Francisco. During those seven days on the road from Invercargill to Picton there passed before our eyes one picture postcard view after another. There were views of mountains and lakes; views of waterfalls and bouldered streams; views of rivers that wound their way through quiet valleys or between limestone cliffs; views of broad, pebbly estuaries; views of fields divided by rows of giant poplars; views of bald green hills on which grazed flocks of sheep and herds of cows; views of distant snows; views of deserted beaches strewn with white driftwood; views of distant islands; views of fantastic rock formations; views of slender bridges over deep ravines; views of glaciers; views of avenues of magnificent beeches; views of dense native bush, where the graceful fronds of the tree fern showed vividly green in the sunlight; views of unfrequented roads bordered by tiger lilies, blue hydrangeas, and pink rambler roses – all growing wild in the utmost profusion; views of tiny wooden churches perched on the hillside; views of acre upon acre of blazing yellow gorse; views of parks and formal gardens; views of historic buildings. So many views were there, often of such extraordinary beauty, that there is no question of my trying to describe even some of them in detail, and anyone who is interested will have to have recourse to one or other of the many lavishly illustrated books on New Zealand that are available, or, better still, make the same journey that Paramartha and I made. In giving an account of that journey I shall, therefore, not be attempting to paint any poetic word-pictures but instead will sim-ply describe our route and comment, from time to time, on points of interest.

One of our principal objectives was to see Milford Sound, 'the most accessible of the fjords through which the Tasman Sea permeates Fjordland'. Originally we had planned to see it on the second day of our trip, but on our arrival at Te Anau, where we had arranged to spend that and the following night, Paramartha suggested that we should press on and see Milford that very day. He did not mind the extra driving, he said, and in any case, the weather might not be so fine tomorrow. The result was that the next two hours were among the most enjoyable of my life, at least in recent years. From Invercargill we had taken the scenic route to Tuatapere, and later we had eaten our picnic lunch on the sun-drenched shores of Lake Manapouri, the deepest lake in New Zealand, and, it was said, the most beautiful. Thus our journey that morning had certainly not been devoid of outstanding views. But the views on the journey from Te Anau to Milford, especially coming as they did one after another, in rapid succession, were of an entirely different order. For about twenty miles the road ran parallel to Lake Te Anau, the largest lake in the South Island, after which it struck inland, following the Eglinton River up the valley and crossing numberless streams and creeks. On the way, we passed conical green hills, huge expanses of gorse in full bloom, and flocks of sheep. After an hour came a beech forest, and in the beech forest, not far from the road, were the Mirror Lakes, so called because – as we saw – they reflected in their brown depths a neighbouring snow peak. We then drove through 'the avenue of the disappearing mountain', as it was called, an optical illusion in which the peak at the head of the road kept appearing and disappearing. By this time we were, in fact, in more mountainous terrain, and passing from the world of the beautiful to the world of the sublime. Mountains rose more and more steeply all round us, their sides covered with dark green bush. Waterfalls fell from precipitous heights. Having passed two or three small lakes, the road dropped abruptly into a valley, then rose by a series of sharp bends to the Homer Tunnel.

The tunnel, which was situated 3,000 feet above sea level, was just wide enough for two-way traffic, and sloped downwards towards the Milford end. On either side of its mouth rose grey cliffs so bare of vegetation as to seem more like the sides of a stone quarry. Down the face of these cliffs coursed innumerable waterfalls, all glittering like quicksilver in the brilliant sunshine. On the ground lay heaps of half melted snow, and great boulders, either blasted from the tunnel or fallen from the cliffs, were strewn about, one boulder being as big as a two-storeyed house and almost as square. On passing through the tunnel, rock-hewn and without lining, we emerged into the spectacular Claddau Valley and commenced the steep, winding descent to Milford. Twenty minutes later we had reached our destination. As it was mid-afternoon, we were too late for a steamer trip round the Sound. But we did not mind. We were quite content to wander up and down the rocky foreshore, every now and then raising our eyes to the celebrated Mitre Peak, whose truly episcopal contours dominated the scene and were reflected in the waters at our feet.

The road terminating at Milford, we returned to Te Anau by the same route and checked in at the motor camp where we were to stay. A short rest, and we were ready for dinner. This we eventually found in one of the township's two Chinese restaurants. Unfortunately, our vegetarian fried rice turned out to contain prawns. In the Far East prawns are apparently regarded as vegetables. Finding a vegetarian meal in the evening was in fact the only real difficulty we encountered in the course of our tour (we had encountered a similar difficulty when travelling in the North Island). Sometimes, especially in the case of the smaller towns, which closed down at six or even earlier, we had difficulty finding a meal in the evening at all. And only when we were lucky enough to find a Chinese or Thai restaurant was there more than one vegetarian option. On the present occasion we finished our meal as best we could, picking out the prawns, and spent the rest of the evening strolling round Te Anau, a township of about 3,000 people which was, it appeared, popular as a resort. The streets were full of tourists and holidaymakers, the souvenir shops of kitsch, much of it featuring cartoon versions of the unfortunate kiwi – the flightless bird, not the native New Zealander. Among the tourists were a number of Asians, including quite a few Japanese. This led me to wonder what the attitude of the average citizen of New Zealand was to these strangers from the Land of the Rising Sun. The Japanese were still extremely reluctant to express remorse for their wartime atrocities, the victims of which had in many cases been Australian and New Zealand prisoners of war. Some commentators attributed this reluctance to the fact that Japanese culture is a shame culture, not a guilt culture. Others ascribed it to the Japanese habit of simply ignoring anything unpleasant or embarrassing and behaving as though it did not exist or had not occurred. To me the reluctance suggested that Buddhist ethics, especially Mahāyāna Buddhist ethics, were not very influential in the domain of Japanese public life. After all, the Germans had repeatedly expressed their remorse for having persecuted the Jews and had given enormous sums to the State of Israel by way of compensation. Why could the Japanese not behave similarly in respect of the crimes they had committed against Chinese civilians, Korean 'comfort women', and Allied prisoners of war? Did it mean that in Germany, for all the horrors of the Nazi period, Christian ethical teaching had struck deeper root than Buddhist ethical teaching had succeeded in striking in Japan? After all, did not the *Sūtra of Golden Light* teach confession of, and repentance for, one's sins of body, speech, and mind, and was not this sūtra supposedly one of the most important sūtras in the history of Japanese Buddhism and, therefore, in the history of the Japanese people in so far as they were Buddhist? These reflections of mine, which I shared with Paramartha, may well have been prompted by the fact that recently I had seen a review of a book that gave, for the first time, an account of the incredibly brutal treatment meted out by their Japanese captors to a group of some 300 Allied prisoners of war. Only five of the prisoners had survived (by managing to escape), the Australian author of the book being one of them.

The following day the weather was very changeable, being cold, windy, and rainy, with intervals of brilliant sunshine, and we congratulated ourselves on having made the trip to Milford Sound when we did. But changeable as the weather was, it did not prevent us from getting out and about. In the morning, after breakfasting at the local bakery and café, we drove fifty or more miles up a gravel side road to see the Mararoa Lakes. For much of the way the road followed the windings of the river, and we had pleasant, pastoral views of meadows where sheep and cows grazed. In the background were low blue hills, and beyond the hills ranges of snowy mountains. There were few signs of human habitation, and a kind of breathless hush prevailed. At one point, though, the road was bordered by a line of magnificent poplars that continued for a mile or more and led to what appeared to be a fruit farm. By the time we reached the lakes the sky had more or less cleared. Tents and trailers were visible here and there among the trees, the spot apparently being a popular one with weekend campers. The second lake was very much larger than the first, and like the first it was bordered with thick forest. Many of the trees, I noticed, were hung with moss, which also covered much of the ground. Owing to the recent heavy rains, the road through the forest had turned into a muddy track and we were unable to follow it all the way to the head of the second lake, where it terminated, as we had hoped to do. We therefore turned round and made our way back along the gravel road to its junction with the highway. From here we proceeded not to Te Anau but to Mossburn, which was situated at about the same distance in the opposite direction. The sun was now quite hot, and after eating our picnic lunch in the rather bleak little park-cum-children's playground we adjourned to the very 'English' tea and gift shop nearby and sat outside enjoying the heat as we drank our tea. On our way back to Te Anau, however, the clouds suddenly gathered, the sky darkened, and the rain began to fall, and we spent the rest of the afternoon in our cabin at the motor park reading.

I was then reading Lloyd Geering's *Tomorrow's God*, which several people had recommended to me. Lloyd Geering could be described as the Don Cupitt of New Zealand, and 'the Dogmaless Dean' is in fact quoted a number of times in his book. Less subtle but perhaps more honest than Don Cupitt, he resigned as Professor of Old Testament Studies and Principal of the Theological Hall at Knox College in Dunedin upon losing his faith and is well known as a commentator on religious and theological issues. According to the book's blurb, Geering

> argues that the world we live in is largely a product of our own
> making, and that we supply its meaning. Thus 'God', a central
> symbol of meaning, is entirely a human creation. He traces the
> collective 'drift towards meaning' that gave rise to the various
> religions, and explores the reasons they are now in decline.

Further,

> Geering argues that, for our own survival, we must consciously
> create new meaning for our lives. We must focus – and urgently – on
> caring for the earth. But new systems of meaning can only evolve out
> of our cultural past, and Geering shows how the Christian tradition
> may lead towards a new world of meaning.

I found the book interesting, informative, and an easy read, and would certainly recommend it as a highly accessible introduction to Sea of Faith type thinking. In two central chapters he proposes what he calls a Three World model of reality, the three worlds being those of physical objects, states of consciousness, and knowledge, and describes the phases of human culture, the ethnic (tribal), the trans-ethnic (religious), and global (secular). Like me, he emphasizes the importance of the Axial Period, and views the transition from consciousness to self-consciousness as absolutely crucial. Nonetheless, for all its intellectual honesty, and despite points of agreement, I found *Tomorrow's God* a deeply unsatisfactory book. The author seemed to have no actual feeling for religion. He seemed to be devoid of any higher sensibility, any awareness of a transcendental dimension, 'the Transcendental' being for him, no doubt, only a symbol of meaning and as such a human creation. His approach to the basic questions of human existence is in fact entirely rational. For him 'trans-ethnic religion', the product of the Axial Period, has been superseded, ever since the seventeenth- to nineteenth-century Enlightenment, by secular modes of thought, Christianity itself now surviving in the West only as a folk religion. Tomorrow's 'God' is the Earth, and tomorrow's secular 'religion' no more than what might be described – the characterization is mine, not his – as environmentalism touched with emotion. Personally, I cannot imagine man's quest for ultimate meaning finding satisfaction in 'our utter dependence on the earth, accompanied by a sense of reverence for the earth,' any more than I can envisage concern for the environment, however important this may be, as being an adequate substitute for the leading of the spiritual life. On Geering's terms, the problem of birth, old age, disease, and death remains unsolved.

Late that afternoon, the weather having apparently changed, we drove into Te Anau and saw the miniature wildlife park, which was located on the outskirts of the town, not far from the lake. Before we could see very much, however, the rain started to descend and we were obliged to take refuge in the car. Before so doing we did nonetheless manage to have to have a good look at a rare flightless bird. This was the takahe or notornis. About the size of a large hen, it had a short beak and dark, smooth plumage in which there was a metallic blue-green tint, and pecked about on the other side of the wire mesh without taking any notice of us.

Queenstown, which was also situated on the edge of a lake, was bigger than Te Anau and much more of a tourist centre. The guidebook went so far as to declare it the premier holiday resort of the South Island, and as having 'an international flavour'. Paramartha and I arrived there at about 11 o'clock, having left Te Anau soon after breakfast and come by way of Mossburn, Five Rivers, and Kingston. For the latter part of the journey the road skirted Lake Wakatipu, on the eastern shore of which Queenstown was situated, so that we were able to enjoy fine views of woods, waters, and mountains. Earlier, I had noticed many poplars, willows, and hawthorns – trees I associated with England rather than with New Zealand. In Queenstown we found the holiday season already in full swing, and the international flavour of the place very much in evidence. Pavement cafés were crowded; steamers and launches furrowed the placid surface of the lake, which was almost entirely surrounded by mountains; sightseeing helicopters and biplanes droned overhead. After walking along the promenade, and exploring the quayside area, we therefore drove out of town and up into the mountains in the direction of Skippers, where in the eighteenth century men had dug for gold. Our rental car contract prevented us from going all the way and seeing the Skippers Canyon, but we went far enough and eventually, having climbed to a height of about 4,000 feet, we drew up on the far side of the road and had lunch sitting in the long grass at the edge of the cliff. It was a very hot day, the hottest we had experienced since our arrival in New Zealand six weeks earlier, and the hot weather was to continue unabated for the remainder of our stay in the South Island. What with the warm sunshine, the scent of the grass, and the sound of the skylarks high in the air (in England I had not heard skylarks since I was a boy) the spot we had selected could hardly have been more idyllic. Below us lay the valley, with its green fields, its dark lines of trees, and its little white dots of farmhouses. In the background, at the foot of the mountains, a broad river wound in great shining loops towards Queenstown, the position of which was indicated by a triangle of silver between two hills.

From the Skippers road we drove down to the historic village of Arrowtown, fifteen or twenty miles north of Queenstown, on the outskirts of which we were to stay the night. Arrowtown was a charming place, perhaps the most charming we saw in the course of our travels in the South Island. Much of its charm was due to its being an old mining town, gold having been discovered there in 1862, and to the fact that a number of the original buildings were still standing. Paramartha and I spent an hour strolling up and down the main street looking at these buildings, many of which had been converted into cafés and souvenir shops, after which we spent another hour in the very interesting Lakes District Museum, formerly the bank, where a unique variety of displays presented, in the words of the brochure, an authentic picture of the harsh pioneering days and the exciting gold rush era of the 1860s. One saw the conditions under which the early settlers lived and worked, while sketches, photographs, paintings, and explanatory notes brought to life their characters and personalities.

In the evening, after checking into the motel and resting for a while, we took a walk down a sort of continuation of the main street, where stood a row of some two dozen single-storeyed cottages belonging to its early mining days. Now protected buildings, and obviously well cared for, they were for the most part built of wood. Some were so small as to seem like large doll's houses; a few were occupied. Having seen the cottages, and admired the magnificent trees that lined the road on both sides, forming a splendid avenue, we decided it was time for dinner. Charming though Arrowtown was, however, it seemed unable to provide a vegetarian meal, and we therefore drove into Queens-town, where eventually we located a pizzeria with a vegetarian option.

On Monday, it being the fourth day of our tour, and my sixth in the South Island, I woke feeling quite ill. There were no particular symptoms, and no cause that I could identify. It was simply that I felt ill. As this had happened to me before, and as I attributed it to old age, I was not unduly worried. We therefore set out for Wanaka and Haast as planned, and in the course of the day the unpleasant feeling gradually wore off. A few miles from Arrowtown we passed the so-called Bungee Bridge and actually witnessed a bungee jump. Having plummeted from the bridge and almost touched the surface of the river sixty or more feet below, the jumper seemingly *bounced* all the way back as the rubber bungee cord contracted – to the cheers of a small group of spectators. Paramartha explained that bungee jumping – now a popular sport in many parts of the world – had its origins in a traditional Fijian initiation ritual. Whatever its origins, the sport was obviously a dangerous one, and I wondered what led people to risk life and limb in this way. Some years ago, I told Paramartha, the rock-climbing activities of a small minority of (male) Order members had given me cause for concern, especially as there had been one or two nasty accidents. Did such Order members not appreciate the preciousness of this human life of ours, which according to the scriptures gave one the rare opportunity of making progress towards Enlightenment? By this time we were travelling through green valleys where sheep grazed and which commanded fine views of the distant snows. At one point in the journey we saw, on the other side of the river, the remains of an old goldfield. Shafts had been sunk in the mountainside, and tumble-down miner's huts stood here and there among the rubble.

Wanaka, which we reached two hours after leaving Arrowtown, was situated on the southern shores of Lake Wanaka, another major lake. Though a tourist resort, it had no international flavour but instead possessed, according to the guidebook, the flavour of a typical New Zealand holiday town. Whether because of the smallness of the place, or because of its relaxed atmosphere, or because of the majestic mountain scenery by which it was surrounded, both Paramartha and I rather liked Wanaka and could easily have spent more time there. But we had a long way to go that day, and after walking around a little and having a drink we left for Haast.

Less than an hour later we were at Hawea, at the southern tip of Lake Hawea, and had begun following the road that ran along the western side of the lake, which extended thirty or more miles in a northerly direction. The weather was even hotter than it had been the previous day, and the sun shone down from a virtually cloudless sky. On account of its intense blueness, its calm breadth, and the softness with which it reflected its few islands and the surrounding mountains – as well, perhaps, on account of the quality of the light in which it was bathed – Lake Hawea struck me as being even more beautiful than Lake Manapouri. But we pressed on. Soon we came to a narrow neck of land that divided an arm of Lake Hawea from the upper reaches of Lake Wanaka. Having crossed this, and having skirted the upper reaches of Lake Wanaka, we left the lake to follow the Makarora River, through an open valley, to a township bearing the same name. From Makarora the road led through scenery hardly less spectacular than that between Te Anau and Milford Sound – scenery it is impossible to describe but to which a Turner might have done justice. A number of flats and a gradual ascent at length brought us to the summit of Haast Pass, after which, crossing 'The Hinge' and the Gates of Haast chasm, we began the steep winding descent to Burke Flat. We now were in the valley of the Haast River, where, for the next two hours, we enjoyed view after magnificent view of rivers, valleys, mountains, and forests. At one point we stopped for lunch at a picnic area behind which there was a walk through dense native bush (it felt cold among those ancient trees), and from whose front entrance we could see, on the other side of the river, above the dark foothills, the white mass of a whole range of snow peaks. On another occasion we left the car and descended into a boulder-strewn gorge. Here, passing underneath the bridge high overhead, we walked up to where a seething mass of waters came cascading down over the rocks to become a turbulent stream. At 3 o'clock, having emerged from the mountains with the Haast River, we reached our immediate destination.

We had seen many small townships, but Haast was probably the smallest, having as it did a population of little more than 200. There were several rows of bungalows, a petrol station, and a newly-built police station that seemed much too big for such a small place. There was also a café, in a quiet sunny corner of which we refreshed ourselves before driving on to the motor camp, which was situated twenty miles down the coast. The road, sealed and evidently quite new, ran straight through dense native bush, of which a green wall rose sheer on either side. Every few miles a rough track gave access, through the bush, to the beach. We were indeed a long way from civilization, and were not surprised, therefore, when the motor camp turned out to be the most isolated we had as yet encountered, as well as the smallest and the least well equipped. It was also the noisiest, in that the three masculine occupants of the room next to ours talked so loudly that we could hear almost every word they said. However, we were not unduly disturbed, and after a short rest went out and made our way along the estuary walk, as it was called. This was a very extensive circular walkway that led first over mud-flats and swampy ground and then through what was probably the densest and most luxuriant bush I had yet seen – bush that rose to cover the neighbouring hills in a mantle of dark green. Handsome native trees towered fifty or sixty feet in the air, their twisted trunks wrapped round with thick creepers. Tree ferns lifted their green fronds; the clumps of New Zealand flax raised their spears. It was hardly possible, I felt, to get closer to nature than this – to nature, that is, as vegetation, for we saw no wild life other than a bird or two. From the bush we passed to the beach, the grey sands of which were strewn with enormous quantities of driftwood, including the bleached skeletons of whole trees.

Our next day's journey, from Haast to Hokitika – a distance of roughly 250 miles – was dominated by glaciers. There were two of these: Fox Glacier and Franz Josef Glacier. We reached the first of them at about eleven o'clock, after passing though scenery so beautiful, and withal so varied, that I was no more able to take it all in than I am able to describe it all now. Or rather, we reached the township of Fox Glacier, where we had a cup of tea before driving four or five miles up a side road, between precipitous grey cliffs, to the parking area, from where a steep track led over very rough, rubble-strewn ground to the foot of the glacier itself. We did not go all the way, the track being so very steep (for me, at least), but instead contented ourselves with gazing up at the great river of grey ice from a distance of about three-quarters of a mile. The road between the township of Fox Glacier and the Franz Josef settlement was a mountainous one, climbing up and down a number of times in rapid succession. We did not stop to see the Franz Josef Glacier, on the rather dubious principle that one glacier was pretty much like another and that if you had seen one you had seen them all. After crossing over Mount Hercules (had a roaming classicist once passed that way?), and driving through magnificent bush, mountain, and river scenery, we did, however, stop for our usual picnic lunch at a rest area beside a lake. By this time it was very cloudy, and the light had changed, turning the lake and its surroundings into a harmony in black and silver that Whistler would have appreciated. By contrast, Hokitika, into which we drove not long afterwards, was bathed in sunshine. It was a bigger and more upmarket place than we had expected, with an imposing Boer War memorial in the form of a clock tower, shops selling greenstone jewellery and decorative items of an unusually high quality, and a Chinese restaurant where, after checking in at the holiday park, we eventually had dinner. When actually driving from one place to another Paramartha and I did not talk much, but occasionally a thought or a reflection would come to one of us which he would proceed to communicate to the other. Thus it was that on the morning of that, the fifth day of our tour, there had occurred to me – I do not know why – the thought that at this very time thirty years ago I had been travelling in India with Terry Delamare, saying goodbye to friends and teachers, and explaining that I had decided to shift my personal headquarters to the West and to work for the Dharma from there. It being the first week of January, I was probably still in Kalimpong, and seeing Dhardo Rimpoche and Yogi Chen, as well as the Kazi and Kazini of Chakhung and my former students. Thus much had I communicated to Paramartha, when the recollections started coming thick and fast and were being communicated to my companion in their turn. Thirty years ago I had just been informed by the English Sangha Trust that my services were no longer required at the Hampstead Buddhist Vihara and that I would not be welcome back (they suggested that I should remain in India and tell everyone I had changed my mind about returning to England!) and on receiving the news had turned to Terry and said 'Do you know what this means? It means a new Buddhist movement.' Thirty years ago I had returned to England on the very day I had originally said I would, without money, without influential friends, without any supporting organization, and in the face of the united opposition of the then British Buddhist establishment. Thirty years ago I had founded the FWBO, to be followed a year later by the WBO. Since then a great deal had happened. So much has happened that, having handed over the last of my responsibilities to a group of senior disciples, I am presently in the position of being able to go on a seven-month tour of the United States, Canada, Australia, and New Zealand secure in the knowledge that the new Buddhist movement of which I had spoken to Terry Delamare, all those years ago, was now a reality and that on my return to England in March I would be returning to a state of affairs very different from that to which I returned in March 1967. One of my few

Pancake Rocks

A typical view of South Island

regrets in this connection is that Terry, who for four years was my closest friend, did not live to see the FWBO in its present state of development. He died in 1969. Had he lived, he would now have been 61.

The following day, Wednesday, we travelled the greatest distance in one day of our whole tour, covering about 400 miles in a little less than nine hours, including stops. We stopped at Shantytown to see the old gold-mining town, at Punakaiki to see the Pancake Rocks, and having left the coast at Westport and turned inland, through the Buller Gorge, we stopped in Murchison to look round the museum. All these places were known to me, Purna, Vijaya, and I having followed the same route in 1977, after we had left Christchurch and crossed the Southern Alps to emerge at Kumara Junction, a few miles above Hokitika. I have written about that earlier trip in *Travel Letters*, and sights described then I shall not attempt to describe again now (though I shall have something to say about the Murchison Museum), the more especially as the region appears not to have changed much in the course of the last twenty years. Not that there had been no changes at all during that period, or that such changes as had taken place were without significance. The most noticeable change was in the area of tourism. In 1979 there had been very few tourists, but now places like Shantytown, Punakaiki, and Murchison were full of them, as Paramartha and I noticed that morning, and as we had already had occasion to observe in Te Anau, Queenstown, and Hokitika, and other towns along the way. Many of the tourists were from Singapore and Taiwan, and signs in Chinese – and Japanese – could be seen outside a number of shops and restaurants. There had in fact been a dramatic increase in tourism, and in tourist facilities and amenities, throughout New Zealand, and when people asked me, as they sometimes did, what changes I thought had taken place in the country since my last visit, increase in tourism was always first on my list. Second on my list came the greater attention now being paid to the Maori language and Maori culture. Then again, there were more new churches, some of them very imaginatively designed, more deer farms, and more Japanese cars. Other changes, I was aware, had also taken place, but my knowledge of these was a matter not so much of personal observation as of hearsay. The gap between rich and poor had widened, crime – and drug-taking – had increased, and in New Zealand, as in Australia, the merits and demerits of what had come to be called multiculturism were being vigorously debated.

The Murchison Museum, which I had not seen on my previous visit to the town (at least, there was no mention of it in *Travel Letters*), was situated next to the local garage and contained a collection of memorabilia from the place's early history, including its gold-mining and earthquake days. Much of this material consisted of sets of newspapers and magazines published locally and clippings from the New Zealand press. These were of particular interest to Paramartha, who was looking for information relating to his Italian great-great-grandfather, who had lived and worked in the area in the 1860s. He had been a ferryman, and was famous for having refused, one dark night, to ferry across the river part of the armed gang which had committed a cold-blooded multiple murder and was fleeing from justice. Very likely as a result of his refusal, all four members of the gang were caught and three of them eventually hanged. Though the two women assistants were familiar with the story of the murder, which had created a sensation at the time, and though they were positive they had seen something about it somewhere in the Museum's archives, their search proved fruitless, and Paramartha and I left without his having been able to find out more about the murder – or about his Italian great-great-grandfather – than he already knew.

The distance between Murchison and Nelson, where we were to spend our last night in the South Island, was rather greater than that between Westport and Murchison, and we covered it in about three hours, arriving at our destination at 5.30, after a very pleasant drive. But pleasant though our drive was, to me it was a trifle tedious, and I was not sorry when we reached Nelson. There a shock awaited me. The 'prosperous and even fashionable little place' (thus *Travel Letters*) of twenty years ago had since expanded enormously, in the process losing much of its character and charm. So much had it expanded, indeed, and so greatly had it changed, that as Paramartha and I trudged the shop-lined streets of the city centre in the late afternoon heat I failed to recognize a single landmark. Only the Anglican cathedral, prominent at the top of a flight of steps, and glimpsed down a side street, seemed at all familiar. But not all the changes were for the worse. At the time of my previous visit Nelson had boasted only one second-hand bookshop. Now there were two, and Paramartha and I spent half an hour browsing in them before heading for Tahuna Beach Holiday Park, which was situated a few miles south of the city. This was the biggest holiday park we had yet stayed at, and very security-conscious. But though it was the biggest it was also the quietest, as we discovered on returning to it that night after having dinner at a Thai restaurant in Nelson.

So far as our travels in the South Island are concerned, there is not much more to relate. We left Nelson at 10 o'clock the next morning, after paying another visit to the better of the two second-hand book-shops, which was really quite a good one, and before long were driving through scenery of the type I had characterized, in *Travel Letters*, as 'Mediterranean'. It was Mediterranean still, with green hills and glimpses of the snows, and for the last lap of our journey was increas-ingly so. Emerald green hills still ran down into waters of sapphire blue, and every turning of the road still revealed vistas more enchant-ing than the last. But there had been changes. The serpent of urbani-zation and 'development' had insinuated itself into this southern paradise. There were more houses, more hotels, more cars and, of course, more tourists. This was particularly the case in Picton, which we reached soon after midday, after stopping for a drink at Havelock, and where I picked up the tickets for the Lynx, as the faster inter-island ferry was called, while Paramartha returned the rental car. There were now two hours to go to the departure time. We passed them by walking round, having a leisurely meal at a pizzeria, and looking in a bookshop, where I bought a copy of *Asia Pacific: Its Role in the New World Disorder* by M.S. Dobbs-Higginson (Mandarin, 1995), which according to the back cover blurb was 'part business book, part cultural history,' and which a review in *The European* described as offering 'a comprehensive and coherent view of the religion and a detailed historical, economical and cultural analysis of the individual nations.' Having now read it, I can strongly recommend the book to all who are interested in the Asia Pacific region, and in particular to those within the FWBO who have regular dealings with India, South Korea, Taiwan, and Indonesia.

In 1977 the Picton ferry building comprised, besides the ticket office, little more than a bleak waiting room and a nondescript café. Now it was like an airport terminal, with baggage check-in, escalators, a smart restaurant, a departure lounge, and an air bridge to the waiting ferry. We embarked at 3 o'clock, together with four or five hundred other people. So long as we were in the Queen Charlotte Sound all was well, but on our entering the more turbulent waters of the Cook Strait, the ferry, which was a hovercraft, began to lurch and roll. A number of people vomited, many of them children. Despite having taken a travel sickness tablet, I myself felt rather queasy. At Wellington we were met by Rohit, a Mitra, and driven to the men's community at Hataitai, where I had spent two weeks while Paramartha was in Invercargill visiting his parents. After we had enjoyed the hospitality of the community for ten days, and I had given a poetry reading at the Centre and conducted a question-and-answer session for the women Order members and Mitras, Paramartha and I left Wellington for Auckland on Monday, 20 January, spending three nights on the road, two of them at Wanganui and one at New Plymouth. *En route* we saw the principal Ratana temple – with its twin towers, stained-glass windows, and graves of the founder of the religion and his sons – a black ironsand beach, and, most unexpectedly, an exhibition of Len Lye's kinetic sculptures. For me the most memorable part of our brief tour, however, was the visit we paid to Jerusalem and the views we had of Mount Egmont, the Fujiyama of New Zealand.

Jerusalem was upwards of fifty miles from Wanganui. In the early 1970s it had received a lot of publicity on account of the presence there of a commune for 200 people run by James K. Baxter (1926–72), New Zealand's greatest poet. It was because of its association with Baxter that we wanted to see the place, and we had arranged to spend an extra night at Wanganui so that we could do this. The day following our departure from Wellington, therefore, we left the Aramoho Holiday Park after breakfast and made our way up the Wanganui River Road, described by the guidebook as 'a rugged road winding round bluffs above the historic Wanganui River' – the third longest river in New Zealand and, it was said, the most beautiful. The road was certainly rugged, and it certainly wound a lot. But we did not mind. At every turning of the road – and the river – there was yet another vista to admire. In 1843 the Reverend Richard Taylor had travelled up the river establishing a chain of mission stations to which he had given Western, even biblical, names – names that had since been 'Maori-ized'. Thus we passed, in succession, Atene (Athens), Koriniti (Corinth), and Ranana (London), none of which appeared to consist of more than a few dozen houses. Eventually, the road having wound round yet another bluff, we saw across a bend in the river, high on the hillside to our right, and surrounded by trees, the tiny steepled church that told us we were not far from the Hiruharama (Jerusalem on the map) of James K. Baxter's later poetry. The Roman Catholic mission had been established in the 1880s by Mother Mary Aubert, founder of the religious order known as the Daughters of Our Lady of Compassion. On driving up into the village, an affair of some two or three dozen shabby buildings scattered over the hillside below the church, we found nothing to indicate where Baxter's commune had been located nor anyone who seemed at all likely to be a source of information on the subject. The whole place had, in fact, a derelict and neglected air. By contrast, the convent and church, to which there was a separate entrance from the road, were very spick and span. The nuns were out, but a plump little Maori girl who was playing outside the convent told us that the church was open and that we might go in and look around. This we accordingly did, spending some time inside the little wooden building looking at the Maori-style carving on the front of the altar (or was it, now, a communion table?), at the rather bizarre painting of Christ, again in Maori style, on the wall above the main entrance, and at the photograph of a bearded James K. Baxter reading the lesson in that same church.

Between the church and the convent, but nearer the convent, lay a small, secluded garden in which there was a Rosary Walk – a path up and down which one could stroll while saying the rosary. A notice-board to the left of the entrance listed all the dangers from which the Virgin Mary gave protection – provided, of course, one said her rosary regularly. Paramartha remarked that these were very similar in kind to the dangers from which Tārā delivered her devotees. At intervals along the walk, on the right-hand side, standard rose bushes had been planted. There were seven of them, all of the same height, each slender trunk being crowned by a profusion of pure white blossoms, so that I was reminded of Rossetti's 'white rose of Mary's gift, For service meetly worn.' Half-way along the Walk, the rose bushes to the right and left of her, stood the blue-robed figure of the Blessed Virgin herself, rather less than life-size. On the pedestal beneath her feet were inscribed the words 'I am the Immaculate Conception.'

Being unwilling to retrace our steps, we decided to make a detour and return to Wanganui via Raetihi. From Jerusalem we therefore pressed on to Pipiriki. Between Pipiriki and Raetihi stretched thirty or so miles of the worst roads and ruggedest mountain scenery we had yet seen. From Raetihi we made a secondary detour to Ohakune in order to take a closer look at Mount Ruapehu, a volcano which, to the consternation of the local skiing industry, had erupted several times during the last two years, the latest eruption having occurred six months earlier. We did not go up as far as the snow line, but we went far enough to see the great white mass of Mount Ruapehu, 9,175 feet above sea level, towering ahead of us. A plume of smoke (or was it a cloud?) showed it to be still mildly active. Returning to Ohakune, through dense native bush, we rejoined the loop of our original detour and made our way, via Kakatahi, back to Wanganui, having travelled about 300 miles that day.

The following day, on our way to New Plymouth, we saw Mount Egmont. Or rather, we saw the broad, forest-clad base of the mountain, the rest of it being hidden by a low-lying blanket of grey cloud. As we circled the mountain clockwise, however, driving from south of it to north-east and finding our way through a perfect maze of roads in dense bush, it eventually revealed itself to us. At 8,260 feet it was not so high as Mount Ruapehu, but what it lacked in height it more than made up for in symmetry, its gently sloping sides rising to form an almost perfect cone. In the course of the day we saw it a number of times and from many different angles. Now it dominated a pastoral landscape dotted with sheep and cows, now rose majestic above the roofs of New Plymouth, its peak a dazzling white against the intense blue of the sky, now looked down from the other side of a lake, that same peak glimmering in ghostly fashion above a mass of dark foliage as the shadows lengthened and the air grew colder. A New Zealand Hokusai, I reflected, had ample material for an album of Thirty-six – or One Hundred – Views of Mount Egmont. Perhaps our most impressive view of the Fujiyama of New Zealand was vouchsafed us as we drove back to the motor camp that night after eating at an Argentine restaurant in New Plymouth and seeing the rather perfunctory illuminations in Pukekura Park. The sky had turned a deeper blue, and now that we were closer to the peak we could see that its sides were streaked with snow rather than covered with it. Catching the last of the daylight, it rose luminous from a wreath of bronze-coloured cloud above the long dark mass of the foothills.

The last day of our tour was the least rewarding, at least as regards scenery. Between New Plymouth and Hamilton there were mountains and a broad plain, but after Hamilton, where we stopped for lunch, and which Paramartha said had changed a lot since the days when he worked there in a photographic studio, the story was one of increasingly dense urbanization – dense, that is, by New Zealand standards. As we drove through Ngaruawahia, a township a few miles out of Hamilton, Paramartha told me that it was here, when walking past the abattoir and experiencing the smell, that he had decided to become a vegetarian. He was then twenty-one. Shortly afterwards we passed through Huntly, five miles west of which was the pit where he had worked as a coal miner for six months. (Paramartha seemed to have had quite a varied experience of life before coming to England, and I suggested he should write his memoirs – an idea that did not meet with a very favourable response.) Urbanization meant more roads, more roads meant more traffic, and more traffic meant more accidents. In both the North and the South Island, as well as while travelling in the United States, I had noticed little white crosses by the roadside from time to time, some of them decorated with flowers. They marked the spot where a fatal accident had occurred, there being one cross for every person killed. After leaving Hamilton we saw more white crosses than we had yet seen in New Zealand. By the time we reached the outskirts of Auckland we had counted more than thirty of them. Twice we passed a cluster of five crosses, indicating that five people had been killed in a single accident, and once we passed a cluster of six. Drunken driving? Sleeping at the wheel? Whatever the cause might have been, it was dreadful to think of lives being lost in this way. Once we were in Auckland, however, the crosses disappeared – not so much, I suspected, because there were no fatal accidents as because there was no place for such crosses in a modern city. We also found ourselves being caught up in the rush hour traffic, so that it was another half hour before we were at Saranadipa and being welcomed by Taranatha and Akashagarbha, the only community members not on retreat.

After dinner Paramartha returned the rental car and saw a friend. I spent the evening reading. It was Thursday, 23 January. In a few weeks' time, on Sunday, 16 February, the portion of Dhardo Rimpoche's ashes I had brought from England would be enshrined in the stupa currently being built at Tararu Retreat Centre, and one calendar month after that Paramartha and I would be returning to England after an absence, in my case, of exactly seven months. Though looking forward to seeing Prasannasiddhi, Kovida, and other friends, I would be sorry to leave New Zealand, and would be taking back with me a host of positive impressions of the country – especially of my nine days in the South Island.

Urgyen Sangharakshita

August 1997

Travels of a Bibliophile in North America and Australasia

Books: travelling companions of another kind – New Hampshire – the Bodhicaryāvatāra – Santayana – Henry Shuckman and D.H. Lawrence – celebrating my birthday – Concord – Walden Pond – Missoula – Keckemet – Kodaly – In Memory of Haydn – from Tucson to San Francisco via the Painted Desert, the Grand Canyon, and Death Valley – D.H. Lawrence and the Lawrence Memorial Chapel – Taos Pueblo – D.H. Lawrence's paintings – San Francisco – the Buddhist Churches of America bookstore – Oregon – Alain Danielou's While the Gods Play – Seattle – Don Castro – Museum of Asian Art – 'Kesa: The Elegance of Japanese Monks' Robes' – prayer and worship – Vancouver – Visionary, teacher, and healer, Omraam Mikhael Aivanhov – The Buddha Tree – Sydney – Pure-Land Zen and Zen Pure-Land: Letters from Patriarch Yin Kuang – reflections on other-power and self-power – Ku-ring-gai National Park – Katoomba – the Blue Mountains – Norman Lindsay – Melbourne – Ballarat – Alan Walker's Franz Liszt – The Myths of Plato – The Vision of Piers Plowman – George Moore's Esther Waters – The Hazards of Being Male and Goldberg's buddyship – Auckland Buddhist Centre – Dante's Divine Comedy – Mike Johnson's Dumb Show – the poetry of James K. Baxter – Wellington – David Copperfield and reflections on betrayal – Beerbohm, Swinnerton, Freeman, Drayton, and Hazlitt – the poetry of Alistair Te Ariki Campbell – Witi Ihimaera's The Matriarch – A Vindication of Charles the First – incense – Friedrich von Hardenberg (Novalis)'s Henry von Ofterdingen – the fifty-one Epistles of the Sincere Brethren or Brethren of Purity – Veronica de Osa's The Mystic Finger Symbol – Edward John Trelawny's Records of Byron, Shelley and the Author – Milton's Paradise Lost and Paradise Regain'd – a tour of Northland – Cymbeline – Narziss and Goldmund – Abdullah Dougan's Forty Days

Dear Dharmacharis and Dharmacharinis,

On 19 August 1996, I left England on a seven-month tour of North America, Australia, and New Zealand. I did not go alone. With me was Paramartha, who, having just qualified as an osteopath after four years of study, was visiting North America for the first time, Australia for only the second time since his departure from that country for England (and ordination) in 1987, and New Zealand, where he was born, after an absence of almost ten years. There could not have been a better travelling companion. But with me on the plane I also had travelling companions of another kind. These were the half-dozen books that formed part of my hand luggage and included, besides my much-loved *Milton's Poetical Works* with the original spelling and punctuation, the Ñāṇamoli-Bodhi translation of *The Middle Length Discourses of the Buddha*, and Donald S. Lopez's anthology *Buddhism in Practice*, both recently published, and a copy of *Plotinus*. Books have always been my constant companions and friends and when, as an eighteen-year-old conscript, I left England for India in 1943, it was not without half a dozen pocket-sized volumes representative of my devotion to poetry, philosophy, and religion. On that occasion I had not known when I would see a library or bookshop again and was making sure I would not find myself bookless in a strange land. On this occasion there was no such danger. I knew from previous experience that in North America, at least, there were excellent bookshops (or bookstores, as they call them over there), as well as beautifully organized second-hand book warehouses of enormous size and incredible variety, and the half-dozen volumes in my cabin luggage were intended simply as a stand-by and for dipping into along the way. Moreover, just as I would be seeing other people in the course of my journey, though Paramartha was my travelling companion, so there would be new books to buy and read, despite the fact that I already had plenty of reading material with me. After all, one cannot have too many friends.

In New Hampshire, which was our first stop, and where we spent ten days in the men's community at Aryaloka, I was too busy seeing people to have time for serious reading. I did, however, manage to read a few of the contributions to *Buddhism in Practice*, which unlike most previous anthologies and standard accounts of Buddhism does not attempt to represent systematically the various Buddhist traditions, but offers instead, as its title suggests, a selection of texts, in the broadest sense of that term, in order to provide the reader with a sense of the remarkable diversity and range of the practices of persons who over the course of 2,500 years have been identified, by themselves or by others, as Buddhists.[*]

Some of the practices of persons identified as Buddhists are rather odd, though others belong to mainstream Buddhism. At Aryaloka I also started reading the new Crosby–Skilton translation of the *Bodhicaryāvatāra*, going through it a chapter at a time. My acquaintance with this precious work – in some respects the Buddhist counterpart of Saint Augustine's *Confessions* – goes back a very long way, but there is always something new to discover in it. This time I was particularly struck by two verses, both from chapter 9, 'The Perfection of Understanding'. The first half of the first of these, verse 44, reads,

The dispensation [sāsana] is rooted in the monkhood and the monkhood itself is imperfectly established,[†]

on which the translators comment

The Buddhist monastic community has undergone schisms in the course of its history. These schisms have taken place as a result of disagreement over the interpretation of the monastic rules which define the institution of monkhood. The different ordination lineages resulting from such schisms do not accept each other's monastic code as valid. In this way the monkhood is imperfectly established.

In view of what I have said in *Forty-Three Years Ago* and in *Was the Buddha a Bhikkhu?* this is interesting, showing as it does that as early as the eighth century CE when Shantideva wrote his celebrated treatise, doubts were being entertained as to the technical validity of monastic ordination. The second verse, verse 93, reads,

If a sense organ and an object are separated by a space, how can there be contact between the two? Furthermore, if they are not separate they are one, so what is in contact with what?[‡]

In the case of this verse what struck me was the fact that the urge of lovers to 'become one' through the sense organs is doomed to failure, for the object of their respective sense organs is another body, and two

---

* Donald S. Lopez, *Buddhism in Practice*, Princeton 1995, p.3.

† Kate Crosby and Andrew Skilton (trans.), *The Bodhicaryāvatāra*, OUP 1995, p.184.

‡ ibid., p.124.

bodies cannot occupy the same space. Oneness is possible, if at all, only on a mental or spiritual plane where, as the archangel Raphael explains to Adam in *Paradise Lost*,

> *Easier then Air with Air, if Spirits embrace,*
> *Total they mix, Union of Pure with Pure*
> *Desiring; nor restrain'd conveyance need*
> *As Flesh to mix with Flesh, or Soul with Soul.*

This is why the long-distance sexual relationship, as it has come to be called, can be an important stage in the emotional and spiritual development of the individual. By giving the parties to such a relationship the opportunity to see each other less as bodies and more, to use Milton's language, as spirits, a prolonged physical separation enables them to start replacing lustful affection *(pema)* by loving-kindness *(mettā)* and to raise themselves and their relationship, at least temporarily, from the kāmaloka or 'realm of sensuous desire' to the rūpaloka or 'realm of (archetypal) form.'

As I was seeing a lot of people, both individually and in groups, it was not until Paramartha and I had spent four or five days at Aryaloka that I was able to get to a second-hand bookshop. This was when Vidyavati took me to have lunch in Portsmouth, an attractive little town some fifteen or twenty miles away, which I had visited several times before and with whose second-hand bookshops I was already familiar. In one of these bookshops I found a copy of George Santayana's *Persons and Places: The Background of My Life*. Santayana was not one of my favourite philosophers, though I was acquainted with his *Platonism and the Spiritual Life* and *Scepticism and Animal Faith*, while as readers of *Learning to Walk* (now included in *The Rainbow Road*) may remember, his *Egotism in German Philosophy* had featured in a romantic episode belonging to my early life. I had also encountered a few chapters from *Persons and Places* a few years ago, in a volume of selections from his writings, and having found these chapters interesting and couched in an admirable style, I therefore bought the book. It was a first edition, and at three dollars was extremely cheap by English standards, and in the course of the next few days I dipped into it extensively.

26 August was my birthday and cards, flowers, and messages arrived from various quarters. Paramartha gave me a copy of Henry Shuckman's

---

* *Paradise Lost*, book VIII, lines 626–9.

Savage Pilgrims on the Road to Santa Fe and Paramashanti a copy of *Paradise Lost* with Blake's illustrations. Paramartha's choice of gift was prompted by the fact that we were planning to visit New Mexico and hoped to see the ranch where D.H. Lawrence had lived in the twenties and the memorial chapel in which his ashes were enshrined. Meanwhile, I plunged into *Savage Pilgrims* and finished it the following day. The title of the book was a reference to the fact that when he reached New Mexico in 1922 Lawrence decided that his 'savage pilgrimage', his rambling worldwide search for a powerful pre-civilized culture, was finally over. Whether because I read it so quickly, or because it was rather lacking in depth, the book did not make much of an impression on me, and nine months later I have had to look at it again in order to refresh my memory of what it was about. Shuckman is a young man from England who, realizing his long cherished ambition to visit New Mexico (an ambition inspired by a reading of D.H. Lawrence's works), encounters on the road to Santa Fé a rich variety of fellow travellers, from a piscatorial film producer to the bizarre Greek owner of the Lawrence oil paintings, and from the hospitable but sinister Fat Man to the writer Natalie Goldberg, whom he finds living in a house made of tyres and beer cans and smothered in adobe. He also goes in search of the Flying Father, a priest who pays his pastoral visits by aeroplane, and has his first experience of Zazen. The edition of *Paradise Lost* given me by Paramashanti was published in New York by the Heritage Press in 1940 and in it Blake's watercolour illustrations to Milton's epic poem were printed in colour for the first time. These illustrations had long been great favourites of mine, together with Blake's designs for the *Book of Job*, and I was particularly glad to have this finely-produced volume. Apart from the fact that it was my birthday, 26 August passed much like any other day. In the morning Vidyavati photographed me in the garden and I saw a few people individually, in the afternoon I saw more people, and in the evening I dined with the members of the Jayamala women's community. The following day, in the evening, my birthday was celebrated at the Center with a programme that included violin duos, a poetry reading, American Indian flute music, and short speeches. I particularly enjoyed the flute music, which created an atmosphere of calm and concentration comparable to that of a meditation session.

The following day Vidyavati drove Paramartha and me to Concord, famous for its association with Emerson, Thoreau, and Hawthorne, and for being the place where 'the shot heard round the world', was fired. The purpose of our visit was to see Walden Pond, on the edge of which, in a wooden hut of his own construction, Henry Thoreau lived for two years experimenting in self-sufficiency. It was raining heavily when we arrived, so that we were obliged to seek shelter first in the Visitor Centre and then in a pizzeria in town. Besides luxury items of which Thoreau would have surely disapproved, there were several shelves of books. Resisting the temptation to buy a souvenir of *Walden*, which I had read some years ago and not liked very much, I confined myself to buying a recent (1992) book by Harold Bloom, author of *The Western Canon* and *The Book of J*. This was *The American Religion: The Emergence of the Post-Christian Nation*. I have not read it properly yet, but according to the back cover blurb,

> Harold Bloom finds that although America considers itself a Christian
> nation, in fact, American civilization has spawned its own peculiar
> theology, a spirituality that Bloom classifies as a form of Gnosticism.

The rain having more or less abated, we drove back to the Visitor Centre, saw the replica of the hut (it was closed, but we could look through a window and see Thoreau's bed, table, chair, and lamp), inspected the standing bronze statue of the author, and walked round Walden Pond, which was several miles in circumference and in England would have been called a lake. Half-way round we came to the site of the original hut, which was surrounded by trees and commanded a fine view of the calm silver waters of the Pond. As I had learned at the Visitor Centre, the house in which Thoreau's parents lived was situated only two or three miles from the hut and he had, apparently, taken his washing home to his mother every week. Self-sufficiency is not so easily achieved! Before leaving Concord we explored the town centre a little, saw two dazzlingly white New England churches, with their austere classical façades and elegant, slightly frivolous steeples, searched in vain in the churchyards for Emerson's grave, and visited a couple of second-hand bookshops, in one of which I found a copy of *The Last Puritan*, Santayana's only novel, which I had long wanted to read, and a copy of the 1895 Bodley Head edition of John Davidson's *Ballads and Songs*, which contained his well-known ballad 'Thirty Bob a Week' and the scarcely less well known 'Ballad of Heaven', together with the much anthologized 'In Romney Marsh'. By this time the rains were over and gone, and we returned to Aryaloka beneath triumphantly blue skies.

Blue skies were very much in evidence during our four days in Missoula. Hot sunshine was very much in evidence too, so that I was obliged to buy a straw hat (Paramartha insisted on sticking to his baseball cap). Thanks to the fine weather we were able to spend much of our time out of doors, though I still saw a good many people, both individually and in groups, as I did at all FWBO centres we visited in the course of our tour, besides officiating at two Mitra ceremonies. On one occasion we were taken up into the mountains to see Garnet Ghost Town, a derelict gold-mining settlement, and on another for a cruise on Flathead Lake, which was twenty-eight miles long and fifteen miles wide. There being no men's community in Missoula, we stayed at Punya and Lee's condominium, which they kindly placed at our disposal for the duration of our visit. Punya is English, but Lee is an American of Hungarian descent. She is also a musician, and upon investigating her and Punya's library I came across *The Selected Writings of Zoltan Kodaly*. This was of particular interest to me. Kodaly was one of the two greatest modern Hungarian composers, the other being Bela Bartok. Not only that. He had been born in Kecskemet, an agricultural town situated fifty or sixty miles south-east of Budapest, and it was from Kecskemet that my mother's paternal grandfather had come to England in 1844 at the age of twelve. I therefore dipped into the *Selected Writings* with great interest. Besides learning about Kodaly's – and Bartok's – work as a recorder and transcriber of Hungarian folk music, I came to know something about his attitude to music and other composers. I was particularly pleased with what he had to say about Haydn, whose music I sometimes think I love as much as I love Mozart's. In his *In Memory of Haydn* (1959) Kodaly writes:

> He did not write for the understanding minority but for everyone.... How many present-day composers could learn from Haydn's remark if instead of merely interesting music they tried to express great thoughts in generally understood language.
>
> For Haydn, however, this was not just a question of style: it came from his explicit interpretation of the purpose of art.
>
> In a letter written in his later years he says: Frequently when struggling against all sorts of obstacles my mental and physical strength flagged and I found it hard to proceed further on the career I had started, an inner feeling inspired me: there are so few happy and satisfied people on earth, they are pursued everywhere by sorrow and care. Perhaps your work could be sometimes a spring in

which the heavy-laden could find for a few minutes peace and rest.

This thought inspired him to further work. He wanted to be the benefactor of mankind. And he achieved his end. There has been hardly any composer who in the past two hundred years has caused more people delight and comfort.[*]

Haydn, it would seem, was one of those for whom religion and art overlap.

In the course of my previous visit to the States I had spent six days on the road with Manjuvajra and Kulananda, travelling from Tucson to San Francisco via the Painted Desert, the Grand Canyon, and Death Valley. This time I was eager to see even more of America and eager, too, that Paramartha should have an opportunity of seeing the Grand Canyon, which I was more than happy to see for the second time. In Missoula we were accordingly joined by Manjuvajra and his big comfortable station wagon, and on 1 September the three of us set out on our journey, in the course of which we drove through eight states (Montana, Wyoming, Colorado, New Mexico, Arizona, Utah, Nevada, and California), spent several days in the Rocky Mountains, visited a whole series of National Parks, including Yellowstone and Yosemite, watched a variety of wild animals, from bison to rock squirrels, and experienced an astonishingly wide range of climate, landscape, and weather. And of course we saw the Grand Canyon, as well as the nearby Monument Valley, which I had not seen before, where enormous crimson-coloured rock formations rose at intervals sheer from the vast crimson-coloured plain. Except for the three days we spent in Boulder, where we met Reginald A. Ray, author of *Buddhist Saints in India*, and where I bought a copy of Porphyry's *Against the Christians: The Literary Remains*, we were on the road for the greater part of each day, stopping only for a picnic lunch (and for such sightseeing as had to be done on foot), and in the evening finding a motel for Paramartha and me (Manjuvajra slept in the station wagon) and a restaurant for our evening meal. During the two weeks of our trip I therefore had hardly any time for reading. Not that I minded. I was perfectly content to look out of the window at the scenery, while Manjuvajra drove and chewed gum and Paramartha, stretched out on the back seat, either read or wrote or made up for the sleep he had lost due to his final examinations. (Dr Johnson once said that if he had no duties, and no reference to futurity, he would spend his life driving briskly in a

---

[*] *The Selected Writings of Zoltan Kodaly*, Boosey and Hawkes, London 1974.

post-chaise with a pretty woman. With a similar proviso, I would spend mine driving slowly with one or two good friends through the wide open spaces of America.) What little reading I did was done by night, before sleeping, when I dipped into what remained of Porphyry's scholarly critique of Christianity or turned the leaves of a lavishly illustrated book on D.H. Lawrence and America. Writing to Catherine Carswell in November 1916, he said,

> In short, I want, immediately or at length, to transfer all my life to America. Because there, I know, the *skies* are not so old, the air is newer, the earth is not tired.

But he added

> Don't think I have any illusions about the people, the life. The people and the life are monstrous.

It was no less clear that while Lawrence loved America he was *in* love with New Mexico, and it was principally on Lawrence's account that I had for so many years wanted to visit that part of the United States and see with my own eyes the landscape that had inspired some of his finest writing.

During the two days that we spent driving through New Mexico the sky was overcast, and every now and then it rained, at times quite heavily. The atmosphere was gloomy and oppressive. Henry Shukman had encountered a rich variety of fellow travellers on the road to Santa Fé, but the most colourful character we met, the day before crossing the state border into the Land of Enchantment, was the elderly proprietor of a rock shop who not only believed in UFOs but maintained that the lump of vitrified rock on his desk was the product of extraterrestrial technology. Having seen our first adobe dwelling and picnicked beside a river beneath sheltering trees, at 2 o'clock in the afternoon we booked ourselves into a motel in Questa and an hour later were heading, through intermittent rain, in the direction of Taos and Santa Fé. Half-way between Questa and Taos we saw the signboard for which we had been looking and turned left, leaving the highway. The Kiowa Ranch, as it was called, was situated up in the Sangre de Christo Mountains, at the end of a winding, seven-mile track. First came a ramshackle two-storeyed building that we at first thought was the object of our quest but which was not. To the left of this building there was a gate. Passing through the gate, we climbed the raised concrete path that ran in wide, steep zig-zags between the

The shrine to D.H. Lawrence near Taos, New Mexico

Manjuvajra and Paramartha at the Kiowa Ranch

pine trees up to the Lawrence Memorial Chapel. This was a modest, whitewashed affair, its gable surmounted by the carved white figure of a phoenix with half-open wings, Lawrence's emblem, and one stepped straight through the doorway into the building's one room. Facing the entrance there was a squat, silver-coloured altar, on the front of which, on a white background, the letters DHL had been painted. Large green vine leaves flanked the letters, and above them and below there was a half sunflower. A bigger sunflower adorned the top of the altar, which sloped up to a niche containing another carved white phoenix. Above the niche could be seen a round, painted window at the centre of which there flared the orange disc of an enormous sunflower. A lamp hung from the wooden ceiling. In its austerity and 'primitiveness' the chapel was a fitting memorial to the great writer, but though his ashes were presumably enshrined there, I did not have a feeling of his being, in a sense, present. Perhaps too few pilgrims ever came to the place to create that kind of atmosphere. Not that it mattered. One can feel Lawrence's living presence in his books.

In front of the chapel, to the left, was the grave in which Frieda Lawrence was buried. The area was cordoned off, so that in order to get to the chapel one had to walk round the three wooden posts on the right-hand side of the grave, which were in line with the middle of the chapel door. In death, as in life, Frieda was rather in the way, though this did not mean that Lawrence's emotional dependence on her had not been such that he was unable, as I well knew, to get on without her. A few yards from the chapel stood the tiny, one-roomed cottage occupied by Dorothy Brett the artist, Lawrence's faithful but at times unwanted disciple (unwanted by Frieda, at least), and not far from that stood the famous ranch. The latter was a low, two-storeyed structure, much smaller than I had expected, and in a very poor state of repair and decoration. Work of some kind was being done on it, for pots of paint, together with planks and other materials, lay scattered around, and it was not possible to get in at the blue-painted door. At one end of the rickety veranda stood the wooden armchair Lawrence had made for himself. It had once been painted white, and on the square ends of the two uprights that went to form its back there were red hearts (or was it shields?) framed in green and yellow. At the edge of the little courtyard, only a few yards from the veranda, grew a magnificent pine tree, five feet across at the bottom and proportionately tall. It was famous for having been painted, from an unusual angle, by Georgia O'Keefe, who visited the ranch after Lawrence's death. A poster of a poppy by the same artist was nailed to the wall behind Lawrence's armchair.

From the threshold of the chapel, and from the concrete path as we made our way back to the station wagon, we had what would have been a splendid view – the kind of view that Lawrence must have enjoyed – had the sky been not so overcast and the distant horizon not obscured by a thin veil of fine rain. Through the veil, we could just make out the shadowy forms of successively lower foothills and, beyond, the blue-grey levels of the desert. I was glad to have come, glad to have seen the place Lawrence had loved so much, where he had lived and laboured and where he had produced some of his finest work. My connection with Lawrence went back a long way. It went back to the time when, as a teenager, I bought the Phoenix edition of his poems, in three volumes, and borrowed Mabel Dodge Luhan's *Lorenzo in Taos* from the Tooting Public Library. The latter I have not encountered since, and it was probably not the best book with which to begin the study of Lawrence's life, but rarely have I been without a copy of at least a selection from his poems. It was also as a teenager that I first read *The Rainbow*, which affected me like an emotional depth charge and was the strongest literary influence on the novel I completed shortly before joining the army. In the seventies and eighties I read practically everything Lawrence had written, including all three versions of *Lady Chatterley*, besides reading some of the more important biographies and studies, from John Middleton Murry's *Son of Woman* to Keith Sagar's *D.H. Lawrence: Life into Art*. I also saw the film versions of *Women in Love*, *The Fox*, and *The Rainbow*.

From the Kiowa Ranch and the Lawrence Memorial Chapel we drove to Taos, on the way stopping only to visit the Taos Pueblo. As we drove round the place I could not help thinking we really had no business to be there. It was not that we were made to feel unwelcome. This was certainly not the case. As the notices at the entrance showed, the pueblo was accustomed to visitors. But it seemed wrong to treat people's homes as a kind of tourist attraction, even though the people themselves did not object and though tourism might benefit them economically. Be that as it may, it was obvious that notwithstanding its picturesque appearance the pueblo had lost much of its traditional character. The raven-haired men wore jeans and drove trucks, and as our station wagon slowly circled the irregular, multi-storeyed adobe dwellings I could see through doors and windows refrigerators and washing machines. The numerous crosses in the graveyard showed that the community had long been Christianized. In Taos we walked down what seemed to be the original main street, with its memories of Kit Carson, and round the Spanish-style plaza, where outside the entrance to one of the hotels we saw a notice that said 'D.H. Lawrence Paintings.' They were the oil paintings that had been confiscated by the London Police in 1929 on account of their alleged obscenity and returned to the artist on the condition that they were not again exhibited in England. I had forgotten about them, or forgotten they were in Taos, though Henry Shukman had described how he had seen them and how he had met the self-promoting expatriate Greek who was the proprietor of the hotel and the painting's legal owner. Though familiar with the paintings in colour reproduction, mainly from Keith Sagar's *D.H. Lawrence*, I was curious to see the originals. Having paid our three dollars each (Henry Shukman had paid one dollar), we found them in a large room to the rear of the foyer dominated by enormous portraits of the expatriate Greek when young, and various members of his family. They were located in a corner, but the electricity having failed in that part of the room we were unable to see them properly. All the same, seeing the paintings gave me a better idea of Lawrence's highly-developed colour sense than I could otherwise have obtained. I was also pleased to see two or three of Dorothy Brett's paintings, one of them being her 'big picture of the desert, with all our ranch life going on.'

The following day we drove from Questa to Santa Fé, which though bigger than Taos was quieter and much less commercialized, and from Santa Fé to Farmington. The day after, having left Farmington amid thunder and lightning and seen Monument Valley in brilliant sunshine, we joined up with the route that Kulananda, Manjuvajra, and I had followed two years earlier. Travelling through Arizona, Utah, Nevada, and California, spending two nights in Williams, one night in Las Vegas, and one in Bishop, we saw the Grand Canyon, the Mohave Desert, Death Valley, and the Yosemite National Park, and on 17 September reached San Francisco, after covering nearly 5,000 miles since leaving Missoula. In San Francisco, where we spent nine or ten days, Paramartha and I stayed in the men's community above the Center and Manjuvajra with a Mitra. I was accommodated in Paramabodhi's room, which he kindly vacated for me. In the room there were a few books, one of which I was soon reading. This was Kurt Vonnegut's *Slaughterhouse Five*, which interested me mainly because of its first-hand account of the bombing of Dresden by the Allies in 1945, the

The Grand Canyon

author having been a prisoner of war in the city at the time. I had visited Dresden earlier in the year, on my way back to Berlin from Prague, and had seen both the Opera House and other restored buildings and the as yet unrestored Frauenkirche, as well as the famous art gallery. San Francisco appeared not to abound in second-hand bookshops, but Paramartha, Manjuvajra, and I paid a visit to the Buddhist Bookstore, run by the Buddhist Churches of America and located in their spacious headquarters building. The BCA is the national Buddhist organization of the various Jōdo Shin Shū or True Pure Land congregations, and it was therefore natural that their bookstore should be well stocked with Pure Land literature, though the literature of other schools was by no means unrepresented. It was in fact the best and most comprehensive Buddhist bookshop I have come across. As Jōdo Shin Shū literature is not easily available in England I was particularly interested in works dealing with this school and eventually left with a copy of *Shinran: An Introduction to His Thought* by Yoshifumi Ueda and Dennis Hirota, the second part of which contained selections from Shinran's writings. Had I not been travelling, and not wanted to run the risk of incurring excess baggage charges when we flew to Australia, I would have bought all four volumes of Shinran's *Kyogyoshinsho* or *The True Teaching, Practice and Realization of the Pure Land Way*. As things turned out, by the time our travels ended I had dispatched to England no fewer than four boxes of books new and second-hand. Japan and Japanese Buddhism were very much the order of the day in San Francisco, it seemed. From the Buddhist Bookstore the three of us went to Japan Town, which I had seen on an earlier visit, and two days later (or was it two days earlier?) Paramartha and I visited the Asian Art Museum and the Japanese Tea House and Garden, both situated in Golden Gate Park. The Japanese Tea House, where I had once talked with the poet and Zen priest Philip Whalen, was a disappointment. Or rather, the waitresses were a disappointment. Though Japanese, they clearly were not accustomed to wearing the kimono, and their movements, far from being graceful, were clumsy and awkward. One of them was wearing trainers. Hardly less disappointing was the sushi bar to which the local Order members took Paramartha and me towards to end of our visit. Here it was not the service bar but the food that was disappointing. Though quite tasty, it consisted of tiny round cakes of cold rice, with a vegetarian topping (normally it was raw fish), which one ate with chopsticks after dipping them in a hot sauce. Since each cake was hardly bigger than a thimble we were glad to go back to the community afterwards and partake of Karunadevi's pumpkin pie.

Second-hand bookshops may not have abounded in San Francisco, but at least there was one in the little coastal town of Coos Bay, where Paramartha, Manjuvajra, and I stopped on our way to Seattle. It was the second day of our journey. That morning, having seen the giant redwoods (including the Big Tree, more than 300 feet high), we had crossed the state border into Oregon, and the air was now much colder. We were therefore glad to stop for a hot drink, and gladder still that we could find it in a second-hand bookshop the proprietor of which ran a coffee bar for the benefit of his customers. Though the town was small, the bookshop was a big one, with a very varied stock. Paramartha and I were soon browsing in the 'Alternative' section, where we found an astonishingly rich collection of books on Indian philosophy and religion. Paramartha bought four volumes on yoga, I a copy of *The Way to the Labyrinth: Memories of East and West* by the French musicologist Alain Danielou, whom I had once heard playing the vina at a concert in Benares, as well as a copy of the same author's *While the Gods Play*, a scholarly study of certain aspects of South Indian Shaivism. Like me, Danielou had spent twenty years in India, and knew some of the places, and even some of the people, I had known, and I therefore lost no time in plunging into his memoir, with the result that at intervals during the next few days I lived more in India than in America. It was a very orthodox India, for Danielou was a traditionalist of the doctrinaire Guenon type, with a penchant for the darker, more sinister side of Hinduism (he would probably have loved the Thugs). The book read well, even though it was a translation, and with some, at least, of the author's attitudes and ideas I found myself in whole-hearted agreement. All the same, I did not find the Frenchman's character a very pleasant one; at times it even repelled me. Though well informed and highly intelligent, he was arrogant and supercilious and one could imagine him recording his memories with a sneer on his face. Some of his strictures were unduly harsh, even in cases where harshness was justified to an extent, such as those on Gandhi ('this skinny, puritanical, and neurotic little man') or Nehru ('haughty, inaccessible, and self-important' once he came to power), and on the modern Western world. He was also guilty of the occasional inaccuracy, as when he described Lama Govinda as marrying a 'rich Parsee widow from Bombay' (Li Gotami was neither rich nor a widow) and 'this peculiar couple', as he called the Govindas, as creating 'a kind of ashram in California' of which 'the Parsee lady became [the] goddess', which was a ridiculous distortion of the true facts. About the gentle, saintly Sri Sunyata, whom I had also known, Danielou was positively slanderous, so that it was difficult for me to resist the conclusion that for all his culture and sophistication there was in the make-up of the distinguished musicologist an unpleasant streak of viciousness.

In Seattle, which we reached late the following afternoon, we were accommodated in the men's community above the spacious new centre. Sea fog had prevented us from having, that morning, more than a few glimpses of the Pacific Ocean, but it had not prevented us from stopping and seeing Cape Foulweather, where Captain Cook had landed and 'discovered' Oregon. Nor did the weather prevent us, once we had driven inland and passed through Portland, from seeing in the distance the shining white summit of Mount Rainier, the ethereal shape of which was visible on fine days from Seattle itself. On the second or third afternoon of our stay Aryadaka took Paramartha and me to the Jōdo Shin Shū church for a meeting with its minister, Don Castro, whom I had met on my previous visit (in San Francisco, I had renewed acquaintance with Buddhist friends at the Zen Center and the Nyingma Institute), and Paramartha had his first experience of a Pure Land place of worship. By this time I had finished reading *Shinran*, which gave an excellent short account of the Master's life and work, the Mahāyāna mode of thought, the emergence of the Pure Land Path, and the structure of Shinran's thought, and I was looking forward to having a discussion with a Jōdo Shin Shū follower who, as I knew from my previous contact with him, was both friendly and well informed. In the event, the discussion was a very good one, though shorter than we could have wished, as Don Castro had to leave for another appointment. Since our last meeting he had evidently been reading FWBO literature, particularly *The History of My Going For Refuge*, and at one point in the discussion he commented that he thought my spiritual experience had followed a course similar to that of Shinran's. From the Pure Land church (as Spenser speaks of 'Isis church' I am less resistant to the idea of applying the term to a Buddhist place of worship than I used to be) the three of us – Paramartha, Aryadaka, and me – drove to the Museum of Asian Art, where besides the permanent collection, which contained many fine Buddhist images, we saw the special exhibition on 'Kesa: The Elegance of Japanese Monks' Robes'. In Seattle, as in San Francisco, Japan and Japanese Buddhism seemed to be the order of the day! Since the abbreviated kesa worn by members of the

Western Buddhist Order derives from a Japanese original, the exhibition was of special interest to us, particularly as the organizers had produced an illustrated brochure that not only described the kesa in full detail but explained its symbolism and traced the three periods or stages of kesa development in Japan, from the introduction of Buddhism from Korea in the sixth century CE down into modern times. There was also a section on 'Contradiction in Japanese Kesa', the opening paragraph of which read:

> Originally made of old textile patches to symbolize vows of poverty, the patches used in Japan were lavishly made of the most elegant and gorgeous brocade in the land and show superb workmanship. When examining the kesa of Japan, the first thing that impresses us is the beauty of the textiles. These textiles represent the top quality of what could be produced in a certain era. They are expensive and display magnificent designs. At first it might come as a big surprise and even seem a contradiction that such extravagance would be spent on garments worn by Buddhist monks who have made the vow of poverty.

The brocades from which the kesas were made were elegant and gorgeous indeed, and the designs truly magnificent, and it was difficult to imagine a greater contrast than that between those splendid garments (all of them versions of the full kesa, of course, not the abbreviated one) and the plain cotton robes currently worn by Theravādin monks in Sri Lanka, Burma, and Thailand – not to mention the rag robes favoured by their ascetic predecessors in ancient India. The contrast is illustrative of two different attitudes to prayer and worship. For some people, a colourful religious ceremony, with robes, lights, incense, and music, is nothing less than an earthly reflection of an archetypal, imaginal realm, and participation in it can be a profound spiritual experience. Such, it seems, were the envoys whom a pagan Russian prince sent out in search of the true religion. Dissatisfied with the Muslims of Bulgaria, and complaining that worship in Germany and Rome was lacking in beauty, they came at length to Constantinople, where they attended the Divine Liturgy in the great Church of the Holy Wisdom. Here they found what they were looking for, reporting, 'We knew not whether we were in heaven or upon earth, for surely there is no such splendour or beauty anywhere.'* The result

---

* Timothy Ware, *The Orthodox Church*, Harmonsworth 1963, p.269.

was that Russia embraced Orthodox Christianity. For those of the opposite temperament, religious ceremonies get in the way of direct experience of Reality, things like robes being a frivolous distraction from the true business of the spiritual life. And of course, it is possible for even the most sacred ceremonies to degenerate into a species of entertainment to be performed in a mechanical or slovenly manner. Within the Christian communion, the two extremes are represented by the Orthodox Church and the Roman Catholic Church on one hand, and the Puritans, Calvinists, Quakers, and Nonconformists on the other. Anglicans – and perhaps Lutherans – come somewhere in between. Among Buddhists the extremes are represented, respectively, by the Lamaists and the Theravādins. In the FWBO it will, I hope, be possible for us to have ceremonies that are neither gaudy nor bleak but which, following the middle way, manage to combine richness with simplicity, aesthetic appeal with significance.

Half-way through our stay in Seattle Aryadaka drove Paramartha and me up the coast to Vancouver, where we spent two nights at the small centre-cum-community. Our visit being such a short one, we had little time for sightseeing or for looking in bookshops, but Aryadaka drove us round the very beautiful Stanley Park, where we saw, through the rain, a number of black squirrels, which apparently are unique to the area. In Seattle, both before and after our Canadian excursion, we had better luck with bookshops. At the Theosophical Society's Quest Bookshop I found a copy of *The Mystery of Light: The Life and Teaching of Omraam Mikhael Aivanhov* by Georg Feuerstein, the yoga scholar and historian who with Karel Werner translated *The Three Jewels* into German, while Paramartha, in the course of one of his solo outings in the city, came across a Japanese novel he thought would interest me. Aivanhov (1900–86) was a Bulgarian-born master who, at the behest of his teacher, went to France in 1937 and lived and taught there for fifty years. I had first heard of him some years earlier, when an American Friend left the FWBO to become his disciple, and I was naturally desirous of learning more about him. Feuerstein's book proved to be very informative, as regards both the man and his teaching. The teaching turned out to be a kind of Christian Gnosticism in which the sun, in its spiritual aspect, played a significant role. Aivanhov in fact described his teaching as solar yoga and I was interested to note that, like Plotinus, he regarded the sun as an intelligent entity. As for the man himself, the picture that emerged from the first part of the book was both impressive and attractive. Visionary, teacher, and healer, Omraam Mikhael Aivanhov was at the same time a simple and direct man whose simplicity and directness were, in Feuerstein's words, 'the fruits of a wonderful mental lucidity and great personal integrity.' I could not help thinking that our American ex-Friend was probably safer in his hands than she would have been in those of certain other teachers I could name. *The Buddha Tree* was translated from the Japanese of Fumio Niwa, who is described in the translator's Introduction (1965) as 'one of contemporary Japan's most prolific novelists'. It tells the story of handsome and effete Soshu, a hypocritical Buddhist priest who, riven by guilt, tries to reform but instead is caught up in a web of intrigue and deceit. Though the story is well told, and though Soshu and the other principal characters come very much alive, it was not the story that interested me so much as the setting. This was the Japanese countryside and the Pure Land temple of which Soshu is hereditary priest. Since the author was brought up in a Pure Land temple and served there as a priest for several years, before leaving at the age of twenty-eight to become a creative writer, he is able to give a graphic account of traditional temple life, with its time-honoured customs, its daily and seasonal rituals, and its colourful festivals, as well as of the kind of relations obtaining between the temple and its priest on the one hand and the parishioners and their various interests on the other. It was like being in the Japanese Buddhist equivalent of a parish in Barsetshire. But whereas Anthony Trollope tells us nothing about Anglicanism as a religion, Fumio Niwa manages to impart a great deal of information about the Jōdo Shin Shū faith. Indeed he from time to time communicates valuable insights into Shinran's teaching on such subjects as sin, repentance, grace, and compassion. I therefore read *The Buddha Tree* with great interest, and continued reading it with undiminished interest in Sydney, where Paramartha and I arrived on 10 October and where we stayed two days at Chittaprabha's house in the suburbs and a week at Vijayaloka, the retreat centre and men's community outside the city.

At Vijayaloka we were accommodated in the cottage normally occupied by Dipankara and one or two other members of the community. At the back of the cottage there was a broad wooden deck and here, weather permitting (there was much rain during our stay and a couple of thunderstorms), I sat and read. A few dozen yards away, on the far side of an expanse of grass, began the native bush, which was quite dense and sloped sharply down to the invisible river. Sulphur-crested white cockatoos flew past, as well as the occasional king parrot or rosella. Once, Paramartha, wandering in the bush, came across an echidna or spiny anteater, one of Australia's two egg-laying mammals. On several occasions, I saw – and heard – the famous kookaburra or laughing jackass, a solitary member of that species being in the habit of occupying a low branch on a dead tree immediately opposite the deck. Having finished *The Buddha Tree* I started on *Pure-Land Zen and Zen Pure-Land – Letters from Patriarch Yin Kuang*, which I had found in a bookcase in the cottage's lounge. Together with Abbot Tai Tsu and the great Ch'an meditation master Hsu Yun, Yin Kuang was one of the three most influential figures in modern Chinese Buddhism. He was the current patriarch of the Pure Land School in China, and his letters were addressed to various disciples. A teaching that particularly struck me was that one should read the Mahāyāna sūtras *without thinking of their meaning*. This I took to mean that one should read them without engaging in discursive mental activity, so that the transcendental import of the sūtra, bypassing the rational mind, would be able to penetrate directly to the imaginal faculty of the reader and even to awaken his or her innate Buddha-wisdom. Such a way of reading would be particularly appropriate, I thought, in the case of those sūtras in which the Buddha, or great bodhisattva, who is the preacher of the sūtra, expresses himself in the language of myth and symbol rather than in that of concepts. It was also clear from the Introduction (which I think was by the translator of the *Letters*) that for the Chinese Pure Land School, as for the patriarch himself, self-power and other-power were not incompatible, so that Ch'an/Zen and Pure Land Buddhism were themselves not incompatible. Hence the title of the book – *Pure-Land Zen and Zen Pure-Land*. According to the Introduction, Zen and Theravāda adopt the self-power approach, whereas the more flexible Pure Land and Esoteric (i.e. Tantric) schools combine self-power with other-power. However, Pure Land differs from Zen in not stressing the master–disciple relationship and in 'de-emphasizing' the role of the sub-gurus/roshis and rituals. I found this interesting for several reasons. For one thing, the four schools referred to were the very four which, in my recent paper *Extending the Hand of Fellowship*, I had examined in respect of the different ways in which they were unorthodox, that is, the different ways in which they emphasized what was secondary in the Buddhist life at the expense of what was primary. It was therefore interesting to look at them from a different point of view and to see which of them depended on self-power and which on other-power. Zen and Theravāda clearly depended on the former, as the author of the Introduction had said. The Jōdo Shin Shū or True Pure Land School, the specifically Japanese form of Pure Land belief, no less clearly depended on the latter. That left Tantric Buddhism, which in the Introduction had been categorized as combining self-power with other-power. In view of the fact that this school *did* stress the master–disciple relationship, the guru being regarded as the Buddha and therefore infallible, and *did* emphasize the role of such things as lineage, blessing, and ritual 'empowerment', I was inclined to regard it as being, on the whole, dependent more on other-power than self-power. The Chinese Pure Land School, which I had not mentioned in my paper as it was not the form of Pure Land Buddhism we were most likely to meet in the West, explicitly combined both approaches. In the words of the Introduction to the *Letters*, the main aim of (Chinese) Pure Land was 'rebirth in a Buddha land through self-effort and the power of Amitābha Buddha's Vows.' Earlier on, the writer had connected the self-power approach with the spiritually more advanced, identified as the monks and nuns, and the other-power approach with spiritually less advanced, identified as the lay followers. I would reverse this. In my opinion the path of dependence on self-power is for the spiritually *less* advanced, and the path of dependence on other-power for the spiritually *more* advanced.

Except for visits to the Art Gallery of New South Wales, where I admired the work of Arthur Boyd, and to the local FWBO centre, where I gave a poetry reading one evening, Paramartha and I did not go much into town. This was partly because I found Sydney a very speedy place (in this respect it resembled San Francisco) and partly because it was more convenient for people who wanted to see me individually to do so at Vijayaloka. Vajrasuri having lent us her car, we visited the Mount Annan Botanical Garden, near Campbelltown, and explored some of the beautiful bays and beaches to the north of the city, with which Paramartha was well acquainted, he having spent two years in Sydney before coming to England. The most memorable of these explorations was the one when, in perfect weather, we spent the greater part of the day driving round the Ku-ring-gai National Park, where the road wound round creek after picturesque creek and where we followed a few trails into the bush – a bush in which the only sound was that of the cicadas and where there was an amazing variety of wild flowers, as of trees and shrubs. Walking along the beach at the end of another day we saw, as the light faded, two or three black and white ibises scavenging the rubbish bins, poking their long curved bills through the wire to get at whatever savoury morsels the beach-goers had deposited there. For me these stately birds were associated with the Egyptian god Thoth, the god of wisdom and learning, and I was taken aback – even rather shocked – to see them seeking their supper in this degrading fashion.

The trip that took us farthest afield was the one we made to the charming little town of Katoomba, up in the Blue Mountains, some hundred miles from Sydney, where we spent two days with Dharma-mati, who showed us the Three Sisters rocks and took us for a ride on the virtually perpendicular scenic railway; where we saw bright-hued galahs, rosellas, and king parrots, and where I finished reading *The Buddha Tree*. The Blue Mountains owed their name, we were told, to the fact that the eucalypts with which their sides were densely covered emitted a blue vapour, so that the predominant colour of the breath-takingly beautiful landscape, with its extensive ranges and lofty peaks, was blue rather than green. On the way there we had seen a signboard saying 'Norman Lindsay Gallery'. Norman Lindsay (1879–1969) was an Australian artist and novelist best known for his classic children's story *The Magic Pudding* and for the fact that the first volume of his autobiography had been banned. In England I had read, and admired, some of his literary criticism (*The Mask of Robert Browning* was a feast in itself), but except for a few black-and-white book illustrations I was unfamiliar with his art. As Paramartha and I were both keen to see what we could of this, on the way back to Sydney we stopped at the gallery. Unfortunately the place was closed, it being a Tuesday, and Tuesday being the day the committee that ran the gallery held its weekly meeting. Elderly, well dressed men and women of 'middle-class' appearance (I put the words in inverted commas as Australia has a classless society) were even then turning up in their gleaming new cars. We therefore had to be content with wandering round the well-kept grounds looking at the clumsy, rather crude statuary groups, all the work of Robert Lindsay and all depicting one or more naked nymphs being leered at by a lurking satyr. Glancing from the statuary to the committee members, and from the committee members to the statuary, I wondered if yet another rebel was in process of being posthumously co-opted by the establishment.

Melbourne was much less speedy than Sydney and therefore much more enjoyable. It was also rather an 'English' city, even as Sydney was rather an 'American' one. The men's community was tucked away at the end of a quiet cul-de-sac in Brunswick, a suburb full of Greeks,

Turks, and Cypriots, and abounding in ethnic shops, restaurants, and places of worship. Trams ran straight to the city centre, and it was not long before Buddhadasa had taken us to see the National Art Gallery of Victoria, which was part of Melbourne's 'South Bank' complex (though in this case the complex happened to be sited *north* of the river) and which could boast several excellent European paintings, including a Burne-Jones. He also took us to the famous Hanging Rock and to Ballarat, and towards the end of our stay Vidyaratna and Dayamegha took us to Healesville Sanctuary for the day. Ballarat was founded in the 1851 goldrush, and the open-air museum, or historical park, of Sovereign Hill, situated in an early gold-digging area, portrayed the way of life on the goldfields in those days. In Ballarat itself we visited the Fine Art Gallery and saw Nicholas Chevalier's *Buddha's Renunciation* (1884), a greatly enlarged photograph of which Buddhadasa had sent me some months previously. The Healesville Sanctuary was a wildlife park, and in the course of our visit we saw kangaroos, wallabies, dingoes, echidnas, duck-billed platypuses, and koala bears, as well as pelicans, cranes, and wedge-tailed black eagles. We were especially fascinated by the echidnas, balls of brown spines from which protruded a long black snout and who moved about in the pit-like enclosure without any visible means of locomotion.

Neither in Melbourne nor in Ballarat did Paramartha, Buddhadasa, and I omit to explore the second-hand bookshops, and when Paramartha flew to Perth to spend a couple of weeks with his brother and sister Buddhadasa and I extended our explorations from the city centre to various suburbs and even to one or two neighbouring townships. Melbourne was well provided with second-hand bookshops, and as prices were generally lower than in London I soon acquired a whole boxful of treasures for Buddhadasa to dispatch to England after Paramartha and I had left for New Zealand. Not that I was able to dive into all of them straight away, or that I even wanted to, especially as in the rooms in which Paramartha and I were staying, rooms usually occupied by Buddhadasa and Siladasa, I had found several books that I wanted to read before my departure. The most important of these were the first two volumes of Alan Walker's *Franz Liszt* (the third and final volume was yet to come) and T.A. Stewart's *The Myths of Plato*. Liszt was a composer to whom I had not paid much attention, though I was familiar with the well-known pieces, but after making my way through the two bulky volumes, the second of which concluded with the frustrations of the Weimar period, I resolved that as soon as I had the opportunity I would get to know his work better, especially the B minor Piano Sonata, of which Walker spoke highly. Liszt was a fascinating character. I had not realized before that, while not conventionally moral (in the eyes of the Church he was a fornicator and adulterer), he was nonetheless a fervently devout Roman Catholic who at times of crisis was capable of spending hours together in an agony of prayer. *The Myths of Plato* (1970) was the second edition of a work which on its publication in 1905 'first recalled the attention of English scholars to the organic importance of Plato's *Myths*, as a unit in the upsurge of discovery which was just then opening a vista of the emotional and spiritual aspects of Greek religion, long buried under the pressure of Olympian orthodoxy.' Professor Stewart not only assembled the myths from various Platonic dialogues, and treated them as so many aspects of a consistent system of thought; he also discussed them, both collectively and individually, at some length, pointing to the existence of parallels in such diverse sources as Dante, the English Romantic poets, and the *Kalevala*. In his view Plato used myth to communicate a vision of Truth or Reality that was incommunicable by any other means. Reason might take you to the top of the mountain, but it was myth that provided you with the wings with which you launched yourself into the empyrean. I at once saw the relevance of Stewart's understanding of myth to my own studies of the mythic element in Buddhism, particularly the biography of the Buddha, and as soon as I had finished reading the book I started copying lengthy extracts from it into one of my notebooks with a view to making use of the material later on. When Siladasa, to whom the volume belonged, came to know of this, he generously presented it to me, so that it now occupies a place on one of the bookshelves in the room where, nine months later, I am writing this article.

Other books read during my five weeks in Melbourne, whether purchased or borrowed from Buddhadasa's and Siladasa's collections, included *The Vision of Piers Plowman, Esther Waters*, and *The Hazards of Being Male*. *The Vision of Piers Plowman* is a fourteenth-century alliterative poem attributed to William Langland, about whom we know little more than what he tells us himself in the poem. The work is divided (in its most extended version) into a prologue and twenty-two passus or 'steps', and according to the *Wordsworth Companion to Literature in English* it 'manifests a passionate concern for the corruption of secular society, the regular clergy and the mendicant orders, and its consequences for the spiritual welfare of the populace. His dreamer-narrator's search for "true" Christianity and the path to salvation includes an introspection and a condemnation of the established Church which also characterize the writings of Wyclif and the Lollards and inspired the mystical writers of the period.' I had wanted to read the poem for some years, but had been unable to find a satisfactory rendering into modern English verse. Henry W. Wells's translation, published in London by Sheed and Ward in 1935, was exactly what I had been looking for. *Piers Plowman* is an allegorical poem, but since Langland had a racy style, and a gift of graphic description, his personified virtues and vices possess a preternatural, Hogarthian vitality. One of the leading characters in his allegorical *dramatis personae* is Mede the Maid, who makes her appearance in *Passus II* and is said to have been modelled on Alice Perrers, the greedy and corrupt mistress of the aged Edward III.

> *The finest of furs were affixed to her garments.*
> *She was crowned with a coronet that a king might envy,*
> *Her fine fingers were fretted with gold wiring*
> *And red rubies upon it red as coal brands:*
> *Dazzling diamonds, double sapphires,*
> *And blue beryls from the East to ban diseases.*
> *Her robe was rich, ingrained with red scarlet,*
> *And ribands of red gold, and rich jewels.*
> *Her raiment ravished me; its richness amazed me.*
> *I wondered who she was, and who was her husband.*

Since in Middle English the word *meed* or *mede* signifies both reward and bribe, Mede the Maid is a dangerously ambivalent character. So dangerous is she that Conscience refuses to wed her on any account, even though she brings with her as her portion

> *the earldom of Envy and Wrath, its neighbour,*
> *With the castles of Chiding and Chattering-out-of-reason,*

and much else besides, and though the king orders him to take her. Some of Langland's satirical allusions are still topical, as when he says of Mede the Maid:

> *Those who wait in Westminster worshipped her wholly.*
> *All the gentle justices were joyous at her coming,*
> *And bustled to the bower where their bride was dwelling,*
> *To comfort her and be kind to her, with Clergy's permission.*

He also has a keen eye for people's weakness and capacity for self-deception, and for the pretensions of the learned professions, including the medical profession.

> *Age had good hope, and hastily shrived himself,*
> *Drove off Despair and dared Life in battle.*
> *Life fled for fear and sought physic to help him,*
> *He besought him for succour and got salves and syrups.*
> *He gave physicians the gold that gladdened their spirits,*
> *And they gave him against Age a glass helmet.*
> *Life believed that Leachcraft would lead Age captive,*
> *And drive away Death with drugs and powders.*

The physicians giving Life a glass helmet against the assaults of Age is a particularly nice touch. In the lines that follow Age not only attacks Life but batters 'a physician in a furred hood' so badly that he falls in a palsy and dies three days after. Yet Life 'still hoped for good health and held his heart merry,' after which there comes a sudden change and with it a dramatic shift, on the part of the narrator of the poem, from the third person to the first person singular.

> *But Age was soon after me, and walked on my brain pan.*
> *He made me bald before and bare on the crowning.*
> *He walked so heavily on my head that it will be seen forever.*
> *'Sir-ill-mannered Age,' I said, 'woe be with you!*
> *How long has your way been upon the heads of the people?*
> *If you had acted courteously you would have asked permission.'*
> *'Yes, dear sluggard!' he said and struck me harder.*
> *He hit me under the ear so that I am hard of hearing.*
> *He buffeted me about the mouth and beat out my teeth.*
> *He gyved me in gouts; I could not walk freely,*
> *And this woe that I was in moved my wife also.*
> *She wished heartily that I were already in heaven.*
> *The limb that she loved was no longer able.*
> *Age and she had enfeebled it together.*

But Langland is not always satirical. He can admire the flowers of the field and wonder at the way Reason (or as we would say, instinct) teaches the magpie 'To build and to breed where the thorn-bush shields him'. Moreover, he was evidently a man of genuine Christian conviction who felt for the poor and oppressed and who, though himself something of a scholar, was far from looking down on the unsophisticated faith of the unlettered majority.

Shoemakers and shepherds and such simple peasants
Pierce with a pater noster *the palace of heaven,*
And pass purgatory penniless at their earthly parting,
Go into the bliss of paradise for their pure faith,
Who were imperfect here in knowing and living.

This is reminiscent of *The Cloud of Unknowing*'s 'short prayer pierceth heaven,' as well as the Jōdo Shin Shū's belief that a single heartfelt repetition of the name of Amitābha is sufficient to ensure rebirth in the Pure Land.

Esther Waters, said to be George Moore's finest work, was one of those classic English novels one is always intending to read but somehow never gets around to. It had been on my reading list (though never very high up on it) for years, and despite the fact that editions of the work were easily available it was only when I saw it on Siladasa's bookshelves that I took it up. I had read *Conversations in Ebury Street* when I was fourteen or fifteen, and *Confessions of a Young Man* only two years ago, but this was something very different. It is a realistic novel – realistic in the Zolaesque sense of the term. It tells the story of a religious-minded girl – Esther Waters – who is seduced by a fellow servant: her lover deserts her, she bears a child, and endures a bitter and humiliating struggle to bring their boy up. Life in the family for which she works in the early part of the story centres on their racing stables, and there hangs over them the black shadow of a fatal addiction to gambling. Moore had first-hand knowledge of the so-called sport of kings, his Irish MP father having been the proprietor of a racing stable, and the picture he paints of a way of life dominated by horses and horse racing is a vivid one. It was a way of life about which I knew nothing, and the reading of *Esther Waters* served to remind me that a good novel can be a means of widening our mental horizon by acquainting us with modes of life and types of character outside our personal experience. It also served to remind me that a good novel can teach a moral lesson, though it will do this indirectly, by enlisting our sympathies on behalf of what is truly positive in life. As well as showing the evil of gambling, which can bring bankruptcy and ruin upon whole families, Moore's story depicts, in the person of humble, illiterate Esther, the heights of heroism to which a single mother (as we would now call her) is capable of rising in order to keep, protect, raise, and educate her child. The novel closes on what I thought was a note of pathos, perhaps unintended by the author. Her great task accomplished, Esther has found peace with an old friend, the widow of her first employer, and her son, now a handsome young man, has come to see her. He has joined the army, and stands before his mother in all the glory of his brand new regimentals. He is full of youthful hope, she of maternal pride. But what of the future, I wondered? Has she sacrificed and suffered for his sake, all those years, only for him to die on some distant battlefield, fighting in a war he does not understand?

Although *The Hazards of Being Male: Surviving the Myth of Masculine Privilege*, by Herb Goldberg, PhD., was published in 1976, I found it to be highly relevant to some of the concerns of the present-day Men's Movement. It was also astonishingly close, in certain respects, to some of my own thinking, even though the author seems not to have heard of Buddhism, much less still of the FWBO. Nowhere was this closeness more evident than in the chapter on what Goldberg calls buddyship. But instead of trying to summarize his views on the topic I shall reproduce a long and important extract that I copied into one of my notebooks and which needs to be seriously pondered by men and women alike.

> Buddyship is the deepest of male–male interactions. Buddyships, which already have endured crises, have rich dimensions that generally cannot exist even in the deepest male–female relationships. For example, it has facets of a good father–son and a loving brother–brother interaction. Each buddy, at alternate times, may assume the role of teacher or guide to the other and will revel in the other person's development and expanded skills. And there is also a sense of warmth and empathic understanding and comfort when one person is feeling weak, acting foolish, or being vulnerable. In these instances, one buddy gets stability and nourishment from the other. There is a happy, mutual sharing of resources, both material and emotional. The competitive element is inconsequential and a win for one becomes a win for both.
>
> The brother–brother dimension of buddyship is one in which each looks out for the other, protecting him from exploitation. It is this phase of the male–male interaction that tends to be the most threatening to a wife or girl friend of one of the buddies. That is, a buddy will not hesitate to tell the other when he sees him allowing himself to be manipulated and self-destructively controlled by a woman.

Buddyship may also be threatening to an involved woman because many of its dimensions are not shared with her. Buddies will share deepest feelings about their relationships, personal fantasies, private or secret experiences. This may be very disturbing to an involved woman and her jealousy over the relationship may be deeper even than jealousy over a man's girl friend – partially because a relationship with another woman can be righteously attacked as being a betrayal of trust while a buddyship cannot.

Consequently, the woman may consciously or unconsciously attempt to undermine or destroy the buddyship. This may be attempted through derogatory comments, flattery, or suggestive innuendos. 'What do you need him for? He's a big baby,' 'He just uses you,' 'You're like two overgrown adolescents,' 'He's not good enough for you,' 'He's jealous of you,' 'He's a loser,' 'You're always kissing his ass,' 'Why don't you got to bed with him? You spend more time with him than you do with me!' Suggestive remarks may be made implying latent homosexuality. Explosive arguments will occur particularly if a wife or girl friend sees 'her man' do something for a buddy that he might not do for her or lend money or material possessions that she feels will cause her to be deprived in some way.

Female jealousy and resentment over a buddyship may also reflect her awareness that its roots may be deeper, because the relationship has more room for freedom, is less possessive, and does not have the components of jealousy and role rigidity that often exist in male–female relationships.

Buddyships are relatively role free. Each male feels safe enough to be open to act silly, stupid, and in spontaneous, child-like and affectionate ways which he may not feel safe enough to show anyone else.

The art of buddyship in our culture is undeveloped because it requires time, a willingness to work through crises, to upset one's heterosexual partner, to endure hostile suggestions and innuendoes about latent homosexuality, and a social maturity and competence that is not culturally recognized or rewarded the way that, for example, marriage is. If anything, a buddyship, if it is particularly intense, is embarrassing to others. Buddies are accused of delayed emotional development and of neglecting more important activities and relationships. Buddyships are often viewed as a threat to the 'mature' husband–wife relationship because they require time, cultivation, commitment, mutual nourishment, and love. Their rewards, however, if achieved, are great because of their mutually supportive, nourishing, no-strings-attached aspects. They can endure stresses that few male–female relationships can because they do not have legal, contractual binds that force them to remain together.

The lack of such a relationship makes a man particularly vulnerable. It over-intensifies his dependence on his woman, placing an emotional burden on her that can suffocate and destroy their relationship. Once a primary relationship with a woman breaks down the man has no one to turn to. In addition, once the male has totally and solely become reliant on a woman for the satisfaction of his emotional needs, he cannot afford to risk losing her. Consequently, he will be more prone to cling to an unhappy, unfulfilling relationship out of desperation and the frightening fear of being cut off from all emotional nourishment.

I believe that the lack of buddyship is also an important factor in the significantly higher male suicide rate and the significantly higher rate of death of divorced males as opposed to divorced females. Instead of reaching out for help, comfort, and nourishment from a buddy, he hides behind a façade of strength and independence. Or he desperately reaches out for another woman, often throwing himself prematurely into another relationship. When no woman is available to him he may become engulfed in his isolation and alienation and become suicide prone.

It is my belief that the male needs to realize the importance of a buddyship relationship and learn to develop one. The path toward a buddyship relationship is a difficult and hazardous one that requires an awareness of the great need and survival value of such a relationship. It is much more difficult to launch because while the male–female relationship tends to begin on the basis of a sexual attraction, the initial reaction between males tends to be one of cautiousness, anxiety about openness and getting close, and some distrust. Therefore, while a male–female relationship can arrive at a state of intimacy fairly rapidly, the male–male relationship must endure various phases of development and be tested before the intimacy of buddyship can be achieved.

The continuing impact of a buddyship is the development of a deep mutual respect, trust, and pleasure in each other's company. Envy and competitiveness will increasingly recede into the background while your buddy's growth and achievements will begin to make you feel as good as if it were happening to you. You will find

growing interest in each other as total people and the specific things
you do together will become significantly less important than the
simple joy and comfort in being with each other. A real buddyship
will last a lifetime, remaining in the face of even massive personal
changes in every other aspect of life.

Besides visiting bookshops and reading books, during my time in
Melbourne I read the weekend *Australian* and back numbers of *Quad-
rant*, a cultural monthly with which I was already familiar as Buddhadasa was in the habit of sending me photocopies of any articles of
special interest. Reading the two latter gave me a clearer understanding of political and economic conditions in Australia and of the
kind of problems its people were having to face. Britain, I realized, was
politically and economically, though not culturally, at the periphery of
the collective Australian consciousness, which tended to be more
occupied with the threat posed, potentially, by its bigger Asian neighbours. I also attended two receptions at the Melbourne Centre, one for
me and one for representatives of other Buddhist groups. There were
afternoon and evening walks in the community's immediate neighbourhood, where outsized roses bloomed in every front garden, and
longer walks down to the tree-bordered canal, beside which stood a
big, newly-built Orthodox church, with high white walls and golden
onion domes that gleamed in the sun. In Melbourne there were 300,000
Greeks, I was told – more than in any other city in the world except
Athens.

In New Zealand I had two lengthy sojourns in Auckland and two in
Wellington, the two in Auckland being separated by the time Paramartha and I spent in Wellington and the South Island, and the two in
Wellington by our nine-day tour of the South Island and the two days
which, immediately before that, I spent in Invercargill with Paramartha and his parents. On our arrival in Auckland on 25 November my
friend and I had been met by Dharmadhara, Guhyasiddhi, Taranatha,
and others and taken from the airport to the men's community at Point
Chevalier, where we were to stay, and from there, after we had rested
and refreshed ourselves, to the Auckland Buddhist Centre, where
members of the local sangha were gathered in force. After eight colourfully clad 'offering goddesses' had one by one presented me with
the traditional eight offerings to the honoured guest, Dharmadhara as
chairman of the Centre delivered a short speech of welcome to which
I replied. I then led a short puja in the shrine-room and spoke a few

more words. It was an emotional occasion. People were overjoyed to see me, especially, perhaps, those who hitherto had known me only through my writings and from photographs. For my part, I was glad that I had been able, after an interval of seventeen years, to redeem my promise to visit New Zealand again, glad to see the Centre's spacious new premises, and glad to meet so many friends both old and new.

The following day Dharmadhara and I discussed arrangements for interviews. Many people wanted to have a personal talk with me, and it was arranged that I should see the women at Aniketa's place, which was fifteen minutes' walk from Saranadipa, the men's community, as the latter had a rule prohibiting women visitors and it was thought best not to violate this. Two or three afternoons a week, therefore, I made my way to Aniketa's secluded bungalow and saw two or three women there, sometimes staying on for a cup of tea with my hostess afterwards. Men I of course saw at Saranadipa. These arrangements left me with plenty of time for visits to nearby Coyle Park, with its rows of giant macrocarpa pines and view of the Harbour Bridge and the city centre, and for strolls along Point Chevalier Beach, where scores of tiny shells crunched underfoot with every step one took. They also left me with plenty of time for reading. Having dipped into N.K. Devaraja's *An Introduction to Sankara's Theory of Knowledge* and read the *Katha Upanishad*, both of which I found lying in a cardboard box in my room together with other dust-covered books on Hinduism, I started on the Dorothy Sayers translation of *The Divine Comedy*.

What prompted me to read Dante I am not sure. It may be that I felt it was time for me to renew my acquaintance with his masterpiece. Or my interest may have been aroused by the many references to the great Italian poet in T.A. Stewart's *The Myths of Plato*, which I had read in Melbourne a few weeks earlier. Whatever the reason may have been, it was the first volume of the Sayers translation that I took from one of the bookcases in the hallway downstairs, on my second day in New Zealand, and for the next two or three weeks I remained immersed in it and the two succeeding volumes. My acquaintance with Dante went back a long way. I first read *The Divine Comedy* when I was thirteen or fourteen, in a copy of the Cary blank verse translation, with Flaxman's illustrations, that I had borrowed from the Tooting Public Library. About the same time, or a little later, I also read Maria Francesca Rossetti's *The Shadow of Dante*, borrowed from the same invaluable institution, and a year or two after that I read the *Convitio* and Dante Gabriel Rossetti's classic version of the *Vita Nuova*, second-hand copies of both of which I had been able to acquire. But in fact my acquaintance with Dante went back a long way before any knowledge of his works. In the passage between my own room and my parents' bedroom, in our upstairs flat at 23 Selincourt Road, hung small reproductions of two well-known Pre-Raphaelite paintings: Holiday's *Beatrice Refuses Dante Her Salutation* and Rossetti's *Dante's Dream*. I must have looked at these hundreds of times, and the latter, in particular, with its rich hues and mysterious personages, was among the most familiar objects of my childhood. Who knows what part it may have played in my lifelong admiration for Rossetti, both as a painter and as a poet?

So far as I remember, I did not again accompany Dante on his celebrated journey through Hell, Purgatory, and Paradise until the eighties, when I read I.C. Wright's version of *The Divine Comedy* while on one of the Tuscany ordination retreats. Like the original it was in *terza rima*, and like the Cary version I had read forty or more years earlier it was illustrated by the engravings after Flaxman. Some of these were admirable, but this time, at least, I felt Flaxman's neoclassical style was incompatible with the medieval spirit of Dante's great poem. What kind of impression *The Divine Comedy* made on me when I first encountered it, at thirteen or fourteen, it is now impossible for me to say. Perhaps I could never say. At that time of my life I did not clearly distinguish between poetry and religion, and in *The Divine Comedy*, as in Milton's *Paradise Lost* and Aeschylus' *Oresteia* trilogy, I sought as much for spiritual enlightenment as for aesthetic enjoyment. Reading them, my experience was predominantly one of being caught up into a world of images and archetypes of overwhelming beauty and profound significance. Doctrinally, they were all on much the same level. I no more believed in the objective truth of Dante's vision than I believed in that of Milton or Aeschylus. Beatrice and the Virgin Mary were no more – and no less – real to me than were the figures of Satan and Messiah, the Eumenides and Pallas Athene. Beauty was Truth, Truth Beauty – though the Truth in question was not that of science or even philosophy in the usual sense of the term. When I reread *The Divine Comedy* in Tuscany I had long been aware that ordinarily poetry and religion, symbol and fact, history and legend, were distinguishable the one from the other, but I was still able to experience the work as though the seamless garment had not been rent, albeit I experienced it with, perhaps, a lesser degree of intensity. Of the three parts of the poem it was the second, the Purgatorio, over which I lingered with the keenest feelings of admiration and delight. Even though what I was reading was not the original but a translation, it seemed I had hardly ever encountered anything so beautiful. It was surprising that while Dante himself called his work simply *La Commedia* (since it ends happily, at least for the hero, he could not call it a tragedy) succeeding generations should have rejoiced to bestow upon it the epithet 'Divina'.

On the occasion of my present rereading, in Auckland, it was again the Purgatorio that I admired and delighted in most. I was particularly moved by the poet's treatment of the relationships between himself and Virgil, a relationship wherein Virgil's solicitude for Dante, and Dante's reverence for his master and guide, are overshadowed by the sadness of their common knowledge that being respectively Christian and Pagan they are doomed to be eternally separated. Virgil can guide Dante through Hell; he can accompany him up the side of Mount Purgatory; he can even bring him to the terrestrial Paradise, where he will meet Beatrice; but he cannot ascend with him into Heaven. His mission accomplished, he must return to Limbo, the abode of just men who died before the coming of Christ. Dante's treatment of the relationship between himself and Beatrice struck me as being less successful. This was due, I thought, to the fact that the Beatrice who personifies Theology was not fully integrated, in the poet's imagination, with the Beatrice who is the idealized human object of his love, so that the lady who bitterly upbraids Dante the lover for his infidelity and the lady who instructs Dante the Christian in the mysteries of the Faith seem to be not quite one and the same person. A few years earlier I had detected what I felt was a discrepancy, of much the same kind, in the character of Virgil's Aeneas. I found it difficult to believe that the Aeneas who was the lover of Dido was the same person who was the slayer of Turnus. In this case the cause of the discrepancy was the fact that whereas the Aeneas of the first half of the *Aeneid* is modelled on Odysseus, the hero of the *Odyssey*, the Aeneas of the second of the epic is modelled on Achilles, the hero of the *Iliad*, and that Virgil, for all his genius, had been unable fully to integrate Homer's two heroes in the person of his own 'pious Aeneas'.

The Divine Comedy was not my only reading matter during those first days in Auckland. While still on the Purgatorio I read Mike Johnson's *Dumb Show*, which Punyasri had given me and which she warmly recommended. Johnson was a New Zealand writer who lived on Waiheke Island. He was known to Punyasri and I believe he had once or twice participated in Arts events at the Auckland Centre. Despite the recommendation I took up the novel rather doubtfully, thinking that perhaps here was another local author whose friends were inclined to overestimate his achievement, but a few pages were enough to convince me that Johnson was a writer of substance and I did not put the book down, except for lunch, until I had finished it. Written in a brutally demotic but frequently poetic style, and containing a strong element of Magic Realism, *Dumb Show* is a story of a macabrely dysfunctional family holed up in an isolated farm house in South Island, not a hundred miles from Christchurch. Grandfather has exiled himself to the glass tower built on top of the house, Mother is Aunty Pi's slave, Father's mind is shattered by shell-shock, and Uncle Honk is wont to punish the children – Maverick, Judd, Princess, and Nerida – with the help of Seth, his bloodthirsty leather belt, which possesses almost a life and personality of its own. Other characters are Aunty Grin, who invariably echoes Aunty Pi, drink-sodden Uncle Owl, Mut the dog, and Croak the cat. There also is the ghost child Pito, the circumstances of whose death some years earlier are gradually revealed in the course of the story. Friends warned me that the family was not very representative, and that I should not think that sadism, incest, and infanticide were usual features of life on a New Zealand farm.

The day on which I read *Dumb Show* happened to be Sangha Day, and in the evening I went along to the Centre and joined in the celebrations. Dharmadhara launched the newly-published *Great Buddhists of the Twentieth Century*, after which I signed copies of this and *Extending the Hand of Fellowship*, as well as other titles, then led a sevenfold puja – a puja that included a Mitra ceremony and a number of Mitra reaffirmations. A week or so later Paramartha and I went into the city centre, looked round the (old) Art Gallery, and visited a few bookshops. I had already seen the bookshops with Dave Rice, an Auckland Mitra (now Dharmachari Jayaghosa) but had not bought anything. This time I bought James K. Baxter's *Collected Poems* and Frank McKay's *Life of James K. Baxter*. The name of James K. Baxter (1926–72), generally considered to be New Zealand's greatest poet, was well known to me. I had initially encountered his work in 1974 or 1975, at the time of my first visit to the Land of the Long White Cloud, and only a few days before Paramartha and I made our little excursion a friend had lent me his *Selected Poems* and this had revived my interest in him. According to his biographer, in the course of his short life Baxter became, more than any other New Zealand writer, a national figure:

a social prophet; a conspicuous irritant to established society (an academic critic called him 'a hairy nuisance'); a cult leader and founder of a commune at Jerusalem [in the South Island]; he was well known by name to most New Zealanders through the press, the radio, and television.

He was also 'a pioneering dramatist, an essayist, a lecturer with genuine charisma,' as well as an alcoholic by the time he was thirty, when he joined Alcoholics Anonymous, and a devout convert to Roman Catholicism who was sometimes at odds with his fellow Catholics. Not surprisingly, especially in view of its bulk (the *Collected Poems* comprises than 600 pages), Baxter's poetry as a whole is uneven in quality, though certain poems are miracles of perfection and though even the 'failures' are interesting. In this respect his poetry resembles that of D.H. Lawrence. He also resembles Lawrence in his variety and in the breadth of his concerns, as well as in the fact that in his case, too, the poet is very much the prophet, raging against the iniquities of Babylon. His rage is if anything even more violent than Lawrence's. It is also more controlled and more focused, so that some of his poems of social and political protest, besides being more effective than Lawrence's, must surely be among the most virulent ever penned in English. Principal target of his attacks is the average conservative, complacent, reactionary white New Zealander, who appears in Baxter's poetry as the character Harry Fat. Harry Fat likes the kind of country where 'the little man is king', thinks Communists should be weeded out of the Civil Service with a strong hand, and evidently is a supporter of the National Party. He is a racist and a militarist and he believes in the rope. He is also great friends with Uncle Sam.

> Said Uncle Sam to Harry Fat,
> 'Your folks are fine to know
> And it's great the way your island
> Keeps afloat there Down Below,
> But you need the global attitude
> To produce a first-class show.'
>
> 'Just give me the time,' said Harry Fat,
> 'And the tourist trade will grow.'

The tourist trade has certainly grown since Baxter wrote those lines in 1956, as Paramartha and I observed in the course of our travels, especially in the South Island. What would the poet have thought, I

wondered, of the mushrooming hotels and holiday resorts, of the
greatly extended road network, and of the enormous increase in the
numbers of cars and coaches?

> *'You folks don't know,' said Uncle Sam,*
> *'What entertainment means*
> *For a trigger-happy tourist*
> *With a dollar in his jeans.*
> *No whorehouse on the corner*
> *Was a grief to our Marines.'*

> *'Try Mazengarb,' wrote Harry Fat,*
> *'For some talent in the teens.'*

Now there is a casino in Auckland, in a controversial tower that is the
tallest building in the city and dominates the skyline, and the moneyed
tourist, who is more likely to come from Japan or South-east Asia than
from the United States, has little cause for complaint.

But Baxter was not always in a rage, any more than Lawrence always
was, and not all his poems are poems of protest, even though social
and political concerns are never very far away. He is often tender, often
lyrical (for the *Hutchinson's Encyclopaedia*, I note, he is simply the
author of 'fluent lyrics'). Among his tenderest poems are those in
which he addresses, or remembers, his father, whom he greatly admired for his having refused to fight in World War I, despite being
shanghaied, sent to the front, and sentenced to No.1 Field Punishment
(a kind of crucifixion, with ropes instead of nails).

> *At times when I walk beside the budding figtree*
> *Or on the round stones by the river,*

> *I meet the face of my dead father*
> *With one or two white bristles on his chin*

> *The safety razor missed. When he was younger*
> *He'd hold the cut-throat with the ivory handle*

> *And bring it with one deft stroke down his jowl,*
> *Leaving the smooth blue skin. 'Old man,' I say,*

> *'Long loved by me, still loved by many,*
> *Is there a chance your son will ever join you*

In the kingdom of the summer stars?' He leaves me
Without a word, but like a touch behind him,

Greener the bulge of fruit among the figleaves,
Hotter the bright eye of the noonday sun.

In Baxter's later work his Roman Catholic faith is very much in evidence – a faith by no means inconsistent with sideswipes at the Church, and at priests and nuns. It is especially evident in 'Jerusalem Sonnets' and in 'Autumn Testament' (of which the poem just quoted is part), the two sequences that between them constitute what is probably his finest poetic achievement. One poem in 'Autumn Testament' is in the form of a dialogue between the poet and the Blessed Virgin Mary.

'Mother, your statue by the convent path
Has chips of plaster scattered round it

'Where rain or frost have stripped you of your mantle –'
'It doesn't matter.' 'As you know, in winter

'I often kneel there under the knife-edged moon
Praying for —' 'I hear those prayers.'

'Mother, your blue gown seems like stone,
Too rigid —' 'What they make of me

'Is never what I am.' 'Our Church looks to the young
Like a Medusa; they want to be –'

'Free, yes; Christ is the only Master.'
'They are taught to judge themselves.' 'Suffer it.'

'But sin —' 'I see no sin. My secret is
I hold the Child I was given to hold.'

A few weeks later Paramartha and I were to visit Jerusalem, the Maori settlement where from 1969 to 1971 Baxter had run his controversial commune. No chips of plaster were scattered round the 'statue by the convent path.' The nuns must have tidied the place and tried to make their patroness look more respectable. They may even have installed a new statue, for the one we saw was brightly painted and held no Child. Did this mean that the Virgin no longer had a secret? In another poem, one that forms part of the 'Jerusalem Sonnets', Baxter interrogates the portrait of Mother Aubert, who in the nineteenth century established the Roman Catholic mission at Jerusalem, of which the convent was part.

'Mother Mary Joseph Aubert, did you come here
To civilize the Maoris?' – 'No my son,

'I came from my native France to these rough hills
Only to make them Christian' – 'Why then, mother,

'Are the corners of your mouth drawn down,
Why do you frown a little, why are your old hands folded

'In a rheumatic clench?' – 'Work, work;
Without work nobody gets to Heaven' –

'There's no work for the Maori in the towns' –
'Nonsense! There is always work, if one can

'Be tidy, chaste, well spoken' – 'The pa is all but empty,
Old woman, where you fought your fight

'And planted cherry trees – Pray for the converts' great-grandchildren
Who need drugs to sleep at night.'

Devout Roman Catholic though he was, Baxter was appreciative of other faiths. At the age of fifteen, according to his biographer, he had written a poem on the Buddha (unpublished) which called him the ever-wise, while the *Collected Poems* contains, besides passing references to the Buddha and Buddhism, a 'Song for Sakyamuni', and a poem in which he alludes to the fact that his son had become a Buddhist.

My son's room smells of incense that he burns
Before the Buddha – as good a way as any
Of yoking the demons that rise at puberty,

Not demons, other selves.

Frank McKay also informs us that in November 1968 Baxter had reviewed Edward Conze's *Thirty Years of Buddhist Studies*, writing in it that although he was not a Buddhist scholar he had met people who had been cured of serious mental disturbances through Buddhist disciplines. Christians could not dismiss the Buddhist approach to attachment, 'since it is precisely attachment that exhausts and dismembers the souls of many in this destructively activist age.'

Ten years before he wrote that review Baxter had visited Japan and India, and his first volume of poetry after his return to New Zealand was entitled *Howrah Bridge and other poems*. He stayed five months in India, visiting Delhi, Bombay, and Calcutta, and seeing something of life in the villages. He also met several village holy men, one of whom lived in a glass hut alongside a temple and impressed Baxter by his replies to questions; and he was fascinated by Shantiniketan, Rabindranath Tagore's rural university. Broadly speaking, Baxter's overall impression of India was that of many other Western visitors. He was overwhelmed by the heat, the smell, and the dust, and shocked by the extreme poverty of cities like Calcutta, where people died in the streets and were ignored by passers-by. But he also found that even the most disadvantaged had an air of joy about them, and that the people in the villages were warm and hospitable and that, though poor, they were deeply in communion with their environment. With his extreme sensitivity, Baxter was affected by his Indian experience not only more profoundly than are most Western visitors but also more lastingly. His time abroad in fact changed him. The visit to Asia had given him a new perspective. After India, writing was no longer the main thing in his life. His chief concern became people and how to help them.

On 15 December Paramartha and I left for Wellington, driving round the eastern edge of the North Island, via Hicks Bay, Gisborne, and Napier, and taking a leisurely three days to reach our destination. On our arrival at the men's community at Mount Victoria we were welcomed by Achala and Rohit Vig and afterwards had dinner with them and the rest of the community. Two days later Paramartha flew down to Invercargill, to see his parents, leaving me to follow in a fortnight's time. During that period I saw a number of people individually, was given a reception at the spacious new Wellington Centre, spent an evening in discussion with men Mitras and Friends, and was taken for walks and outings by Achala and Rohit Vig. Rohit, a Mitra hailing originally from Delhi, also lent me his CD player and borrowed discs for me from the Public Library. In this way I was able to follow up the interest in Liszt and his music that I had developed in Melbourne and listen not only to the B minor Piano Sonata but also to a number of the Hungarian composer's other works, including his 'Funérailles' and 'Bénédiction de Dieu dans la solitude'. Since I have no technical musical vocabulary at my disposal I cannot say much about them, but they were quite different from what I had expected (they were not at all 'Romantic') and communicated a sense of grandeur and solemnity that was deeply moving. During most of the time that I was alone, however (and generally I was alone for the greater part of the day), I simply read. My principal reading was *David Copperfield*, on which I started within two hours of arriving in Wellington. Why I should have elected to reread this much-loved classic I do not know. Achala had thoughtfully placed in my room a collection of books by New Zealand authors, both of his own and borrowed from friends, but having dipped into *The Penguin Book of New Zealand Verse* it was the fat green volume of *David Copperfield* that I drew from the bookcase and in which I remained immersed for the next week or more.

I had last read *David Copperfield* in Tuscany, on one of the men's ordination retreats. Though I had enjoyed reading it again (it must have been the second or third time), I cannot remember thinking of it as having a definite theme. But this time the thought struck me that it did have a *theme*. It's theme was *betrayal* – especially the betrayal of the innocent and trusting. The characters could in fact all be classified according to how they were situated in this respect. There were those who were betrayed but did not betray in turn, those who neither betrayed nor were betrayed, and those who both betrayed and were themselves betrayed. David Copperfield is betrayed by his weak-minded mother and his sadistic stepfather, by the friendly waiter at the inn, by his brilliant and fascinating friend Steerforth, and by the educational system in the form of Mr Creakle and Salem School. But he does not betray others, though perhaps he betrays himself by idolizing first Steerforth and then Dora, his first wife. Betsey Trotwood, David's strong-minded paternal aunt, has been betrayed by the man she married, as a result of which she hates men, but she herself betrays no one. The saintly Agnes Wickfield, who eventually becomes David's second wife, betrays no one either, though she is in danger of being betrayed by her doting father, who loves her not wisely but too well, and who is himself being systematically betrayed (deceived, cheated) by his whilom clerk now partner, the unspeakable Uriah Heep, who in turn is betrayed (deceived and unmasked), in the interests of justice, by the ebullient and optimistic Mr Micawber, David's former landlord. Mr Micawber, who is always expecting something to turn up, is betrayed by life itself, in that his expectations are invariably disappointed – at least until he emigrates to Australia. Peggotty, David's old nurse, betrays nobody, neither does her brother Mr Peggotty or their nephew Ham, though Ham is betrayed by Little Em'ly in a way that affects all three of them, as well as David. Almost the only characters in the novel who neither betray nor are betrayed, so far as I remember, are Dora's two elderly maiden aunts, Traddles's betrothed down in remotest Devonshire, and the mentally retarded Mr Dick, as if to suggest that betrayal is inseparable from ordinary human existence and can be avoided only by those who live in obscurity or retirement or who are imbeciles. Steerforth not only betrays Little Em'ly and the blindly devoted David; he also 'betrays' his proud mother and, in a different way the fiercely passionate Rosa Dartle, her companion, by eloping with Little Em'ly, who is only a fisherman's daughter. In the end he himself is betrayed by the elements, so to speak, when the ship in which he is returning to England is wrecked in a storm and his body is cast up at the very spot where he and David had strolled together and where, as though in an anticipation of his fate, they once had watched the 'cruel sea'.

At least one critic of *David Copperfield* is of the opinion that the theme of the novel is what one of its characters calls 'the undisciplined heart'; another, that it is about prudence and, conversely, about the dangers of imprudence and trust. Neither reading is incompatible with my own. It is the undisciplined heart that disregards considerations of prudence, thereby exposing itself to the possibility of betrayal, and it is the undisciplined heart that is more likely to betray. The disciplined heart, on the contrary, betrays neither itself nor others and is less likely to be betrayed.

Though *David Copperfield* was my principal reading, this did not preclude my dipping into other things, especially after Achala had driven me to the city centre and we had visited the second-hand bookshops, of which there were seven in one street alone. Among my discoveries were Max Beerbohm's *Works and More*, Frank Swinnerton's *The Georgian Literary Scene*, John Freeman's *Last Poems* (apparently a first edition), Drayton's *The Barons' Wars*, and Hazlitt's *The Plain Speaker*. Beerbohm was a favourite minor author of mine (I also admired his caricatures), and I particularly enjoyed the essay 'King George the Fourth,' a spirited, if not altogether serious, defence of that much maligned monarch, in which he examines some of the principal accusations that have been brought against him, and points out in what ways he has been harshly and hastily judged. It has to be admitted that the incomparable Max's wit has worn a little thin in places (unlike Oscar Wilde's) and that he occasionally strikes what to modern ears sounds like a wrong note. Frank Swinnerton, critic and prolific novelist, has been described as 'a familiar figure in the literary life of the first half of this century,' and *The Georgian Literary Scene* is a very thorough, well organized, and lively account of the period in question, a period starting (according to the author) with the 'artful virtuosity' of Henry James and concluding with the 'later visions' of T.S. Eliot and the New Academicians. I enjoyed the book immensely, and found myself very much in agreement with most of Swinnerton's literary judgments which, though at times severe, were always fair and free from any hint of partisanship. John Freeman was only a minor Georgian poet, and Swinnerton mentions him only in passing, but his work appeared in *Georgian Poetry* as well as appearing in later, more general anthologies and I was glad to have *Last Poems*. The volume concludes with 'Last Lines', written after a walk in Norfolk. It was Freeman's last poem, and includes the following anguished verses:

Age, with unabating passions,
Narrows upon me; yet I cry
Unending for youth's fresh devices
That lit my past and made this 'I'.

Is it the petty scourge of thought,
This malady of small regrets,
Misfeatures all I dream upon
And mars the joy that sight begets?

How great the puny Ego swells
In the distinction of Remorse!
Shadows grotesquely darken over,
Clear eyes grow dim, pure voices coarse.

Oh folly! self-forgetting is sole bliss,
Self-idolism the steepest hell,
Like the East Wind that seres the earth,
Self dries up every human well.

In the remaining verses the poet loses himself in the contemplation of the natural world: a young bull, a herd of cows, and the summer clouds on their journey to the ocean.

Michael Drayton was a contemporary of Shakespeare who produced a huge quantity of work in a variety of forms. Though I was familiar with his sonnet sequence 'Idea' (to which belongs the famous and much anthologized 'Since there's no help, come let us kiss and part'), as well as with the *Carcanet Selected Poems*, I had not before had the opportunity of reading *The Barons' Wars* in its entirety and therefore was glad to have come across the old Morley's Universal Library (1887) edition of the work. The wars in question are those between Edward II and his discontented barons led by Mortimer, the queen's lover. The sufferings of the unfortunate king, after his deposition, at the hands of the 'crew of ribalds' sent to conduct him to Berkeley castle, where he is to be murdered, are graphically described.

> *With shameful scoffs and barbarous disgrace,*
> *Him on a lean ill-favoured jade they set,*
> *In a vile garment, beggarly and base,*
> *Which it should seem they purposely did get;*
> *So carrying him in a most wretched case,*
> *Benumbed and beaten with the cold and wet,*
>   *Deprived of all repose and natural rest,*
>   *With thirst and hunger grievously opprest.*

No less graphic is Drayton's description of the adulterous queen's chamber, the walls of which he represents as being adorned with a series of paintings of scenes from classical mythology.

> *There Mercury was like a shepherd's boy,*
> *Sporting with Hebe by a fountain brim,*
> *With many a sweet glance, many an amorous toy;*
> *He sprinkling drops at her, and she at him:*
> *Wherein the painter so explained their joy*
> *As he had meant the very life to limn:*
>   *For on their brows he made the drops so clear*
>   *That through each drop their fair skins did appear.*

It is in this chamber that Mortimer is seized by the young king, Edward III, and his men, who have entered by a secret passage. Before their arrival Mortimer and the queen have been looking – prophetically, as it turns out – at the painting depicting the Fall of Phaethon.

> *Looking upon proud Phaëton wrapped in fire,*
> *The gentle Queen did much bewail his fall;*
> *But Mortimer commended his desire,*
> *To lose one poor life or to govern all:*
> *'What though,' quoth he 'he madly did aspire,*
> *And his great mind made him proud Fortune's thrall?*

> *Yet in despite, when she her worst had done,*
> *He perished in the chariot of the sun.'*

Besides the title poem, *The Barons' Wars* contained Drayton's 'Heroical Epistles', 'Nymphidia', 'Idea', 'Elegies', and other poems, all well worth reading. 'Nymphidia' is a delightful fairy poem, reminiscent of *A Midsummer Night's Dream* in much the same way that the *The Barons' Wars* is reminiscent of *The Faerie Queen*. The description of the arming of the fairy knight Pigwiggin, Queen Mab's champion, is well known.

> *His helmet was a beetle's head,*
> *Most horrible and full of dread,*
> *That able was to strike one dead,*
>   *Yet did it well become him;*
> *And for a plume a horse's hair*
> *Which, being tosséd with the air,*
> *Had force to strike his foe with fear,*
>   *And turn his weapon from him.*

> *Himself he on an earwig set,*
> *Yet scarce he on his back could get,*
> *So oft and high he did curvét*
>   *Ere he himself could settle:*
> *He made him turn, and stop, and bound,*
> *To gallop and to trot the round,*
> *He scarce could stand on any ground,*
>   *He was so full of mettle.*

Like all men of his generation, Drayton was intensely patriotic ('Poly-Olbion', his most ambitious work, describes the beauties and glories of England), and his 'Ballad of Agincourt' (not included in *The Barons' Wars*) breathes a spirit similar to that of Shakespeare's *Henry V*. The first and last verses (two out of a total of fifteen) are characteristic of the poem as a whole.

> *Fair stood the wind for France,*
> *When we our sails advance,*
> *Nor now to prove our chance*
> *Longer will tarry;*
> *But putting to the main*
> *At Caux, the mouth of Seine,*

With all his martial train,
Landed King Harry.

* * *

Upon Saint Crispin's day
Fought was this noble fray,
Which fame did not delay
To England to carry;
O, when shall English men
With such acts fill a pen,
Or England breed again
Such a King Harry.

There are not a few classic English authors whose writings, in these hasty days, are available only selectively. One is William Hazlitt, prolific journalist, dramatic and literary critic, essayist, and lecturer, and I was therefore glad to have acquired the complete, 1870 edition of *The Plain Speaker: Opinions on Books, Men, and Things*, and thus to be able to read all the essays in the collection, both those with which I was already familiar and those with which I was not. In neither case was I disappointed. Here are some of Hazlitt's opinions on a variety of topics, extracted from the notebook into which I had copied them at the time.

> True friendship is self-love at second-hand; where, as in a flattering mirror, we may see our virtues magnified and our errors softened, and where we may fancy our opinion of ourselves confirmed by an impartial and faithful witness. He (of all the world) creeps closest to our bosoms, into our favour and esteem, who thinks of us most nearly as we do of ourselves. Such a one is indeed the pattern of a friend, another self – and our gratitude for the blessing is as sincere, as it is hollow in most other cases!...

> Few things tend more to alienate friendship than a want of punctuality in our engagements....

> The petty and the personal, that which appeals to our senses and our appetites, passes away with the occasion that gives it birth. The grand and the ideal, that which appeals to the imagination, can only perish with it [i.e. with the imagination], and remains with us, unimpaired in its lofty abstraction, from youth to age; as wherever we go, we still see the same heavenly bodies shining over our heads!...

There is no language, no description that can strictly come up to the truth and force of reality: All we have to do is to guide our descriptions and conclusions by the reality.... Logic should enrich and invigorate its decisions by the use of imagination; as rhetoric should be governed in its application, and guarded from abuse by the checks of the understanding....

Men act from passion; and we can only judge of passion by sympathy....

In morals, the cultivation of a *moral sense* is not the last thing to be attended to – nay, it is the first. Almost the only unsophisticated or spirited remark that we meet with in Paley's *Moral Philosophy*, is one which is always to be found in Tucker's *Light of Nature* – namely, that in dispensing charity ... we are not to consider so much the good it may do the object of it, as the harm it will do the person who refuses it. A sense of compassion is involuntarily excited by the immediate appearance of distress, and a violence and injury is done to the kindly feelings by withholding the obvious relief, the trifling pittance in our power.

We actually injure ourselves, morally speaking, by suppressing our own impulse to be generous! This is an insight worthy of Śāntideva and deserving to be reflected on by all Buddhists....

In the hurry of composition three or four words may present themselves, one on the back of the other, and the last may be the best and right one.

First thoughts are *not* necessarily best thoughts!

Proper expressions rise to the surface from the heat and fermentation of the mind, like bubbles on an agitated stream. It is this which produces a clear and sparkling style....

Give a man a motive to work, and he will work.

Of course this has to be a motive that he himself experiences as such, not one that you think he ought to experience.

Fancy, feeling may be very inadequate tests of truth; but truth itself operates chiefly on the human mind through them....

The greater a man is, the less he necessarily thinks of himself, for his knowledge enlarges with his attainments. In himself he feels that he is nothing, a point, a speck in the universe, except as his mind reflects that universe, and as he enters into the infinite variety of truth, beauty, and power contained in it....

Argument, again, is the death of conversation, if carried on in a spirit of hostility: but discussion is a pleasant and profitable thing, where you advance and defend your opinions as far as you can, and admit the truth of what is objected against them with equal impartiality: in short, where you do not pretend to set up for an oracle, but freely declare what you really know about any question, or suggest what has struck you as throwing a new light upon it, and let it pass for what it is worth.... As a general rule, there is no conversation worth anything but between friends, or those who agree in the same leading views of a subject. Nothing was ever learnt by either side in a dispute....

The soul of conversation is sympathy.

In his younger days Hazlitt greatly admired Coleridge, and Richard Holme's excellent short study of Coleridge, in the Past Masters series, happened to be one of the last books I read before joining Paramartha in Invercargill. During our nine-day tour of the South Island I did not have much time for reading. In fact I read only at night, before sleeping, and once or twice in the afternoon when we were resting in our motel. I read Lloyd Geering's *Tomorrow's God*, which Achala had given me on the eve of my departure from Wellington, and M.S. Dobbs-Higginson's *Asia Pacific*, which I found in a bookshop in Picton. About both these books I have written elsewhere.* Back in Wellington, where we spent only ten days, I browsed through the selection of New Zealand literature Achala had assembled for my benefit, in particular sampling *Into the World of Light*, an anthology of contemporary Maori writing edited by Witi Ihimaera, gave a poetry reading at the Centre, and spent an evening with the women Mitras. I also discovered a new poet. This was Alistair Te Ariki Campbell. Born in Rarotonga in the Cook Islands in 1925, of a Scots father and Polynesian mother, he had been sent to New Zealand at the age of eight after losing both parents. I 'discovered' him by accident, as it were, when the women Mitras presented me with his pocket *Collected Poems* (1996). Though a much less prolific poet than James K. Baxter, and possessed of a narrower range, in his own way he was almost as good as his more famous

---

* See p.261.

contemporary and at times struck, I thought, a more purely lyric note. He seemed also to have a stronger feeling for nature than Baxter. 'At a Fishing Settlement' is an early poem, but apparently one of his best known.

> *October, and a rain-blurred face,*
> *And all the anguish of that bitter place.*
> *It was a bare sea-battered town,*
> *With its one street leading down*
> *On to a shingly beach. Sea winds*
> *Had long picked the dark hills clean*
> *Of everything but tussock and stones*
> *And pines that dropped small brittle cones*
> *On to a soured soil. And old houses flanking*
> *The street hung poised like driftwood planking*
> *Blown together and could not outlast*
> *The next window-shuddering blast*
> *From the storm-whitened sea.*
> *It was bitterly cold; I could see*
> *Where muffled against gusty spray*
> *She walked the clinking shingle; a stray*
> *Dog whimpered and pushed a small*
> *Wet nose into my hand – that is all.*
> *Yet I am haunted by that face,*
> *That dog, and that bare bitter place.*

At times Campbell strikes a note of pathos or, to speak more accurately, a note of what Indian aesthetics terms *karuṇā-rasa* – the sentiment of pity. We hear this note in the last poem in the volume, 'To Saddler a Puppy.'

> *We had to give you away.*
> *We couldn't keep you*
> *and your brother.*
> *We already have your mother,*
> *your father, your aunt,*
> *And your big brother.*
> *Two more would have been*
> *two too many –*
> *you had to go.*
> *But when I carried you*

> *to the petshop, feeling*
> *like an executioner,*
> *why did you lick me?*

The fact that a dog features in both the poems I have quoted does not mean that dogs play a particularly large part in Campbell's poetry, or even that the animal world does. The majority of his poems recall Polynesian myths and legends or adumbrate themes of separation or loss (often the two overlap), and the best of them are too long to be quoted in full, while partial quotation would not do them justice.

On 20 January 1997 Paramartha and I left Wellington for Auckland, travelling via Wanganui and New Plymouth and making a detour inland in order to visit Jerusalem, as related elsewhere. My second sojourn in Auckland lasted nearly two months. When we had been there for exactly four weeks, and had enjoyed outings to Western Springs, the Auckland Zoo, and the local bookshops, both new and second-hand, besides spending a day with Malini and Purna on Waiheke Island and taking part in the enshrinement of Dhardo Rimpoche's ashes in the new stupa at Tararu, my friend flew down to Invercargill to spend a second two weeks with his parents, leaving me at Saranadipa with Dharmadhara, Taranatha, and other members of the community. During those four weeks, despite our various outings and the fact that I had begun writing an account of our nine days in the South Island, I did a fair amount of reading, especially at the weekends when Paramartha was away visiting old friends. To begin with, I started, but did not finish, Witi Ihimaera's *The Matriarch*, which I had bought in Wanganui. I bought it because I had recently read and enjoyed the same author's *Nights in the Gardens of Spain*, a well written novel about the double life of a bisexual middle-class Maori with a wife and children (the 'Gardens of Spain' was a men's sauna), and *The Matriarch* had been hailed as an 'uncompromising masterwork' (thus a review quoted on the back cover). At first I found the book's wealth of information about Maori customs, myths, and history extremely interesting, but after a while it became impossible to tell what was historical fact and what authorial invention. Moreover the figure of the black-veiled Matriarch herself, who besides being the author-narrator's grandmother apparently also functioned as a symbol of Maoridom and its values, became more and more grotesque and incredible. Among other things she was an expert fencer, and there were times when I thought she resembled nothing so much as a cross between Rider Haggard's She and John Betjeman's Joan Hunter Dunn. Reading the book confirmed me in my view that faction is an illegitimate, even an immoral, literary genre, confusing as it does two orders of truth that need to be kept apart. (Magic Realism does not confuse them, because the particular truth of a novel or story in this genre does not purport to hold good beyond the boundaries of the novel or story itself, i.e. in 'real life'.)

Among the books I did finish reading were *A Vindication of Charles the First* and *A Guide to the Practical Use of Incense*, both of which I had found in a second-hand bookshop in Hamilton, Novalis's *Henry von Ofterdinger*, which was one of the books Paramartha had left behind in Auckland many years ago, a translation of *The Epistles of the Sincere Brethren*, a historical novel about El Greco entitled *The Mystic Finger Symbol*, and Trelawny's *Adventures of a Younger Son* in the old two-volume Bell (formerly Bohn) edition. Thus my reading at this time was of a sufficiently miscellaneous character. *The Vindication* was based on contemporary sources and vindicated Charles as prince, as king, as husband, as churchman, and as martyr. There were also informative chapters on the rival parties in the Long Parliament, on Charles and the Civil War, and on the Roundhead and Cavalier generals, as well as a concluding chapter on Charles and Cromwell in which the former emerges as very much the better man and the better ruler. The author of the book, published in 1934, was Joshua Brookes, and his short preface seems curiously relevant at the present time (October 1997), especially the last sentence.

> That history repeats itself is abundantly illustrated by the troublous period of Charles I. The conflict of political and religious opinions that culminated in the Civil War still exists, though in the more tolerant atmosphere of the present day these differences excite less bitterness. The Cavaliers of Charles the First became the Tories and Conservatives of later days, while the Roundheads developed into Whigs and Liberals. Pym was the forerunner of Fox, as Hyde was of Peel and Salisbury. It is still the duty of the somewhat emasculated Conservatives of the present day to defend the liberty that is inherent in the British Constitution, and preserve those rights and privileges of the Monarchy, the House of Lords, and the Church of England, for which Charles I fought and died.

Despite my admiration for Milton, my sympathies are very much with the Cavaliers, though much less with their modern descendants, and

I have never forgiven the Roundheads for having destroyed or damaged so great a part of the artistic heritage of medieval England.

Incense has long been of interest to me, and in the late sixties I sometimes held Japanese style incense-smelling parties at my flat in Highgate, when with half a dozen friends I experimented with the different psychological effects that could be produced by burning different aromatic substances. I was therefore pleased to have come across the little *Guide to the Practical Use of Incense* by Sally E. Janssen, Principal of the Triad Yoga School of Australia and 'an authority on the subject of Incense.' The two most interesting chapters of the book were the ones devoted to the olfactory sense and to the spiritual significance of perfume. In the first of them the author draws attention to the importance of the sense of smell for both animals and human beings, and to the fact that 'perfumes and radiations from natural substances encourage the natural energies and spirit of man'; in the second she enlarges on the theme: 'as incense and beautiful perfumes help to attract spiritual powers, so it has been observed that spontaneous emanations of perfumes can manifest in connection with those of spiritual nature such as the saints and mystics.' She concludes this latter chapter by quoting a remarkable passage from one of Montaigne's essays.

> Physicians might in mine opinion draw more use and good from
> odours than they doe. For myself have often perceived that according
> unto their strength and qualitie, they change and alter and move my
> spirits, and worke strange effects in me which make me approve the
> common saying that the invention of incense and perfumes in
> churches, so ancient and so far dispersed throughout all nations and
> religions, had a special regard to rejoice, to comfort, to quicken, to
> rouse and to purify our sense, so that we might be the apter and
> readier unto contemplation.

Physicians, in the broader sense, evidently have taken Montaigne's words to heart. There is a growing interest not just in incense but in perfumes and aromas generally, and on our visits to bookshops, especially New Age ones, whether in North America, Australia, or New Zealand, Paramartha and I were struck by the enormous number of books on aromatherapy that are now available.

The German Romantic Movement was one of the most important cultural and spiritual movements of modern, i.e. post-Renaissance, times and the poet and writer Friedrich von Hardenberg (1772–1801) known to literature as Novalis, was one of its most interesting and significant figures. I had long wanted to read *Henry von Ofterdingen*, which with *Hymns to the Night* was Novalis's major literary work, and I was glad to be able to read Paramartha's old copy of the book. The theme of the work is nothing less than the ideal education of the poet, of whose vocation Novalis has a very high notion indeed. It was an education that included, in the words of the work's American translator, 'not merely academic learning and cultural polish but also the widest possible savouring of all sorts and conditions of experience.' Young Henry, a medieval poet who seeks the mysterious Blue Flower, is therefore represented as setting out on 'a journey that is interspersed with beautiful tales and exquisite songs'. One of these tales, which according to the translator is one of the strangest and most complicated fairy tales in all literature, is a symbolical portrayal of the struggle between eighteenth-century Rationalism and the Romantic reaction that set in thereafter. Unfortunately, *Henry von Ofterdingen* is incomplete, Novalis having lived to finish only a portion of the first chapter in the second part, so that Roger Cardinal, a modern writer on the creative imagination in poetry and the visual arts, is justified in describing it as 'a curtailed poem which gestures magically towards a hypothetical completeness, which would embrace infinity.'

The Islamic world is often thought of as having been rather static, but it too had its cultural and spiritual movements. One of these was the movement associated with the Sincere Brethren, or Brethren of Purity, who are said to have been a group of scholars in tenth-century Basra, now in Iraq.

> They are the authors of an encyclopedic collection of fifty-one Epistles (Arabic *Rasa'il*) which deal with every aspect of exoteric and esoteric knowledge available at the time. The Epistles reflect the intellectual fermentation and syncretism of the Islamic civilisation of that Era. Through their writings, the Brethren intend to guide their readers or followers, in successive stages, to the purification of their immortal Soul and an understanding of its spiritual nature. On the other hand, they also offer a comprehensive political theory on the Islamic State. Although the Pythagorean and Neoplatonic overtones of the Epistles made the collection suspect in the eyes of many orthodox Muslims, the *Rasa'il* apparently circulated throughout the entire Islamic world.

Thus Eric van Reijn, in the introduction to *The Epistles of the Sincere Brethren*, 'an annotated translation of Epistles 43–47.' I was interested in the mysterious Brethren principally on account of the Epistles' 'Neoplatonic overtones', and was in fact already acquainted with I.R. Netton's *Muslim Neoplatonists: An Introduction to the Thought of the Brethren of Purity*. The five Epistles translated by van Reijn on the whole are of a theological character, but Epistle 45 is entitled 'On Friendship', and much of it is indeed devoted to this topic.

> If you wish to become someone's friend, you should have a good look at him, just as you would do with any coin which comes into your hands, or with plants and seedlings for your garden. Choosing a friend is as important as selecting a bride or buying slaves or provisions. It is very important for us Brethren too; we help one another in secular as well as in spiritual affairs, and our cohesion is stronger than red brimstone. If you ever find such a friend, make sure that you keep him. A true friend is more precious than the apple of your eye, more precious than the Bliss of Paradise....

> If called to the rescue, a true friend will help you. If you are forgetful, he will remind you. By his own example he will encourage you to perform good works. He will inspire you to do what is proper, and guide you towards it. He will spend his money on your behalf and even risk his life to protect you....

> If you find such a friend, you should give him preference over all your acquaintances, relations, kinsfolk and neighbours. He is more precious to you than your own son, your full brother, and your wife, the sole recipient of all your earnings and the incentive of your striving. Give him the same consideration as you give them, no, give him preference!... [A true friend] loves you, because he believes that he and you are one Soul in two bodies. Whatever pleases you is also pleasing to him; what you dislike is also grievous to him. He wishes you well, as you wish him well. True friends are always sincere at heart because their Souls are pure. They know each other thoroughly. Just as the external aspects of Creation are no secret to you, so you should not try to conceal from your Brethren what is already known to them.

After reading *The Epistles of the Sincere Brethren* I discovered that Eric van Reijn, who was a Senior Lecturer in Indonesian Studies at the University of Auckland, was known to Dharmadhara who met him from time to time. Subsequently Dharmadhara told him that I had read his book, and he was both intrigued and delighted to think that a Buddhist should have found it of interest.

Veronica de Osa's *The Mystic Finger Symbol*, subtitled 'A Novel of El Greco,' could be described as an imaginative reconstruction of the life of the great artist. The authoress has access to the Spanish-language literature on him and his period and tells us, in the Bibliography, that she has 'tried to follow as closely as possible the few facts that are known about El Greco's life.' She also saw Toledo, Madrid, Venice, etc., and most of El Greco's pictures mentioned in the work. The result is very readable. We learn a lot about the cities in which El Greco lived and worked, about Titian and Tintoretto, about the court of Philip II, about the post-Tridentine Catholic Church, about the Inquisition, and about Ignatius Loyola's 'spiritual exercises'. We are also made aware of the deeply religious nature of El Greco's inspiration, though she sees it fit to associate this with his love for Jeronima de las Cuevas, the mother of his son, and moreover would have us believe that it is Jeronima's features that are reflected in his depictions of the Virgin Mary. Some of de Osa's comments on individual paintings are illuminating, especially those on *The Burial of Count Orgaz*. She puts them into the mouth of the Franciscan Friar who, in the novel, poses to El Greco for the figure of St Francis on the left of the painting.

> Two Saints, St Augustine and St Esteban, are burying Spain's 'Golden Age'. And those who stand behind its corpse, Spain's best minds of our own time, look down upon it and speak only through the gestures of their gracefully poised hands. But they are all forced to remain in one long line, for the Church does not permit them to move out of their present position. On the right are the priests and, on the left, we, the three friars. We love Spain – but we jealously guard everybody's thoughts and actions. Note how you have lined up these minds, as if the Grandees were all hanging on one long chain without any breathing space between them, in truth without any freedom of action or thought. Only a few carefully moving hands, and the flames of the torches, so well placed, on the right and on the left. There, where the representatives of the Church stand, holding tight the line of the Spanish Grandees, so that none of them dares to leave it, because there is always the vigilant eye of the Inquisition. Only the child, holding a torch, is free to come and go as he pleases – your son, who will live in another century.

The interpretation is an ingenious one, and though differing from the one I give in 'A Note on The Burial of Count Orgaz' (in *The Priceless Jewel*) it is not really in conflict with it. Reading *The Mystic Finger Symbol* renewed my feeling for El Greco's ecstatic and sublime art, much of which (including the *Burial*) Paramartha and I had seen in Spain in the autumn of 1990, and deepened my appreciation of its spiritual significance. (The 'mystic finger symbol' of the book's title, by the by, is the particular disposition of the fingers – index finger and little finger separate from the joined middle fingers – that one sees in many of El Greco's paintings and which de Osa seems to regard as a kind of signature.)

Edward John Trelawny's *Records of Byron, Shelley and the Author*, with its vivid account of the cremation of Shelley's body on the beach at Viareggio, is a primary source for the history of the English Romantic Movement. His *Adventures of a Younger Son* is less well known, and less easy to obtain. In those days the lot of a younger son of good family was not a happy one. After being brutally treated at home and at school, the thirteen-year-old Trelawny was sent into the navy and in the words of H.N. Brailsford, in his introduction to my edition of the book, 'its savage discipline completed what the stupid tyranny of home and school had begun'. The book covers a period of some five years, up to and including the author's return to England at the age of eighteen. Says Brailsford,

> In this breathless chronicle of events there are few tranquil pages. Lengthy as it is [there are more than 600 pages], the young hero is always rushing with the ardour of a great boy in his teens from revolt to battle, from battle to love, and from love to tragic loss. He is nearly everything by turns. He is angry; he is drunk; he is savage with the fury of battle; he is tender with the chivalry of a noble rebel; he has his moods of Byronic cynicism; he has his moments of passionate and resentful sorrow. But there is one note missing in the gamut of his moods. He is never tired and he is never bored.

The chronicle also contains vivid characterization and passages of magnificent description, for Trelawny is a splendid writer. The boisterous teenage Trelawny reminded me, in some ways, of the rip-roaring teenage Jack London, but whereas London became an alcoholic and died at forty Trelawny lived to be eighty-eight, the last surviving member of the Byron-Shelley circle. Apart from its literary value, which is considerable, *Adventures of a Younger Son* is worth reading as the revelation of a character of exceptional independence and force.

New discoveries did not cause me to neglect old favourites. Even while reading *The Matriarch, A Vindication of Charles the First*, and the rest, I dipped into the copy of *Milton's Poetical Works* with the original spelling and punctuation that I had brought with me from England, as I had already done on various occasions during the earlier part of my travels. This time I read several books of *Paradise Lost*, as well as *Comus* and *Paradise Regain'd*, and was more than ever amazed by Milton's superb artistry. I also appreciated, to a greater extent than before, the excellence of *Paradise Regain'd* considered purely as a narrative poem. Milton's depiction of the character of Jesus was interesting, and there were times when the latter seemed more like the Buddha than the Christ of orthodox Christianity, as when the poet describes how, in the wilderness, the Tempter seeks to frighten the 'patient Son of God' first with a storm that tears up pines and oaks by the roots and then by means of supernatural terrors.

> *Infernal Ghosts, and Hellish Furies, round*
> *Environ'd thee, some howl'd, some yell'd, some shriek'd,*
> *Some bent at thee their fiery darts, while thou*
> *Sat'st unappall'd in calm and sinless peace.*
> *Thus pass'd the night so foul till Morning fair*
> *Came forth with Pilgrim steps in amice grey;*
> *Who with her radiant finger still'd the roar*
> *Of thunder, chas'd the clouds, and laid the winds,*
> *And grisly Spectres, which the Fiend had rais'd*
> *To tempt the Son of God with terrors dire.* *

Here one cannot but be reminded of the *Lalitavistara's* – and Sir Edwin Arnold's – description of Māra's attack on the Buddha prior to the Enlightenment. Besides dipping into *Milton's Poetical Works* again, I reread four or five chapters of *Buddhist Saints in India* and much of the *Samdhinirmocana Sūtra*, both of which, too, I had brought with me from England.

After Paramartha's return from Invercargill we had only two weeks left before our departure for England. They were two quite busy weeks. Almost immediately after his return we spent three days touring Northland, which we had long planned to do, going up the east

---

* Book IV, 422–31.

coast via Whangarei, Paihia, Kaeo, and Cable Bay, and coming down the West coast via Kaitaia, Broadwood, Omapere, and Dargaville. It was an interesting trip, and I wish I could write more about it. Apart from the scenery, the highlights were visiting the Paihia Aquarium, seeing the historic Stone House and *pa* at Kerikeri, stopping in the kauri forest to pay our respects to Tane Mahuta, the Father of the Forest, and spending an hour in the Kauri Museum at Matakone, with its extraordinary collection of objects made from fossil kauri gum or 'New Zealand amber'. Back in Auckland, where we had already seen an exhibition of photographs by Robert Morrison, we paid our last visit to the second-hand bookshops (in one of which I found two books by Edith Sitwell for which I had been looking), had our last walk round the ornamental lake at Western Springs, with its sixty or more black swans, attended a performance of Tom Stoppard's *Arcadia*, and were given a grand ceremonial farewell at the Auckland Buddhist Centre, complete with poetry readings and musical items, in the course of which I was presented with a *mere* or Maori ceremonial baton of New Zealand jade. Despite our being so busy (Paramartha was the busier of the two, as there were old friends to whom he wanted to see before we left), I managed to get in a fair amount of reading. This included *Cymbeline*, and *Henry V*, J.B. Priestley's *Literature and Western Man*, which I had read before, Hermann Hesse's *Narziss and Goldmund*, and Abdullah Dougan's *Forty Days*. That I read *Cymbeline* was due to Kovida. In an e-mail he had told me that the RSC's new production of the play was worth seeing, and since I hoped to be able to see it on my return to England I lost no time acquainting myself with the work, which I believe was the only Shakespeare play I had never read. Two passages in particular arrested my attention. In Cymbeline I. vi, the Queen declares her intention of experimenting with the effects of the 'poisonous compounds' with which the court physician, at her command, has supplied her, on

such creatures as
We count not worth the hanging, but none human.

To which the physician replies:

  Your highness
  Shall from this practice but make hard your heart.

Cruelty to animals can lead to cruelty to human beings! The second passage is in Act IV, Scene II, when Belarius, in admonishing his two foster-sons that

reverence ... doth make distinction
Of place 'tween high and low

(i.e. recognizes the principle of hierarchy), parenthetically characterizes reverence as 'That angel of the world.' There could hardly be a more beautiful or more appropriate description of that virtue. Reverence is the guardian angel, so to speak, of our human world. Without the spirit of reverence there can be no social or religious life, no civilization or culture, no art. Shakespeare's great phrase served to remind me that in Buddhism *hiri* and *ottappa*, shame and fear of wrongdoing, are known as the two *lokapālas* or 'guardians of the world' in the sense of their being the upholders of the moral order that alone makes truly human existence possible.

My response to Herman Hesse has been somewhat mixed. His earlier work, not excluding his famous *Siddhartha*, I thought rather weak; but in the seventies I was a great admirer of *The Glass Bead Game*, though I found *Steppenwolf* so unappealing that I failed to finish it. *Narziss and Goldmund*, which I came across in Saranadipa library, is the story of Narziss, a teacher in a monastery in medieval Germany, and Goldmund his favourite pupil. While Narziss remains in the monastery, eventually to become abbot, Goldmund runs away to live a picaresque, wandering life in the course of which he has numerous adventures, amatory and otherwise, lives through an outbreak of the plague, and becomes a sculptor. In his broken old age he returns to the monastery and is reunited with his friend. The story is beautifully told, and I think I enjoyed the novel even more than I had enjoyed *The Glass Bead Game*. Inevitably, I was reminded of what I had written in *The Thousand-Petalled Lotus* (now *The Rainbow Road*) about Sangharakshita I and Sangharakshita II, and this led to a series of reflections on the nature of the relation between spiritual life, on the one hand and, on the other, the life devoted to art.

Forty Days: An account of a discipline was given me by an old friend and his wife, with whom I twice had dinner during my stay in Auckland. The wife belonged to a quasi-Sufi group that had been led by the author, Abdullah Dougan, who I gathered had died eight or ten years earlier and who seems to have been a remarkable man. The 'discipline' of the book's subtitle was the forty-day fast on water alone that he had undertaken while travelling in India and Afghanistan with two pupils in 1974 and the journal he had kept of this fast formed the central part of the book. Before it came some short chapters of autobiography (he began life in New Zealand as Neil in 1918) and these were followed by an account of Arabia and the Hajj pilgrimage, which the three of them actually made, and a chapter of impressions by the pupils. In India they stayed at the Anandashram, where I had stayed twenty-five years earlier, and met Mother Krishnabai, and in Afghanistan they officially converted to Islam in order to obtain their visas for Arabia. The High Court Judge who gave them their certificates told them with 'a straight face' that now they were Muslims, by Koranic law they could be killed if they decided to return to being Christians. Though Dougan was an initiated Naqshibandi Sufi, he and his pupils were highly critical of what they saw of organized Islam and of the ordinary Muslim believer. In particular they were horrified by the wholesale ritual slaughter of animals that went on in Mecca. Back in New Zealand Dougan devoted himself to teaching a mixture of Gurdjieff's ideas, Sufism, and Gnosticism. Apart from the chapter contributed by the two pupils, *Forty Days* is written as if by Abdullah, who invariably refers to Neil in the third person. In Freudian terms, Abdullah is Muslim Superego to Neil's unsanctified Id, and he in fact gives Neil quite a hard time.

On the morning of Monday, 17 March, Dharmadhara and Akashagarbha accompanied Paramartha and me to Auckland airport and saw us off. So sorry was I to leave New Zealand, where I had just spent some of the most carefree months of my life, that I was only half glad to be returning to England. On the twelve-hour haul between Auckland and Los Angeles, in the airport hotel where we spent two nights, and on the ten-hour haul between Los Angeles and London, I read Czeslaw Milosz's *The Captive Mind*. At Heathrow we were met by Kovida and Prasannasiddhi, faithful as ever, who drove us to Sukhavati where we found the passage between the community and the flat decorated with balloons and 'Welcome' signs. The following afternoon, having slept reasonably well during the night, I went into town with Kovida and explored some of the bookshops in the Holborn area. In the newly-open Antiquarian Bookshop Arcade in Great Russell Street I found, to my delight.... But that is another story and one that will have to be told, if at all, another time.

Urgyen Sangharakshita

November 1998

SECOND LETTER FROM SPAIN

Guhyaloka – memoirs – London – Nottingham caves and castle – Malvern Hills with Dick McBride – Worcester – Stratford-upon-Avon – Goldsmith – films at the Midlands Arts Centre – a northern tour, visiting Liverpool, Blackburn, Lancaster, Glasgow, Dhanakosa, Edinburgh, Newcastle, and Leeds – Rosslyn Chapel – Liverpool's Walker Art Gallery – the National Gallery of Scotland and Rubens' The Feast of Herod – Edinburgh – Munich – Glyptothek – Lenbachhaus – meeting with Heinz Roiger – Augsburg – Buddha-Haus – Ulm Cathedral – Nuremberg – Würzburg: the Residenz – Essen – Minden – return to Guhyaloka

Dear Dharmacharis and Dharmacharinis,

I am writing from the veranda of my cottage at Guhyaloka. After an absence of three years I am once more in the magical Valley, looking up at the sunlit limestone cliff opposite, resting my eyes on the vivid green of the pine trees, breathing in the aromatic air, and enjoying a silence broken only by the chirruping of birds and the occasional tinkle of a distant goat-bell. I arrived two days ago, on Friday 10 July, and will stay for altogether four weeks. Before my departure from England friends were asking, 'What will you do at Guhyaloka? Will you be working on your memoirs? Or catching up with your correspondence? Or …?' To all such enquiries I replied that I did not plan to do anything, but that there were several things I might do. One of them was to write a short account of my recent travels in Germany, and this is in fact what I have sat down at my table this morning to do. But before writing about my travels in Germany I must write, however briefly, about my travels in the North of England and in Scotland, as well as say a few words about earlier happenings.

Fifteen months have passed since Paramartha and I returned from New Zealand. My intention, originally, had been to start work on another volume of my memoirs as soon as I had settled into my new quarters in the Madhyamaloka annexe, which thanks to Windhorse Trading, Marpa builders, Subhuti, Kovida, and others, had been enlarged and decorated during my absence, and where I had at last all my books under one roof, but for various reasons this proved to be out of the question. There were people to be seen, letters to be answered, books to be reviewed for the *Times Higher Educational Supplement*, and the Order Convention to be prepared for and attended. I also decided to write 'Travels of a Bibliophile in North America and Australasia' for the Articles edition of *Shabda*. Thus it was not until the first week of October that I was able to start work on the new volume of my memoirs, about which I had been thinking for several years, making notes, recalling incidents, and trying to decide how best to organize my material. By the late spring of this year I had written 30,000 words, comprising Part One of the new volume (I had decided it should consist of four or five parts, each divided into sections of unequal length) and covering the period of August 1964 to March 1965. In other words, Part One told the story of my return to England after an absence of twenty years and the first seven months of my incumbency of the Hampstead Buddhist Vihara, thus laying the foundation for my account of my friendship with Terry Delamare and the circumstances that led to my not returning to the vihara in March 1967, after my farewell visit to India. I did not find the writing of those 30,000 words easy. This was principally because, as I wrote, more and more memories kept crowding in on me, and I had continually to resist the temptation to include material that would only clutter my narrative and obscure its main line.

Having completed Part One, I was therefore not altogether sorry to have to put the memoirs aside for a few months. I had to put them aside, partly because there were letters to be answered and page proofs to be corrected, and partly because I was due to visit FWBO centres in the North of England, in Scotland, and in Germany.

The visit to Scotland had been planned some months earlier, when I promised to take part in the celebrations marking the twenty-fifth anniversary of the FWBO's arrival in Scotland by attending the special weekend event that was being held at Dhanakosa. My visits to

Germany – for there were two of them – were in fulfilment of promises made earlier in the year, namely, that I would take part in the opening of the new Berlin Centre and that I would visit the Minden Centre, which I had not yet seen. Shortly before embarking on these more extensive travels, however, I visited a few places nearer home, spending a fortnight in London and a day each in Nottingham and Malvern.

The purpose of my visit to London was to 'open' the four community houses in Approach Road, recently acquired by the FWBO in order to guarantee the women occupying them security of tenure, as well as to give a reading from 'work in progress' at the London Buddhist Centre. The work in question was, of course, my new volume of memoirs, on which I had until recently been engaged and from which I read five sections. I also read five recent poems, after which Sumangala launched *What is the Dharma?* and I signed copies. During the rest of the fortnight I had dinner or tea with various communities, spent a few hours in Epping Forest with Prasannasiddhi and Ziya, and saw the 'Icons from Moscow' exhibition at the Royal Academy with Paramartha, who on account of his work as an osteopath is now mainly based in London and comes to Birmingham only occasionally.

In Nottingham I gave the same reading that I had given in London, to an only slightly smaller audience. Earlier in the day Kovida and I had been entertained to lunch by Arthadarshin (now temporarily resident in Nottingham for the sake of his daughter), who afterwards took us to see the Caves and the Castle. I had heard of Nottingham Castle before (Charles I had raised his standard there, thus finally breaking with the Parliament), but I had not heard of the Caves, which proved to be something of a revelation. There were more than 400 of them beneath the city centre, all scraped and hacked out of the soft sandstone rock on which the city was founded. People had lived and worked in them for at least a thousand years, right into the twentieth century. During the war they had been used as air raid shelters. Naturally we could see only a small proportion of them – fifteen to be precise. These were situated directly beneath the new shopping centre (we could hear people's footsteps above us) and either led into one another or were connected by tunnel-like passages and flights of steps, all hewn out of the rock. One of the caves, the roof of which was supported by a round central pillar, also carved out of the sandstone, had formed part of a tannery – the only underground tannery known in Britain. One could still see the vats in which the hides were soaked. As we left the Caves and started climbing up to the Castle I reflected that, worthwhile as it might be to visit foreign countries, there were still many places of interest in Britain that I had not only not seen but of which I had not even heard.

Malvern was a place of which I had certainly heard, even though I had not seen it. Kovida and I saw it, or rather drove through it, on our way to visit Dick McBride, an American Beat poet who, with his wife, had settled on the outskirts of the picturesque little hillside town. Dick had lived in San Francisco, had managed the famous City Lights bookshop, and had been closely associated with Allen Ginsberg, Lawrence Ferlinghetti, Gary Snyder, and other luminaries of the Beat Generation. We therefore had a lot to talk about. After lunch Dick and Pat took us on a tour of the Malvern Hills, their car guiding ours. It was a perfect May day. At one point we stopped and sat down on a wayside bench to admire the view, which was as spectacularly beautiful as any I had ever seen in England. It was among the Malvern Hills, on such a day as this, that the poet of *Piers Plowman* had fallen asleep and seen his visions of the Field Full of Folk, of Mede the Maid, of the Seven Deadly Sins, and of Piers Plowman himself, and it was not difficult to believe that the atmosphere of the spot was conducive to dreams and visions.

Though our visit to Dick McBride made the day a full one, it was sandwiched between two other visits, so that the day was a very full one indeed. On the way to Malvern we stopped at Worcester, which I had not seen before, and Kovida and I spent a couple of hours exploring the town and looking round the Cathedral, surely one of the most beautiful in England, where we saw the tombs of King John and Prince Arthur, the eldest son of Henry VII. But beautiful as was the (mainly) Norman and Early English interior, with its slender, soaring multiple columns, its pointed arches, and its Victorian stained glass, the part of the building that impressed me most was the crypt. This is the largest Norman crypt in England, and with its thirty-odd stumpy Romanesque columns it reminded me, despite the vast difference of scale, of the Great Mosque at Cordoba. In both there was a whole forest of columns, among which one could wander, and which at times seemed to extend indefinitely in all directions.

Our last visit of the day was to Stratford-upon-Avon, where we saw *Measure for Measure*. The performance was not a particularly good one. The actress playing Isabella was weak, the interpretation of the part of the Duke lacked depth, and the RSC gave yet another demonstration of its tendency to shout when emphasis was needed – or even when it was not. Nevertheless I was glad we went. *Measure for Measure* has long been one of my favourite Shakespeare plays, and I was happy to see it again. Reading Shakespeare in one's closet is certainly no substitute for seeing him performed in the theatre, and one of the advantages of living in Birmingham is that Stratford-upon-Avon is just down the road. Besides *Measure for Measure*, since returning from New Zealand I have seen, with various members of the Madhyamaloka community, *Henry VIII* (Jane Lapotaire was outstanding as Queen Katherine), *Cymbeline* (a Kabuki-style production that did not quite come off), *Twelfth Night*, *The Merchant of Venice* (on the whole a good performance), and *The Tempest* (a realistic opening scene and an interesting Ariel). I also saw, again with Kovida, three one-act plays. These were J.M. Synge's *Riders to the Sea* and *The Shadow of the Glen*, and W.B. Yeats' *Purgatory*, and we saw them not at the Memorial Theatre but at the Other Place, where I had not been before. *Purgatory* was of special interest to me, it having been studied in the drama group that used to meet in my Highgate West Hill flat in the early days of the FWBO, and I believe Vangisa and Devamitra once gave a performance of it.

Not that our play-going was confined to Stratford-upon-Avon. Birmingham has two repertory theatres, the Old and the New, and at the former a party of us saw a fine performance of Oliver Goldsmith's comedy *She Stoops to Conquer*, which I had read in Barnstaple as a boy but never seen performed. So much did I – and others – enjoy the play that I at once reread some of Goldsmith's other works, including the delightful *Citizen of the World* (a series of essays), and the famous *Vicar of Wakefield*, which Goethe so much admired, besides rereading John Forster's classic biography. These, together with the play itself, served to give me a renewed appreciation of Goldsmith, of whom Dr Johnson said, after his death, 'Let not his frailties be remembered; he was a very great man.'

In addition to its two repertory theatres and its new Symphony Hall, Birmingham possesses, in the Midlands Arts Centre, an important venue for cultural activities. The 'mac' – as it is familiarly known – is even closer to Madhyamaloka than are the two theatres, being situated in the nearby Cannon Hill Park, and since my return from New Zealand I have seen a number of films there. These were mainly classic films, such as Eisenstein's *Battleship Potemkin*, Orson Welles's *Citizen Kane*, and Tarkovsky's *Stalker*, though I also saw a reasonably faithful adaptation of Thomas Hardy's *The Woodlanders*. – But I fear I digress.

Kovida and I left for our northern tour, as we called it, on the morning of Tuesday 26 May, less than twelve hours after I returned from my weekend visit to Berlin, about which I shall write later. In the course of twelve days we visited Liverpool, Blackburn, Lancaster, Glasgow (for the sake of the Art Gallery, the Centre being closed for the week), Dhanakosa, Edinburgh, Newcastle, and Leeds – to mention only those places where there is an FWBO centre or, in the case of Lancaster, a group. Besides spending time with the local Order members and Mitras, with many of whom we shared a meal, we saw parts of the country with which I, at least, was unfamiliar, and did a certain amount of sightseeing. I also gave personal interviews, performed Mitra ceremonies, held question-and-answer meetings, and, on one occasion, dedicated twelve Buddha images. The Buddha images were dedicated at Dhanakosa, the farthest point of our tour and, in many ways, its highlight. The attractive, Burmese-style figures were all replicas of the image in the shrine-room of the Glasgow Buddhist Centre and they were to be installed in the respective shrine-rooms of the twelve FWBO centres that had been, or were to be, established in different parts of Scotland. This was, I thought, an excellent way of demonstrating the Scottish Sangha's determination to spread the Dharma as taught and practised by the FWBO throughout the length and breadth of the Highlands and Lowlands. The dedication ceremony was held in a marquee that had been erected in the grounds of the retreat centre, on the banks of Loch Voil, and was attended by a hundred or more people, most of whom were spending the weekend at Dhanakosa. Kovida and I stayed at a quiet guest house two miles up the road, at the head of the loch, coming down to Dhanakosa each day to take part in the celebrations.

Throughout our travels we were accompanied by Bryan Stephens, a member of the Clear Vision team, who in his usual unobtrusive way made a video recording of the whole tour, besides giving us his very agreeable companionship. By the time we parted he had accumulated twenty-two hours' worth of material.

I returned from the tour convinced that, all things considered, the FWBO was in a reasonably healthy state in the North of England and Scotland. Some of the centres I visited, two at least of them for the first time, were bigger – and more beautiful – than I had expected, and some were attended, moreover, by more people than I had realized. I was also struck by the sincerity and enthusiasm of the Mitras I met, many of them for the first time, at least on their own ground. I also met Order members who, I must confess, previously were little more than names to me, but whose abilities, and commitment to the Three Jewels, were very much in evidence.

Besides returning from our tour assured of the health of the Movement in the North of England and Scotland, I returned with vivid memories of some of the places of interest we had seen. Among these were the new Tate Gallery in Liverpool; the magnificent Ashton Memorial, near Lancaster; the recently opened Ruskin Library building, at Lancaster University; Rosslyn Chapel, near Edinburgh; the Angel of the North sculpture (or construction) on the outskirts of Gateshead; Durham Cathedral; the Parsonage Museum at Haworth, where the Brontë sisters had lived and worked; and the 1853 Gallery at Saltaire, a vast Victorian factory now dedicated to the work of David Hockney but also run as a bookshop. Except for the Angel of the North, all these impressed me deeply, in their different ways. My most vivid memory, however, is of Rosslyn Chapel, and certain paintings I saw in the Walker Art Gallery, Liverpool, and the National Gallery of Scotland in Edinburgh.

Rosslyn Chapel, which features in the poetry of both Scott and Wordsworth, is situated on the edge of the Esk valley, and was built in 1446 by William St Clair, third and last Prince of Orkney. According to the publicity leaflet,

> Rosslyn Chapel conforms neither to contemporary architecture nor to any fashion. Rich in ornament its exact place in the creation of mankind still remains difficult to estimate. The carvings themselves, including the famous 'Apprentice Pillar', are endless in variety and full of symbolism. Many of the Biblical stories are portrayed and there are frequent references for those interested in the Knights Templar and Freemasonry, equally there are Pagan symbols and Rosslyn Chapel has the largest number of 'Green Men' found in any medieval building. There are also carvings of plants from the New World which pre-date the discovery of that land by Columbus by one hundred years.

The interior of the Chapel, in particular, was rich indeed. So rich was it, that to me the place seemed more like a South Indian Hindu temple than a Christian place of worship, besides perfectly exemplifying Blake's dictum 'Exuberance is beauty'. Moreover, whether by means of its aesthetics, or in some other way, it communicated a sense of mystery, even of magic, such as I had not experienced elsewhere.

I had visited the Walker Art Gallery and the National Gallery of Scotland before, and in the case of the former I knew what I particularly wanted to see. This was Rossetti's *Dante's Dream*, with a small reproduction of which I had been familiar since my earliest days. This was only the second time I had seen the original, and again I was not disappointed. The National Gallery of Scotland contained some surprises in the shape of three paintings that had either not been on display at the time of my two previous visits or of which I had then failed to take proper notice. The three were Rubens' *The Feast of Herod*, Guercino's *Erminia Finding the Wounded Rinaldo*, and Tintoretto's *Deposition*. Rubens is by no means one of my favourite artists, but when I saw *The Feast of Herod* I stood transfixed. The feast was that at which Salome asked Herod to give her, as the reward for her dancing, the head of John the Baptist on a dish – a request he reluctantly granted. Now, clad in a blood-red gown, and occupying the centre foreground of the painting, she shows her ghastly present to the king. The expressions on the faces of the guests at the feast are wonderfully portrayed, especially the triumphant smirk on the face of the stout and sumptuously dressed Herodias, the mother of Salome, at whose instigation the dancer made her monstrous request. Most wonderful of all is the way the great artist has depicted the conflict of the emotions in the face of the king himself, whose thoughts, as he sits there at the head of the table, chin in hand, can only be guessed at.

I had become familiar with Guercino's work only recently, when I saw some fine examples of it in an exhibition of seventeenth-century Italian painting at the National Gallery in London. Then I had greatly admired, in particular, the faultless beauty of his *Cumaean Sibyl with a Putto* and *Hagar in the Wilderness* and hence was delighted to encounter, there in Edinburgh, the almost equally beautiful *Erminia Finding the Wounded Rinaldo*. Tintoretto I learned to appreciate, not so much from the National Gallery as from the Palazzo Ducale and Scuolo di S Rocco in Venice, which Prasannasiddhi and I visited in 1982, on our way to the second men's ordination retreat in Tuscany. Though the *Deposition* was not to be compared with the masterpieces I saw on that occasion, and though it was hung too high up for comfort, I was nevertheless glad to renew my acquaintance with the artist.

While in Edinburgh we also visited the Writers' Museum, a seventeenth-century stone building containing, in three separate sets of rooms, mementoes of Scott, of Burns, and of Stevenson. Round the corner from the museum, so to speak, in a busy thoroughfare, stood a statue of another famous Scottish writer, the philosopher and historian David Hume. We were curious to see this statue, which had been erected only recently, but it turned out to be a great disappointment. The seated figure wore a sort of loose classical robe, and its face, I thought, bore no resemblance to portraits of the philosopher I had seen.

It was Hume, probably the greatest British philosopher, who awoke Kant, probably the greatest German philosopher, from his 'dogmatic slumber' (as Kant himself called it), and it was to Germany that, less than a week after Kovida and I returned from our northern tour, I flew from Birmingham on Saturday, 13 June. I flew to Munich. Anomarati was at the airport to meet me and took me to the hotel which was to be our base for the next three days. I had seen him less than three weeks before, when I was in Berlin for the opening of the Berlin Buddhistische Tor or 'Buddhist Gate', the FWBO's new centre in Germany's new capital city. It was a quick weekend visit. I opened the Centre and gave a talk, saw the nineteenth-century German Romantic paintings (mainly Friedrich's and Schinkel's) at the Charlottenburg Palace, had dinner at a crowded Indian restaurant with some twenty Order members, Mitras, and Friends, visited the Botanical Gardens with Anomarati – and that was about all. At the Botanical Gardens Anomarati and I had discussed our forthcoming trip to Munich, the capital of the Free State (formerly Kingdom) of Bavaria and Germany's third largest city, which I had long wanted to see, and now we were installed at its very heart.

First impressions are important, at least subjectively. The first thing that struck me about Munich, as we strolled round part of the city centre that evening, was that it was very different from Berlin. There was a mildly carnival atmosphere, which may or may not have been due to the fact that it was Saturday. Stalls with red and white striped awnings lined the street, as though some kind of fair was in progress, and the crowds seemed to be in a holiday mood. One stout, red-faced old gentleman wore Bavarian peasant costume – black shorts and red braces, and a little feathered cap. Buildings were of a handsome size, architecturally uniform, and in marked contrast to Berlin there were no construction sites and no giant cranes above the skyline.

The following morning was devoted to the arts. Proceeding chronologically, we visited first the Glyptothek, or Sculpture Gallery, then the Städtische Galerie, or Municipal Gallery in the Lenbachhaus, the Alte Pinakothek, or Old Picture Gallery, unfortunately being closed for restoration work. Said to be one of the finest neoclassical buildings in

Germany, the Glyptothek is laid out round a central courtyard and fronted by an Ionic portico. The rooms are all lit from the courtyard, the exterior walls being windowless. In these rooms were some of the finest Greek sculptures I have seen – Archaic, Classical, and Hellenic, as well as models of Greek temples and a collection of Roman portrait busts. There were several splendid *kouroi*, the *Barbarini Faun* (also known as the *Sleeping Satyr*), an amazingly expressive head of Homer, a torso that was said to have been a source of inspiration to Michelangelo, sculptural groups from the east and west, pediments of the temple of Alphaea in Aegina – and much besides. The figures in the two temple pediments were archaic in style, the central figure of Pallas Athene in each case being flanked on both sides by a line of armed warriors in various attitudes.

Before making our way to the Lenbachhaus, where the Municipal Collection was to be seen, we sat out in the spacious cobbled courtyard, enjoying the sunshine and absorbing what we had seen, and contemplating, in my case, the careworn features of the emperor Hadrian, a bronze head of whom stood on a pedestal beneath the trees.

The Lenbachhaus, modelled on an Italian country villa of the Renaissance period, was named after the painter for whom it was built and whose studio it had contained. The gallery was rich in paintings of the Blauer Reiter, or 'Blue Rider', school, particularly those of Kandinsky, whose development could be traced, from its earliest to its latest period, in a series of several hundred colourful works, including items in other media. The most famous painting in the collection, however, was Marc's *Blauer Reiter*, which had given the school its name. At first we had difficulty seeing this work, as our view was blocked by a group of earnest-looking art students to whom the elderly woman lecturer was, no doubt, explaining why it depicted not a blue rider but a blue horse.

In the afternoon, after a short siesta, we had the pleasure of seeing Heinz Roiger, a disciple of the late Ayya Khema, and one of the vice-presidents of the European Buddhist Union, with whom Kulananda and Bodhimitra had developed a friendship and who was anxious to meet me. Our discussion covered a range of topics, mostly Buddhistic, and so engrossing did all three of us find it that after a while we adjourned, at my suggestion, from the hotel reception room to a café in order to continue the exchange over a companionable cup of coffee. Before we eventually parted it was agreed that on Tuesday, the day after next, Heinz should interview me on the subject of ordination for the next issue of *Lotusblätter*, the quarterly magazine of the EBU's German affiliate, and then show us some of Munich's numerous churches and cathedrals.

Sunday having been devoted mainly to seeing works of art, Anomarati and I decided that Monday, when the principal museums and art galleries would be closed, should be devoted mainly to seeing a little of Nature. We accordingly spent much of the morning exploring some of the 150 acres of the Englischer Garten or 'English Garden' (actually more park than garden), where we saw the Chinese Tower (a less elegant version of the pagoda at Kew) and climbed up the artificial hill on which stood the Monopteros, a classical-style rotunda, from which there was a fine panoramic view of the garden and of the neighbouring Munich skyline – a skyline dominated by the twin towers of the Frauenkirche with their blue-grey cupolas. From the English Garden we made our way to the Stuck Villa Museum, *en route* crossing the Isar by the Leopold Bridge and climbing, past the fountain, up to the Angel of Peace monument, from the foot of the square base of which we could look back down the whole length of Prinzregentenstrasse. Unfortunately, our guidebook was out of date: the Stuck Villa Museum, too, closed on Mondays. We therefore went by underground train and tram – quite a long journey – straight to the Botanical Garden. Here we saw more of Nature than we had bargained for, as it rained heavily much of the time. In between the showers we circumambulated the lily pond, wandered round the Alpinium and the rose garden, had lunch in the open-air café, and finally visited the hothouses, where we found an incredible variety of flowering stone plants, cacti, palms, bamboos, orchids, insect-devouring pitcher plants, and other amazing products of the Torrid Zone.

The evening was spent at the Nationaltheater or Bavarian State Opera, where we heard a three-movement work by Gabrieli, arranged for brass, Haydn's 'Drum' Mass, parts of which were of an angelic beauty, and Verdi's 'Four Religious Pieces'. The conductor was Zubin Mehta who, obviously a great favourite with the music-loving Munich public (ours were the last two tickets available), received four calls at the end of the performance. I was glad to have had the opportunity of hearing some music live, as distinct from hearing it on CD or cassette or on the radio, as in the course of the year I had been able to go to only three concerts. I heard Bela Bartok's *Bluebeard's Castle* (an electrifying performance under the baton of Simon Rattle), at the Symphony Hall, Birmingham; Monteverdi's *Coronation of Poppea* at the Birmingham

Hippodrome; and at the Adrian Boult Hall, also in Birmingham, I attended the first performance of David Earl's Cello Concerto, together with some twenty Order members and Mitras.

Anomarati and I spent our last day in Munich with Heinz, who, after interviewing me at the hotel for an hour, took us on a kind of guided tour of some of Munich's churches, in one of which he had once served as an altar boy. Exactly how many churches we covered that morning and afternoon I cannot be sure, for we saw so many towers, domes, façades, naves, arches, statues, altarpieces, organs, stained-glass windows, pulpits, and tombs, that after a while I found it difficult to remember which church was which and where we had seen what. In retrospect three churches do, however, stand out. The first of these was the Cajetan Church of the Theatines, a basilica in the style of the Italian high baroque to the façade of which twin late-rococo towers – one on each side – had subsequently been added. The spacious interior, with its double pillars, round arches, and enormous crossing dome, was most impressive. Yet the place had a shabby, neglected air. The once white walls were grey, the gilt of the rich stucco ornamentation faded. It was in this church, I think, that we saw a statue of the Virgin Mary that may have been of the so-called 'Black Madonna' type. According to Heinz, it was of black stone and both very ancient and very holy. Before it burned several rows of votive candles.

The gilded interior of the eighteenth-century Asamkirche, named for the two Asam brothers who were its architects, has claims to be considered one of the most astonishing church interiors in Europe. A rococo extravaganza of wildly twisting columns, sunbursts, balconies, garlands, wreaths, and statues, it was lit from the east end by a small oval window above which God the Father, wearing a splendid papal tiara, presented his Crucified Son to the world. Though the rococo style of architecture and decoration is certainly not my favourite one, I had to admit that the interior of the Asamkirche, unified as it was by the predominance of gold and the subdued lighting, possessed a bizarre beauty of its own, and I was glad to have seen it. The Frauenkirche or Cathedral Church of Our Lady, the third of the churches of which I have a distinct recollection, was a brick-built Late Gothic structure whose vast well-lit interior was as different from that of the Asamkirche as it was possible to be. Rows of white octagonal pillars of enormous height, all completely free of ornament, supported the lofty roof. Though there were numerous side chapels, and many notable works of art, including the remarkable monument to the

Emperor Ludwig the Bavarian, these in no way detracted from the overall impression of simplicity and austerity conveyed by the place.

In between churches we spent an hour looking round the Stuck Villa, built in 1898 for the wealthy painter Franz von Stuck and furnished in predominantly Art Nouveau style. The rather gloomy downstairs rooms, the walls of which were decorated by the artist himself in 'Pompeiian' style, contained several of his paintings, including versions of *Guardian of Paradise* – an idealized male figure with a flaming sword, and the famous *Sin* – a woman with an evil-looking snake draped around her neck. Fascinating though the villa and its contents were, I could not help feeling that Stuck must have been a strange man.

From the last of the churches, after a farewell coffee, Heinz drove Anomarati and me to the railway station, where we caught the train to Augsburg. It was a very crowded train, and I was glad that thanks to Anomarati's foresight we had reserved seats and were able to sit down.

Augsburg was known to me principally as the city that had given its name to the Augsburg Confession, 'the most important statement of Protestant belief drawn up at the Reformation', and as the home of the Fugger banking family, which at one time was advancing loans to half the princes of Western Europe, as well as to the Papacy. It was a historic old place, full of interesting buildings, and having checked into our hotel Anomarati and I lost no time in sallying forth into the warm evening sunshine. Soon we found ourselves on the Maximilianstrasse, by which much of the older part of Augsburg was bisected. Said to be the longest medieval street in Europe, it was of unusual width, cobbled, and lined with fine buildings, several of them former palaces. Half-way up, a monumental fountain divided the infrequent traffic into two streams, while at the top of the street rose the massive bulk of the Basilica of St Ulrich and Afra, the lofty tower of which was capped with the characteristically Bavarian onion dome.

We explored the basilica the following morning, having watched the service for a few minutes through the ornamental iron grille that extended the whole width of the nave, just inside the entrance. There were very few worshippers, I noticed, most of them elderly women. We also visited the much smaller Protestant Evangelical church next door. It was literally next door, having been built right up against its Catholic neighbour. Had this been done deliberately, in a spirit of sectarian rivalry? Protestantism was certainly more in evidence in Augsburg than in Munich. The city had, in fact, associations with

Martin Luther, the great reformer having preached a number of times in the Heiligkreuzkirche or Church of the Holy Cross where, that afternoon, we saw his and Philip Melanchthon's portraits, both painted by Cranach.

The remainder of the morning was spent in the Schaezler Palace on Maximilianstrasse, which housed a fine collection of German baroque and rococo paintings, plus many works by Hans Holbein the Elder, Lukas Cranach the Elder, and certain of their contemporaries. Once again I admired – as I had admired in Cologne, Dresden, and elsewhere – the work of the older German masters, which seemed to underline the significance of the term 'Pre-Raphaelite' and give it, perhaps, a broader reference than was dreamt of by the English founders of the school of that name. I was particularly impressed by three large paintings of scenes from the life of St Valentine by Bartholomaeus Zeitblom, in which the saint's handsome, ascetic features were represented with incredible sensitivity and refinement. In the afternoon, having visited the Heiligkreuzkirche, we made our way to the magnificent Town Hall, said to be the most significant Renaissance secular building north of the Alps, where we admired the splendours of the restored Golden Hall. On returning to the hotel we saw that Dhammaloka had arrived, as planned, and the three of us went for a meal at a restaurant where, as Anomarati and I had discovered, several vegetarian options were available. This restaurant was connected with the brewery next door, which had been founded in the fourteenth century and was still functioning.

The following day, Thursday 19 July, was devoted to a visit to Buddha-Haus, the retreat centre in the foothills of the Bavarian Alps founded by Ayya Khema, who had died the previous year. Since our 1992 Berlin meeting she and I had corresponded regularly, and even met a few times in London, and she had more than once invited me to visit Buddha-Haus. After her death Nyanabodhi, her leading disciple, invited me to contribute to the memorial volume they were bringing out, which I was happy to do. This led to an exchange of letters between us and, eventually, to my promising that after seeing Munich and Augsburg I would visit Buddha-Haus with my two companions. It was a beautiful morning, and Anomarati, Dhammaloka, and I were in high spirits as, with Dhammaloka at the wheel, we left Augsburg and headed due south, in the direction of the Alps. Our route lay through green, hilly countryside, with here and there a dark stretch of forest and, when we had been an hour or so on the road, a view of the first range of foothills in the distance. Once we passed a long grey castle, perched high up on the hillside a few miles away. By the time we reached Buddha-Haus, two-and-a-half hours after leaving Augsburg, the sun was high in the sky, it was very hot, and we were fifteen hundred feet or more above sea level.

Nyanabodhi and his two colleagues, Nyanachitta and Sanghamitta (the latter a novice nun), received us very cordially, and after I had been shown round the garden and had seen the Sinhalese-style stupa containing Ayya Khema's ashes we all sat on the veranda where, over a cup of tea, we were soon deep in matters of common spiritual interest. Unfortunately, our discussions were interrupted by the arrival of an unexpected visitor (unexpected in the sense of not being expected until the following day) in the form of a much-travelled Dutch monk whose appearance on the scene gave a different turn to the conversation. I did, however, manage to have a further exchange of views with Nyanabodhi when he gave me a guided tour of Buddha-Haus, which was a three-storeyed building of the 'Swiss chalet' type that had once been a hotel. The rooms were all decorated and furnished to a very high standard and evidently were the object of much loving care. After lunch Nyanabodhi and Nyanachitta took us to see the Metta Vihara, which was about half an hour's drive away. It was a building of the same type as the Buddha-Haus, but more isolated (Buddha-Haus was part of a small village), and commanding even finer views. Here we all said goodbye, mutually promising to stay in touch, and soon Anomarati, Dhammaloka, and I were on the road to Memmingen.

In Memmingen, after eating at a pizzeria, we spent an hour wandering round the charming old market town, with its rococo façades, its onion domes, its canal, and its towered gates. Of exceptional interest was the magnificent vaulted ceiling of the Kreuzherrnkirche, which was covered with elaborate plasterwork and supported by four columns of a beautiful pink-and-grey mottled marble.

The following morning, after another look at Memmingen, we drove to the Benedictine abbey of Ottobeuren, which was only a few miles away. Here we saw the baroque basilica, said to be one of the biggest churches in Germany, the white and gold interior of which was lavishly decorated in a style I could not help thinking of as unsuitably 'operatic'. An hour later we were in the ancient city of Ulm, a place that was not only bigger than Memmingen but much busier. In Ulm we had eyes only for the Cathedral, the tapering west tower of which, with its pointed arches, its slender buttresses and pillars, and its lofty pierced-stonework steeple, rose to a height of more than 500 feet. At the time of the Reformation it had been converted from a Catholic to a Protestant place of worship, and many altarpieces and statues of saints were either destroyed or removed. But though much had been lost, much remained, as we saw when, walking round the four-aisled Gothic interior, we saw the delicately carved limewood pulpit canopy, with its forest of turrets and finials, and the tabernacle, a miracle of stone carving the slender pillars and traceries of which rose to a height of eighty feet, as well as seeing the fifteenth-century fresco of the Last Judgement over the choir arch, the sixteenth-century choir altar by Martin Schaffner and the original of Hans Multscher's famous *Man of Sorrows*, a masterpiece of late Gothic realism that formerly stood in the main porch until, the stone having eroded by pollution, it was moved to its present position inside the Cathedral.

Most interesting of all, however, at least to me, were the two rows of fifteenth-century carved wooden busts, almost life-size, that decorated the choir stalls. The busts on the left, the men's side, represented famous figures from classical antiquity, including Virgil(?), Seneca, Ptolemy, Cicero, and Pythagoras, while those on the right, the women's side, represented the various Sibyls, the Phrygian, the Cumaean, the Delphic, and so on. The work of Jörg Syrlin the Elder, the busts were all executed with an astonishing degree not only of realism but of expressiveness, especially, perhaps, those of Seneca and Pythagoras and the Phrygian and Tiburnian Sibyls. Describing the Phrygian Sibyl, the eloquent author of the Cathedral guide wrote:

> She closes her mouth as if she had just spoken. Her eyes, earnest and intent, look to see if anyone will disagree. Shoulders erect and strained, pulled to the front, she extends her left hand as if to strengthen her argument. The right hand holds the manuscript rolled up. She does not need it. The sleeve is pushed back, the folds show the passion of her speech. Otherwise the dress is plain and hemmed only with a fur trimming. She is not concerned about her external appearance but only about what she is saying. She has tied the somewhat large turban at an angle with a cloth. Sliding would divert attention. Thus she appears self-confident and convinced by her own speech. The nose and mouth are also energetic. A woman who knows what she wants, what she does and what she has to say. One might also call her an intellectual.

I was reminded of a certain Dharmacharini.

Next to the women's side of the choir, and hardly less interesting than the busts, was the Besserer Chapel. It was of interest mainly on account of its stained-glass windows by the fifteenth-century master Hans Acker, the different panels of which depicted scenes from the Old and New Testaments. Though the panels were well designed, some Biblical episodes being depicted quite dramatically, the most striking thing about them was the jewel-like richness and brilliancy of their reds, blues, violets, greens, and yellows, which surpassed those of the older stained-glass windows we had seen in the choir.

Our real objective that day being not Ulm but Nuremberg, we were unable to spend as much time in the Cathedral as I, for one, could have wished, and having seen the Besserer Chapel we walked back to the car park and were soon again on the road. Nuremberg in a way was two cities, one inside and one outside the ring of massive walls from which there rose, at intervals, the imposing bulk of a round watch-tower. Having checked in at our hotel, and had a meal, we drove through one of the old gateways into the inner city and had a look round. With their lofty peaked gables, oriel windows, and red-tiled roofs, the older houses certainly presented a picturesque appearance. There were also some interesting Gothic churches, all with richly carved porches, and it was not too late for us to be able to visit two of them. In St Sebald's we found a number of fine altarpieces, while in the other, whose name I forget, a rehearsal of what seemed to be a modern oratorio was in progress. It was in one of these churches, I think, that Anomarati asked me how one could tell the difference between a Catholic and a Protestant church, especially as they both contained statues and altarpieces, which the Reformation had suppos-edly banished from its places of worship. In the end I replied that if there were candles burning before the altar one could safely assume that the church was not Protestant. All were indeed well equipped with statues and altarpieces, but only in one of them did we find candles burning. Nuremberg was a Reformation stronghold. On our way back to the car we passed through a cobbled square in front of a restaurant. Perhaps because it was Friday night, several dozen young people, of both sexes and several nationalities, were engaged in a drunken revel. It was the only time during our trip that I witnessed such behaviour.

In the later Middle Ages the castle of Nuremberg was a favourite Imperial residence, and Anomarati, Dhammaloka, and I spent much of Saturday morning there as part of a tour group, visitors not being allowed to explore the place on their own. Built principally in the twelfth century, and seeming on one side to form part of the city wall, it consisted mainly of a series of huge rooms unfurnished except for a few faded tapestries and, in some cases, an enormous pot-bellied iron stove in the corner. Of much greater interest to me was the Romanesque chapel, with its chunky pillars and round arches. It consisted of two storeys, the two being connected by a square balustraded aperture. The nobles heard mass in the upper storey, where the altar was, whereas the commoners attached to the Imperial court heard it from below, through the aperture. As for the Emperor, he heard it in the upper storey with the nobles, but from a balcony high above their heads.

After lunch we visited Albrecht Dürer's House, the German Museum, and the thirteenth-century Lorenzkirche, a three-aisle Gothic basilica where there were many fine statues and altarpieces but no lighted candles, besides spending a few minutes in the Frauenkirche. Dürer's House was a five-storeyed building with the traditional peaked gables and red-tiled roof, and like Dr Johnson's birthplace in Lichfield, which I had visited the previous year with Paramartha, it occupied a corner site. After watching a documentary film on the great artist's life and work we explored the different rooms. These contained, besides various displays, copies of some of his paintings, a printing press of the kind on which his engravings were produced, and an exhibition of the engraving themselves, including the illustrations to the *Apocalypse* and the *Great and Little Passions*. In the German Museum we confined ourselves to the section dedicated to Dürer, the Renaissance, and the baroque, where we saw many fine paintings by Dürer and Cranach. At 4 o'clock we left for Würzburg.

It so happened that on my return to England I found on my desk, among the books I had recently ordered, a copy of the poet Edwin Muir's *An Autobiography*. Casting my eye down the index I saw a reference to Nuremberg, and at once turned to the relevant page. Muir had passed through the city shortly after the war, when on his way to Prague. Or rather he passed through what was left of it.

> We stopped at Nuremberg [he wrote] and clambered over the ruins of
> the old town. I remembered a few days I had spent there with my
> wife during our stay in Hellerau. The town had enchanted us; so
> much affection had gone into the building of it; every house was a

simple embodiment of the impulse which makes people create a little world around them to which they can attach their affections. Now nothing was left but jagged blocks of masonry. As I clambered over the debris I tried to find Dürer's house and the little fountain in the square, but nothing seemed to be left except some fragments of the city wall.

That was more than fifty years ago. Now there were no jagged blocks of masonry, no debris, and the city wall was certainly not in fragments. Nuremberg was its old smiling self (the little fountain in the square was again playing), and I reflected with admiration on the energy and resourcefulness – and the love – that must have gone into the restoration of the city, as into its original creation. Not that Nuremberg was by any means the only city in Germany to have suffered dreadfully as a result of the war. Muir had passed through Aachen, where there were crowds at what had once been street corners, and through Cologne, of which he wrote:

> All the houses were standing, and for a moment the sense of a settled peaceful life came back. It was an illusion. The spacious houses were roofless, the windows empty gaps. Presently the sour stench of corpses buried under the ruins rose about us. The stench, the unreal houses, the crumbling pavements, prepared us for a dead city; yet people were out as usual for their Sunday evening walk in their Sunday best, the children decked in chance remnants of finery. It was a lovely late summer evening, and the peaceful crowds in that vast graveyard were like the forerunners of a multitude risen in a private resurrection day to an unimaginable new life.

Yet Aachen and Cologne, too, had been restored, as I saw when I visited them. The people who inhabited them had indeed risen to a new life. But as well as reflecting with admiration on the energy and resourcefulness that had gone into the restoration of Nuremberg, as well as into that of Aachen and Cologne and all the other devastated German cities, I reflected with some sorrow that restorations could not, by their very nature, be complete or perfect. Some things were gone for ever. Apart from the millions of human beings killed, thousands of works of art had been destroyed or badly damaged, as the photographs of shattered churches I had seen in Munich and elsewhere mutely witnessed. In Germany, as elsewhere in Europe, war had resulted in the loss of much that was most precious in the cultural heritage of the West.

The ancient university town of Würzburg straddles both banks of the River Main, its two halves being linked by the Romanesque Alte Mainbrücke, or Old Main Bridge, and it was across the bridge that, having checked into our hotel, I found myself walking with Anomarati and Dhammaloka that fine summer evening. Like the much bigger Charles Bridge in Prague it was adorned on both sides with life-size statues of saints, some of them in dramatic attitudes. Straight ahead of us, at the far end of the street into which the bridge led, rose the lofty façade and turreted twin towers of the Romanesque cathedral. Turning left at the end of the bridge we made a circuit through the quarter, eating at an improbable Mexican restaurant and looking at a few churches before returning over the Alte Mainbrücke to our hotel.

The next day we did not have much time for sightseeing, as Anomarati had to catch the midday train to Berlin, while Dhammaloka and I wanted to be in Essen in time for dinner. We therefore confined ourselves to the Residenz, the eighteenth-century baroque palace of the prince-bishops of Würzburg, said to have been built in imitation of Versailles, and the Marienberg fortress, which the prince-bishops occupied before the construction of the Residenz on the other side of the river. The Residenz was indeed a magnificent building, even a beautiful one. Having entered from the formal garden at the rear, we climbed the great five-bayed staircase, gazed up at the Tiepolo frescoes in the vast cupola, and so passed through the White Hall, with its highly elaborate stucco decorations (white on a pale grey ground) by Antonio Bossi, who died insane, and the Imperial Hall, with its splendid gold, agate, and violet colour scheme and its huge frescoes – also by Tiepolo – glorifying the idea of the Holy Roman Empire. Here we left the tour party and passed through the Northern Imperial Apartments. These were much more to my liking, being smaller and more intimate and decorated and furnished, in rococo style, with superlative good taste. From them we made our way through the servants' rooms and so down to the ground floor and out into the cobbled *cour d'honneur*, from where there was a fine view of the Marienberg fortress, brooding upon its rock some miles away.

Unfortunately, the fortress's Mainfränkisches Museum, which contained masterpieces by Tilman Riemenschneider, Bavaria's greatest sculptor, was closed for a few months, so that we saw only a few works by lesser artists and an antiques fair that was in progress. Having seen these, and had a farewell drink on the spacious terrace of the café, from which the whole city could be seen, as well as the vineyards on the hillside beyond, we drove to the railway station. Here Dhammaloka and I dropped Anomarati off and, sightseeing over for the time being, took the motorway to Essen. It was a hot day, certainly the hottest of our tour, and probably the hottest I had experienced that year. Nor was it surprising: it was Sunday 21 June – the day of the summer solstice. Having stopped for lunch at a little walled town where we found a Greek restaurant, we drove on through the green, densely forested hills, halting only for a cool drink, and at 5 o'clock reached 13 Herkulesstrasse, where we were welcomed by Bodhimitra and Guhyaratna.

During the next four days I saw people rather than buildings. After breakfast on Monday there was a meeting with the local Dharmacharis, then one with the Dharmacharinis. This was followed by lunch with three women Mitras, after which I gave personal interviews and Dhammaloka and I had dinner with the Sumandala (women's) community. In the evening I was given a reception at the centre, which had undergone many improvements since my visit two years before. Bodhimitra spoke with great feeling, I replied, after which I led a sevenfold puja that was attended by some eighty people and in the course of which three men became Mitras. The ceremony should have been followed by the launch of Do's new publication *Mensch? Gott? Buddha*, the material for which had been taken from *The Buddha's Victory* and *Who is the Buddha?*, but unfortunately copies did not arrive from the printers in time (I received my own copy the day after I returned to England). All the same, a number of people still wanted me to sign copies of my books, both German and English, and this I happily did.

The following morning Dhammaloka and I left for Minden, a hundred or more miles to the north-east, which I had not seen before. The purpose of my visit was not so much to see the town itself as to see the FWBO centre there and meet members of the local sangha. On the way we stopped at Recklinghausen. Here, as arranged, we met Jayachitta, and the three of us spent an hour looking round the Icon Museum, which was said to be the largest collection of icons outside the world of Orthodoxy. The icons were of many different types, periods, and provenance, but few of them, I thought, were as fine as the best of those I had seen in the 'Icons from Moscow' exhibition in London. Arriving in Minden at 3 o'clock, Dhammaloka and I had tea with Prasadavati and her husband Arno, with whom we were to stay (lunch we had eaten *en route*), after which we had dinner with them and half a dozen friends – though not before I had given a few personal interviews. The rest of the evening was spent at the Centre. Here, as in Essen, there was a reception, a sevenfold puja (beautifully led by Prasadavati), Mitra ceremonies (conducted by me), and a book-signing session. About sixty people attended, and I was delighted to see that the Centre was in such a flourishing condition, despite having been opened only two years ago and having only one permanently resident Order member – Prasadavati.

Wednesday 24 June was my last full day in Germany. Dhammaloka and I left Minden at 10 o'clock, after I had given more personal interviews, arriving back in Essen in time for lunch, which we had with the Centre team – Bodhimitra, Kulanandi, and Shantipada. In the afternoon came further personal interviews, after which Dhammaloka and I had dinner with the members of the Akashadhatu (men's) community. The evening was devoted to a question-and-answer meeting at the Centre. Questions had been handed in beforehand, in English. They were of a higher standard than I sometimes get, and I was glad to spend nearly two hours answering them, with Jayachitta as my very competent translator.

The next day the sky was overcast. Having visited the Evolution shop in the nearby shopping mall, Dhammaloka and I did our last sight-seeing. This took the form of a visit to the Romanesque cloister of a church situated round the corner from the shop, so to speak. Thomas Schwarte acted as our guide, the place being well known to him. After lunch Guhyaratna and Peter drove me to Gruga Park. Here there was heavy rain, and the three of us had to wait in the car for a while before being able to walk around the park and see the Japanese garden. We also saw two pelicans preening their feathers beside the ornamental lake. At 4 o'clock Dhammaloka drove me to Düsseldorf airport, Thomas Sopp accompanying. Having said goodbye to them, I made my way to the departure lounge. Here I discovered that the plane would be leaving three hours late – not one as I had been told at the check-in counter. But unlike some of my fellow passengers I did not mind. I had the experiences of the last two weeks to reflect on, and assimilate, and to me the three hours seemed to pass quite quickly. At Birmingham airport I was met by Kovida and his friend Mark and driven to Madhyamaloka, where I was soon making a hot drink before going to bed after a long day.

Two weeks later, having spent a few days in London and seen Prasannasiddhi and Paramartha, I was on my way to Spain. The Iberia plane was an hour late in leaving Heathrow. On our departure from Düsseldorf the captain of the Lufthansa aircraft had given a full explanation of the reason for the delay and had apologized for the inconvenience caused. This time no explanation was forthcoming and not so much as a word of apology. Did the two airlines have different policies, or was it that their respective crews had different attitudes to their work? At Alicante I was met by Yashodeva, and soon we were speeding along the highway to Villajoyosa. From time to time the sea appeared between the low hills, and I could see the light of the (almost) full moon reflected in its still waters.

Now the calm of Guhyaloka enfolds me. I have read a few books, written two poems, and compiled this Letter, the writing of which has given me the pleasure of living my travels in the North of England and Scotland, and in Germany, all over again. On my return to England I shall take up my memoirs, put aside four months ago, and hope that, health permitting (my blood pressure medication was doubled recently, and I have been advised to avoid stress), it will be possible for me to work steadily on them during the autumn and winter.

Urgyen Sangharakshita

INDEX OF MAIN REFERENCES

The Windhorse symbolizes the energy of the enlightened mind carrying the Three Jewels – the Buddha, the Dharma, and the Sangha – to all sentient beings.

Buddhism is one of the fastest growing spiritual traditions in the Western world. Throughout its 2,500-year history, it has always succeeded in adapting its mode of expression to suit whatever culture it has encountered.

Windhorse Publications aims to continue this tradition as Buddhism comes to the West. Today's Westerners are heirs to the entire Buddhist tradition, free to draw instruction and inspiration from all the many schools and branches. Windhorse publishes works by authors who not only understand the Buddhist tradition but are also familiar with Western culture and the Western mind.

For orders and catalogues contact

WINDHORSE PUBLICATIONS
11 PARK ROAD
BIRMINGHAM
B13 8AB
UK

WINDHORSE BOOKS
PO BOX 574
NEWTOWN
NSW 2042
AUSTRALIA

WEATHERHILL INC
41 MONROE TUNRPIKE
TRUMBULL
CT 06611
USA

Windhorse Publications is an arm of the Friends of the Western Buddhist Order, which has more than sixty centres on five continents. Through these centres, members of the Western Buddhist Order offer regular programmes of events for the general public and for more experienced students. These include meditation classes, public talks, study on Buddhist themes and texts, and 'bodywork' classes such as t'ai chi, yoga, and massage. The FWBO also runs several retreat centres and the Karuna Trust, a fund-raising charity that supports social welfare projects in the slums and villages of India.

Many FWBO centres have residential spiritual communities and ethical businesses associated with them. Arts activities are encouraged too, as is the development of strong bonds of friendship between people who share the same ideals. In this way the FWBO is developing a unique approach to Buddhism, not simply as a set of techniques, less still as an exotic cultural interest, but as a creatively directed way of life for people living in the modern world.

If you would like more information about the FWBO visit the website at www.fwbo.org or write to

LONDON BUDDHIST CENTRE
51 ROMAN ROAD
LONDON
E2 OHU
UK

ARYALOKA
HEARTWOOD CIRCLE
NEWMARKET
NEW HAMPSHIRE
NH 03857
USA

ALSO FROM WINDHORSE

SUBHUTI

SANGHARAKSHITA:
A NEW VOICE IN THE BUDDHIST TRADITION

Sangharakshita was one of the first Westerners to make the journey to the East and to don the monk's yellow robe. In India he gained unique experience in the main traditions of Buddhist teaching and practice. His involvement with the 'mass conversion' to Buddhism of the most socially deprived people of India, frequently treated as untouchables, exposed him to a revolutionary new experiment in social transformation. More recently he founded one of the most successful Buddhist movements in the modern world – pioneering a 'living Buddhism' that seems ideally suited to our times.

Highly respected as an outspoken writer and commentator, he has never been afraid to communicate his insights and views, even if they challenge venerated elements of Buddhist tradition.

But what are those insights and views? How have they arisen and developed? Here one of Sangharakshita's leading disciples offers an account of his evolution as a thinker and teacher.

336 pages
ISBN 0 904766 68 3
£9.99/$19.95

SANGHARAKSHITA

THE RAINBOW ROAD
FROM TOOTING BROADWAY TO KALIMPONG
MEMOIRS OF AN ENGLISH BUDDHIST

At the age of sixteen, Dennis Lingwood discovered that he was – and always had been – a Buddhist. This realization was to act as the motive force behind a life in which Lingwood, now better known as Sangharakshita, has played a major part in the introduction of Buddhism to the West.

The Rainbow Road traces Sangharakshita's development from a childhood characterized by his insatiable appetite for books to his homeless wandering across India and eventual ordination as a Buddhist monk. It takes us from the streets of wartime London to the dusty villages, ashrams, and mountain caves of India. Full of fascinating characters and keen insights, *The Rainbow Road* is as finely observed – and as entertaining – as a first- rate travel book. More than that, it is a remarkable and refreshingly candid record of a journey of spiritual exploration.

496 pages, with photographs
ISBN 0 904766 94 2
£16.99/$33.95

SANGHARAKSHITA

FACING MOUNT KANCHENJUNGA: AN ENGLISH
BUDDHIST IN THE EASTERN HIMALAYAS

In 1950 Kalimpong was a lively trading town where India runs into Nepal, Bhutan, Sikkim, and Tibet. Like a magnet, it attracted a bewildering array of guests and settlers: ex-colonials, Christian missionaries, princes in exile, pioneer Buddhologists, incarnate lamas from the Land of Snows – and Sangharakshita, the young English monk who was trying to establish a Buddhist movement for local youngsters.

In a delightful volume of memoirs, glowing with affection and humour, the author shares the incidents, encounters, and insights of his early years in Kalimpong.

Behind the events we witness the transformation of a rather eccentric young man into a unique and confident individual, completely at home in his adopted world, and increasingly effective as an interpreter of Buddhism for a new age.

512 pages, with photographs
ISBN 0 904766 52 7
£13.99/$27.95

SANGHARAKSHITA

IN THE SIGN OF THE GOLDEN WHEEL: INDIAN
MEMOIRS OF AN ENGLISH BUDDHIST

This engaging volume of memoirs recounts the unique experiences of an English Buddhist monk working in the mid-1950s to revive Buddhism in the land of its birth.

We follow Sangharakshita in his quest – from his hermitage in Kalimpong in the Himalayas to collaboration with a film star in Bombay, a visit from the Dalai Lama, and involvement in the spectacular festivals to celebrate 2,500 years of Buddhism.

Brimming with life and colour, this book is a notable addition to the canon of travel literature as we follow the spiritual adventures of an unorthodox and extraordinary Englishman.

384 pages, with photographs
ISBN 1 899579 14 1
£14.99/$29.95